Japanese Antitrust Law Manual

Law, Cases and Interpretation of Japanese Antimonopoly Act

International Competition Law Series

Volume 27.

The titles published in this series are listed at the end of this volume

Japanese Antitrust Law Manual
Law, Cases and Interpretation of Japanese Antimonopoly Act

By

Akira Inoue

KLUWER LAW
INTERNATIONAL

Published by:
Kluwer Law International
P.O. Box 316
2400 AH Alphen aan den Rijn
The Netherlands
E-mail: sales@kluwerlaw.com
Website: http://www.kluwerlaw.com

Sold and distributed in North, Central and South America by:
Aspen Publishers, Inc.,
7201 McKinney Circle
Frederick, MD 21704
USA

Sold and distributed in all other countries by:
Turpin Distribution Services Ltd.
Stratton Business Park
Pegasus Drive
Biggleswade
Bedfordshire SG18 8TQ
United Kingdom

ISBN 978 90 411 2627 6

To my wife, Yuko

Table of Contents

Chapter 3
Procedure of the Japanese Antimonopoly Act 103

Preface

It has been my firm belief over the past five years that the Japanese Antimonopoly Act must be known to those who would participate in competition in the Japanese market from overseas. Although the Japanese Antimonopoly Act was modelled after the American Antitrust Law, it evolved uniquely with its major amendments and developments of case law. As the Japanese Antimonopoly Act is now starting to be enforced strictly, especially after its amendments in 2005 (taking effect on 4 January 2006), it is worth learning where the land mines of legal risks lie. Several successful revelations of cartels by the Japanese Fair Trade Commission in 2006 urge me to conclude this book so that it can be offered to the potential participants in the Japanese market at the earliest convenience. I am fully convinced that this book realizes my belief.

The fundamental approach of this book is very simple. It provides the landscape of the Japanese Antimonopoly Act, pointing out where the legal risks lie and how to escape them. To lawyers, the Japanese Antimonopoly Act is a complex subject, which necessitates careful analysis not only on the statute and guidelines but also on case law, and in reference to the congressional debates and the reports that preceded the enactment. This book, however, is purported to be read not only by lawyers but also by *homme d'affaires* and anyone interested in learning more about the Japanese Antimonopoly Act. As such, each analysis in this book is kept as simple as possible. In terms of topics covered in this book, although the book may not exhaust all possible aspects of antitrust issues in Japan, it touches on what seems to be the major problems within the antitrust field. Particular attention is paid to the sample compliance manual under the Japanese Antimonopoly Act where the ultimate purpose and the analysis described in this book are condensed. The practical wisdom gained though my professional life are capitalized in the sample manual so readers can get maximum benefit from the book.

There are special individuals who supported me and I would like to thank each of them.

It is difficult to express adequately and accurately my gratitude to Dr. Charles J. Goetz, Hertfield Professor of Law, at the University of Virginia School of Law, who supervised me in drafting my master's thesis. He took great pains in teaching me; but as I cannot affirm that what I learned was all he was particularly meant to be teaching me, I wish to thank him and at the same time to exonerate him. Also, I would like to thank Liam Gilchrist of Blake Dawson Waldron in Melbourne, Australia for the number of informal discussions on the subject and for proof-reading the manuscript. Special thanks are also due to Steven J. Robinson of Davis and Company LL.P. in Vancouver, Canada, for his interest in my work, informal discussions on the subject, and for proofreading the manuscript. Although I have learned much from them, they cannot be held responsible for any of my errors or omissions. I would also like to thank Takayuki Shibashi, professor of law at Chuo University, for his unfailing encouragement on my behalf.

In addition, I would like to thank Paul Kinna and Marilyn Posten for their friendship and interest in my work.

Finally, I would like to express my special thanks to Karel van der Linde, who gave me the very opportunity for this publication, and my editor Ghazaleh Dabiran for her excellent editorial work and courage. Active free competition in the publishing sector is, indeed, realized by businessmen like Karel ver der Linde who, to be successful, are brave enough to venture into a field where angels may fear to thread.

Akira Inoue,
Tokyo, February 2007

About the Author

Attorney at law in Japan and New York State, working with the Tokyo based law firm of Anderson Mori & Tomotsune; Admitted as an attorney at law in Japan in 2000 and in New York State in 2006. LL.B. (Chuo University Scholarship Student) 1996, Chuo University; LL.M. (Chuo University Scholarship Student) 1998, Chuo University Graduate School; LL.M. 2005, University of Virginia School of Law. Passed the Chuo University Faculty of Law Assistant Professor Examination in 1999. From 1988 to 2000, trainee at the Legal Training and Research Institute of Supreme Court of Japan.

Chapter 1

The History and Development of the Japanese Antimonopoly Act

I. OVERVIEW

A. The Basic Structure of the Japanese Antimonopoly Act

The 'Law Concerning Prohibition of Private Monopolization and Maintenance of Fair Trade' (Law No. 54 of 1947) (the 'JAA'), like antitrust regimes in other jurisdictions, is an economically important law which aims to promote free and fair competition in markets, thereby stimulating the creative initiative of entrepreneurs and assuring the protection of the interests of consumers in general.

The model for the JAA is American antitrust law, that is, the Sherman Act, the Clayton Act and the Federal Trade Commission Act. When enacted, the JAA was expected to develop and be applied in the same way as the American antitrust laws. However, the JAA proved incompatible with the real operation of the Japanese economy and the dire economic situation just after World War II. As a result, it was amended significantly in 1953 to introduce several exceptions to the prohibition of cartels and to allow some collaboration among competitors with regards to such things as researching and developing new technology ('R&D'), something that was previously banned. These amendments, and further deregulation of cartels and enterprise combination, have been said to have facilitated the formation of cartels and the concentration of markets, reflecting a competition policy designed to reconstruct the national economy.[1] As a result of these measures, however, cartels have been established as general business practice in Japan beyond the boundaries of the regulations. This cartelization is clearly illegal under the Act.

---

1. *See e.g.*, TOYOKI WATANABE, SIN DOKUSENKINSHIHOU NO JITUMU [THE NEW PRACTICE OF THE JAPANESE ANTIMONOPOLY ACT] 10 – 14 (Shojihomukenkyukai 1981).

Primarily, the JAA prohibits a business from (1) preventing 'free and fair competition' by consulting with other entrepreneurs (the 'Cartel Regulation'),[2] (2) unjustly maintaining its monopolistic position or unjustly excluding other competitors (the 'Monopoly Regulation'),[3] or (3) distorting competition by using any of the sixteen types of unfair trade practices (the 'Unfair Trade Practice Regulation').[4] Also, the JAA provides the substantive rules concerning market concentration (the 'Merger Regulation').[5]

The conduct dealt with by the Cartel Regulation provisions is also described as 'unreasonable restraint of trade', which means to mutually restrict business activities by making cooperative decisions concerning sales price, sales volume, consolidation of manufacturing facilities, and restriction of business partners among competitors, thereby substantially restricting competition in any field of trade. Unreasonable restraint of trade includes conduct such as 'bid rigging', 'price cartelization', 'market segmentation cartelization', 'transaction terms cartelization', 'supply restriction cartelization', 'trading partner restriction cartelization', and others.

The conduct set out in the Monopoly Regulation is called 'private monopolization', which means that entrepreneurs exclude or control the business activities of other entrepreneurs, thereby causing, contrary to the public interest, a substantial restraint of competition in any particular field of trade. Specifically, this means any conduct by a company with a large market share that seeks to exclude the participation of new entrants or restrain the business activities of other competitors by using unjust means (in many cases, but not limited to, any means that violate the Act) in order to increase or maintain market share.

The conduct forbidden by the Unfair Trade Practice Regulation includes the sixteen types of conduct designated by the Japanese Fair Trade Commission ('JFTC') as a hindrance to efficient competition. The types of conduct that are prohibited are: (i) concerted refusal to deal; (ii) other refusals to deal; (iii) discriminatory pricing; (iv) discriminatory treatment of transaction terms, etc; (v) discriminatory treatment in a trade association; (vi) unjustly low price sales; (vii) unjustly high price purchasing; (viii) deceptive customer inducement; (ix) customer inducement by unjust benefits; (x) tie-in sales, etc; (xi) dealing on exclusive terms; (xii) resale price maintenance; (xiii) dealing on restrictive terms; (xiv) abuse of dominant bargaining position; (xv) interference with a competitor's transaction; and (xvi) interference with the internal operation of a competitor's company.

Under the Merger Regulation provisions of the JAA, market concentration which is caused by a business combination such as merger, stock acquisition, or asset acquisition is prohibited when it is likely to substantially restrain competition in any particular fields of trade. The JFTC has primary jurisdiction over the

2. Japanese Antimonopoly Act, Art.3.
3. Japanese Antimonopoly Act, Art.3.
4. Japanese Antimonopoly Act, Art.19.
5. *See e.g.*, Japanese Antimonopoly Act, Art.10.

enforcement of Merger Regulation. However, the JFTC regularly holds 'informal' consultations with relevant Ministries and other sector-specific regulators and, in practice, when ruling on a certain transaction, the JFTC may (and does) take into consideration relevant public and industrial policy issues. Among the various government Ministries, it is generally considered that the Ministry of Economy, Trade and Industry ('METI') has a comparatively strong influence over competition policy. According to the guidelines concerning mergers and acquisitions issued by the JFTC in 1998 and amended in 2004 ('Merger Guidelines'),[6] market concentration is deemed illegal when it appears that market dominant conditions could arise due to one company coordinating with another. It is now understood, even in Japan, that market concentration which results in an oligopolistic market structure entailing oligopolistic price coordination is illegal.

B. The Development of the Japanese Antimonopoly Act

1. Enactment of the Japanese Antimonopoly Act

The original JAA, modelled on the American antitrust laws, contained several unique features not found in the current legislation. Examples of these features are (i) adoption of a *per se* rule against cartels, (ii) stringent control over mergers and acquisitions, (iii) prohibition on an unreasonable difference in terms of economic power among enterprises, and (iv) severe limitations to exceptions to the regulation.

Under the influence of the occupation forces, the JAA was strictly enforced for the first few years after its enactment. From around 1950, however, enforcement was significantly relaxed as a result of the Truman Doctrine and the Korean War. United States' policy changed from discouraging Japan from recovering as an economic power to rebuilding Japan and turning it into a heavily industrialized county which would serve as a bulwark against communism. Also, it was realized that the strict enforcement of the JAA was unrealistic since the Japanese economy had been shattered by World War II and its rehabilitation was still in its infancy.

2. 1953 Amendment of the Japanese Antimonopoly Act

In 1953, the JAA was amended and the major provisions of the Act were relaxed. First, *per se* prohibition of cartels was changed to a prohibition of cartels if they substantially restrained competition contrary to the public interest. Second, the

---

6. The Japanese Fair Trade Commission, *Dokusenkinshihoujouno Kigyoketugosinsa Nikansuru Unyohshisin* [*The Guideline Concerning the Examination on Merger and Acquisition under the Antimonopoly Law in Japan*], (2004), *available at* <http://www2.jftc.go.jp/pressrelease/04.may/04053101.pdf> (last visited 28 February 2005) [hereinafter *Examination Concerning Merger and Acquisition*].

strict regulation of mergers and acquisitions was relaxed. Third, the prohibition on undue difference among enterprises in terms of economic power was abolished. Fourth, depression cartel and rationalization cartel were exempted from the JAA under certain conditions. Fifth, resale price maintenance was also conditionally admitted. Sixth, the provisions dealing with unfair business practices were amended. On the whole, the 1953 amendments were generally regarded as a major relaxation of the JAA. In this regard, it must be noted that the regulation of unfair business practice was the exception. Before the amendments, only unfair methods of competition were prohibited, whereas, after the amendments, unfair business practices became illegal, widening the ambit of regulation.

From around 1960, the JAA was more strictly enforced. Several factors contributed to this change. First, due to strong inflationary pressure at that time, consumer prices continued to rise. Observers thought that the JAA should be more actively applied to price cartels and resale price maintenance, and used to police administered prices. Second, liberalization of capital transactions occurred around this time. This was accomplished through the relaxation and ultimate abolishment of the Japanese Foreign Investment Act. When this Act was strictly enforced, international agreements, including technology licensing agreements, were closely scrutinized and if the provisions of these agreements were deemed to constitute unreasonable business practices, the requisite government approval was not granted unless the provisions at issue were removed. As the regulations pursuant to the Japanese Foreign Investment Act were relaxed, it was considered necessary to provide for the screening of international agreements, including technological licensing agreements, under the JAA. For this reason, the JFTC became very active in applying the JAA. Third, it can be said that Japan became an affluent society in the late 1960s. However, as the society became more prosperous, consumers became increasingly aware of their right to be protected from the exercise of market power by manufacturers. This Japanese consumerism was clearly another factor leading to the strict application of the JAA.

3. 1977 Amendment of the Japanese Antimonopoly Act

The Oil Crisis in 1973 ushered in a new era for the enforcement of the JAA. Hidden cartels, formed by the oil industry in Japan with the intention of fixing price, were discovered and the resulting public outcry included demands for the strict enforcement of the JAA against price manipulation in private industry. Study groups were formed by the JFTC to seek the possibility of an amendment to the Act, and several proposals were made with the aim of making enforcement more effective against market concentration. The government took up this issue and amendments to the JAA were made in 1977. The amendments in 1977 were significant in the history of JAA because it was the first time that amendments were made in order to strengthen the regulations. Among the many amendments of 1977, two reforms are worth close attention. First, the surcharge was introduced. When a price cartel fixed the price by collusion, the JFTC was empowered to order participants of the cartel to pay an administrative fine in order to deprive them of excess profit resulting from cartelization. Second, the price reporting system was introduced, which was subsequently abolished by amendment in 2005. Under this system, when major companies raise prices simultaneously in an oligopolistic market, the JFTC may order them to provide reasons justifying the price increase. This is simply a reporting system which does not involve substantial control over corporate behaviour. However, in view of the fact that firms usually do not wish to provide detailed financial data to the JFTC, this system served as a limited deterrent against simultaneous price increases in oligopolistic markets.

4. 2005 Amendment of the Japanese Antimonopoly Act

In 2005, the JAA was further amended to make enforcement of the Act more effective. More specifically, the amendments, proclaimed on 27 April 2005 and effective from 4 January 2006, aimed primarily to strengthen the regulation of cartels. The magnitude of the power given to the JFTC is said to be the most in the Japanese Antitrust law history. Through the amendment, the antitrust regulations of cartels have become considerably stricter, and the JFTC was given the power to exercise its authority to crack down on cartels much more aggressively. Regarding these amendments, three reforms in particular should be noted. First, the JFTC is now able to exercise compulsory measures to investigate possible antitrust violations for which criminal sanction is imposed (e.g. violation of the Cartel Regulation). Second, the amount of surcharge applicable to cartels has been increased. Third, the Leniency Program has been introduced. This program allows for the reduction of the amount of surcharge imposed on violators of the Act when they voluntarily inform the JFTC of their violations. These amendments will be explained in more detail *below*.

C. Market Power under the Japanese Antimonopoly Act

Under the JAA, market power is defined as the ability to raise the price of a product significantly above the competitive level without losing much business. Some antitrust experts have suggested that price discrimination among consumers implies market power. It should be noted that under the JAA, market power is treated differently from bargaining power. The effects on a market caused by the exercise of market power are anticompetitive in that social welfare losses will occur, that is, diminishing the quantity of goods and services available to society. The effects of bargaining power could be largely pro-competitive, increasing the quantity of goods available to society. Therefore, even when the prices of commodities in a market seem to be below a competitive level, it is necessary to examine what caused this effect so as not equate regular bargaining power with the illegal exercise of market power.

In order to analyze the market power of given parties in Japan, the most important factor is market share, which is often said to be a proxy for market power. A large market share has often been used in evaluating the danger of the exercise of market power in a given market. As a general rule, a significant market share is necessary for a firm to have the kind of market power with which the antitrust laws are concerned.

There is no clear consensus, however, on any specific point below which market power cannot exist. It would be rare to find that a firm with 50 per cent market share could control price over any significant period without substantial cooperation from other firms, although market power is also closely related to the ease of market entry.

Theoretically, in order to assess market power accurately, it is vital to delineate the relevant market. The Japanese courts and the JFTC often adopt this market delineation-market share measurement approach. Therefore, it is necessary to define the relevant market accurately when analyzing market power.

Under the JAA, 'market' is defined as a 'particular field of trade' and is equivalent to 'relevant market' under the US antitrust law. A particular field of trade is the place where the transaction of goods and services between suppliers and purchasers is conducted. In delineating a particular field of trade, it is necessary to take into consideration factors such as the objects of transactions, geographical area of transactions, steps of transactions, the counterparties to transactions, the nature of business activities in question, and the form of transactions. According to Japanese judicial precedents, other factors to define a particular field of trade include suppliers and purchasers, whether or not products are substitutable from the consumers view point, and the difficulties of new entry. Concerning the difficulty of entry into a relevant market, under the JAA, it is generally considered that if entry into the relevant market is so easy that market participants, either collectively or unilaterally, could not increase the price above a competitive level, the entry will likely deter any anticompetitive effects. Relevant case law provides that a particular field of trade is defined by the product and the geographic area, which are the most important considerations. A particular field of trade should be first delineated with regard to products and then geographical area. A particular field of trade may be defined as a market at the manufacture level, a market at the wholesale level or a market at the retail level. It may also be defined as a market for a particular customer or a market for a group of customers.

After defining a particular field of trade, it is then possible to measure market power. In so doing, under the JAA, the general approach is first identifying market participants and then assigning market share to each participants. If the relevant party's market share is more than 80 per cent, it can be inferred the existence of market power. Also, it is generally accepted that the downward sloping curve in the diagram for the market would suggest that market power exists. Also, price discrimination and profit well above the marginal cost would imply market power. Note that in examining the shape of demand curve and whether or not price discrimination has been occurred, it is the pre-condition to delineate relevant market accurately.

Another way to measure market power is the market power index ('MPI'). In order to analyze MPI, it is first necessary to define a relevant market accurately and then to examine the market's supply and demand curve.

MPI is represented in the following equation:

$$MPI = 1/epsilon$$

The epsilon means the elasticity of supply or demand. The elasticity of supply is the measure of the responsiveness of quantity supplied to change in price, whereas the elasticity of demand is the measure of the responsiveness of quantity demanded to change in price. The elasticity of supply is used to measure buyers' market power, while the elasticity of demand shows the suppliers' market power.

With regard to measuring buyers' market power, the elasticity of supply varies with the ability of marginal suppliers to put their resources to alternative uses producing other products or services. Suppliers with highly specialized and immobile equipment might be vulnerable to exploitation by buyers because they have no alternative but to continue supplying their products as long as they can recover their initial investment. As the elasticity increases, buyers' market power declines. In the event that the supply curve is flat and the supply elasticity is infinite, the MPI will be zero, which means no buying power exists in the relevant market. As suggested *above*, when examining the elasticity of supply, the ease of exit from the market should be taken into consideration. The easier it is to exit, the more elastic the supply response would be. In so doing, it would be necessary to consider such factors as how long it takes to convert a plant to new uses, whether or not a production technology is available or subject to patent control, whether or not a converted facility would be sunk, whether or not brand preferences must be established, and whether or not a firm must go into the new industry on a relatively large scale. Also, the higher the elasticity of demand, the more willing other buyers in the market would be to increase their purchases if prices should fall, meaning lower buying power. This would be reflected in the calculation of the MPI. In other words, given that other buyers would increase their consumption substantially at moderately lower prices, suppliers could resist most of the concessions demanded by buyers. As a result, the overall output in a relevant market would not be reduced appreciably, so assuming that buyers try to exercise their market power, it would be difficult for them to affect the quantity and price. In this case, the MPI would be low. Should other purchasers not be able to substitute easily when demand is reduced, decrease of price would not lead to an increase of purchases. In this case, the elasticity of demand would be low, which will, in turn, indicate that the MPI would be high.

On the other hand, with regard to measuring suppliers' market power, the elasticity of demand varies with the ability of marginal buyers to purchase alternatives. The lower the market elasticity of demand and the lower the elasticity of supply of the competitive fringe, the smaller is the market share that will enable a firm to raise price substantially above the competitive level. As the elasticity increases, suppliers' market power declines. In the event that the demand curve is flat and the demand elasticity infinite, the MPI would be zero, which means no suppliers would have significant power in the relevant market. Assessment of barriers to entry is also important in measuring the elasticity of demand. It should be noted that the extent to which established suppliers are constrained by the prospect of new market entry is a key factor in measuring whether or not the demand curve is downward sloping. In some markets, demand curves are downward sloping and prices do not equal marginal cost, but entry is easy and thus, when in equilibrium, firms make only competitive profits, increasing the elasticity of the demand curve and diminishing the MPI. Also, it should be noted that the MPI will increase in markets where entry is easy but the competitors in the market do not sell perfect substitutes. An example would be restaurants, where there are many different competitors but each one is differentiated by several factors, such as cuisine, service, and location. Because no restaurant faces competition from a perfect substitute, each restaurant likely faces a downward sloping demand curve, thus making it possible to exercise market power.

D. Similarities Between the Japanese Antimonopoly Act and United States Antitrust Law

In the JAA, the Cartel Regulation corresponds to section 1 of the Sherman Act, the Monopoly Regulation corresponds to section 2 of the Sherman Act, and the Merger Regulation corresponds to section 7 of the Clayton Act.

In the United States, two antitrust enforcement agencies, the United States Department of Justice ('DOJ') and the United States Federal Trade Commission ('FTC'), coexist. Section 5 of the Federal Trade Commission Act, which bans unfair method of competition, gives the FTC almost the same authority as the DOJ with respect to antitrust enforcement.

In Japan, however, the JAA established only one antitrust agency, namely the JFTC. Under the structure of the JAA, almost all basic antitrust violations are covered by the Cartel Regulation, the Monopoly Regulation and the Merger Regulation. The Unfair Trade Practice Regulation is not an integral part of the JAA. It is a historical relic relating to section 5 of the Federal Trade Commission Act in the United States, which is not needed in Japan as there is only one antitrust agency.

Under the structure of the JAA, antitrust violations other than those covered only by the Cartel Regulation, unfair inducement and intimidation, and the Merger Regulation are covered doubly by both the Monopoly Regulation and the Unfair Trade Practice Regulation. In addition, the Cartel Regulation and the Monopoly Regulation should have been the core regulation of antitrust violations, given the history and structure of the United States Antitrust Law, whereas the Unfair Trade Practice Regulation was expected to play a supplemental role in the antitrust enforcement in Japan. However, the Unfair Trade Practice Regulation has long been considered to be the core regulation of the antitrust enforcement in Japan. As such, the Unfair Trade Practice Regulation has caused substantial confusion regarding the application of the Act.

II. DEVELOPMENT OF THE CASE LAW UNDER THE JAPANESE ANTIMONOPOLY ACT

A. INTRODUCTION

The development of the case law under the JAA can be divided into three stages. The first stage is from 1947 to 1955, during which a considerable number of Tokyo High Court[7] decisions were rendered. The second stage is from 1955 to the mid – 1980s, when no important antitrust decisions were made. The third stage is from the mid – 1980s until the present day, which is a period of significant and important advancement in the development of case law under the JAA.

B. THE INITIAL DEVELOPMENT OF THE CASE LAW UNDER THE JAPANESE ANTIMONOPOLY ACT

The older decisions of the Tokyo High Court handed down during the first stage lacked an understanding of the United States Antitrust Law on which the JAA was based. They also completely distorted the basic idea behind competition regulation. These earlier Tokyo High Court decisions gave rise to much confusion regarding antitrust enforcement in Japan.

The most notable older decisions reflecting this misunderstanding of competition regulation are Newspaper Distribution Conspiracy Case,[8] Toho-Subaru Case,[9] and Toho-Shintoho Case.[10]

The Tokyo High Court in Newspaper Distribution Conspiracy Case ruled that the mutual restriction, one of the constituent elements of the Cartel Regulation, required that the restricted activities be exactly the same business activities or be within the same level of activities (production level, distribution level, wholesaler level, or etc). The Tokyo High Court decided that the conspiracy among newspaper publishers and their distributors did not satisfy the mutual restriction requirement under the Cartel Regulation because it was a conspiracy concluded between different levels of business activities, and this did not constitute a violation of the regulation. According to the ruling, only when either an agreement among newspaper publishers or an agreement among distributors is concluded, the mutual restriction requirement will be fulfilled and a violation of the Cartel Regulation can be found. This ruling adopted an extremely narrow interpretation concerning the

---

7. The High Court in Japan means the court in which appeals against the decision made by the court of first instance can be made, thus similar to appellate courts in the United States.
8. *Asahishinbun K.K. v. Japanese Fair Trade Commission*, 4 GYOSAISHU 609 (Tokyo Hi. Ct. 9 March 1953).
9. *Toho Co. v. Japanese Fair Trade Commission*, 35 GYOSAISHU 144 (Tokyo Hi. Ct. 19 September 1951).
10. *Japanese Fair Trade Commission v. Subaru Kogyo K.K*, 19 HANREIJIHO 11 (Tokyo Hi. Ct. 9 December 1953).

mutuality of restriction requirement. Under this ruling's interpretation, firms which are engaging in agreements restricted by the Cartel Regulation must be in a competitive relationship with each other, essentially meaning that the Cartel Regulation is supposed to prevent only horizontal restrictions.

The Tokyo High Court decision on Toho-Subaru Case and Toho-Sintoho Case established the following rationale concerning the interpretation of 'substantial restraint of competition', one of the constituent elements of the Merger Regulation. First, the Tokyo High Court ruled that substantial restraint of competition meant that a particular firm or firms could control the relevant market by means of determining price, quality, transaction terms and conditions independently from other competitor or consumers, with the effect of lessened competition. This is a very narrow definition of substantial restraint of competition. Second, the *above* definition of substantial restraint of competition was made equally applicable to the Cartel Regulation, the Monopoly Regulation, and all forms of Merger Regulation because of the same term used in each of the regulations.

The initial older case law did help to distinguish the areas covered by each regulation. The Cartel Regulation had been made to cover hard core cartels in which the combined market share of the cartel members exceeded 80 per cent. The Monopoly Regulation had been made to cover only unilateral conduct employed by a monopolist who had a market share in excess of 80 per cent. The Merger Regulation was made only to prevent the creation of a monopolist or a market dominant power in the relevant market. On the other hand, the Unfair Trade Practice Regulation was made to broadly cover all typical unilateral conducts and vertical restraints. Under the old case law, antitrust enforcement by the JFTC inevitably concentrated on challenging hard core cartels based on the Cartel Regulation and unilateral conduct, as well as vertical restraints based on the Unfair Trade Practice Regulation, until the 1980s.

C. The Recent Development of the Case Law under the Japanese Antimonopoly Act

1. Classification of the Conduct Prohibited by the Japanese Antimonopoly Act

Antitrust case law in Japan began to positively develop in the mid – 1980s.

The landmark decisions are the Supreme Court decision on price fixing of petroleum products by oil companies (1984)[11] and the Tokyo High Court decision on exclusive dealing by Toyo Seimaiki (1984).[12] The Tokyo High Court decision on exclusive dealing by Toyo Seimaiki (1984) and both the

11. *Japanese Government v. Idemitu Co.*, 33 KEISHU 1287 (Sup. Ct. 24 February 1984).
12. *Toyo Seimaiki Co. v. Japanese Fair Trade Commission*, 35 GYOSAISHU 144 (Tokyo Hi. Ct. 17 February 1984).

High Court decision (1986)[13] and the Supreme Court decision (1989)[14] on low price sales by a public slaughter house further contributed to the development of the case law regarding unfair trade practices.

These cases made it clear that a market definition and a market analysis (adverse effect on competition) were in principle required to adjudicate an antitrust violation, especially in the case where the Monopoly Regulation or the Merger Regulation is at issue. Originally, the definition of unfair trade practices had been considered not to require a market definition. However, it is becoming clear, with the development of the case law, that most unfair trade practices require reference to market definition and market analysis. In this respect, Toyo Seimaiki Case and Tokyo Shibaura Public Slaughterhouse Case played decisive roles.

As a result of recent case law developments, the JAA is said to be comprised of four main areas, that is, unilateral action, horizontal restraints, vertical restraints, and market concentration. This classification approach is similar to that of the United States Antitrust Law.

With respect to horizontal restraints, cartels are the main targets of the regulations. The *quasi per se* rule is adopted in such a way so that cartels are deemed immediately illegal upon formation, except in extraordinary situations in which cartels are permitted on the ground of public interest. The combined market share of cartel participants, however, must effectively exceed 50 per cent for the *quasi per se* rule to apply.

With respect to vertical restraints, vertical price restraints systematically imposed on distributors or dealers are *quasi per se* violations. Exclusive purchase agreements are illegal if distribution channels to customers are foreclosed to competitors. It is not a violation of the JAA if a manufacturer cuts off transaction with a distributor or a dealer who has failed to comply with requirements given they are imposed on all distributors or dealers of the manufacturer, in order to provide a service that, for a legitimate business purpose, facilitates the distribution of the manufacturer's products.

With respect to unilateral conduct, the use of exclusive dealing or tie in sales by market dominant firms with significant influence in the market is in principal illegal. The JAA has not yet incorporated, however, rules regarding predatory pricing by manufactures operating on a nationwide scale. In addition, it is not clear at what level of market dominance, that is, at what percentage of market share, entities are subject to unilateral conduct rules.

In Japan, there are also regulations on unfair business transactions, aimed at maintaining the fairness of an individual transaction, but the importance of these regulations has diminished considerably since the 1980s.

13. *Mikawashima Meet Plant Co. v. Tokyo-to*, 1182 HANREIJIHO 34 (Tokyo Hi. Ct. 24 February 1984).
14. *Mikawashima Meet Plant Co. v. Tokyo-to*, 43 MINSHU 2078 (Sup. Ct. 14 December 1989).

2. Double Coverage for Unilateral Conduct and Vertical Restraints

Since the mid – 1980s, interpretation of the JAA has begun to return to the basic idea of competition regulation, with the courts recognizing that most of the unilateral conducts and vertical restraints would be covered by both the Monopoly Regulation and the Unfair Trade Practice Regulation.

The Tokyo High Court decision in the bid rigging case in 1993[15] constituted a rejection of the rationale which was adopted in the Tokyo High Court decision in Newspaper Distribution Conspiracy Case.[16] The court found that firms which engaged in restricting the business activities of other firms do not have to be within the same level of the distribution chain or conducting the same kind of business activities. In addition, the court ruled that a particular firm which had not been nominated as a bidder had conspired with the other officially nominated bidders and thus violated the Cartel Regulation. Further, the court rejected the idea that the area covered by the Cartel Regulation should be limited to hard core cartels in which participants of cartels should be in a competitive relationship. The decision rendered by the court suggests that the narrow ambit of the relationship among firms in the context of the Cartel Regulation could not be justified under the JAA.

Currently, based on the analysis of court precedents, the misunderstanding that the Cartel Regulation would be able to cover only horizontal restraints has begun to break down at an academic level, leading most observers to find that the Cartel Regulation covers both horizontal restraints and vertical restraints, although this is not still completely settled in the case law.

3. Definition of Substantial Restraint of Competition

Regarding substantial restraint of competition, the current case law establishes a unified definition for when a particular firm or firms could control the relevant market by means of determining the price, quality, volume and transaction terms with the effect of lessened competition. Furthermore, the case law takes the position that the *above-mentioned* current definition of substantial restraint of competition was equally applicable to the Cartel Regulation, the Monopoly Regulation, and the all forms of business combination covered by the Merger Regulation.

It should be noted that the current case law has begun to adopt a more flexible definition of substantial restraint of competition, one of the examples of which is Asahi Kohmatsu Case.[17] In this case, the agreement involved a related but completely separate product market. Two monopoly firms in these markets made an agreement that each party would not enter into the other party's product market.

15. *Japanese Fair Trade Commission v. Toppan Mua K.K.*, 840 HANREITIMES 81 (Tokyo Hi. Ct. 14 December 1993).
16. *Asahi shinbun K.K. v. Japanese Fair Trade Commission*, 4 GYOSAISHU 609 (Tokyo Hi. Ct. 9 March 1953).
17. *Asahi Kohmatsu K.K. v. Japanese Fair Trade Commission*, 1199 HANREIJIHO 41 (Tokyo Hi. Ct. 13 June 1986).

However, in fact, there was no possibility for these firms to enter into the other party's market. Based on this premise, the Tokyo High Court ruled that the agreement fulfilled the requirement of substantial restraint of competition and was a violation of the Cartel Regulation.

4. Raising the Standard of Illegality for Likelihood of Impeding Fair Competition

On the other hand, the standard of illegality for the likelihood of impeding fair competition, one of the constituent elements of the Unfair Trade Practice Regulation, was raised in the mid – 1980s and now requires an adverse effect on competition in the relevant market.

The landmark cases are the Tokyo High Court decision on exclusive dealing by Toyo Seimaiki (1984)[18] and the Supreme Court decision on low price sales by a public slaughterhouse (1989).[19] These decisions established the principle that in order to analyze the Unfair Trade Practice Regulation case, it is necessary to define the relevant market and examine the competitive effect caused by the conduct at issue.

The Tokyo High Court decision on Toyo Seimaiki case reversed the JFTC's formal decision and remanded the case to the JFTC for further examination. In this case, the JFTC decided that Toyo Seimaiki, which was alleged to have market share of 28 per cent in the relevant market, violated Art. 11 of the general designation (dealing on exclusive terms) by employing exclusive dealing contracts with its distributors. The court held that the foreclosure effect of the exclusive dealing contract in the relevant market needed to exist in order to satisfy the likelihood of impeding the fair competition requirement. The court then decided that the JFTC needed to calculate the market share of Toyo Seimaiki more accurately and examine both the number of distributors in the market and the competitor's distribution method in order to determine whether or not significant foreclosure effects would be caused.

The Supreme Court decision on Tokyo Public Slaughterhouse Case came from a private action for damages, alleging that the Tokyo Public Slaughterhouse violated Art. 6 of the general designation (prevention of unjust low price sales) by charging extremely low slaughter fees as it received subsidies from the Tokyo local government compensating it for its losses. The Tokyo District Court held that Tokyo Public Slaughterhouse was liable for violating Art. 6 of the general designation and awarded compensation to the plaintiffs, the private slaughterhouses which were the sole competitors in the Tokyo metropolitan area.

The Tokyo High Court and the Supreme Court reversed the District Court's decision and denied the liability of the Tokyo Public Slaughterhouse. They found that they were also competing with 59 other slaughterhouses situated in the surrounding Kanto and Tohkai areas. Both courts found that, among the 59 competing

18. *Toyo Seimaiki Co. v. Japanese Fair Trade Commission*, 35 GYOSAISHU 144 (Tokyo Hi. Ct. 17 February 1984).
19. *Mikawashima Meet Plant Co. v. Tokyo Public Slaughter House*, 43 MINSHU 2078 (Sup. Ct. 14 December 1989).

slaughter houses, the slaughter fees paid to 47 slaughter houses were below those of the plaintiffs and the slaughter fees paid to 11 slaughter houses were below those of the defendant. Furthermore, the decisions stressed the fact that, as a general trend, slaughterhouses in big cities were suffering losses because farmers preferred sending livestock to those located in rural areas due to technological developments in transportation devices for frozen block meat. The court held that the definition of the geographic market had a decisive role even when adjudicating Unfair Trade Practice Regulation violation cases.

Furthermore, the Supreme Court decision in both Shiseido Case (1998)[20] and Kao Case (1998) affirmed the ongoing movement.

The Supreme Court stated that, in general, stricter proof should be required to fulfill the illegality requirement of the likelihood of impeding fair competition standard, even when adjudicating whether or not the business activities at issue constitute a violation of the Unfair Trade Practice Regulation. Also, the Supreme Court ruled that the cosmetic sales distribution contract, which necessitated face-to-face counselling in selling products, does not violate Art. 13 of the general designation (prohibition on dealing on restrictive terms) inasmuch as the face-to-face sales meet the two prong test. The first test is whether or not there is some justification for imposing the duty to conduct face-to-face counselling in selling the products. The second test is whether or not such a duty is imposed upon all other dealers. Based on the analysis concerning the two prong test, the court decided that the requirement to conduct the face-to-face counselling in the cosmetic distribution contract fulfilled the two conditions and that termination of the contract with discount stores due to their non-compliance with the obligation did not violate the Unfair Trade Practice Regulation.

As a result of these decisions, it became apparent that adverse effects on competition in the relevant market need to be examined in order to analyze whether or not 'likelihood of impeding far competition' will occur.

III. TRANSFORMATION OF 'UNFAIR METHOD OF COMPETITION' INTO 'UNFAIR TRADE PRACTICE' AND LATER DEVELOPMENT

A. Changes in Characteristics of the Unfair Trade Practice Regulation

1. The 1953 Amendment-Creation of the Unfair Trade Practice

As mentioned *above*, the Unfair Trade Practice Regulation has played a major role in the unique development of the JAA. A brief overview of the history of the Unfair Trade Practice Regulation is required to the extent necessary to understand the JAA.

20. 1234 HANREIJIHO 7 (Sup. Ct. 18 December 1998).

In 1953, the words 'unfair method of competition' found in Art. 19 of the JAA were changed to 'unfair business practices or unfair trade practice'. This significant change is one of the keys to understanding the unique development of antitrust enforcement in Japan.

Unfair trade practice was different from unfair method of competition in three ways. First, the substantive standard of illegality has changed from a standard of 'contrary to public interest' to a standard of 'likely to impede fair competition'. At the time the change was made, the likelihood of impeding fair competition was considered to be a much lower standard than the substantial restraint of competition in the relevant market. Second, the authority of the JFTC to designate illegal conduct to be an unfair trade practice is limited. The JFTC can only designate illegal conduct to be an unfair trade practice if the conduct is provided for in the JAA Art. 2, para. 9. Prior to the 1953 amendment, the JFTC had the power to designate any conduct contrary to the public interest to be an unfair method of competition in addition to the conduct provided for in the JAA Art. 2, para. 9. Judging from the types of conduct provided for in the JAA Art. 2, para. 9, it is clear that unfair trade practice does not include horizontal restraint on competition, particularly for hard core cartels.

Third, the illegal conduct provided for in the JAA Art. 2, para. 9 includes the new pattern of conducts such as dealing with another party by unjust or undue use of one's superior bargaining position, unjustly or unduly interfering with a transaction between a competing firm and any other trading party. As a result, unfair trade practice restrictions were considered to be the fundamental rules of day-to-day transactions with which every firm had to comply.

Unfair trade practices designated by the JFTC are divided into two categories. One category is a general designation which is applied to all industries and the other category is a sector-specific designation, that is, a special designation which is applied to a particular industry. This will be explained in detail *below*.

2. General Designation and Designated Conducts

In 1953, for the first time in the Japanese antitrust law history, the JFTC designated nine patterns of conduct under the general designation of unfair trade practices. In 1982, the JFTC replaced these by designating sixteen patterns of new conduct under a new general designation of unfair trade practice in order to clarify each violation in more detail, reflecting past decisions and experience concerning the practical implementation of the Act. Both the old general designation and the new general designation cover concerted refusal to deal, unjust low price sales, tie-in sales, dealing on exclusive terms, unilateral refusal to deal and all typical types of vertical restraints.

Almost all unilateral conduct is covered by the general designation on unfair trade practice. Also, Vertical restraints are fully covered by Arts. 11, 12, and 13 of the general designation. Regarding horizontal restraint, Art. 1 covers concerted refusal to deal against both a particular trading party and a particular competitor-secondary boycott.

As a result, the general designation of unfair trade practice does not cover *per se* illegal hard core cartels and rule of reason type horizontal restraints such as restriction on information exchanges, research and development agreement and standard setting agreement among competitors, which are exclusively governed by the Cartel Regulation. The general designation also does not cover unilateral conduct which does not conform to the designated typical unilateral conducts, which are covered by the Monopoly Regulation.

Furthermore, Art. 8 of the general designation covers deceptive customer inducement and Art. 9 of the general designation covers customer inducement by unjust benefit. These are typical customer projection clauses which correspond to section 5 of the US Federal Trade Commission Act.

3. Unique Regulation Based on Art. 14 of the General Designation

Art. 14 of the general designation established a type of regulation unique to Japan, as it prohibits unfair transaction and practices between two contracting parties. Under the article, a dominant bargaining position means that one contracting party has a stronger bargaining power over another party. It is different from market dominance or market power. In practice, it is assumed that in each particular type of transaction, one party always has a superior bargaining position and, based on that assumption, fair transaction rules are determined by either statutes or the guidelines of the JFTC. The regulation based on Art. 14 protects the party with the weaker bargaining position.

The types of transactions primarily targeted by the regulation were (i) international licensing agreements, (ii) international sole distributor agreements, (iii) supplying agreements with large scale retailers, and (iv) subcontract transactions between a parent manufacturer and a subcontractor.

In an international licensing transaction, a foreign licensor was presumed to be in a superior bargaining position to a Japanese licensee. A set of rules were established under the guidelines regarding grant back (obligation to grant a license for patents on improvements or developments), non-competition and tie-ins in order to maintain fair licensing transactions.

In an international sole distributor transaction, a foreign firm was also presumed to have a superior position over a Japanese sole distributor. A set of rules were established under the guidelines, including rules on resale price maintenance and tie-in aimed at maintaining fair distribution transactions.

In order to maintain the effectiveness of Art. 14, parties to international agreements such as licensing agreements, distribution agreements, and joint venture agreements between a foreign firm and Japanese firm were required to notify the JFTC within 30 days after signing the agreement. After receipt of notification, JFTC officials examined each notified agreement pursuant to the guidelines. When an official found guideline violations, the official requested the Japanese firm to renegotiate and to delete or revise the clauses in question. In this way, the purpose and effect of the *above* delineated regulation pursuant to Art. 14 had been the protection of Japanese firms from foreign firms.

The aforementioned two types of regulation were criticized and finally abolished in 1997.

In a supply type transaction with a large scale retailer such as a department store, a chain store or a supermarket, it is assumed that the large scale retailer is always in a stronger bargaining position than the supplier. The JFTC issued a special designation on unfair trade practice concerning supply type transactions with a department store.[21] The special designation prohibits a department store from engaging in actions such as unduly returning the purchased products, unduly refusing to accept the ordered product, unduly reducing the agreed price and coercing the seller to send salespeople. The JFTC has applied the same special rules to supply type transactions with other large scale retailers.

In a subcontract transaction between a parent manufacturer and its subcontractor, the parent company is presumed to have a stronger bargaining position than the subcontractor. The same idea concerning the disparity between them in terms of bargaining power was adopted in the 'Act Against Delay in Payment of Subcontract Proceeds, etc. to Subcontractor' ('Subcontractor Act') enacted in 1956. The Subcontractor Act purports, by preventing delay in payment of subcontract proceeds, etc., to protect the interests of subcontractors, thereby contributing to the wholesome development of the national economy. In order to achieve the ultimate purpose, the Subcontractor Act prohibits unduly refusing to accept ordered products, unduly delaying payment, unduly returning accepted products and unduly reducing the agreed upon price.

In practice, Art. 14 of the general designation had the purpose and effect of protecting firms with a weak bargaining position against firms with a strong bargaining position.

4. Unique Japanese Style Regulation

The aforementioned unfair business contract and transaction regulation has an extremely weak connection with the relevant market. This is true even if the unfair transaction may be employed simultaneously to all or many contracting firms. It should be noted, however, that there is an argument that unfair trade practice might have the dangerous potential to become a common practice in the industry and therefore should be banned. In handling each case concerning unfair trade practice, when the JFTC found that an unfair trade practice existed, it rendered an administrative warning[22] to violators, demanding them to take corrective measures rather than issuing the formal order. This practice had been considered appropriate and

21. The Japan Fair Trade Commission, *Designation of Specific Unfair Trade Practices by Large-Scale Retailers Relating to the Trade with Suppliers,* (2005), *available at* <http://www.jftc.go.jp/e-page/legislation/ama/large_scale_retailers.pdf> (last visited on 23 March 2006).

22. It should be noted that in Japan an administrative warning by the JFTC, which is sometimes used to terminate a formal proceeding after commencement of an investigation, is a completely different administrative measure from an elimination order. An administrative warning will

efficient because the effect on the relevant market caused by each transaction might be minimal.

In terms of the restriction on supply type transactions and subcontract transactions, the competition laws of each country have unique regulations reflecting their own historical development, such as the price discrimination regulations pursuant to the Robinson Patman Act in the United States and special rules for promoting market integration in the EU competition law. Competition authorities of each country, however, are increasingly reluctant to implement those unique regulations. It can be said that the unique restriction pursuant to Art. 14 of the general designation brings about the same reluctance as such rules in competition regulation regimes of other countries.

5. Likelihood of Impeding Fair Competition

The general designation provides a diverse array of conducts as constituting unfair trade practice. It is almost impossible to give a unified definition of the likelihood of impeding fair competition for unfair trade practice.

However, it was widely believed until around 1980 that the likelihood of impeding unfair competition was a much lower substantive standard than the substantial restraint of competition standard of the JAA Art 3. It was also widely believed that unfair trade practice in general did not require adverse effects on the relevant market. One of the justifications for the aforementioned interpretations of the JAA is that it had been considered in Japan that an administrative remedy given by the antitrust agency is a more effective way to restore fair competition than a judicial remedy rendered by a court. This approach generated the tendency to lower the threshold for the JFTC to bring an action to prevent unfair trade practices. It should be noted that, in terms of antitrust enforcement, judicial remedies have not functioned effectively until recently.

B. Related Provisions and Problems

Based on the aforementioned idea that the Unfair Trade Practice Regulation governs day-to-day business transactions and this type of regulation provides the principal competition rules in the Japanese market, prohibition on unfair trade practices was incorporated into the following main regulations and provisions of the JAA in 1953.

---

be issued when an investigation has been initiated but sufficient evidence has not been found to establish the case, and the JFTC has made successfully suspected parties correct their business activities voluntarily. In Japan, administrative warnings have been criticized in that they are used frequently so that the JFTC settled cases even when it found a violation. *See e.g.*, TADASHI SHIRAISHI, DOKUKINHOH KOUGI [The Lecture of Japanese Antimonopoly Act] 169 (3d edn. 2005).

First, under the Merger Regulation, business combinations were prohibited when market concentration would be likely to substantially restrain competition in any particular field of trade. In addition, employing unfair trade practices in the process of market concentration, such as in mergers and acquisitions, was prohibited.

Second, under the JAA Art. 6, international agreements which contained unfair trade practice-type agreements, as well as international agreements which contained unreasonable restraint of trade-type agreements, were prohibited as illegal international agreements.

Third, under the JAA Art. 8, transactions by trade associations were prohibited when they would substantially restrain competition in the relevant market.

Fourth, under the JAA Art. 24, which governed the actions of cooperative actions by partners, small and medium sized firms, the act of unduly raising sales prices by substantially restraining competition in the relevant market was prohibited as an exception to the general exemption from the regulations under the JAA. In addition, it was also prohibited for partners, small and medium sized firms to be engaged in unfair trade practices as an exception to the general exemption from the regulation under the Act.

These newly incorporated unfair trade practice provisions were unnecessary and redundant in nature and have inevitably brought much confusion in interpretation of each regulation.

Chapter 2
Substantive Rules of the JAA

I. HORIZONTAL RESTRAINT

A. Hard Core Cartel-Quasi per se Rule

In Japan, hard core cartels have been a major enforcement target of the JFTC since the enactment of the JAA and especially after 1989, which was triggered by the United States' discovery of bid rigging cases in construction industries in the Structural Impediments Initiative Talks between the Japanese and United States governments. Actually, the JFTC was well aware of the problem, but its previous response had been to issue extremely weak warnings on construction bid rigging rather than taking an active prosecutorial approach. The JFTC's enforcement on bid rigging in the post – 1989 period became more vigorous.

Under the JAA, the principle known as the quasi per rule is applied to hard core cartels, typically price fixing and bid rigging. As such, the case law establishing the *quasi per se* rule has been developed in cases concerning price fixing and bid rigging cases.

Under the JAA, horizontal restraints are covered by the Cartel Regulation. The Cartel Regulation was defined in the JAA art 3.

The JAA Art. 3 provides that no entrepreneur shall effect private monopolization or unreasonable restraint of trade. With regard to 'unreasonable restraint of trade', the JAA Art. 2, para. 6 clarifies its definition and adds that it shall mean 'such business activities, by which any entrepreneur, by contract, agreement or any other concerted actions, irrespective of its names, with other entrepreneurs, mutually restrict or conduct their business activities in such a manner as to fix, maintain, or increase prices, or to limit production, technology, products, facilities, or customers or suppliers, thereby causing, contrary to the public interest, a substantial restraint of competition in any particular field of trade'.

In Japan, the condition of 'in any particular field of trade' is always construed together with the condition of 'substantial restraint of competition' and has no independent significance.[1]

Therefore, in order to determine whether certain business activities constitute an 'unreasonable restraint of trade', three main conditions are looked at, namely, (i) substantial restraint of competition in any particular field of trade, (ii) mutually restrict or conduct their business, and (iii) against the public interest.

Hereinafter, three elements will be explained separately and, concerning their application, along with how the *quasi per se* rule has been established in the Japanese case law.

1. The Interpretation of 'Substantial Restraint of Competition in Any Particular Field of Trade'

Generally, 'substantial restraint of competition' means that a competitive function in a given market is substantially restrained or that an important function of a given market is lost.

More precisely, the Tokyo High Court in Toho-Subaru Case[2] made the definition of a substantial restraint of competition in any particular field of trade clearer.

It should be noted that although Toho Co. ('Toho') appealed to the Supreme Court seeking to reverse and have the court enter a new judgment, the judgment at the Tokyo High Court was affirmed by the Supreme Court.[3]

The essential facts of this case are as follows.

Toho concluded a lease agreement with Subaru Co. ('Subaru') to rent two theatres located at Yurakucho and Thiyodaku in Tokyo on 26 January 1950. The JFTC decided that the concluding of the lease agreement would cause substantial restraint of trade because through the agreement Toho would have come to operate eight theatres out of ten located in the Yurakucho and Marunouchi area. The total seating capacity of the ten theatres was 10,787. On the other hand, the eight theatres operated by Toho already had a fixed seating capacity of 9,742 seats. This was 90.4 per cent of total numbers in the area. As Toho refused to accept the recommendation from the JFTC, it initiated the hearing. Toho filed the litigation seeking reversal of the judgment by the JFTC at the Tokyo High Court on the ground that its order lacked sufficient evidence to prove that competition in that area would be substantially restrained.

The Tokyo High Court, however, dismissed Toho's claim. Since the JFTC intervened in this case at the time when the lease agreement between the two parties was concluded and before the actual lease had begun, the elimination orders

---

1. MASAHIRO MURAKAMI, DOKUSENKINSHIHOH [The Japanese Antimonopoly Law] 69 (Hirobundou 2000) (1996).
2. *Toho Co. v. Japanese Fair Trade Commission*, 4 MINSHU 497 (Tokyo Hi. Ct. 19 September 1951).
3. *Toho Co. v. Japanese Fair Trade Commission*, 8 MINSHU 950 (Sup. Ct. 19 May 1954).

pursuant to the JAA Art. 7 was issued in the form of a prohibition of leasing two theatres from Subaru to Toho, participating in the management of two theatres, and engaging in any business activities having the same effects as the lease agreement. Although the Tokyo High Court determined that through the lease agreement at issue, Toho would come to dominate the relevant market; the actual market share of Toho would increase by only 7.7 per cent even when the lease agreement was executed. Based on the foregoing facts, the Tokyo High Court ruled as follows:

'Substantial restraint of competition stipulated in the JAA Art. 15, para. 1 does not mean each action conducted by an entrepreneur as the plaintiff argued, but means the situation where in fact the competition in the relevant market has been reduced substantially and a business or a body of business has a power to control a market by changing a price, quality and quantity of goods and so on, at its will, or is about to have such a power ... Although the number of seats increased through the transaction by the plaintiff was small, considering the location of both theatres, their high reputation, and the fact that they have been used to show a lot of foreign movies, when the plaintiff comes to have a substantial control over the two theatres, in addition to the fact that the plaintiff has a majority of number of seat in the area, it can be found that the plaintiff has great influence in deciding price and number of movies shown in the area. Therefore, we conclude that the competition in the relevant market will be substantially restrained by the lease agreement. The argument by the plaintiff that there is insufficient evidence to support the fact that competition will be substantially restrained on the ground that the increased number of seats through the transaction was minimal is not persuasive'.

Even though Toho-Subaru Case judgment was not made concerning the interpretation of the JAA Art. 2, para. 6, since the same language is used, the prevailing view in Japan is that the definition established in the judgment concerning 'substantial restraint of competition in any particular field of trade' shall apply to the interpretation of the JAA Art. 2, para. 6.

From this judgment, however, the meaning of the words 'situation where in fact competition in a certain market has been reduced substantially and a body of business has the power to control a market by changing a price, quality and quantity of goods and so on, at its will or is about to have such a power' is not completely clear.

Due to this opaqueness, commentators and scholars have been trying to clarify the meaning of the aforementioned language.

Today, it has been pointed out that this condition should be interpreted by taking into consideration other factors, such as market share of relevant parties, several factors concerning suppliers and purchasers, whether or not there are substitutes, and the difficulties of new entry.[4]

In addition, it has been indicated that the condition of 'any particular field of trade' should be construed as the place where the transaction of goods and services between suppliers and purchasers is conducted. Economically speaking, this has

---

4. *See e.g.*, MURAKAMI, *supra* note 1, at 70.

the same meaning as 'marketplace'. Further, it has been noted that, in interpreting this condition, such factors as objects of the transaction, geographical area of the transaction, steps of the transactions, counterparties to the transaction, nature of business activities in question, and form of transaction should be taken into consideration.

The Supreme Court, as explained in detail later in this study, adopted the idea that, in price fixing cases, when a price fixing agreement is found, except for in the case where parties apparently have no power to implement their agreement to restrain competition, the requirement of 'substantial restraint of competition in any particular field of trade' is deemed to satisfy the claim and the burden of proof shifts to the defendant's side to demonstrate that they were unable to affect competition.

In other words, under the established case law, when a hard core cartel agreement is found, except for in bid rigging cases, the condition of 'any particular field of trade' is automatically determined as commodities or services and geographical area purported in the agreement at issue and the condition of 'substantial restraint of competition' is also automatically satisfied by assuming that the agreement contained such an anticompetitive effect. To put it another way, in hard core cartel cases, when a cartel agreement is found, this condition is automatically fulfilled without an elaborate examination.

Based on the *above*, it has been evaluated that the Supreme Court adopted a principle similar to the American *per se* rule (the '*quasi per se* rule') and detailed examination of this condition is no longer necessary in hard core cartel cases.

2. The Interpretation of 'Mutually Restrict or Conduct Their Business'

The Supreme Court in Oil Industry Case clarified the condition of 'mutually restrict or conduct their business'.

The facts of this case are as follows.

After the price increase of crude oil by OPEC in late 1970, it was feared in Japan that the price of commodities made of oil would increase dramatically. In fact, in late 1973, social disorder arose because of the sharp increase in the price of oil-related products. In 1971, the METI issued a large amount of administrative guidance, including a directive requiring wholesalers in the oil industry to bear ten cents per barrel of the price increase of OPEC at that time. In addition, the METI required that the wholesalers informed it when they would raise the price of oil, and sometimes directed them as to how much to raise the price. After 1971, pursuant to the directions of the METI, the wholesalers raised the price several times. Neither the JFTC nor the Prosecutors Office raised antitrust concerns about these practices.

In 1973, before consultation with the METI, the people in charge of each wholesaler company frequently met to discuss and decide on when and by how much to raise the price of oil. Following these meetings, and after obtaining permission from the METI, the wholesalers did in fact raise the price five times. At that time, the METI also directed them not to raise the price due to the new pact concluded among the nations of the OPEC, and requested them to report the METI prior to their price rises.

In this case, the defendants argued that their agreement and subsequent price rises did not constitute a violation of the JAA because they were just following the directions of the METI and they had obtained permission before raising their prices.

The Tokyo High Court held that all the defendants were guilty, rejecting their arguments. On appeal, the Supreme Court found that 20 out of 23 of the defendants were guilty. In handing down its judgment, with regard to the justification defence, the Supreme Court stated that 'The defendants concluded the agreements by which they would raise the price of the oil simultaneously, with strong intent to implement it and anticipating that other participants of the agreement would follow the execution. Therefore, it is explicit that the agreement had an effect of restricting their business once they concluded it. Their agreement satisfied the condition of "mutually restrict or conduct their business" and constituted unreasonable restraint of trade stipulated in the JAA Art. 3. The fact that there were no sanctions which guaranteed the implementation of the agreements does not affect the conclusion of this judgment'.

The Supreme Court adopted the view that a strong binding power was not required to meet the condition of 'mutually restrict their business' and that when a price fixing agreement is concluded this condition would be automatically met. This reasoning is said to be the ground on which the Supreme Court adopted the *quasi per se* rule in hard core cartel cases.

3. The Interpretation of 'Against Public Interest'

The Supreme Court in Oil Industry Case defined the condition 'against public interest' and said 'judging from the purpose, the keystone and the progresses of the JAA, 'against public interest' stipulated in the JAA Art. 2, para. 6, in principle, means against the establishment of free competition which the Act seeks to accomplish. However, even if a certain action should appear to be against the public interest formally, such an action should not be regarded as 'against the public interest' when it is not substantially against the ultimate purpose of the JAA Art. 1, which says that the Act 'aims to promote free and fair competition, to stimulate the creative initiative of entrepreneurs, to encourage business activities of enterprises, to heighten the level of employment and people's real income, and thereby to promote the democratic and wholesome development of the national economy as well as to assure the interests of consumers in general, which requires a comparison of the principal purpose of the Act and the interests protected by such a business activity ... when businesses agree to restrict each other by fixing the prices through mutual consultation, provided that it should be found that the competition in the relevant market place has been restrained substantially against the public interest by their agreement, it would become immediately a violation of the Act and there is no need to examine an actual implementation of the agreement'.

The Supreme Court judgment *above* impacts Japanese antitrust policy in three significant ways.

First, the Supreme Court demonstrated its view that public interest in the JAA Art. 2, para. 6 meant the promotion of the democratic and wholesome development of the national economy as well as assuring the interests of consumers in general, which are stipulated in the Act Art. 1. Before this judgment, there were two views concerning the definition of the public interest. The first view was to regard the public interest as an economic order based on free competition and assumed that, by promoting it, the purpose of the JAA stipulated in Art. 1 would be realized.[5] The JFTC had adopted the first view before the Supreme Court judgment.[6] According to the first view, restraint of competition is deemed against the public interest without exception. The second view was to regard it as the promotion of the general interest of the public in addition to realizing free competition.[7] The second view could lead to a greater possibility for a restraint of trade to be justified on the ground that it was not against the public interest.

Judging from the language of the JAA Art. 1, it is clear that the Act's purpose would be realized by a sound economic order based on free competition, the basic policy of the JAA. Therefore, the first view is more in line with the inherent intention of the JAA.

However, as the Supreme Court judgment suggested, the assumption that carrying out the policy always contributes to the purpose of the JAA is not necessarily true because that hypothesis has not yet been verified even after almost fifty years since the JAA's enactment. It might be argued that the Supreme Court adopted the middle course between the first and the second view because it admitted the possibility that a cartel might be justified, whereas it denied the general interest of the public should be included in the concept of the 'public interest'.

The second significant impact is that the Supreme Court admitted that, although the JAA purported to realize the public interest, there could be a situation where the public interest would be realized by permitting cartels. In sum, even when hard core cartels are formed, they could be justified as not being against the public interest. When emphasizing the rationale of the judgment which says that after comparing an economic order based on free competition with the interest protected by the business activity in question, given that the latter trumped the former (i.e., it is not 'against the public interest'), the possibility that hard core cartels could be justified would be greater.

However, this judgment admitted that 'against public interest' had the same meaning as against an economic order based on free competition and that justifying a price fixing agreement as not against public interest was an exception. Therefore, the cases where hard core cartels would be justified under the rationale of the

5. *See e.g.*, YOSHIO KANAZAWA, KEIZAIHOH [Law of Economy] 159 (Yuhikaku 1980).
6. See Nodashouyu Co., 4 SHINKETSUSHU 1 (FTC, 4 April 1952). See also *Nodashoyu Co. v. Fair Trade Commission*, 8 GYOSAISHU 2300 (Tokyo Hi. Ct. 25 December 1958).
7. *See e.g.*, YOSHIHIKO RYOKAKU, KYOSOUTO DOKUSENNO HANASHI [The Talk About Competition and Monopoly] 170 (Soukeisha, 1978).

Supreme Court judgment should be very limited.[8] This deliberation is supported by the fact that the price fixing agreement at issue in the Supreme Court judgment in Oil Industry Case in which the raising of prices was implemented in accordance with the direction by the METI was found to be illegal.[9]

It should be noted that with regard to the relationship between the administrative guidance issued by the METI and the price fixing agreement, both the JFTC and the METI issued positioning papers concerning the question of the relationship between administrative guidance and the JAA. The JFTC's memo asserted that if an administrative guidance was not grounded in statutes, antitrust concern should arise since freedom of enterprise would be restricted, adversely affecting price, quantity, and other factors relevant to trading in a market. Also, the JFTC expressed that administrative guidance involving trade association was especially problematic since it was likely to precipitate concerted conduct by members. In addition, the JFTC pointed out that even administrative guidance given on a personal basis to individuals in each enterprise might give rise to anticompetitive conduct if the Ministry employed the standard guidelines concerning price and quantity, since each enterprise would follow such guidelines on the assumption that others would do the same. On the other hand, METI's memo argued that administrative guidance which was not based on statutes was nonetheless issued within the framework of laws conferring the METI's general administrative power and was premised on voluntary cooperation of enterprises receiving such guidance. The METI also expressed that administrative guidance was not binding and guidance given on an individual basis to each enterprise could not violate the JAA as there were no collusive agreements.

Concerning this issue, the Supreme Court in Oil Industry Case said 'when taking into consideration the necessity to cope with the dynamic situation flexibly, there is no reason why administrative guidance having no grounding in the law should be determined as illegal inasmuch as such a way of administrative guidance is within the common idea of the society, and it may not interfere with the ultimate purpose of the law when there is a strong necessity for the guidance to be issued. Although a price fixing agreement seemed to be a violation of thc JAA facially, when such an agreement was concluded by following and cooperating with legitimate administrative guidance, an agreement would be justified'. Although the Supreme Court admitted the legitimacy of the administrative guidance, it denied that the price fixing cartel would be justified, the reasoning of which says 'it is clear

8. *See e.g.*, KENZO SANEKATA, JOHKAI DOKUSENKINSHIHOH [The Interpretation of the Japanese Antimonopoly Law] 37 (Kobundo 1997).
9. MURAKAMI, *supra* note 1, at 66–67. *See also* KAN IJUH, DOKUSENKINSHIHOH NO TEBIKI [The Guidance of the Japanese Antimonopoly Law] 33 (Tokyokeizaishinpousha 1982). According to this article, the practice at the JFTC has been consistently that the fact that a certain business activity was the result of following the direction by the Ministry does not always justify it. Basically the policy taken by the JFTC is correct because whether or not a certain business activity meets the requirement of a justifiable cause is case-by-case judgment and traditionally the courts in Japan tend not to admit the satisfaction of the requirement of a justifiable cause easily.

that their raising of the price was not made by cooperating with the Ministry because they agreed not only to how much to raise the price but also to raising the price of oil from tomorrow on the premise that they would obtain the permission from the Ministry about their price raise'.

There could be an argument against the rationale of the Supreme Court judgment based on the idea that it hindered the stability of the law and it might lead to the arbitrary application of the law because the Supreme Court did not clarify under what cases and conditions a price fixing agreement would be justified.

However, even when adopting the standpoint of the Supreme Court judgment, there would be no changes in that a price fixing agreement in principle is illegal under the JAA, because the justification is only an exception to be permitted in limited and exceptional cases.

In addition, the parties which are going to form a cartel are always compelled to do so at the risk of violating the law, which sometimes triggers the commencement of derivative actions when the parties are corporations, as well as possible criminal sanctions and surcharges. Since it is clear that the party shall bear a huge risk in forming a cartel, the party could easily anticipate whether or not they should form it by taking into consideration the huge legal risk arising out of it. Further, twenty years have passed since the Supreme Court judgment was rendered, and there have been no situations in which the law has been applied arbitrary nor implementation of the law impaired due to the vagueness of the language in the judgment. Therefore, the standpoint adopted in the judgment should be upheld.

The third significance is that the Supreme Court made it clear that, in a price fixing case, when the court finds an agreement, it is deemed to satisfy all the constituent elements of the Cartel Regulation and it will be presumed to be illegal without the court reviewing the real effects of an agreement on the competition and examining whether or not it is against public interest. In this regard, it can also be said that, as to a price fixing case, the Supreme Court adopted the *quasi per se* rule.

It should be noted, however, that the *quasi per se* rule adopted by the Supreme Court is different from the United States *per se* rule in the following three respects. First, as explained earlier in this book, cartels could be justified as being not against the public interest. Second, under the subsequent case law, the combined share of cartel participants must exceed 50 per cent in the relevant market so as to assure the effective implementation of cartel agreements. To put it another way, a cartel agreement could be justified by the fact that the cartel participants lacked enough market power. Third, with respect to bid rigging, individual bid rigging does not constitute a violation of the Cartel Regulation.

The Supreme Court also clarified that establishing the fact that a price fixing agreement was not against the public interest is an issue upon which the defendants bear the burden of proof. In other words, it is presumed that a price-fixing agreement meets the condition of (i) substantial restraint of competition in any particular field of trade, (ii) mutually restrict or conduct their business, and (iii) against public interest. Thus, the agreement is presumed to be illegal and the burden of proof to verify that the agreement will not cause a substantial restraint of competition or promote public interests shifts to the defendant's side as a justifiable cause.

The distribution of the burden of proof articulated in the Supreme Court judgment should be upheld because it is consistent with the traditional interpretation of articles of the law which stipulate a criminal or administrative penalty. This traditional interpretation requires reviewing, separately in this order, three aspects of the law; fulfilment of a constituent element, existence of a justifiable cause, and a cause of non-culpability.[10] Also, the traditional interpretation grants a strong presumption of illegality should all constituent elements be fulfilled.

Before the Supreme Court judgment in Oil Industry Case, there were several views as to at which point in time a hard core cartel agreement will be a violation of the Cartel Regulation. The first view was that a hard core agreement becomes a violation of the Act at the time when an agreement was concluded, which was adopted by the Supreme Court judgment and the subsequent Tokyo High Court judgment. The second view was to regard the commencement of action toward reaching an agreement as a violation of the law. The third view was to regard the real implementation of the agreement as a violation of the Act. The most important grounds of the second and third views is the language of the JAA Art. 2, para. 6, which provides 'causing, contrary to the public interest, a substantial restraint of competition in any particular field of trade', and not 'trying to cause a substantial restraint of competition'. To be sure, it is consistent to interpret the Act in accordance with the second and third views. In addition, before the Supreme Court judgment, the JFTC had rendered a judgment in which not only a conclusion of the agreement but also an implementation of it had been taken as the appropriate time. Further, it had been the common practice at the JFTC to mention real implementation of an agreement. On the other hand, the first view had advocated that it was unrealistic to consider that the JFTC could not do anything even when it could find a hard core agreement before its implementation.

It is not appropriate to construe, however, that this is the decisive ground for the Supreme Court adopting the first view because practically it has been quite rare for the JFTC to expose a hard core agreement before its implementation. Even when it did expose such an agreement, it can be said that in most cases the reason why the JFTC did not issue an elimination order did not lie in the fact that it adopted the first view but because the parties to the agreement complied with an informal direction by the JFTC which made issuing the formal order became no longer necessary. The most important ground for the Supreme Court in adopting

10. *See Idemitsu v. Fair Trade Commission*, 33 KOUKEISHU 497 (Tokyo Hi. Ct. 26 September 1980). In this case, the Tokyo High Court decided that the chairman of the oil union which cooperated the administrative directions by the METI were inculpable because they lacked the recognition of the illegality of their price coordination. The METI had admitted and welcomed the price coordination as a well-organized production for a long period of time. In addition, the JFTC had not initiated any proceedings in spite of the fact that they had recognized that the oil manufacturing corporations had regulated their pricing. Based on these facts, the court decided that it was too much severe to conclude that the defendants should bear the responsibility for their compliance with the directions by the Ministry.

the first view is the basic concept that the effective regulation of cartels is one of the most important subjects of the JAA. Practically speaking, when adopting the second and third view, the JFTC bears the heavy burden of proof to demonstrate an actual commencement and implementation of the agreement, which is no doubt time consuming and has the possibility of lessening the effectiveness of the Act in promoting free competition in the national economy. When considering the illegality of a hard core agreement, it is appropriate to adopt the first view which enables the JFTC to expose a cartel without reviewing the real implementation of an agreement.

4. Finding of Cartel Agreement

Under Japanese judicial precedents, it has been construed that in order to determine that certain business activity constitutes a cartel, a concurring of intent among the parities based on communication is necessary. The Supreme Court clearly requires a concurring of intent among the parties based on communication in order to determine that there has been a violation of the Cartel Regulation.[11] Under the JAA, however, it is not necessary that the finding of a concurring of intent be supported by direct evidence. In other words, under Japanese case law, it is admitted that cartel agreements can be found from circumstantial evidence.

It has also been considered that a mere parallel conduct engaged in by competitors with knowledge of each other's action does not constitute an agreement in the context of the Cartel Regulation. The proof of parallel business behaviour is not by itself sufficient to find an agreement in the context of the Cartel Regulation or, phrased differently, such behaviour itself does not constitute the Cartel Regulation offence. Circumstantial evidence of consciously parallel behaviour may have made heavy inroads into the traditional judicial attitude toward conspiracy, but conscious parallelism has not yet been equated with conspiracy under the Cartel Regulation. Under the JAA, the court adopted the idea that rather than deeming mere conscious parallelism an agreement, it is necessary to find certain additional feature of firms' behaviour called 'plus factors' supporting the inference of agreement.

Hereinafter, this book will introduce some of the judicial precedents demonstrating the *above-delineated* fact-finding practice in Japan.

a. Toshiba Chemical Case[12]

In this case, the JFTC issued a recommendation to companies, including Toshiba Chemical Co. ('Toshiba Chemical'), on the ground that they formed the cartel in violating the JAA Art. 3 on 6 June 1989.

---

11. *Japanese Government v. Idemitu Co.*, 33 KEISHU 1287 (Sup. Ct. 24 February 1984).
12. *Toshiba Chemical Co. v. Japanese Fair Trade Commission*, 906 HANREITIMES 136 (Tokyo Hi. Ct. 25 September 1995).

Seven companies not including Toshiba Chemical accepted the recommendation. Accordingly, the JFTC issued judgments and surcharge orders to seven companies on 8 August 1989 and seven companies accepted these.

However, since Toshiba Chemical refused to accept the recommendation, the JFTC commenced a hearing on 8 August 1989 and rendered the judgment that Toshiba Chemical violated the JAA Art. 3 on 16 September 1992. Toshiba Chemical filed suit in the Tokyo High Court seeking denial of the judgment by the JFTC. The Tokyo High Court rendered the judgment remanding the case to the JFTC on the ground that the hearing proceeding at the JFTC violated the JAA because one of the referees had participated in the investigation conducted before the hearing on 25 February 1994. The JFTC reformed the member of the hearing and rendered the same judgment on 26 May 1994, against which Toshiba Chemical filed suit in the Tokyo High Court. The court rendered the judgment on 25 September 1995 and said that the term 'mutually' used in the JAA Art. 2, para. 6 meant that several businesses recognized and anticipated that others would raise the same kind and content of commodities' prices almost at the same time. It also pointed out that although it was not necessary to communicate explicitly about how much to raise prices, it was necessary for each business to anticipate others would raise prices based on their communication. It should be noted, however, that in this case the court found the contents of communication among competitors from prior to and after the price rises, participants of the communications, dates, places and times of each meeting and the same business conduct adopted by conspirators. Therefore, it can be said that the court found evidence close to direct evidence to infer agreement among competitors. The judgment had recognized the main issue of this case as being whether or not there were enough inferences from communication among the competitors as to their price rises. The court provided the general principle that it was possible to find an agreement from tangential facts. It was not necessary to mention, however, this general principle because it was able to find the agreement from direct evidence. Rather, the main issue of this case was whether or not the withdrawal from the agreement should be admitted because colluding companies except for Toshiba Chemical had already admitted the charge before Toshiba's case had been commenced at the JFTC, and only Toshiba Chemical had contended that it did not conclude the agreement. In other words, since the agreement among parties had been found before the commencement of Toshiba case, the only issue to be discussed at Toshiba case was not whether or not it was possible to find the agreement but whether or not withdrawal from the agreement should be admitted. In this case, Toshiba Chemical exchanged information as to the price rises with seven companies before the meeting held on 10 June 1987 and clearly consented to such price rises before the meeting. In addition, there was no evidence introduced from Toshiba Chemical as to its withdrawing from the agreement. Therefore, even if Toshiba Chemical did not express its view concerning the price rises clearly at the meeting, the argument that it had withdrawn from the agreement, had it been raised, would not have been admitted in this case.

b. *Kyowa Excio Case*[13]

In this case, ten companies formed the body named *Kabutokai* in which they exchanged information and agreed to cooperate to decide which company would obtain orders in bidding.

Based on this agreement, ten companies colluded as to which company would obtain the orders in twenty seven biddings conducted from 1 April 1981 to 15 June 1983. The JFTC, after finding the agreement, rendered the surcharge order to three companies including Kyowa Excio Co. ('Kyowa Excio'), all of which actually obtained orders in the biddings. Two of the three companies accepted the order by the JFTC. Kyowa Excio refused to accept the order by the JFTC, which initiated hearing proceedings and rendered the judgment demanding Kyowa Excio to pay the surcharges on 30 March 1994. Kyowa Excio filed suit seeking the denial of the judgment of the JFTC in the Tokyo High Court, which dismissed all claims by Kyowa Excio on 29 March 1996. In rendering its judgment, the Tokyo High Court detailed its finding of agreements among the parties of *Kabutokai*. Eight of the ten members of *Kabutokai* lacked any intention and capability to get orders as to the given work at the time of forming *Kabutokai*. In this regard, the court said that because even if they lacked the intention and the capability, they were able to expect substantial collateral for their contribution to the efforts of two companies to obtain orders. As the judgment detailed, since it is almost impossible to know the intention and the capability of other competitors and therefore it is quite natural to act on the premise that the competitors have the intention and the capability to get orders, it is appropriate to find that ten companies were parties to the agreement. In this case, although it was assumed that the content of the implicit agreement called for deciding which companies would obtain orders in biddings through consultation among the members and cooperation by other members, not all of them were clear enough in this case (some of them were specified to some extent). In addition, the date, the place and the progress of the meetings in which the agreement was concluded were not specified in the facts of this case. In spite of this, fact-in-issue of the implicit agreement among the parties was found based on the inferences from twenty seven occurrences of collusive bidding from March 1981 to June 1988 as well as numerous communications among the members of *Kabutokai*. Based on this fact-finding, the court determined that the agreement substantially restricted the competition in the industry and violated the JAA. This kind of fact-finding is an effective way to find an agreement among parties, especially in bid rigging cases, because a single occurrence of bid rigging does not constitute a violation of the Act, since 'substantial restraint of competition', one of the elements of the Act, Art. 2, para. 6, requires a certain span of time and geography. In order to judge bid riggings as a violation of the Act, it is indispensable to find a principal agreement based on which members colluded for each bid rigging, and therefore it would be appropriate to find a principal agreement from each occurrence of bid rigging.

---

13. *Kyowa Excio Co. v. Japanese Fair Trade Commission*, 552 KOSEITORIHIKI 25 (Tokyo Hi. Ct. 29 March 1996).

c. *Yuasakizaikohgyo Case*[14]

In this case, although the defendants bid approximately the same price, no definite agreements were discovered.

The referee said that, judging from the fact that the defendants bid approximately the same price, it could be found that, through the two meetings held before the bidding as well as from other communications, the defendants concluded an implicit agreement as to what price they would bid. The referee stated further that, as it was necessary to determine what extent of concurrence was needed to find an agreement, it was not enough to find only the fact that the price they bid was the same, but also that there were communications among the defendants as to price and that each defendant acted the same way with the anticipation that others would act likewise. Based on these fact-findings, the referee concluded that there was an agreement as to price among the defendants. Although it was construed that it is not necessary to find an exact agreement as to price, it is necessary to find communication among the parties as to price and concurrent actions. The expression that each defendant acted the same way with the anticipation that other would act likewise could cover broad business activities. This is, however, a case where purpose, date, time, participants, and content of conversation of each meeting were all specified such that the referee would be able to find an agreement as to price from these tangential facts easily or simply from direct evidence.

However, it should be noted that there is an argument in Japan that since the recommendation procedure (recommendation was abolished in the amendment to the JAA in 2005) is not intended to find facts but simply to give an opportunity to redress inappropriate conduct, it is not proper to examine recommendation cases in the context of analyzing practical trends as to finding an agreement in a Cartel Regulation case.

d. *Hiroshimashisekiyushogyokumiai Case*[15]

In this case, the JFTC adopted a similar framcwork to that explained *above* and found an agreement on price from the content of meetings held by the parties, communications, the price raised after the meeting, the date of the price raise, and from the date, place, and participants of each meeting. The referee in this case noted that communications among the parties involved in the cartel should be necessary to examine in order to find an agreement on price. As explained *above*, in Japan, in order to find an agreement, at least it is necessary to find a communication as to price among parties, and the fact-finding practice used by the courts and the JFTC has followed this principal so far. It should be noted, as briefly explained *above*, that the basic pattern of fact-finding by both courts and the JFTC concerning an agreement has been that, in an industry where agreements on price had been concluded repeatedly after meeting several times among

14. Yuasakizaikohgyo, 1 SINKETUSHU 62 (FTC, 30 August 1949).
15. Hiroshimashisekiyushogyokumiai, 44 SHINKETUSHU 3 (FTC, June 24 1998).

competitors in a given industry and communicating price rises, one of the competitors proposes a price fixing agreement or how much to bid and other participants of meetings consent and follow the proposal.

In addition to *above* cases, there are several recommendation cases in which the JFTC found agreement among competitors using the same method outlined *above*.[16]

e. Mitsubishi Building Maintenance Case[17]

The overall trend of fact-finding by the JFTC is towards acting more carefully after the introduction of the 'surcharge' in 1977. Under the relevant provisions of the surcharge, the JFTC is compelled to order a large penalty compared to the normal administrative or criminal penalty when finding an agreement among competitors. Due to its nature as a penalty, it has been criticized as being against the double jeopardy rule set out in the Japanese Constitution Art. 39. Taking into consideration these factors, the JFTC seems to have adopted a more careful approach to finding an agreement from circumstantial evidence, an approach which is well exemplified in Mitsubishi Building Maintenance Case.

In this case, six companies including Mitsubishi Building Maintenance Co. ('Mitsubishi'), attended several meetings named '*Tohkakai*' to exchange information concerning their business from 31 August 1982. The JFTC issued its recommendation to the participants of the meeting on 9 March 1984 after careful investigation of the case on the ground that the participants agreed to fix the price at that meeting. As six companies refused to accept the recommendation, the JFTC commenced a formal hearing and rendered judgment which stated that there were no agreements as to price among the parties. The referees in this case found that there were some communications as to the price among the parties at the meeting held on 31 August 1982. They added, however, that had six companies actually agreed on a price raise at that meeting, Mitsubishi should have distributed documents reflecting such price raise before or after the meeting and informed the five other companies how much to raise the price. They found no evidence to prove these facts. In addition, they concluded that there was not enough time to examine the price raise considering the number of topics discussed at that meeting and total meeting time. What is notable in this case is that the referees of this case denied finding an agreement among the parties even though they found several communications as to price at that meeting. This case was the first case in which the JFTC initiated a hearing at which the referees did not find a violation of the JAA in twenty nine years since its establishment. This demonstrated that the hearing proceeding at the JFTC was functioning. After this case and up till now, there have been no cases in which the JFTC initiated a hearing on the ground that an exchange of information not leading to an agreement should be considered a violation of the JAA.

---

16. *See e.g.*, Akitashichuoriyokumiai, 13 SINKETUSHU 55 (FTC, 11 August 1965); Asahigarasukabusikigaisha, 22 SINKETUSHU 92 (FTC, 9 December 1975).
17. Mitsubishibiltechnoservice, 41 SINKETUSHU 46 (FTC, 28 July 1994).

5. Conscious Parallelism

Under the JAA, parallel conduct alone is not sufficient to constitute a violation of the Cartel Regulation. If there is no evidence showing an exchange of information or communication of intention among enterprises, an agreement among cartel members cannot be found. In Shodanren Case,[18] major newspaper companies raised their prices simultaneously, but there was no evidence to show that there had been meetings attended by representatives of the companies involved, or communications of intention among them. The Federation of Consumer Groups brought the complaint to the JFTC alleging that a uniform price raise could not have been possible without collusion and that the JFTC should commence an investigation. After concluding its investigation, the JFTC decided not to proceed with an administrative hearing on the grounds that no evidence of meetings or communication among the companies was found. The federation filed suit in court to have the JFTC's decision reversed, which was dismissed. Some scholars argue that under some circumstances, an agreement can be inferred from uniformity of conduct. They argue that if firms suddenly ceased to compete without persuasive justification, the fact that they stopped competing and engaged in uniform conduct should be regarded as evidence of conspiracy. Such uniformity of conduct can be used as evidence to establish the existence of an agreement. However it is doubtful whether or not this fact alone should suffice. If the evidence is combined with some other factors, such as communication concerning price among members, it may possibly be employed as part of the evidence required to prove the existence of an agreement. Other circumstantial evidence from which it is possible to infer an agreement are large market share, a high entry barrier to a relevant market, scarcity of market participants, product homogeneity, inelasticity of the market's demand curve and supply curve and complexity of market participants' behaviour. If the industry structure is not conductive to coordination, it should be recognized that it would be irrational for firms to risk prosecution by engaging in the forbidden process without any hope of gaining market power through agreement.

6. Regulation of Trade Association's Conducts

A trade association is defined in the JAA Art. 2, para. 2 as 'any combination or federation of combinations consisting of two or more enterprises and having as its principal purpose the furtherance of the common interest of its members'. This definition further states that a trade association includes (i) any association, incorporated or unincorporated, of which two or more enterprises are members; (ii) any foundation with or without legal personality of which two or more entrepreneurs control the appointment or dismissal of directors or managers and the execution or existence of business; and (iii) any partnership of which two or more enterprises are members, or any contractual combination of two or more enterprises.

18. *All Japan Consumer Federation v. Japanese Government*, 12 GYOSAIREISHU 933 (Tokyo Hi. Ct. 26 April 1961).

One important element in this definition is that a trade association is an organization composed of enterprises of which purpose is to further the common interest of constituent enterprises. Therefore, a trade association has no business of its own. Typically, the activities of a trade association include research and development, gathering and dissemination of business and political information, unification of technical standards and political lobbying on behalf of its members. The activities of trade associations are very important in the Japanese business community. There are at least one and sometimes several trade associations in every business sector. In automobile manufacturing and retailing, for example, the Japanese Automobile Manufacture's Association and the Japanese Automobile Dealers' Association are trade associations for the sector.

In accordance with the Rules of the JFTC, every trade association shall file a notification of its establishment with the JFTC within thirty days after the date of such establishment. Also, when any change occurs regarding the information filed with the JFTC, the trade association concerned shall, in accordance with the Rules of the JFTC, file a notification of such changes with the JFTC within two months after the end of the business year during which such change occurred. Moreover, in accordance with the Rules of the JFTC, every trade association shall file a notification of dissolution with the JFTC within thirty days after such dissolution.

Trade associations are often used to eliminate and restrict competition among enterprises. If a trade association's activity restricts entry into a market, or expels existing firms from a market, the trade association's activity also exerts a direct influence on the market mechanism.

As such, the JAA Art. 8, para. 1 provides that trade associations shall not engage in any conduct set forth in item 1, 2, 3 and 4.

The JAA Art. 8, para. 1, item 1 is particularly relevant to the prohibition on cartels. It states that if a trade association substantially restricts competition in any particular field of trade, it shall come under the prohibition. The objective of this provision is to prohibit trade association's activities which stifle competition among members, thereby resulting in a substantial restraint of competition in a particular field of trade. Although the purpose of this provision is to prohibit cartels which substantially restrain competition, it is also thought necessary to provide for the control of trade associations in addition to the provision dealing with cartels. Restrictive activities engaged in by trade associations are in substance no different from those of a cartel. The prohibition of a cartel, however, requires evidence that participating enterprises have agreed or at least communicated their intentions to restrain competition among themselves, and obtaining such evidence is not always a simple matter. To prohibit a trade association, however, the JFTC needs only to prove that a decision or resolution of the trade association has been made, which is usually an easier proposition than fulfilling the requirements of the Cartel Regulation.

For this reason, Art. 8. para. 1 was inserted into the JAA, enabling the JFTC to challenge restrictive activities engaged in by trade associations. Examples would include decisions of trade associations concerning price, production quantities and territories of association's members. When trade associations engage in such restrictive activities which substantially restrain competition in any particular field of trade, the JFTC may proceed against the association rather than against its members and render an elimination order to refrain from such activities. There could be cases where it might not be easy to determine whether or not such activities have been decided upon by a trade association and imposed on its members, or whether or not some of the members have decided that the restrictive activities be carried out using the trade association as a vehicle for their plan. In such a case, the JFTC may proceed against either the trade association or the participating members, depending upon the availability of evidence. In Petroleum Industry Price Fixing Case, it could have been found that the Petroleum Association decided to fix the price of oil instead of its members. However, both the Tokyo High Court and the Supreme Court held that the member enterprises fixed the price through the association, thus applying the prohibition to its member enterprises rather than applying it to the association.

The JAA Art. 8, para. 1, item 2 prohibits firms from entering into international agreements which could constitute cartels.

The JAA Art. 8, para. 1, item 3 provides that it is unlawful for a trade association to engage in limiting the current or future number of enterprises in any particular field of trade. Several JFTC decisions involved the medical association's resolution to the effect that no new physicians would be allowed to join the association unless the physician established his clinic at the location determined by the association, which policy was adopted by the association to prevent excessive competition in all areas. Other cases involving the medical association were such that the association decided to require hospitals and clinics that wished to commence operations within the association's business sphere to receive permission from the association and to require that applicants for admission be introduced by a member.

The JAA Art. 8, para. 1, item 4 states that a trade association shall not unduly restrict the function or activities of its constituent members. This article envisages a situation where a manufacturers' trade association prohibits its members from selling products to wholesalers regarded as price-cutters by the association.

It should be noted that the JAA Art. 8, para. 1, item 2 to 4 do not prohibit unreasonable restraint of trade under the JAA, since they do not include the requirement of 'a substantial restraint of competition'.

The JAA Art. 8, para. 1, item 5 prohibits associations from causing members to employ conduct which constitutes unfair trade practices. It is generally construed that, under this provision, individual members shall actually employ unfair trade practices and that this prohibition is part of the Unfair Trade Practice Regulation.

Although the JAA prohibits trade associations from engaging in the aforementioned conduct, it also provides a system that exempts trade associations' activities from the application of the JAA under certain circumstances. Cooperatives may be established pursuant to the provisions of various statutes for the purpose of providing mutual aid among small-scale firms. If the requirements are met, joint economic undertakings will generally be exempted from the application of the JAA. This exemption is for the purpose of allowing small-scale firms that are incapable of competing individually with large-scale firms by themselves to form a mutual-aid business union that is an economically effective unit of competition. However, forming a trade association will not be exempted from the application of the JAA, if it engages in unfair trade practices, or if it substantially restrains competition in a particular field of trade. Similarly, no exemption will be granted to cooperative federations or other organizations that collude with other organizations or firms to fix prices or to restrict the amounts of goods or services. In addition, the JAA contains provisions that exempt concerted activities which would be engaged in to combat a depression and concerted activities to rationalize an industry.

B. Concerted Refusal to Deal

1. Overview

In theory, concerted refusal to deal can be covered by both the Cartel Regulation and the Unfair Trade Practice Regulation.

With regard to the Cartel Regulation, however, there are no court cases which applied the Cartel Regulation to a concerted refusal to deal. All the cases have been dealt with by applying the Unfair Trade Practice Regulation.

Japanese distribution problems, including concerted refusal to deal in the Japanese market, were a major focus on the Structural Impediments Initiative Talks conducted from 1989 to 1992 and have been the subject of complaints made by the United States manufacturers, which were excluded from the Japanese market due to these problems. The fact that the Japanese distribution system was complex was hardly new to the JFTC. The JFTC's study group had reported as much in 1980 and subsequent JFTC's reports acknowledged the connection between a variety of distribution practices and market access by foreign firms. In 1989, in response to Structural Impediments Initiative Talks, the JFTC appointed another advisory group to study distribution issues in Japan. In 1991, after receiving the advisory group's report, the JFTC started preparing to release guidelines concerning distribution systems and business practices in the Japanese market.

The guidelines concerning distribution systems and business practices under the Antimonopoly Act (released on 11 July 1991) ('Distribution Guideline')[19] are the result of these efforts and provide situations where a concerted refusal to deal is deemed to be in violation of the Cartel Regulation.

---

19. The Japan Fair Trade Commission, *Guidelines Concerning Distribution Systems and Business Practices Under the Antimonopoly Act*, (1991), *available at* <http://www.jftc.go.jp/e-page/legislation/ama/distribution.pdf> (last visited 17 March 2006).

According to the guideline, the following types of conduct, if it results in a substantial restraint of competition in the relevant market, constitutes a violation of the Cartel Regulation.

(i) Manufacturers concertedly, in an attempt to exclude price-cutting distributors, refuse to supply products to such distributors;
(ii) Distributors concertedly, in an attempt to prevent new entry by competitors, refuse to supply products to new entrants or cause their suppliers (manufacturers) to refuse to supply products to new entrants;
(iii) Manufacturers concertedly, in an attempt to prevent new entries by competitors, refuse to supply products to new entrants or cause their suppliers (manufacturers) to refuse to supply products to new entrants; and
(iv) Finished product manufacturers concertedly, in an attempt to prevent competitors from entering a market, inform material suppliers of their intention to refuse to deal if the suppliers provide the materials to new entrants.

According to the guideline, in cases where firms concertedly, along with their customers, suppliers, etc., engage in, for instance, the following types of conduct, and if the conduct makes it very difficult for any firm with which there has been a refusal to deal to enter a relevant market, or the effect is to exclude the refused firm from the relevant market, thereby resulting in a substantial restraint of trade, such conduct constitutes a violation of the Cartel Regulation.

(i) Distributors and manufacturers concertedly, in an attempt to exclude price-cutting distributors, undertake conduct whereby the latter refuses or restricts the supply of products to price-cutting distributors and whereby the former refuses to deal in the products of those manufacturers which have supplied their products to those manufacturers which have supplied their products to such distributors;
(ii) A manufacturer and its distributors concertedly, in an attempt to exclude imported products, undertake conduct whereby the latter does not deal in the imported products and whereby the former refuses to supply products to those distributors selling the imported products;
(iii) Distributors and a manufacturer concertedly, in an attempt to prevent other distributors from entering a relevant market, undertake such conduct whereby the latter refuses to supply products to new entrants and whereby the former refuses to deal in products to such new entrants, and whereby the former refuses to deal in the products of those manufacturers which have supplied their products to such new entrants; or
(iv) Material manufacturers and a finished product manufacturer concertedly, in an attempt to exclude imported materials, refuse to supply materials to those finished product manufacturers which have purchased the imported materials.

Note that the guideline provides several examples to show 'a substantial restraint of trade' in a relevant market in concerted refusal to deal cases, such as (i) where it is made very difficult for any firm manufacturing or selling products superior in price and quality to enter a relevant market, or where such a firm is to be excluded from the relevant market, (ii) where it is made very difficult for any firm adopting innovative selling methods to enter a relevant market, or where such firm is to be excluded from the relevant market, (iii) where it is made very difficult for any firm having superior business capabilities to enter a relevant market, or in cases where such firm is to be excluded from a relevant market, (iv) where it is made very difficult for any firm to enter a relevant market where no active competition is taking place, and (v) where a concerted refusal to deal is conducted toward any potential entrant of a relevant market.

On the other hand, with regard to the Unfair Trade Practice Regulation, Art. 1 of the general designation states that a concerted refusal to deal by agreement among competitors shall be unlawful. Also it prohibits from making other firms employ a boycott. Under the general designation, a boycott is regarded as unlawful in principle but could be justified in exceptional cases.

According to the Distribution Guideline, the conduct described *above* concerning the Cartel Regulation shall be a violation of the Unfair Trade Practice Regulation even when it does not cause a substantial restraint of trade.

2. Case Law

a. *Chiba Newspaper Press Case*[20]

The three large national newspaper publishing companies, Asahi Newspaper Press K.K., publisher of the Asahi Newspaper, Yomiuri Newspaper Press K.K., publisher of the Yomiuri Newspaper, and Mainichi Newspaper Press, publisher of the Mainichi Newspaper engineered a sharp drop in sales volume in Chiba Prefecture and conspired to take coordinated measures to exclude a new entrant to this territory, Chiba Nippo Press K.K. ('Chiba Nippo'), the publisher of the Chiba Newspaper in Chiba Prefecture. The publishing companies held separate meetings with their dealers and requested the dealers not to deal with Chiba Nippo. They also forced them to agree not to sell or deliver Chiba Newspaper after 20 March 1955. At the meeting held on the afternoon of 20 March 1955, they made the dealers reconfirm the resolution to boycott Chiba Nippo and had them notify Chiba Nippo of their resolution. As a result of the resolutions, more than 200 dealers quit dealing with Chiba Nippo as per the resolutions made by the publishers.

The JFTC applied for a preliminary injunction order to the Tokyo High Court on 16 March 1955, alleging that the action of the three publishing companies violated the Unfair Trade Practice Regulation and that it would cause irrevocable damage to Chiba Nippo. The JFTC argued that, if the boycott should be

20. *Asahi Newspaper Press K.K. v. Japanese Fair Trade Commission*, 6 GYOSAIREISHU 1076 (Tokyo Hi. Ct. 6 April 1955).

implemented, Chiba Nippo would likely lose its customers and be excluded from dealing newspapers in Chiba Prefecture, which would cause substantial anticompetitive effects in that area.

The Tokyo High Court granted the preliminary injunction ordering the three publishers to refrain from taking their planned action.

Until recently, it has been considered that the Unfair Trade Practice Regulation will exclusively apply to concerted refusal to deal. As explained before, however, the Distribution Guideline acknowledged that certain types of concerted refusals to deal which cause a substantial restraint of trade is a violation of the Cartel Regulation.

b. Toy Gun Association Case[21]

The Tokyo District Court decision on the National Toy Gun Association Case is one of the major concerted refusal precedents coming after the Distribution Guideline was released.

In this case, the Toy Gun Association, whose members comprised of all toy gun manufactures in Japan except Dejicon Denshi K.K. ('Dejicon Denshi'), formulated voluntary safety standards for its members which set caps on the weight of plastic bullets and the initial maximum speed of bullets, and required members to affix a stamped safety seal issued by the Toy Gun Association to the product. The association then organized three associations of wholesalers in order to promote the voluntary safety standard for toy guns. Dejicon Denshi began to market a high grade toy gun, which was more powerful and exceeded the safety standard. The Toy Gun Association urged its member manufactures and the associations of wholesalers to request retailers not to carry the new toy gun produced by Dejicon Denshi. The Toy Gun Association even sent letters stating that its member would not supply their toy guns to retailers who did not comply with the request.

The Tokyo District Court held that the association violated both Art. 8, para. 1, item 1, one of the conditions for finding 'a substantial restraint of competition', and Art. 8, para. 1, item 5, one of the conditions for 'likelihood of impeding fair competition'.

The court ruled that the implementation of a safety standard would not likely violate any provisions of the JAA if the following three conditions were satisfied. First, if the purpose of creating a safety standard is justifiable in light of public policy. Second, if the substance of the safety standard is reasonable. Third, if the implementation method of a safety standard is appropriate. Based on this analysis, the court found that the conduct of the association might meet the condition of justifiable purpose and the reasonable safety standard condition, but that the implementation method was excessive in that the association notified wholesalers of the concerted refusal to supply toy guns, and as such, the third condition was not fulfilled. Also, the court found that even association members often distributed

---

21. *Dejicon Denshi K.K. v. Toy Gun Association*, 1629 HANREIJIHO 70 (Tokyo Dis. Ct. 9 April 1997).

seals to be affixed to toy guns which did not meet the safety standard, as the association did not conduct any inspections.

The decision in Toy Gun Association Case also indicated that, under the JAA, concerted refusal to deal is covered by both the Cartel Regulation and the Unfair Trade Practice Regulation (Art. 1 of the general designation which prohibits concerted refusal to deal).

C. BUYERS' HARD CORE CARTELS

Buyers' cartels formed to drive down the price, as far as the JAA is concerned, would violate the Cartel Regulation. Although there are several recommendations from the JFTC which dealt with joint purchasing,[22] there have been no court cases or formal decisions at the JFTC which dealt with buyers' cartels. Furthermore, although it has been said that generally the economic impact of a buyers' cartel is quite similar to that of sellers' cartel, there has been little academic analysis given to buyers' cartel in Japan.[23]

Hereinafter, economic analysis to show the competitive effects of buyers' price fixing agreements on relevant markets will be introduced. In addition, an argument will be made that the *quasi per se* rule should apply to this type of cartel in Japan.

In competitive markets, willing buyers interact with willing suppliers. It is assumed that no single firm or individual is able to control the price or quantity of available goods. Also, it is supposed that many firms are producing identical products and many purchasers are willing to buy specific products. Further, it is assumed that there are no significant inhibitions to entry into and exit from the market. In addition, competitive markets could benefit both suppliers with a producer surplus and purchasers with a consumer surplus. When operating at a competitive equilibrium of supply and demand, social welfare could be maximized.

On the other hand, buyers' cartel members, when possessing market power, could maximize their profits by manipulation, depressing the quantity of their inputs purchased from suppliers and, thus, producing lower prices.

22. *See e.g.*, Himejisikankogyo, available at <http://sink.jtfc.go.jp/pdfdocs/H120510H2J025.pdf> (FTC, 10 May 2000) (last visited 5 February 2005). In this case, plumbers formed the association to administer their businesses and negotiate their purchase of raw materials from suppliers. In order to implement its policy, the association forced suppliers not to sell raw materials directly to associates. The JFTC determined that such an arrangement was a violation of the JAA Art. 19 because the association purchased the raw materials on the condition that suppliers would accept the unfair competition policy. The JFTC focused on the anticompetitive conditions imposed upon the suppliers by the association and no consideration was made on the joint purchasing activities themselves.
23. *See e.g.*, Akira Inoue, *Antitrust Analysis of B2B Transaction*, NELLO REPOSITORY, 83 – 124, (2005), available at <http://lsr.nellco.org/cornell/lps/clacp/7> (Master's Thesis at University of Virginia School of Law, on file with the University of Virginia School of Law Library).

The consequences of buyers' cartels on social welfare can be understood with the aid of the Figure.

In a competitive market, a firm attempts to maximize profits by setting output levels at the point where the firm's marginal cost equals to its obtainable price. It is also true that, in long-run competitive equilibrium, output permits the firm to provide goods and services with minimum total cost. If each of the firms in the competitive industry follows this rule, we will be able to obtain a market supply curve by adding up the quantities produced by each firm at any given price, which will be the sum of the quantity determined by the marginal cost for each of them.

Therefore, the supply curve in a competitive market is represented as the marginal cost for society, shown as the marginal social cost curve in Figure 1. When firms act in concert to purchase the entire market supply of an input good, the firms' buying decisions reflect the marginal factor cost (the 'MFC') of that input. The MFC is the additional cost which shall be borne by purchasers when buying one more unit. In a competitive market, a firm could obtain all necessary goods at the prevailing market price. Therefore, the MFC of an input is negligible. When a buyers' cartel is formed, the colluding firms purchase close to the entire supply of goods. The MFC curve rises more rapidly than supply curve, because, in order to buy a greater volume of input, buyers must pay a higher price not only for the additional unit but also for all of the other units they have purchased. Therefore,

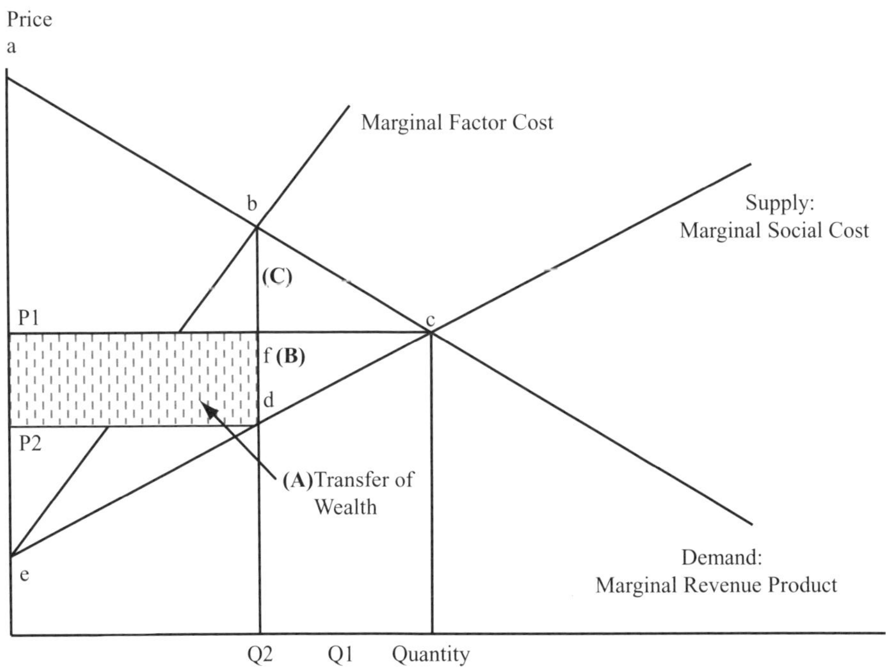

Figure 1. Marginal Social Cost Curve

as the Figure illustrates, the MFC curve is always steeper than the supply curve of the input.

Intermediate goods are valued for their contributions in producing the buyers' final products. As a result, the demand by buyers for intermediate goods is determined by multiplying the increase in output of final products resulting from the use of one more unit of the intermediate goods purchased from suppliers times the output price of buyer's final products. Therefore, the demand is called the value of marginal revenue product (the 'MRP'). In other words, the MRP is an additional revenue which purchasers obtain when buying an input unit.

Buyers' cartel members have market power to establish the price because their purchases influence the price they pay for the products. The more quantity they buy, the higher the price becomes. On the contrary, the less they buy, the lower the price becomes. Buyers achieve a lowered price by buying a lesser quantity of products than would be purchased in a competitive market, so that revenue that once flowed into sellers now flows into the coffers of the buyers in the form of reduced costs. In addition, the oligopsony buying decision will cause a social loss because buyers do not purchase the quantity that society needs, thereby leading to not producing the quantity of final product that a society needs.

In a competitive market, where both sellers and purchasers are assumed to have no market power to control the output price, the price is represented by P1 and the quantity is Q1, whose combination maximizes the social welfare, the sum of consumer and producer surplus. In Figure, the consumer surplus is described in the area under the demand curve and above P1, which is triangle aP1c, while the producer surplus is the area above the supply curve and below P1, which is triangle eP1c.

On the other hand, when faced with a positively sloping supply curve as described in Figure, buyers will discover that they can influence the price they must pay for an intermediate good by adjusting the quantity that they buy.

When a buyers' cartel is formed, participants do not compete with each other in the intermediate good markets. The result is that they will buy where the increase in total cost resulting from the purchase of one more additional unit of input from supplier, the MFC, equals demand, the MRP. This is because profit maximization requires expanding the quantity of inputs purchased until the MRP produced by that expansion is equal to the MFC so that the marginal impact on profit is zero.

Consequently, each firm will demand additional units of the input up to the point where marginal revenue product is equal to marginal factor cost, which is represented in Figure as the intersection of the MFC curve with the MRP curve. As a result, quantity is reduced to Q2 and price becomes P2.

As Figure shows, buyers' cartel causes two kinds of anti-competitive effects: social welfare loss and the redistributive effects.

The social welfare effects are analogous to those of a sellers' cartel, that is, too few resources will be employed. At the point where supply and demand are equal, the total social welfare generated by the operation of the market will be optimal, whereas it is not privately optimal for buyers. In order to maximize the private welfare, buyers will purchase Q2 units of goods at price P2. As a result, the total social welfare will be reduced from the competitive potential by an area (B)+(C), that is, bdc. This is the potential welfare gain to society that is unrealized.

The redistributive effects are the buyers' resulting revenues that once accrued to suppliers from the production and sale of their goods. (A) in Figure, the area P1fdP2, represents these effects of the cartel's behaviour, depicting a portion of what was a producer surplus in a competitive market which flows to buyers as consumer surplus.

As outlined *above*, by the exercise of market power by buyers, both suppliers and society could be harmed. This is the harm which the antitrust laws should protect society against.

Based upon the *above* economic analysis, the *quasi per se* rule established in sellers' price fixing cases should also be applied to buyers' cartel cases in Japan. As shown *above*, when buyers collude, the collusion will almost always cause anti-competitive harm. Also, as the court in *National Macaroni Manufacture Association v. Federal Trade Commission* pointed out, the reason why the illegality of price fixing agreements does not depend on a showing of its unreasonableness is that it is contrary to the policy of competition.[24] There is little difference between buyers' cartel agreements and sellers' cartel agreements in that both cause anticompetitive effects on competition. It is consistent with the principal purpose of the JAA that the *quasi per se* rule established in sellers' price fixing cases should be applied to buyers' cartel cases.

D. Coordination with the Intellectual Property Rights

1. Policy Related Concerns

From the viewpoint of the JAA, there are three characteristics of intellectual property rights that sensible antitrust policy must take into account.

The first characteristic is differences in fundamental economics. Products and services based on intellectual property are usually characterized by large initial investments ('fixed costs') and low costs to reproduce individual items ('variable costs'). It logically follows that competition to be the first to generate products and services covered by intellectual property protection is beneficial for consumers and should be encouraged and preserved.

However, because of the nature of competition in markets characterized by intellectual property, there is a tendency to drift toward single-firm dominance, and even monopoly, for two reasons. First, in order to encourage initial investments, the law provides intellectual property protection and, in effect, precludes competition within the scope of the intellectual property for a period of time. Second, products and services based on intellectual property frequently exhibit 'network

24. *National Macaroni Manufacture Association v. Federal Trade Commission*, 345 F.2d 421 (7 Cir. 1965).

effects', that is, each individual's demand for a particular company's product or service is positively related to its widespread use by others.

In sum, incentives to innovate must be protected in intellectual property intensive markets and innovation competition can yield great consumer benefits. On the other hand, threats to competition can be substantial. For example, the combination of intellectual property protection and network effects will almost inevitably lead to monopoly and monopoly can diminish or eliminate future innovation. The challenge for antitrust is to deal with these economic conditions by preserving competition without unreasonably undermining incentives to innovate.

The second characteristic is the importance of innovation in a dynamic economy. Traditionally, antitrust enforcers ask whether or not a particular transaction is likely to allow the parties to raise price to the disadvantage of consumers, lower price drastically so as to drive out competitors and eventually injure consumers, or achieve comparable effects from other exclusionary conduct. In competition where there are extensive use of intellectual property protection, however, the success of competition is frequently based on qualitative rather than quantitative factors: the key is not so much who can produce the most widgets at the lowest cost, but rather who can be the first to design, protect with intellectual property rights, and bring to market a new and improved widget. Because market participants' incentives and opportunities to innovate are increasingly important in intellectual property-related competition, a rational competition policy will pay more heed to the effects of market structure, competitive conduct, and enforcement on innovation than it pays in industries where cost minimization is the most significant dimension of efficient competition.

The third characteristic is the uncertain durability of market power in intellectual property right-related competition. It is widely accepted in Japan that intellectual property right-related markets are characterized by an increased rate of innovation, relative ease of entry, and instability of market shares. As a result, cartels and monopoly power in intellectual property markets will necessarily be short-lived, and in any event, will be defeated more quickly and efficiently by market forces such as new entry and innovation than by any band of bureaucrats. It should be emphasized that the question of whether or not market power is durable or ephemeral is fact-specific and needs to be addressed on a market-by-market and product-by-product basis. Although this analysis is important in examining intellectual property-related markets, the uncertain durability of market power alone does not automatically exempt the exercise of the intellectual property rights from JAA enforcement.

2. Overview

a. Interpretation of the Japanese Antimonopoly Act Art. 21

Under the JAA, coordination between antitrust enforcement and intellectual property rights is dealt with under the JAA Art. 21.

The JAA Art. 21 provides that provisions of the Act shall not apply to such conduct recognizable as the exercise of any rights under the Copyright Act, the Patent Act, the Utility Model Act, the Design Act and the Trademark Act. On its surface, Art. 21 goes against the basic principle of the JAA in that the exercise of intellectual property rights should be subject to the JAA just like the exercise of any other property right in general. The JFTC released guidelines regarding patent and know-how licensing contracts.[25] In these guidelines, the JFTC took the position called 'Deviation Theory' concerning Art. 21 of the JAA. This view requires two dimensional analyses when dealing with individual cases. As a preliminary matter, Deviation Theory requires a decision to be made as to whether or not the conduct at issue should be protected from the standpoint of the individual intellectual property laws. If the conduct at issue is determined to be outside of this protection, the JAA should apply to the conduct. If the conduct at issue is found to be protected, it must be further decided whether or not the conduct at issue is a violation of any provisions of the JAA. When it is decided that the conduct at issue is a violation of the JAA, the conduct is deemed to be outside of the protection of the intellectual property right laws. In sum, the view acknowledges that the JAA should be applied to any conduct which is regarded as the proper exercise of the intellectual property rights. It is not easy to determine, however, whether or not specific conduct is within the protection of the individual intellectual property right laws. For example, concerning the licensing patent rights, although it is generally accepted that restriction on sales volume and the area of production are within the protection of the Patent Act, and restriction on sales price and sales area are outside of the protection, there is no consensus among scholars on this issue.

The JAA Art. 21 should be interpreted so that it requires consideration of all relevant factors, such as the individual provisions of the intellectual property rights, the purpose of the individual intellectual property law, and the characteristics of the individual intellectual property rights, in applying the JAA. This interpretation is more straightforward and clear.

It should be noted, however, that there is no difference in which view to take in reaching the conclusion that the JAA is applied to conduct which is regarded as a proper exercise of intellectual property right. In sum, Art. 21 does not function as an exemption from the JAA. As such, for longer perspective, it is recommended that the JAA Art. 21 shall be deleted.

b. *Patent Pool Guideline*

i. Overview of the Guideline

Concerning competition concerns about standardization and patent pooling, the JFTC released guideline in 2005.[26]

25. The Japanese Fair Trade Commission, *Guidelines Concerning Joint Research and Development Under the Antimonopoly Act*, (1993), <http://www.jftc.go.jp/e-page/legislation/index.html#ama> (last visited 23 March 2006).
26. The Japan Fair Trade Commission, *Guidelines on Standardization and Patent Pool Arrangements*, (2005), *available at* <http://www.jftc.go.jp/e-page/legislation/ama/Patent_Pool.pdf>.

As explained earlier in this book, standardization shall mean standardizing specifications for new product interfaces, especially in industries experiencing innovation and technical change, whereas patent pooling means establishing an organization to which multiple holders of patents and other rights delegate the authority to grant licenses for use of their patented concepts and other rights, and from which members obtain the requisite licenses.

The guideline states that the standardization of specifications does not necessarily lead to anticompetitive situations, but anticompetitive issues would arise if the standardization of specifications restricts competition in relevant markets or threatens to impede fair competition, especially with where the standardization (i) restricts prices of new products with specifications, (ii) restricts development of alternative specifications, (iii) unreasonably extends the scope of specifications, (iv) unreasonably excludes technical proposals from competitors, and (v) excludes competitors from the standardization of the specifications.

ii. Standardized Specification

Concerning the exercise of patent rights established as a part of standardized specification, the guideline explains that the refusal by a patent holder to grant a license generally does not pose an antitrust problem inasmuch as the patent holder is not involved in the development of the specification. However, it also states that if a patent holder has taken part in the activities and is endeavouring to have its patented technologies adopted by the specifications, refusing to grant a license will pose a legal problem under the JAA. According to the guideline, when specifications are standardized, and if it becomes difficult for companies to develop and produce products with the specifications, then the activities of patent holders do constitute private monopolization when they substantially restrict competition in related markets. Alternatively, they can constitute unfair trade practices when they threaten to impede fair competition. This will also apply when a patent holder nominally has no involvement with the development of the specifications but in practice does endeavour to have its patented technologies adopted in the specification, for example by colluding with a participant in the activity.

iii. Patent Pools

(A) Overview

Concerning patent pools, according to the guideline, in examining whether or not forming patent pools would cause antitrust concerns, it is necessary to take into consideration such factors as to what extent the specifications have become popular in the relevant market and the position of the pool in that market. Generally, even if many competitors pool their patents for specifications, the activity will have little effect on competition if market share of the products with specifications is not high and if several alternative specifications are available or all necessary patents for the specifications are available without obtaining a license from the pool. In particular, if many competitors license their patents for specifications through the pool, imposing on licensees certain restrictions will not pose problems under the

JAA when (i) the market share of the pool is no more than 20 per cent in the relevant market, or (ii) in case where market share is inappropriate for analyzing the effect on competition, if there are at least four other available specifications, except for where a patent pool is concluded with the clear purpose to restrict competition. The guideline also adds that even when these conditions are not met, imposing restrictions on licensees is not necessarily deemed to pose problems under the JAA, and in analyzing the competitive effects, it is necessary to examine such factors as to what extent the specifications have become popular in the relevant market and the position of the pool in that market.

More specifically, concerning a formation of a patent pool, the guideline examines antitrust concerns in the following three respects.

(B) Characteristics of Patent

When only the essential patents are pooled and licensing conditions are fixed, competition among the patented technologies is not usually restricted. In order to eliminate completely the risk of violating the JAA, it is necessary to limit patents in the pool only to essential patents. If patents that are not essential for specifications are pooled, the activity is likely to restrict competition and pose antitrust concerns under the JAA given that anticompetitive effects are caused in cases where a number of patents on alternative technologies are pooled and licensed with fixed conditions. Due to the fact that the patents on these technologies are competing based on their licensing conditions, competition among these alternative technologies is restricted. In addition, if non-essential patents are pooled, antitrust concerns are likely to arise. Anticompetitive effects are caused in cases where there are a number of patents on alternative technologies and some are pooled and licensed as a package with essential patents, because the technologies with the patents not pooled are hardly adopted by licensees of the pool and are excluded from the technology market. To sum, when a patent not essential to the specification is pooled, the anticompetitive effects are not negligible. As a consequence, it is necessary to comprehensively evaluate, on the basis of market conditions, the effect on competition of pooling such patents, taking into consideration factors such as whether or not pooling the patents is reasonably necessary or has pro-competitive effects, whether or not patent holders pooling their patents can license out their patents without going through the pool, and whether or not the businesses can select necessary patents and accept licenses only for them.

(C) Restriction on Participating in Patent Pool

Under the guideline, imposing restrictions, such as imposing rules for managing activities, on those participating in the pool generally does not pose antitrust concerns under the JAA, when the restrictions are recognized as reasonably necessary for managing the activities and are not unreasonably discriminatory against specific participants. However, imposing on participants restrictions on the use of their pooled patents, such as by prohibiting them from licensing their patents without going through the pool, is generally not recognized as reasonably necessary to manage the activity and is likely to have a significant impact on competition. Therefore, imposing such restrictions poses the risk of violating the JAA.

(D) Management of Pooling Activities

Normally, in the operation of a pooling activity, a management organization grants a license, collects licensing fees and audits the licensees' business to check compliance with the conditions. Through these activities the organization gathers confidential information on licensees' businesses, such as production volume and sales prices of their products. If participants or licensees of the pool can access this confidential information, there is a risk they will use it to commit activities in violation of the JAA. In complying with the JAA, it is important to limit access to confidential information on licensees' business activities gathered by the management organization. It is also advisable to outsource the management of the pooling activities to a third party that has no human or capital connection with participants of the pool.

(E) Licensing Through Patent Pools

Moreover, concerning licensing through patent pools, the guideline examines antitrust concerns in the following five situations.

(1) Setting Different Licensing Conditions

There is not necessarily an issue under the JAA when patent holders on technologies for specification pool their patents and license them with different conditions, such as the scope of authorized use of the patents and with different licensing royalties. The impact on competition is examined on a case-by-case basis with a view to the reasonable necessity for making such differentiations. However, in licensing agreements through a pool imposing different conditions on specific businesses without due cause, such as refusing to license the patents, requiring extremely high licensing fees compared with other licensees and limiting the scope of authorized use of the patents, there would be the risk of violating the JAA given that such activities have a direct and serious impact on the competing functions of licensees that are suffering discrimination.

(2) Restricting Research and Development Activities

In the case of licensing patents for specifications through a pool, any restriction on licensees with respect to research and development concerning the technologies for the specifications or competing technologies independently or jointly with third parties will make it difficult to develop those technologies or specifications and will run the risk of restricting competition in the product and technology market. If developing specifications is regarded as substantially a joint research and development activity such that a small number of competitors confidentially develop core technologies for the specifications, restricting research and development of technologies for the specifications or competing technologies independently or jointly with third parties could be recognized as falling within reasonable restrictions. However, even in a case such as this, once the specifications have been developed, limiting research and development by licensees in the licensing agreements through the pool may not be deemed to be reasonably necessary and will pose a legal problem under the JAA.

(3) Obligation to Grant a License for Patents on Improvements or Developments of the Technologies for the Specifications Through a Pool (Grant Back)

When licensing patents through a pool, requiring licensees to grant licenses for patents on improvements or developments of the technologies for the specifications through the pool will restrict competition in the technology market, causing such anticompetitive effects as reinforcing the advantageous position of the pool in the markets associated with the specifications by accumulating in the pool the improvements or developments. This would make it difficult to develop alternative technologies for the specifications or alternative specifications and restrict competition among technologies based on patents having similar functions and effects given that these similar patents are pooled. On the other hand, there may be cases in which patents on improvements or developments by licensees are essential to the specifications. In this case, imposing the obligation on the licensees generally does not pose antitrust concerns under the JAA if it means obliging a licensee to pool the essential patent and license it non-exclusively through the pool, and if it is accompanied by no other restrictions on the use of the essential patent and imposes on the licensee non-discriminatory treatment in, for example, the distribution of licensing fees compared with others pooling their patents.

(4) Measures Against an Application for Invalidation of Patents

In cases of licensing through patent pools, imposing on licensees a non-challenge clause will deprive licensees of the opportunity to contest the validity of any patent included in the pool if doing so is accompanied with a measure to terminate licensing agreements with the licensee for all the patents in the pool. Imposing on licensees a non-challenge clause will create a legal issue under the JAA if it is accompanied by a measure to terminate licensing agreements with the licensee for all patents in the pool. On the other hand, if the measure is to terminate licensing agreements with the licensee only for the patent subject to the invalidation claim, for instance by taking out the patents from the pool, imposing on licensees a non-challenge clause will not deprive licensees of the opportunity to contest the validity of any patent included in the pool. Imposing such a clause does not pose antitrust concerns under the JAA.

(5) Non-assertion of Patent Rights against Patent Holders and Other Licensees

There would be a huge risk of violating the JAA if a non-assertion of patents clause was imposed on licensees which prohibited the exercise of patent rights licensees could obtain against patent holders in the pool, since this arrangement would have the effect of accumulating patent rights other than those managed in the patent pool. On the other hand, there may be cases in which licensees obtain or will obtain an essential patent associated with the specifications. In this case, imposing on licensees a non-assertion of patent clause generally does not violate the JAA if it means obliging a licensee to pool the essential patent and license it non-exclusively through the pool, provided it is accompanied by no other restrictions on the use of the essential patent and imposing on licensees non-discriminatory treatment in, for example, the distribution of licensing fees compared with the others pooling their patents.

3. Case Law (Pachinko Machine Patents Pool Case)[27]

As explained *above*, the enforcement of the JAA needs to be coordinated with the exercise of intellectual property rights. Pachinko Machine Patents Pool Case is one of the leading cases which make the necessity of coordination clear.

The factual background of this case is as follows:

The ten manufactures produced and sold approximately 90 per cent of Pachinko machines in Japan.[28] The ten manufactures held more than half of the shares in the Japanese Machine Patent Administration Federation, a patent pooling company, and controlled the company substantially. Also, the ten manufactures entrusted their individual proprietary patents concerning Pachinko machines to the pooling company. It is almost impossible for new producers to manufacture Pachinko machines without obtaining licenses from the pooling company. Under these circumstances, the ten manufactures and the pooling company reconfirmed their policy not to give licenses to any party other than current licensees in order to prevent new entry into the market. In accordance with the policy, the pooling company refused to license patents to two firms which hoped to produce Pachinko machines and who offered to make license agreements with the pooling company. Also, when another firm which intended to produce Pachinko machines acquired more than 50 per cent of the shares of one of the licensees, the pooling company refused to renew the license.

The JFTC decided that the conduct of the ten manufactures and the pooling company was in the violation of the Cartel Regulation by excluding new entrants from the relevant market. The JAA Art. 3 should have been applied to the conduct of the ten manufactures and the pooling company for their concerted refusal to deal since the ten manufactures controlled the pooling company. In the decision, the JFTC ordered the ten manufactures and the pooling company to revoke their policy and not to prevent new entry by refusing to license the patents. It should be noted, however, that the albeit JFTC should have put in place a compulsory licensing order as a remedy to restore competition in the relevant market, a step was not taken by the JFTC.

27. Sankyo, 44 SINKETUSHU 238 (FTC, 6 August 1997).
28. Pachinko machines are a very popular Japanese game machine, similar to a slot machine.

E. Rule of Reason Type Horizontal Restraint

The guideline released by the JFTC recognizes that an exchange of information sensitive to competition among competitors and joint research and development agreements among competitors may be regulated by the Cartel Regulation.

On the other hand, some scholars admit pro-competitive aspects of information exchange. Indeed, through the exchange of information, they may be able to use their resources more effectively, rendering the relevant market more competitive. Although the JFTC seems to recognize pro-competitive aspects of information exchange, it takes the position that whether or not an information exchange is a violation of the Cartel Regulation depends upon the structure, rules or whether information exchange might facilitate price coordination.

Until now, however, there have been no decisions concerning exchange of information among competitors and joint research and development agreements among competitors. Even if competitors are only exchanging information, it could become illegal under the JAA as cartel practices given that the parties form implicit understandings or common intentions as to price through the information exchange. As such, a reasonable inference could be made so that the parties have reached a cartel agreement. When communications among parties include information as to price, such practices are likely to be in violation of the JAA Art. 3, since they would be regarded as agreements on price.

II. VERTICAL RESTRAINT

A. Overview of the Monopoly Regulation and Unfair Trade Practice Regulation

Under the JAA, vertical restraints are covered by both the Monopoly Regulation and the Unfair Trade Practice Regulation.

As a premise to explain the 'double coverage' of the two regulations, this book will seek to provide a brief overview of the Monopoly Regulation and the Unfair Trade Practice Regulation.

1. The Monopoly Regulation

The Monopoly Regulation is defined in the JAA Art. 3. The conduct set out in Art. 3 is called 'private monopolization', which means that entrepreneurs exclude or control the business activities of other entrepreneurs, thereby causing, contrary to the public interest, a substantial restraint of competition in a particular field of trade. Specifically, this means any conduct by a company with a large market share that excludes participation of new entrants or restrains the business activities of other competitors by using unjust means (in many cases, but not limited to, any means that violate the Act) in order to increase or maintain its market share. Although the phrase 'contrary to the public interest' is used, since exclusion and control entails wrongful conduct on the part of the monopolizing party, this conduct is regarded as inherently contrary to the public interest. The term 'private monopolization' used in the JAA seems to indicate that publicly created monopolies are not subject to the Monopoly Regulation. Publicly created monopolies are usually based on national laws established by the Japanese Diet and their activities are regarded as being within the ambit of powers conferred by the JAA. Note that public enterprises, in which the Japanese government owes a majority of equity, are not automatically exempt from the application of the JAA.

As stated *above*, one of the two types of conduct which is deemed to be monopolization under the JAA is the 'exclusion' by a powerful enterprise of the business activities of other firms. Although the JAA does not provide the definition as to what is 'exclusion', predatory pricing is sometimes deemed to be 'exclusion', and therefore it is a Monopoly Regulation violation. This is a price manipulation exercised by a powerful firm, often accompanied by below-cost selling and price discrimination. Although predatory pricing is also regulated by the Unfair Trade Practice Regulation, if it creates a situation where competition in a particular field of trade is substantially restrained, it would constitute a violation of the Monopoly Regulation as exclusionary conduct. Exclusive dealing agreements and tie-in arrangements may also be deemed to be 'exclusions'. In a typical exclusive dealing agreement, for example, a manufacture imposes certain obligations on dealers which often prohibit them from handling competitors' products. In a typical tie-in arrangement, firms offer their products on the condition that the purchaser would accept additional products or services. The arrangement might tend to exclude competitors of the tied products. Although both exclusive dealing and tie-in arrangements are also regulated by the Unfair Trade Practice Regulation, if they would create a situation where competition in a particular field of trade is substantially restrained, they would constitute a violation of the Monopoly Regulation as exclusionary conduct.

Another form of conduct which is deemed to be monopolization under the JAA is the 'control' of business activities of other firms. Generally, 'control' entails a situation in which a powerful enterprise imposes its will on another enterprise and coerces it to engage or not to engage in certain activities. For example, if a powerful enterprise acquires stock in a competing corporation, and through the influence made possible by the acquisition coerces the latter to refrain from establishing its branch office in a certain area where the former has already been providing its services, this conduct would be regarded as 'control' and therefore deemed to be a violation of the Monopoly Regulation.

2. The Unfair Trade Practice Regulation

On the other hand, conduct prohibited by the Unfair Trade Practice Regulation is defined in the JAA Art. 2, para. 9.

Art. 2, para. 9 defines unfair trade practices as any act which tends to impede fair competition and which is designated by the JFTC. It goes on to list

(i) unjustly discriminating against other entrepreneurs, (ii) dealing at unjust prices, (iii) unjustly inducing or coercing customers of a competitor to deal with oneself, (iv) dealing with another party on such terms as will unjustly restrict the business activities of the said party, (v) dealing with another party by unjust use of one's bargaining position, and (vi) unjustly interfering with a transaction between an entrepreneur who competes in Japan with oneself or the company of which oneself is a stockholder or an officer and another transaction counterparty; or, in case such entrepreneur is a company, unjustly inducing, instigating, or coercing a stockholder or an officer of such company to act against the interests of such company. Art. 19 prohibits firms from engaging in unfair trade practices. The JFTC lists the sixteen types of conduct which constitute hindrances to efficient competition. These are (i) concerted refusal to deal, (ii) other refusal to deal, (iii) discriminatory pricing, (iv) discriminatory treatment of transaction terms, etc, (v) discriminatory treatment in a trade association, (vi) unjustly low price sales, (vii) unjustly high price purchasing, (viii) deceptive customer inducement, (ix) customer inducement by unjust benefits, (x) tie-in sales, etc, (xi) dealing on exclusive terms, (xii) resale price maintenance, (xiii) dealing on restrictive terms, (xiv) abuse of dominant bargaining position, (xv) interference with a competitor's transaction, and (xvi) interference with the internal operation of a competitor's company.

The common condition which applies all types of conduct mentioned *above* is 'the likelihood of impeding unfair competition'. It is almost impossible, however, to give a unified definition of the likelihood of impeding fair competition for unfair trade practice.

It was widely believed until around 1980 that the likelihood of impeding fair competition was a much lower substantive standard than the substantial restraint of competition standard of the JAA Art. 3. It was also widely believed that unfair trade practice in general did not require adverse effects on the relevant market. One of the justifications for the aforementioned interpretations of the JAA is that it had been considered in Japan that an administrative remedy to restore fair competition given by the antitrust agency is a more effective way to deal with anticompetitive conduct than a judicial remedy rendered by a court. This trend generated the tendency to lower the threshold for the JFTC to bring an action to prevent unfair trade practices. It should be noted that, as this book will make clear later, it has become considered necessary to analyze market effects caused by unfair trade practices in order to examine whether or not the condition of the likelihood of impeding unfair competition has been satisfied.

3. Double Coverage of the Monopoly Regulation and the Unfair Trade Practice Regulation

Although it is still not clear from the case law, in theory vertical restraints are covered by Art. 3 and Art. 19 (Art. 11, 12, and 13 of the general designation). Substantive rules concerning vertical restraints would be quite similar to those developed in the United States if Art. 3 were held to cover vertical restraints.

B. Resale Price Maintenance

1. Overview

Resale price maintenance is typically a requirement imposed by a manufacturer on its wholesalers and/or retailers to the effect that such wholesalers or retailers must maintain wholesale or resale prices at the level indicated by the manufacturer.

Resale price maintenance has been the major target of antitrust enforcement in Japan. For example, from 1981 through 1989, the JFTC brought 25 Unfair Trade Practice Regulation violation cases, 16 cases of which involved resale price maintenance issues and 15 cases of which were challenged between 1981 and 1985. Even after the issuance of the Distribution Guideline, the JFTC has been said to focus on resale price maintenance. In 1991, the JFTC brought two resale price maintenance cases, the first such cases in four years, which clearly evidences the JFTC's policy to pursue more vigorous enforcement against resale price maintenance. This is partly because it will likely bring direct benefit to consumers by lowering retail prices. Also, traditionally, the JFTC officials do not see resale price maintenance as a pro-competitive tool of inter-brand competition, or as an efficient way to assure the desired level of pre or post sale service.

In a resale price maintenance case under the JAA, it is usually a requirement that wholesalers or retailers set their prices at or above those set by the manufacturer. Art. 12 of the general designation provides that resale price maintenance is in principle unlawful if parties reselling the product are bound by direction by the manufacturer. However, there must be a binding obligation that the reselling parties must adhere to the price level set by manufacturer. Therefore, mere 'suggested prices' or 'recommended prices' does not amount to resale price maintenance. The rationale for holding resale price maintenance unlawful is that the conduct can only be carried out in a situation where the manufacturer is able to impose such terms and conditions on distributors. In such a situation, the relevant market at the manufacture's level is highly oligopolistic, making it possible for the manufacturer to enjoy monopolistic pricing.

In a manufacture/dealer consignment, title to the commodity does not pass from the manufactures to the dealer. The manufacturer reserves title, which passes from the manufacturer to the purchasers to whom the dealers sell the article as an agent. It could be argued that in a contract of this nature, the dealer does not purchase the commodity but only acts as an agent and there is no sale or resale as far as the manufacturer and the dealers are concerned. However, if the purpose of the consignment is to evade prohibition on resale price maintenance, the JFTC should pierce the corporate veil and determine that the substance of the agreement is de facto a sales contract.

According to the Distribution Guideline, whether or not resale prices have been restricted is to be judged based on the determination of whether or not any artificial means are used to secure effectiveness in attaining sales at the price indicated by the manufacturer. It shall be judged that the effectiveness in attaining sales at the price indicated by the manufacturer is secured in cases where a written or oral agreement between a manufacturer and its distributors causes the distributors to sell at the price indicated by the manufacturer. Examples of this are as follows: (i) where a written or oral contact provides that sales are made at the price indicated by a manufacturer; (ii) where distributors are required to pledge in writing to sell at the price indicted by manufacturer; (iii) where a manufacturer only starts dealing with distributors that accept the condition that they sell at the price indicted by the manufacturer; and (iv) where a manufacturer deals with distributors on condition that the distributors sell at the price indicated by the manufacturer and that unsold goods are not to be discounted but to be repurchased by the manufacturer.

In addition, under the guideline, it shall be judged to be illegal resale price maintenance where any artificial means, such as imposing or suggesting the imposition of economic disadvantages if sales are not made at a manufacturer's indicated price, causing distributors to sell at the indicated price. Examples of this are as follows: (i) where curtailment of shipments or any other economic disadvantage (including reduction of quantities shipped, raising of shipment price, reduction of rebates, and refusal to supply other products) is imposed in the event that sales are not made at a manufacturer's indicated price or where a notification or suggestion to that effect is made to distributors; (ii) where rebates or other economic rewards (including lowering of shipment price and supply of the products) are provided in the event that sales are made at a manufacturer's indicated price, or where a notification or suggestion to that effect is made to distributors; and (iii) where a manufacturer causes distributors to sell at the manufacturer's indicated price by the following means: (a) collecting sales price reports, patrolling retail establishments, conducting price, supervision by salespersons dispatched to shops, examining ledgers or records of retailers, etc. in order to ascertain whether sales are being made at the manufacturer's indicated price; (b) identifying price-cutting distributors by making use of secret marks and requesting wholesalers who supplied the goods to such distributors not to sell to them; (c) buying goods from price-cutting distributors and requesting such distributors or wholesalers who supplied them to buy the goods or pay the cost of their purchases; and (d) transmitting complaints to price-cutting distributors from nearby distributors with regard to low-price sales, and requesting the price-cutting distributors to end such sales.

It should be noted that the guideline provides exceptional situations where it seems that resale price maintenance will not be a violation of Art. 12 of the general designation. First, in case of consignment sales, and if the transaction is made with a consignor at its own risk and account such that a consignee bears no risk beyond that associated with its obligation to exercise the care of a good manager in shortage and handling of goods, collection of payments, and so on and is not liable for loss of goods, damage to them, or for unsold goods, then it is not illegal even when a manufacturer instructs resale price to the direct purchasers. Second, in cases of transactions where a supply price is negotiated and decided directly between a manufacturer and a retailer (or user), and the manufacturer instructs a wholesaler to deliver goods to the retailer (or the user), and if the manufacturer is deemed, in substance, to sell the goods to the retailers (or the user) under such circumstances that the wholesaler is charged only with responsibility for physical delivery of the goods and collection of payment, and a fee is paid for such work, even when manufacturer instructs resale price to a wholesaler, then it shall not be illegal under the JAA.

2. Case Law

a. *Meiji Shoji Case*[29]

When this case arose, there existed four main manufactures in the Japanese powdered milk market. Meiji Shoji K.K. ('Meiji Shoji'), a sales company of Meiji Milk K.K., started to sell a new type of powdered milk, F – II, in September 1964, and took measures to maintain the price level. First, Meiji Shoji determined the suggested wholesale price and retail price of F – II, and then requested retailers to purchase products at the suggested wholesale price and to sell them at the suggested retail price. Second, Meiji Shoji planned to distribute F – II through registered wholesalers who promised to sell to registered retailers, who promised to sell at the suggested retail price, at the suggested wholesale price. Third, Meiji Shoji made it clear that it would cut or reduce the rebate for wholesalers or retailers who did not comply with the promise. Meiji Shoji implemented the aforementioned sales policy. Three other manufactures which were competitors of Meiji Shoji also implemented the identical policy. The Supreme Court ruled that resale price maintenance which is imposed on all distributors systematically is the illegal according to the *quasi per se* rule. The Supreme Court rejected all the justification defences raised by the defendants, most of which were based on Japanese business practices and the need for administration. It was argued that retail price maintenance is necessary to prevent the product from being sold as a loss leader. Also, Wakodo, the forth largest manufacture, whose market share was approximately 10 per cent, also argued that its price maintenance actually promoted competition with the other three large manufactures. The court rejected these arguments, holding that the practices would prevent competition among distributors even if they promoted competition among manufactures. Also, the court ruled that the restriction requirement of Art. 12 of the general designation shall be satisfied not only by incurring the contractual obligation of maintaining the resale price but also by imposing any effective means of economic disadvantage for noncompliance. After the case, resale price maintenance, along with hard core cartels, had become the main target area of Japanese antitrust enforcement. Subsequent cases at the Supreme Court level, however, always found at least one implementation example of resale price maintenance, such as termination of a dealer contract, suspension of the supply of products, unilateral refusal to deal, or threat of termination.

As a result of these precedents, it was widely understood that in order to find a violation of Art. 12 of the general designation (prohibition on resale price

29. 326 HANREITIMES 82, (Supp. Ct. 10 July 1975).

maintenance), it is necessary to prove an example of implementation as well as instruction of maintaining resale price to distributors.

b. Shiseido Case[30]

The consent order of Shiseido Case shows the development of resale price maintenance regulation in Japan.

Shiseido K.K. ('Shiseido') is the largest cosmetic manufacturer in Japan and requires its cosmetic dealers to sell Shiseido products at the suggested retail price and to obtain sales margins which Shiseido deems appropriate. Until 1995, retail price maintenance for certain cosmetic products pricing at less than 1,000 yen had been authorized as per an exemption granted by the JAA and approved by the JFTC. The top five dealers by sales amount of Shiseido cosmetic products were the large scale chain retailers, including Jusco K.K. ('Jusco') and Daiei K.K. ('Daiei'). Jusco tried to discount Shiseido cosmetic products when the number of exempted cosmetic product in terms of retail price maintenance regulation was reduced in 1992 and informed Shiseido of its intention. Shiseido requested Jusco to give up its discount sales and proposed the provision of additional samples for promotion. Daiei also planned to discount Shiseido products in order to compete with other discount stores and informed Shiseido of its intention. Shiseido promised to take appropriate measures against discount stores and requested Daiei to withhold its discount plan by offering to support sales promotion. Jusco and Daiei continued to sell Shiseido products at the suggested resale price in order to avoid any troubles with Shiseido. In this case, no implementation examples were found such that Shiseido threatened the dealers who tried to discount, or persuaded them to sell at the suggested price by notifying them of suspending supply if they would not comply with the instruction. Shiseido proposed, however, to provide benefits to obtain consent to maintain resale price from Jusco and Daiei. The JFTC decided that the conduct of Shiseido satisfied the restriction requirement, which is defined as 'imposing some kind of constraints on activities of distributors' in Art. 12 of the general designation. Thus, it was found to be an Unfair Trade Practice violation.

It is worth noting here that the JFTC found a violation of the resale price maintenance prohibition in spite of the fact that no implementation examples were found.

C. Exclusive Dealing

1. Overview

Art. 11 of the general designation provides that if a party prohibits the other party to a transaction from dealing with the former party's competitors and unduly reducing

---

30. Shiseido, 42 SINKETUSHU 97 (FTC, 30 November 1995).

the business opportunities for the competitors, such an exclusive dealing arrangement would amount to a violation of the Unfair Trade Practice Regulation. Exclusive dealing can be made through contracts between a manufacturer and a dealer, whereby the former prohibits the latter from handling its competitor's services or products. Also, it can be made through an agreement in which the distributor obligates suppliers to provide products or services only to the distributor.

The Distribution Guideline states that where a restriction on handling of competing products is imposed by an influential manufacturer in a relevant market, and if the restriction may result in making it difficult for new entrants or competitors to easily secure alternative distribution channels, such restriction is illegal as a violation of Art. 11 of the general designation. Under the guideline, an influential manufacturer in a relevant market shall be determined in the first instance by the market share of the manufacturer, that is, whether or not it has no less than 10 per cent of market share or its position is within the top three in the relevant market. Nevertheless, under the guideline, in deciding whether or not an influential manufacturer's conducts is illegal, the JFTC will also take into consideration such factors as whether or not the restriction may result in making it difficult for new entrants or competitors to easily secure alternative distribution channels. If a restriction on handling of competing products is imposed by a low-ranked or newly-entered firm which has a market share of less than 10 per cent and whose position is not in the top three largest firms in the relevant industry, the restriction usually would not result in making it difficult for new entrants or competitors to easily secure alternative distribution channels, and such restriction is not illegal under the guideline. In addition, in determining whether or not a restriction 'may result in making it difficult for new entrants or competitors to easily secure alternative distribution channels', under the guideline, the following factors should be taken into consideration: the structure of the market, the position in the market of the manufacturer that imposes the restriction, the number of distributors affected by the restriction and their position in the market, and the impact of the restriction on business activities of the distributors.

2. Case Law (Toyo Seimaiki Case)[31]

The Tokyo High Court decision in Toyo Seimainki Case is the leading case on vertical exclusive dealing.

Toyo Seimaiki manufactured medium-sized rice cleaning machines and sold them primarily to rice sales retailers through distributors. Toyo Seimaiki began to conclude new distribution contracts with its distributors, which provided that the distributors were never to use rice cleaning machines provided

31. *Toyo Seimaiki K.K. v. Japan Fair Trade Commission*, 35 GYOSAIREISHU 144 (Tokyo Hi. Ct. 17 February 1984).

by its competitors. In this case, the JFTC found that Toyo Seimaiki had a market share of approximately 28 per cent, and that the exclusive dealing contract which Toyo Seimaiki demanded distributors to conclude violated Art. 11 of the general designation (prohibition on exclusive terms), as Toyo Seimaiki was regarded as a leading firm in the relevant market. The Tokyo High Court reversed the formal decision by the JFTC and remanded the case to the JFTC for further examination with the following instructions. First, the court said that the JFTC needed to define the relevant market accurately and calculate the market share of Toyo Seimaiki correctly. The court indicated that the relevant market should be defined as the market for selling rice cleaning machines provided to retailers in order to analyze the market foreclosure effects. In the JFTC's decision, the market share of Toyo Seimaiki was computed based on the sales amounts of the distributors. However, Toyo Seimaiki's market share could have been smaller because medium sized machines of Toyo Seimaiki were sold to large scale rice cleaning factories through distributors. Second, vertical exclusive dealing violates Art. 11 of the general designation if it is likely to cause the foreclosure effects. Therefore, the JFTC needed to find out how far and to what extent the distribution routes for the competitors were foreclosed. When the market share of the firm who imposed the exclusive dealing arrangement is very large, foreclosure effects may be presumed to exist. In this case, however, Toyo Seimaiki's market share was not enough to presume foreclosure effects. The JFTC needed to find how many distributors existed in the relevant market and how the distributors were organized by the competitors in addition to the market share of Toyo Seimaiki. In conclusion, according to the court's ruling, the JFTC should have found both the number of distributors in the relevant market and the competitors' distribution methods in order to determine whether or not the foreclosure effects existed. From the Tokyo High Court decision, it was made clear that in Unfair Trade Practice cases, it is necessary to delineate the relevant market. Also, in order to analyze whether or not the impeding fair competition requirement is fulfilled, market analysis is, in principal, required.

D. Sales Area, Customers and Sales Method Restriction

1. Overview

Art. 13 of the general designation provides that restriction on the business activities of another party to a transaction is regulated.

Under the JAA, however, sales area, customers and sales method restrictions are considered to be incidental to resale price maintenance and have gotten little attention in the case law. As such, it is not clear which rule will apply to sales area, customers and sales method restrictions. The Distribution Guideline has been considered the most reliable source on substantive rules.

a. Restriction on Sales Area

The Distribution Guideline classifies restriction on sales area into the following four categories:

(i) Assigning a specific territory to each distributor as the area of primary responsibility and requiring the distributor to carry out active sales activities within each territory ('area of responsibility system');
(ii) Restricting the area where a distributor may establish business premises such as stores, or designating the plan of where such premises are to be established ('location system');
(iii) Assigning a specific area to each distributor and restricting the distributor from selling outside each area ('exclusive territory'); and
(iv) Assigning a specific area to each distributor and restricting the distributor from selling to customers outside each area upon request ('restriction of sales to outside customers').

Under the guideline, it is not illegal for a manufacturer to adopt the area of responsibility system or the location system for the purpose of developing an effective network for sales or securing a better system for after-sales service. It is considered a violation where such restriction falls under exclusive territory or restriction on sales to outside customers.

With regard to exclusive territory, in cases where an influential manufacturer in a market assigns exclusive territory to distributors and if the price level of the product covered by the restriction is likely to be maintained, such restriction is illegal as an unfair trade practice (Art. 13 of the general designation). Whether a manufacturer is influential in a market is in the first instance judged by a the market share of the manufacturer, that is, whether it has no less than 10 per cent of the relevant market or its position is within the top three firms in the relevant market. Nevertheless, even if a firm falls under this criteria, the restriction by the firm is not always illegal. In cases where the price level of the product is likely to be maintained by the restriction, such restriction is illegal. In case of a low-ranked or new manufacturer which has a market share of less than 10 per cent and whose position is the not in the top three largest firms, the price level of the product usually would not be maintained by exclusive territory, and such restriction is not illegal. Also note that whether or not 'price level of the product covered by the restriction is likely to be maintained' is to be determined by taking into account such factors as actual conditions of inter-brand competition (market concentration, characteristics of the product, degree of product differentiation, and distribution channels, difficulty in new market entry), the actual conditions of intra-brand competition for the product (degree of dispersion in price, and business types of distributors dealing in the product), number of distributors affected by the restriction, and their positions in the market, and the impact of the restriction on the business activities of the distributors (extent, and manner of the restriction). In cases where exclusive territory is assigned to distributors by an influential manufacturer in a market under circumstances where inter-brand competition does not work well due to the oligopolistic structure of the market and product differentiation, price competition for the product of the manufacture's brand may be imposed, and the price level of the product is likely to be maintained. In cases of test marketing of a new product or sale of local souvenirs, the price level of the product usually would not be maintained by territorial restriction and such restriction is not illegal.

With regard to a restriction of sales to customers, in cases where a manufacturer imposes restrictions of sales to outside customers, and if the price level of the product is likely to be maintained, such restriction is illegal as an unfair trade practice (Art. 13 of the general designation).

b. *Restriction on Customers*

The Distribution Guideline lists the following three categories of restrictions on customers.

(i) Requiring each wholesaler to supply only to certain retailers, so that the retailers may buy only from that wholesaler ('requirement of designated accounts');
(ii) Preventing distributors from buying and selling products among themselves ('prohibition of sales among distributors'); and
(iii) Prohibiting wholesalers from selling to price-cutting retailers.

With regard to the requirement of designated accounts on wholesalers, if such an obligation is imposed and if the price level of the product covered by the restriction is likely to be maintained, it is illegal as unfair trade practices (Art. 13 of the general designation).

Regarding prohibition of sales among distributors, in cases where a manufacturer prohibits sales among distributors for the purpose of preventing its products from being sold to price-cutting distributors, and if the price level of the product is likely to be maintained, such restriction is illegal as unfair trade practices (Art. 13 of the general designation).

Regarding prohibition on sales to price-cutters, in cases where a manufacturer causes wholesalers not to sell to a retailer on account of the retailer's price-cutting, the price level of the product is likely to be maintained, and such restriction is in principle illegal as unfair trade practices (Art. 2 or Art. 13 of the general designation).

Moreover, in cases where a manufacturer stops shipments to a distributor that has been its direct customer, on account of the distributor's price-cutting, the price level of the product is likely to be maintained, and such conduct is in principle illegal as an unfair trade practice (Art. 2 of the general designation). Whether or not such restriction is 'on account of the retailer's price-cutting' is to be objectively judged based on the actual conditions of the transactions, including the manufacturer's response to other distributors, and related circumstances.

c. *Restriction on Sales Method*

The Distribution Guideline provides the following four examples of restrictions on sales methods.

(i) Calling for demonstration – sales of the product;
(ii) Calling for customer delivery service for the product;
(iii) Instructing conditions for quality control of the product; and
(iv) Calling for shelf space or a display area exclusively for the product.

Under the guideline, in cases where there are restrictions on the retailers' sales methods (excluding those on sales price, sales territory and customers) are recognized to have rational reasons for the purpose of ensuring proper sales of the product, such as those relating to assuring the safety of the product, preservation of its quality, maintenance of the value of its trademark, and so on, and if the same restrictions are applied to other retailers-customers on equal terms, such restrictions in themselves do not present a problem under the JAA. However, in cases where restrictions on retailers' sales methods are used as a means to restrict sales price, handling of competing products, sales territory or customers, their illegality is to be judged with the guidance of Art. 11, 12 and 13 of the general designation set forth in the guideline. Note that, under the guideline, in cases where a manufacturer stops shipments only to price-cutting retailers among those which do not observe the restrictions on sales methods on account of their non-observance of the restrictions, the manufacturer usually shall be found to have restricted sales price by means of the restrictions on sales methods.

Furthermore, under the guideline, in cases where a manufacturer imposes the following types of restrictions on advertisements and representations as a kind of sales method, the price level of the product is likely to be maintained and such restriction is in principle illegal as an unfair trade practice (Art. 13 of the general designation):

(i) Where a manufacturer restricts the price shown at stores or prohibits price advertising: or
(ii) Where a manufacturer causes magazines, newspapers or other advertising media in which the manufacturer puts advertisements, to reject such advertisements for discounted pricing of the manufacturer's products and the price of the products are made clear.

2. Case Law (Kao Case and Shiseido Case)[32] (Restriction on Sales Method)

The Supreme Court decision in Shiseido Case and Kao Case are the main precedents concerning the restriction on sales method.

32. 1234 HANREIJIHO 7 (Sup. Ct. 18 December 1998).

In Shiseido Case, Shiseido Cosmetic Sale K.K. ('Shiseido Cosmetic Sale'), a sales company sold Shiseido cosmetic products to cosmetic dealers under the standard dealership contract, which requires face-to-face counselling sales. The face-to-face sales requirement obligated dealers to prepare themselves to provide product information concerning product characteristics and usage at the request of consumers at the sales location by using trained sales person. In this case, however, Fujiki, one of the Shiseido's dealers, started catalogue sales at a reduced price, circulating catalogues and accepting orders via telephone or fax. In the catalogue sales, Fujiki did not expect to conduct the face-to-face counselling sales as per its obligation. After prolonged negotiation, Shiseido Cosmetic Sale finally terminated the dealership contact with Fujiki.

In Kao Case, Kao sold its cosmetic products to dealers under a similar dealership contract. Kao terminated the dealership contact with one of its dealers, Egawa Kikaku, which was supposed to continue selling a large volume of Kao's cosmetic products to another dealer without performing the counselling sales duty.

In these cases, the Supreme Court upheld the argument of the cosmetic manufacturers and made the following four rulings. First, it is not a violation of Art. 13 of the general designation (dealing on exclusive terms) to impose a duty concerning sales methods such as the obligation for dealers to perform face-to-face counselling of products by a trained salesperson at the location where cosmetic products are being sold so long as the restriction meets a three prong test. The first prong of the test is whether or not there are some justifications in imposing such a duty at issue for distributing cosmetic products. The second prong is whether or not such a duty is imposed on all distributors. Note that regarding the second prong test, it was found that Shiseido Cosmetic Sale concluded the same kind of agreement with all distributors, thus imposing the same obligation on all of them. Second, face-to-face counselling sales methods have itself some justification in maintaining the brand image by instructions to consumers about how to use the products effectively and can prevent skin care problems. Third, so long as the face-to-face counselling requirement is imposed on all distributors lawfully, the cosmetic manufacturers are allowed to demand dealers not to sell their product to the dealers who do not conclude an agreement with them. In addition, the Supreme Court held that although restrictions on sales methods might have the same competitive effects as resale price maintenance in stabilizing the resale price, they should be distinguished from each other under antitrust regulation. Concerning the last prong, it is said that it should apply to all type of vertical restraints. In conclusion, the Supreme Court decided that it was not a violation of Art. 13 of the general designation (dealing on exclusive terms) to impose a duty concerning sales methods such as an obligation for dealers to perform face-to-face counselling for products by trained salespeople at the location where cosmetic products which fulfilled the *above* delineated three prong test. Therefore, it is not a violation to terminate dealership contract with those who did not comply with face-to-face counselling obligation.

III. UNILATERAL ACTIONS

A. Characteristics

Under the JAA, unilateral actions could be covered by both the Monopoly Regulation and Unfair Trade Practice Regulation.

In the following two kinds of cases, however, the Monopoly Regulation is to be applied exclusively. First, the Monopoly Regulation applies to non-typical illegal conduct not covered in any article of the general designation of unfair trade practices. Second, the Monopoly Regulation applies when the combination of many separate types of conduct are assessed as a whole and considered to be exclusionary conduct, which means activities engaged in to exclude the business activities of other firms in private monopolization, which may include non-typical type conduct or non-illegal conduct.

It should be noted, however, that even in the case where each separate type of conduct in combination fulfils any one of general designations, applying the Monopoly Regulation to the combined conduct as a whole may be a more effective application of the law rather than applying the Unfair Trade Practice Regulation to each type of conduct separately. In these two kinds of cases, the JFTC has no choice but to apply the Monopoly Regulation.

B. Exclusionary Conduct

1. Exclusive Dealing

a. Overview

As explained *above*, Art. 11 of the general designation prohibits unjustly dealing with the other party on condition that the said party shall not deal with a competitor, thereby tending to reduce transaction opportunities for the said competitor. The terms 'on condition' have been interpreted so that this condition needs an agreement to be concluded between the parties or intimidation to be used. If this condition cannot be fulfilled, exclusive dealing arrangements will be dealt with under the Monopoly Regulation.

b. Case Law

i. Hokkai Times Newspaper Press Case[33]

Hokkaido Newspaper Press published *The Hokkaido Newspaper* and worked with 90 per cent of the newspaper dealers in the Hokkaido area. It had a market share of approximately 56 per cent in the Hokkaido area. Hokkai Times Press, another

33. *Hokkaido Newspaper Press v. Japanese Fair Trade Commission*, 6 SHINKETSUSHU 89 (Tokyo Hi. Ct. 23 December 1954).

newspaper publishing company, which used to publish only an evening edition, began to publish a morning edition and become a competitor of Hokkaido Newspaper Press. Hokkaido Newspaper Press repeatedly requested its own dealers not to distribute *The Hokkaido Times* and terminated its dealership agreement with the dealers who did not comply with the request. As a result, Hokkai Times Press was forced to establish its own distribution channel. The JFTC decided in 1954 that exclusive dealing of Hokkaido Newspaper Press with dealers violated the Unfair Trade Practice Regulation. The Tokyo High court upheld the JFTC's decision. While the application of the Unfair Trade Practice Regulation is not incorrect, it would also have been possible for the JFTC to apply the Monopoly Regulation to the conduct of Hokkaido Newspaper Press.

ii. Nordian Case[34]

The JFTC decision on MDS Nordian is a typical example of the dual coverage of the Monopoly Regulation and the Unfair Trade Practice Regulation on unilateral conduct.

MDS Nordian, a Canadian company, sold radioactive materials to two Japanese X-ray film companies and had market share of one hundred per cent in the Japanese market, although another foreign company was trying to sell the same materials to one of the Japanese companies. At this stage, MDS Nordian decided to invest in the construction of a new nuclear reactor in Canada and established a sales policy of making long-term exclusive contracts with their main customers. Under the policy, MDS Nordian made offers and executed twenty year exclusive dealing contracts with two Japanese customers. The JFTC decided that the conduct of MDS Nordian violated the Monopoly Regulation and issued a recommendation order. In addition, pursuant to the rationale established in Hokkai Times Newspaper Press Case, the JFTC could have issued the order on the ground that the conduct constituted a violation of the Unfair Trade Practice Regulation, specifically Art. 11 of the general designation (prohibition on dealing on exclusive term).

2. Tie-in Sales

a. Overview

Art. 10 of the general designation prohibits unjustly causing the other party to purchase a commodity or service from oneself or from an entrepreneur designated by oneself by tying it to the supply of another commodity or service, or otherwise coercing the said party to deal with oneself or with an entrepreneur designated by oneself. This is called a tie-in arrangement and is unlawful in principle. For example, if a manufacturer of computers conditions its sale of computers upon the buyer's purchase of computer cards used together with the computer, although

34. MDS Nordian K.K., 45 SINKETUSHU 148 (FTC, 3 September 1998).

it is tie-in arrangement, it is not unlawful. However, if the party offering the tying product enjoys powerful economic position in the market for such product, the purchaser is forced into purchasing the tied product, which it may not wish to purchase. Such contracts may be regarded as unreasonable coercion of consumers and constitute an unfair trade practice.

The Distribution Guideline provides several examples in which tie-in arrangements are deemed to be illegal under the JAA. According to the guideline, tie-in arrangements shall be illegal when a party is compelled to purchase products from the firm in the following situations:

(i) Where the influential firm, indicating that it would terminate or reduce purchases from the other party unless the other party purchases the firm's products, requests the other party to purchase the firm's products;
(ii) Where the procurement personnel in the influential firm, suggesting that the influential firm's purchases would be affected, requests the other party to purchase the firm's products;
(iii) Where the influential firm, setting a sales target of its products for each transacting party on the basis of the amount of purchases from the latter, and indicating that the latter's failure to attain this target would result in a reduction in the volume of purchases by the firm from the latter, requests the latter to purchase a large enough amount to meet the sales target;
(iv) Where the influential firm, revealing the comparative list of each transacting party's purchases from and sales to the firm and suggesting that it would otherwise purchase only a corresponding volume, requests additional purchases by each party;
(v) Where, in response to the other party's offer to sell, the influential firm, indicating that it would purchase the other party's products if the other party purchases services supplied by the firm or its designated firm, requests the other party to purchase the services;
(vi) Where, even though the other party has expressed its intention not to purchase, the influential firm, stating that it has purchased services from that party, makes a request to the party and induces it to purchase the firm's products; or
(vii) Where in spite of the absence of proposal by the other party to purchase, the firm unilaterally sends its products to that party, and offsets the products' total value against an unpaid account that it owes to the latter.

b. Case Law

i. Microsoft Case[35]

Microsoft K.K. ('Microsoft') entered into license agreements with several Japanese personal computer manufactures, including NEC and Toshiba in 1995,

35. Microsoft, 45 SINKETUSHU 153 (FTC, 14 December 1998).

which obligated manufactures to install both Microsoft Excel and Microsoft Word software applications in their personal computers. In the process of negotiation, Microsoft rejected all proposals from personal computer manufacturers which requested licensing of the application software to be undertaken separately. The product market for spreadsheet software and word processing software applications was deemed to constitute separate product markets because of the different usage and demand. In 1995, Microsoft Excel had the largest share of the spreadsheet software market and Lotus 1 – 2 – 3 had the second largest. However, in the word processing market, Ichitaro produced by Just System K.K. had the top market share and Microsoft Word had the second largest. Microsoft tried to increase the market share of Microsoft Word through a tie-in arrangement. As a result of the arrangement, Microsoft Word gained the largest market share in the word processing market in 1997. The JFTC rendered a recommendation decision that Microsoft's tying arrangement of Microsoft Word (the tied product) and Microsoft Excel (the tying product) violated Art. 10 of the general designation and ordered Microsoft to cease the arrangement so that the personal computer manufacturers could install separate software in their computer at their own discretion. Tie-in arrangements of this type have the same effect on the tied product market as exclusive dealing have. Therefore, it would have also been possible to apply the Monopoly Regulation in this case.

ii. Toshiba Elevator Case[36]

The Osaka High Court in Toshiba Elevator Case held that a tie-in arrangement where replacement parts for a manufacturer's elevator were tied to the provision of maintenance services for the elevator by a subsidiary of the manufacturer violated Art. 10 of the general designation (prohibition on tie-in sales).

The factual background of this case is quite similar to the Kodak case in the United States.[37] Toshiba Elevator Technos K.K. ('Toshiba Elevator'), a subsidiary of Toshiba Electric K.K., an elevator manufacturer, intentionally refused or delayed supply of the spare parts to independent maintenance service providers. In the Japanese elevator market, the six main competing manufactures had similar market share in the relevant market, of which Toshiba Elevator had a market share of approximately 20 per cent. Replacement parts were not usable in elevators manufactured by other manufacturers. Toshiba Elevator had a market share of more than 90 per cent in the maintenance service market for Toshiba's elevators.

In this case, the Osaka High Court found Toshiba Elevator liable for the tie-in arrangement and ordered it pay damage awards to the independent maintenance service providers. This is the very first case in Japan in which a damage award was granted for the violation of the JAA. In the court proceedings, Toshiba Elevator argued that the independent service providers did not have the technical

---

36. *Toshiba Elevator Technos K.K. v. Kousei Denki Yugengaisha*, 833 HANREITIMES 62 (Osaka Hi. Ct. 30 July 1993).
37. *Eastman Kodak Co. v. Image Technical Services Inc.* 504 US 451 (1992).

capabilities of performing the maintenance service and that the maintenance service supplied by these providers would increase the danger for users. The court found that the independent service providers had sufficient capabilities to provide elevator maintenance service by themselves.

It should be noted, however, that under the same fact finding inquiry, the Osaka High Court could have held that the tie-in arrangement for replacement parts was a violation of the Monopoly Regulation if the relevant product market was defined narrowly to be the maintenance service market for its own elevators.

iii. ENIX Case[38]

ENIX Corp. ('ENIX'), a software manufacture, was scheduled to begin marketing the new game software 'Dragon Quest IV'. 'Dragon Quest' was such a popular game series that young students were lining up in front of retail stores to purchase the software. The popularity of Dragon Quest IV was reported in newspapers and even debated in the Diet. ENIX directed wholesalers and retailers not to charge more than the suggested price for Dragon Quest IV, taking into consideration the criticism made during the sale of Dragon Quest's previous version. Several wholesalers supplied Dragon Quest IV to retailers under the condition that they would also purchase unpopular software titles. The JFTC rendered a formal decision that the tie-in arrangement of Dragon Quest IV and the unpopular software titles violated Art. 10 of the general designation. This could also be regarded as unfair competition conduct in the form of coercing customers to purchase unnecessary goods.

Neither ENIX game software products nor Dragon Quest IV could be defined as a relevant product market. The relevant market was the game software market, and that being the case, the market share of ENIX was too small to affect the trade terms of the market. Therefore, the arrangement was considered to be a kind of unfair competition violation, under which the conduct itself is deemed anticompetitive by nature. In other words, the conduct was '*per se* illegal' such that market analysis is not necessary.

3. Price Discrimination

a. Overview

Art. 3 of the general designation states that unreasonable price discrimination is an unfair trade practice. According to the designation, both offering a commodity or service at different prices to different customers or territories and accepting such terms are included in this category. It is generally understood that business activity of this kind is unreasonable only when it is detrimental to competition,

38. ENIX, 38 SINKETUSHU 41 (FTC, 28 February 1992).

which only arises when there is a tendency for competition to be restrained and an anticompetitive impact is felt by the majority of enterprises in the relevant market.

b. Case Law (Hokkoku Newspaper Press Case)[39]

The Tokyo High Court decision in the Hokkoku Newspaper Press Case is still a principal precedent for dealing with price discrimination. Hokkoku Newspaper Press K.K. ('Hokkoku Newspaper Press'), which published *The Hokkoku Newspaper* in Ishikawa prefecture and had a market share exceeding 60 per cent there, merged with Toyama Newspaper Press K.K. in neighbouring Toyama prefecture. Hokkoku Newspaper Press continued to publish *The Toyama Newspaper* in Toyama prefecture. In 1956, Hokkoku Newspaper Press increased the number of pages of *The Toyama Newspaper* to the same number as the number of pages of *The Hokkoku Newspaper*, but continued to set cheaper monthly charges for *The Toyama Newspaper* than for *The Hokkoku Newspaper*. The Tokyo High Court ruled on the application for the preliminary injunction by the JFTC that both newspapers were identical, based on the articles, and options in the newspapers and the conduct was in violation of the Unfair Trade Practice Regulation. Consequently, the court ordered Hokkoku Newspaper Press to raise or reduce the monthly charges of one of newspaper to bring them to the same price or to increase or decrease the amount of pages of one of the newspapers to reflect the price difference.

4. Low Price Sales

a. Overview

Art. 2, para. 9 of the JAA provides that unreasonable pricing is an unfair business practice and directs the JFTC to designate specific conduct in this area. Under this heading, the JFTC announced Art. 6 and 7 of the general designation. The former deals with low price sales and the latter prohibits unreasonably high pricing. However, the former is more important than the latter. A sale below cost of production or purchase, as the case may be, is an unreasonable business practice in principle if the price charged is substantially below such cost level and is carried out by an enterprise on a continual basis. Cost in this context is understood to be the sum of the cost of production or purchase plus general overhead expenses.

---

39. *Hokkoku Newspaper Press v. Japanese Fair Trade Commission*, 9 GYOSAIREISHU 443 (Tokyo Hi. Ct. 18 March 1957).

b. Case Law

i. Chubu Yomiuri Newspaper Press Case[40]

Chubu Yomiuri Newspaper Press K.K. ('Chubu Yomiuri Newspaper Press'), a newly incorporated company, planned and advertised the publication of *The Chubu Yomiuri Newspaper* starting 25 March 1975 in the three prefectures of the Tokai region for a monthly charge of Japanese yen (JPY) 500. It was supported by Yomiuri Newspaper Press, the largest national newspaper publishing company and publisher of *The Yomiuri Newspaper*. In that geographic area, that is, the Tokai newspaper market, a local newspaper company, Chunichi Newspaper Press K.K., had the dominant position. At that time, monthly charges of the national newspapers were JPY 1,300 and the local newspapers' monthly charges ranged from JPY 1,000 to 1,200. Before Chubu Yomiuri Newspaper Press began to sell *The Chubu Yomiuri Newspaper*, the JFTC applied to the Tokyo High Court for an order providing that Chubu Yomiuri Newspaper Press should raise the monthly charge up to JPY 812, alleging that the average total cost for the monthly charge was expected to be no less than JPY 812. In reply, Chubu Yomiuri Newspaper Press insisted that the average total cost should be JPY 500 because the newspaper was mainly produced from the faxed materials of *The Yomiuri Newspaper*. The court held that the average total cost of the product was to computed as if the firm at issue was an independent firm and that the conduct of Chubu Yomiuri Newspaper Press violated the Unfair Trade Practice Regulation (Art. 6 of the general designation) because JPY 500 was found to be below average total cost. The court then ordered that Chubu Yomiuri Newspaper Press must raise the monthly charge up to JPY 812. In this case, the JFTC initiated the formal proceedings in 1975 and finally ordered, in a form of consent decree (i.e. consent order in which a defendant needs not to admit the allegation but must take corrective measures.), that Chubu Yomiuri Newspaper Press would set a monthly charge at JPY 1,000 in 1977.

ii. Tokyo Shibaura Public Slaughterhouse Case

The Supreme Court decision in the Tokyo Shibaura Public Slaughterhouse Case arose from a private action for damages alleging that the defendant, the Tokyo Slaughterhouse, violated Art. 6 of the general designation by charging extremely low slaughter fees, which were made possible by the Tokyo local government's compensation for losses through subsidies. The Tokyo District Court held that the Tokyo Slaughterhouse was liable for the violation and granted the damage award to the plaintiff, a private slaughter house which was the sole competitor in the Tokyo metropolitan area. The Supreme Court and the Tokyo High Court reversed the district court's ruling and denied the liability of the Tokyo Slaughterhouse. Both courts held that the two slaughter houses were in competition with 59 other houses in the greater Kanto and Tokai area. They found that, among the slaughter fees

40. *Chubu Yomiuri Newspaper Press. v. Japan Fair Trade Commission*, 26 GYOSAIREISHU 670 (Tokyo Hi. Ct. 30 April 1975).

charged by the 59 competing slaughter houses, the slaughter fees of 47 slaughter houses were below those of the plaintiff, the private slaughterhouse, and the slaughter fees of 11 slaughterhouses were even below those of the defendant, the Tokyo Public Slaughterhouse. The courts also emphasized that as a general rule, slaughterhouses in big cities were suffering from losses because farmers preferred to send their livestock to closer slaughterhouses and then send block meat to big cities due to the rapid advancement in the transportation methods of frozen block meats. The courts held further that whether or not low priced sales violated Art. 6 of the general designation should be determined by considering the intent of the firm concerned, actual competitive relationships with competitors, and conditions in the relevant market. The courts finally denied liability, although they found that the defendant's slaughter fees were significantly below cost.

iii. Maruetsu Case[41]

Complaints are often brought to the JFTC by local small shops where large scale retailers such as chain stores sell consumer products at an overwhelmingly low price, effectively excluding competition with the smaller shops.

In Maruetsu Case, two shops in the vicinity of and competing with the large chain stores Maruetsu and Hallomart, reduced their prices on an 11 carton box of milk as a loss leader in order to attract customers. One shop reduced the sales price to JPY 178, then to JPY 160, then to JPY 155 and eventually to JPY 100 for the first box and to JPY 150 for each additional box, although it purchased milk at a cost ranging from JPY 157 to JPY 160 a box. The other shop reduced the price to JPY 178, then to JPY 156 and finally to JPY 100 for the first purchase and to JPY 150 for each additional box to meet the competition, although it purchased milk at the cost ranging from JPY 155 to JPY 168 a box. The shops sold the milk at a price less than the purchase price from the beginning of July until the middle of November 1981, selling them significantly below cost for the last two months. The two shops increased their sales volume of milk and total sales during the period. Small shops in the area, however, were compelled to reduce their sales amount during the period, as they purchased the milk at JPY 185 and sold at JPY 190 to JPY 200. In this case, the JFTC decided that the low price sales of milk by stores who sold multiple products had put small shops specialized in the sale of milk in an unduly disadvantageous position and violated the Art. 6 of the general designation. Up until this point, it had not been established what rule of case law will apply to predatory pricing by nationwide manufacturers.

In 1984, the JFTC released the guideline on excessively low price sales, which is applicable to low priced sales by retailers.[42] According to the guideline, low price sales violate Art. 6 of the general designation when a retailer sells the

---

41. Maruetsu, 29 SINKETUSHU 13 (FTC, 28 May 1982).
42. The Japan Fair Trade Commission, *Guidelines Concerning Unfair Price Cutting Under the Antimonopoly Act*, (1984), *available at* <http://www.jftc.go.jp/e-page/legislation/ama/pricecutting.pdf> (last visited 31 March 2006).

products at a price lower than the purchase price for a considerable period of time and the low price sales do not have any business justification, such as sales of perished products and sales of non-seasonable products, and the low price sales have the probability of forcing competing retailers to discontinue their business. As stated *above*, under the guideline, a price is considered unfair when products or services are sold 'at a price which is excessively below the cost incurred in the said supply or otherwise unjustly at low prices'. The phrase 'cost incurred in the said supply' refers to the 'cost incurred' by the provider of said products or services 'in the said supply'. It should be noted here that the 'cost incurred in the said supply' are not the costs generally incurred by other companies in the same industry, nor are they the costs of a specific competitor. The phrase, 'at a price which is excessively below cost incurred in the said supply', is understood to refer to prices which fit the classic definition of unjustifiably low prices. Since this, in effect, means prices that are far below the gross cost of sales, in the retail sector this phrase is interpreted as referring to prices which are below purchase price. Thus, a comparison of selling price versus purchase price is always one of the standards by which the JFTC judges the fairness of prices. In this context, the term, 'purchase price' refers to the price paid for the products alleged to have been sold at unfair prices by the company which has carried out the sales in question. Furthermore, this term refers not to the officially listed price of said products, but to the actual purchase price. Any discounts, rebates, or physical goods received by the purchaser in connection with the purchase must be taken into account in calculating the real purchase price. Moreover, if purchase prices of price-cutting products are under prime cost for a certain period of time and manufacturers add the total reduced amount to the price of normal products later, the JFTC shall adjust the reduced price up to the actual price level and determine price fairness on the basis of normal purchase price.

Next, even if products are sold at the type of price described *above*, such pricing is not considered unfair if it occurs infrequently, lasts for only a very short period of time, and does not affect competitors in the manner described *below*. More specifically, price cutting is not unfair unless it is to some extent carried out continuously. The phrase 'continuously' means either that price cutting is carried out continuously over a relatively extended period of time, or that the company carrying out such price cutting has adopted a sales policy which provides an objective basis for expecting such price cutting to be carried out, even though it may not be carried out every day. Thus, a typical example of unfair price cutting involves the sale of a product for less than its purchase price on a more or less continuous basis, but in certain cases, depending on the nature of a product and the purpose and effect of a given price cut, prices which are slightly above purchase price (provided that they are below the gross cost of sales) or which occur only infrequently can still be deemed unfair.

As stated *above*, the second characteristic of unfair price cutting is the fact that it is tending to cause difficulties to the business activities of other entrepreneurs. The term 'other entrepreneurs' generally refers to retailers which sell the same product for which the price has allegedly been reduced unfairly, and other retailers which are competitors of the firm which has carried out the price cutting. However, because price cutting also affects the sale of competing products, the term 'other entrepreneurs' can sometimes also refer to the manufacturers of these competing products. The phrase 'tending to cause difficulties to the business activities of other entrepreneurs' means that a price cutting action need not necessarily create an actual disruption of business operations in order to be determined unfair. It is enough that the price reduction creates a recognized possibility of such disruption. The impact of price cutting upon competitors is determined on a case-by-case basis, taking various factors into consideration, including but not limited to, the size and circumstances of the firm which has carried out the price cutting; the quantity of products subject to the price cut, the duration of the price cut, advertising and publicity associated with the price cut, and the nature of the product. The third important factor which is examined in order to determine the fairness of a price cut is whether there is 'proper justification' for it. Concerning products that are damaged, part of an incomplete set, or otherwise impaired, it is only natural that such imperfections be reflected in the price. Such products should be clearly identified, however, to avoid creating the mistaken impression that a standard product is being sold at a low price.

5. Unilateral Refusal to Deal

a. Overview

To date, in Japan, there have been no cases in which the essential facility doctrine was at issue.[43]

Although the JFTC has the authority to issue a compulsory dealing order and compulsory licensing orders, both of them have never been used.

The Distribution Guideline states that the practice of unilaterally refusing to deal shall be illegal under the JAA, such as when a firm engages in conduct where a manufacturer influential in a relevant market, by causing its distributors not to deal with its competitors, prevents them from easily finding alternative trading partners, and, with a view to ensuring the effectiveness of such conduct, refuses to deal with distributors not yielding to this request. Also, according to the guideline introduced *above*, when an influential firm in a relevant market engages in the conduct described *below* as a means to achieve unjust purposes, such as excluding its competitors from a relevant market, and if such conduct may make it difficult for the refused firm to carry on normal business activities, such conduct shall be illegal under the JAA.

(i) A material manufacturer influential in a relevant market, in an attempt to prevent its customers (finished product manufacturers) from producing some of the materials which they have bought from the material

---

43. In the United States, when the courts found that an access to certain facilities is essential, they have imposed controllers of such facilities a duty to deal. See *United States v. Terminal R. Association*, 224 US 383 (1912).

manufacturer, stops the supply of main materials which have been supplied to finished product manufacturers; or

(ii) A material manufacturer influential in a relevant market, in an attempt to exclude competitors of its customers (finished product manufacturers) who have close relations with the material manufacturer from the said finished product market, stops the supply of the materials which have been supplied to these competitors.

b. Case Law (Toyo Seikan Case)[44]

Toyo Seikan K.K. ('Toyo Seikan') was the largest steel can manufacturer in Japan and sold cans to food processing firms which made canned food, such as meat and vegetables. Toyo Seikan had a 56 per cent share of the national can manufacturing market. If the market shares of affiliated companies were included, Toyo Seikan's market share would have reached 74 per cent. At the time, there were several food processing manufactures which began manufacturing several types of cans for their own use. Toyo Seikan decided to implement the policy of prohibiting the self manufacturing of cans and threatened the food processing manufactures who began to make cans for their own use by suspending the supply of the cans. Toyo Seikan threatened some food processing manufactures by suspending the cans, forcing them to cease producing the cans for their own use.

The JFTC decided that Toyo Seikan's conduct violated the Monopoly Regulation and ordered it not to prevent food processing manufacturers from producing cans for their own use.

6. Interference with a Competitor's Transaction

a. Overview

Interference with a competitor's transaction is regulated by Art. 15 of the general designation. Art. 15 of the general designation prohibits firms from unjustly interfering with transactions between another firm which is in a competitive relationship and another transacting party by preventing the formation of contract, by inducing breach of a contract, or by any other means. The coverage of Art. 15 is very broad because Art. 15 requires only interference with a transaction between a competitor and the other transacting party by any means. As such, Art. 15 of the general designation is construed to apply as a supplement to other articles of the general designation. Otherwise, it would be possible for almost all violations of the Unfair Trade Practice Regulation to be covered by Art. 15 of the general designation. Accordingly, Art. 15 of the general designation is typically applied to interference with a transaction of a competitor by using unethical means such as threats, intimidation or physical force which is not covered by any other articles of the general designation.

---

44. Toyo Seikan, 19 SINKETUSHU 87 (FTC, 18 September 1972).

b. Case Law

i. Kumamoto Uoichiba Case[45]

Kumamoto Uoichiba competed with Daikan Bussan in the fish market of Kumamoto prefecture. The market share of Kumamoto Uoichiba in the relevant market was 85 per cent and the market share of Daikan Bussan was 15 per cent. Kumamoto Uoichiba constructed a wall surrounding Daikan Bussan and tried to prevent dealers from participating as bidders in the auction sales at Daikan Bussan's market. Kumamoto Uoichiba demanded that the dealers who had contracts with Daikan Bussan not renew them. The JFTC decided that this conduct by Kumamoto Uoichiba violated Art. 15 of the general designation.

ii. Tokyo Jyuki Case[46]

In the past, sewing machines were sold under instalment contacts. Under these arrangements, the customer obtained the ownership of the sewing machine after making several instalment payments. One of major sewing machine manufactures, Tokyo Juki K.K. ('Tokyo Juki') began to offer reimbursement of paid instalments when customers cancelled a contract with its competitors in order to induce them into entering into the contact with Tokyo Juki. It is difficult to judge whether or not this sales method was a justifiable sales strategy or an unethical interference with its competitor's business. The JFTC decided that Tokyo Juki's conduct violated Art. 15 of the general designation and issued a recommendation, ordering Tokyo Juki to stop implementing its sales tactics, which Tokyo Juki accepted.

iii. Yashiro Case[47]

Yashiro K.K. had a subsidiary trading company, Yashiro Shoji K.K. (correctively referred to as 'Yashiro'). Yashiro K.K. was a wholesaler of Groom products (Groom is the brand name and its product line-up includes handbags), which were usually purchased through its subsidiary Yashiro Shoji K.K. and sold to prestigious Japanese department stores. In 1989, Groom handbags were sold for a retail price of JPY 28,600 in Paris. At the time, the same handbags were sold for JPY 49,440 in Japanese department stores. Fuji Sankei Living Service planned to sell Groom handbags for JPY 28,840 after negotiating with Groom. Yashiro requested that Groom suspend transactions with Fuji Sankei Living Service, and as a result Fuji Sankei Living Service was not able to purchase Groom handbags. In this case, the JFTC found that Yashiro unduly disrupted the transaction between its competitor and Groom and decided that the conduct engaged in by Yashiro violated Art. 15 of the general designation. In this case, neither Groom handbags nor Groom products were defined as a relevant market because so many other famous handbags and branded products were competing in the Japanese market. The relevant product market would be defined as the branded handbag market, in

45. Kumamoto Uoichiba, 10 SINKETUSHU 17 (FTC, 9 February 1960).
46. Tokyo Jyuki, 11 SINKETUSHU 41 (FTC, 9 June 1963).
47. Yashiro, 37 SINKETUSHU 29 (FTC, 5 September 1990).

which case Groom's market share was too small for the conduct in question to render anticompetitive effects on the relevant market. In addition, an exclusive import distribution contact by a firm with a small market share is regarded as valid by the JFTC. At the time, however, the huge price gap between the domestic and foreign pricing had become a contentious social issue. In this context, the JFTC tried to prevent Yashiro from interfering with the contract between Fuji Sankei Living Service and Groom on the assumption that Groom accepted the offer of Fuji Sankei Living Service through a process of negotiation.

In the context of dealing with concerns as to the difference between the domestic and foreign pricing, the JFTC often prohibits Japanese firms from taking actions which prevent parallel imports into Japan by applying Art. 15 of the general designation.

iv. Kanagawa Raw Concrete Cooperative Case[48]

There are many cases in which the conduct of a cooperative with a dominant position in a relevant market is found to be a violation of the Unfair Trade Practice Regulation. The Kanagawa Raw Concrete Cooperative Case is a typical case dealing with abuse of market power by a cooperative. The Kanagawa Prefecture Cooperative for small and medium sized raw concrete manufactures, as a joint sales organization, sold raw concrete for local construction companies to dealers in Kanagawa Prefecture. The market share of the cooperative exceeded 90 per cent. In defining the relevant market for raw concrete sales, a geographic market should be defined narrowly because the transportation costs make up a high percentage of the total cost. For the most part, local construction companies had to consume raw concrete supplied in the local concrete market due to these transportation costs. Under these circumstances, the cooperative required its dealers not to purchase raw concrete from those manufacturers who were not members of the cooperative. The JFTC found that the exclusive dealing request to the dealers violated Art. 11 of the general designation. Also, the JFTC decided that the request to the local construction companies and cement manufactures separately violated Art. 15 of the general designation because the cooperative did not deal with them directly. While it was not a mistake for the JFTC to apply the Unfair Trade Practice Regulation to the conduct of the cooperative, it would have been more appropriate to apply the Monopoly Regulation since the cooperative clearly tried to exclude its competitors from the relevant market through the use of several different methods.

7. Abuse of Dominant Position

The JAA Art. 2, para. 9 states that, in dealing with another party, unwarranted use of one's bargaining position is an unfair business practice and directs the JFTC to designate specific conduct under this heading.

---

48. Kanagawa Raw Concrete, 36 SINKETUSHU 44 (FTC, 15 February 1990).

The JFTC issued Art. 14 of the general designation, which provides that to engage in the activities enumerated in the designation by unreasonably utilizing superior bargaining position is unfair business practice. Art. 14 of the general designation specifies the following five activities as unreasonable business activities: (i) causing the other party in a continuous transaction to purchase a commodity or service other than the one involved in the transaction; (ii) causing the other party in a continuous transaction to provide the more influential party with money, service or other economic benefits; (iii) setting or changing the transaction terms in a way disadvantageous to the other party; (iv) in addition to any act coming under the aforementioned categories, imposing a disadvantage on the other party regarding the terms or the execution of a transaction; and (v) causing a company which is a counterparty to follow one's directions in advance, or to get one's approval regarding the appointment of officers of the said company.

Art. 14 of the general designation applies when an enterprise with bargaining power, that is, with the dominant position, unduly utilizes such position, thus resulting in unreasonable disadvantage to the other party to the transaction. With regard to 'dominant position', it is generally understood in Japan that the term 'dominant position' shall not mean dominant position in a relevant market but rather dominant position in a particular transaction. Even if a party is a relatively small firm, it can be in a dominant position if the other parties are comparatively smaller, thus making it possible for the dominant party to impose unreasonable transactional terms and conditions.

If there is a difference in bargaining power between the parties to a transaction, naturally the weaker party is compelled to accept terms and conditions disadvantageous to it. It would be excessive intervention of law into freedom of contract if interpreting that any disadvantage incurred by weaker parties is a result of abuse of a dominant position. Therefore, whether or not 'abuse' exists should be determined by the particular circumstances of cases at issue. However, in Japan, it is generally understood that in order to fulfil the condition of 'abuse', suppressive or intimidating conduct is required.

A well known decision in this regard is Mitsukoshi Case,[49] in which the respondent Mitsukoshi chose to settle the case in accordance with the consent decree proceeding (i.e. consent order in which a defendant needs not to admit the allegation but must take corrective measures.). In this case, Mitsukoshi was the largest retailer in Japan and enjoyed tremendous prestige. Suppliers of products clamoured for the opportunity to sell products to Mitsukoshi since it would give them credibility and prestige as a supplier. In this sense, Mitsukoshi was in the dominant position vis-à-vis its suppliers. Using its economic advantage, Mitsukoshi demanded that suppliers purchase certain luxury items, such as paintings and jewels, contribute money for festivals sponsored by Mitsukoshi to promote its business, and bear the cost of repairing and renovating Mitsukoshi retail stores without guaranteeing that the suppliers' products would be exhibited there.

---

49. Mitsukoshi, 29 SINKETUSHU 31 (FTC, 17 June 1982).

The JFTC claimed that if a powerful purchaser such as Mitsukoshi made a request, suppliers had no choice but to accept it. Therefore, the mere fact that Mitsukoshi made the request established that it abused its dominant position. Mitsukoshi made the counterargument that specific evidence of abuse was needed to challenge its conduct. As this case was settled by the consent decree, no formal judgment was rendered.

8. Non Typical Type Conducts

a. Paramount Bed Case[50]

The Tokyo local government was to purchase special care beds for public hospitals through competitive bids. The tenders were limited to local dealers to promote the protection of small or medium sized firms. In Japan, Paramount Beds, France Beds, and Mirkis Beds were the three major manufactures producing special care beds. At the time of this case, Paramount Beds actually supplied most of the beds for special care to the Tokyo local government. In competitive specifications of bids, the policy of the Tokyo local government was to adopt specifications under which multiple bed manufactures could also participate in the bidding. Paramount Beds tried to influence the action of the officials in charge of the tendering process in order to maintain its high market share. Paramount Bed first attempted to have the officers in charge of tendering designate a specification which would make it necessary to use the intellectual property rights owned by Paramount Bed without disclosing its ownership. Second, Paramount Bed attempted to have the officers designate a specification which would match with standard specifications of Paramount Bed but not match with those of its competitors. Furthermore, Paramount Beds prepared the explanatory notes and written materials for officers, which indicated that the functions of the Paramount beds were superior to those of its competitors and made the officers answer questions following prepared model responses at the on site explanatory meeting. As a result, Paramount Beds enjoyed advantageous treatment in the competitive specification bids and Paramount dealers won almost all bids. Paramount Beds also arranged the bid-rigging amount for its own nominated dealers by designating winning bidders.

The JFTC held that Paramount Beds illegally excluded its competitors and thus violated the Monopoly Regulation. Note that because Paramount's conduct (the interference with the actions of officers in order to obtain favourable treatment) did not fall under any articles of the general designation, the JFTC applied the Monopoly Regulation in this case.

50. Paramount Beds, 44 SINKETUSHU 362 (FTC, 31 March 1998).

b. Hakodate Newspaper Press Case[51]

Hokkaido Newspaper Press K.K. ('Hokkaido Newspaper Press') tried to prevent the new entry of competitors in the south eastern region of Hokkaido Prefecture. After obtaining information that a newly formed company was about to enter the market and publish a new newspaper, Hokkaido Newspaper Press undertook several measures to prevent the new entry. First, as a local newspaper publishing company usually names its newspaper after the local geographic area and Hokkaido Newspaper Press was expected to use local names such as Hakodate or Minami Hakodate, Hokkaido Newspaper Press applied to the Patent Office for trademark protection for these names for the purpose of preventing the newly formed company from using these names. After the newly incorporated company selected 'The Hakodate Newspaper' as its name, Hokkaido Newspaper Press demanded in writing that it stop using Hakodate Newspaper as its name. Second, the newly formed company wished to obtain news from Jiji, a large news distribution company. By then, Jiji already had a policy of dealing with only one newspaper publishing company in a specified area and did not deal with another company without the consent of the first company. Hokkaido Newspaper Press, knowing Jiji's policy well, repeatedly reconfirmed the policy and requested Jiji not to distribute news to the newly formed company. Third, Hokkaido Newspaper Press began to issue an additional area specific version of its paper as a supplement to the newspaper in the Hokkaido area and announced that it would charge half the price of the advertisement fees for this area-specific paper in order to block the newly formed company from gaining advertisement fees. As the advertisement fees are one of the major sources of income for newspaper publisher, given that the newly formed company should be excluded from the fees, it was difficult to enter the relevant market. Fourth, Hokkaido Newspaper Press, after being informed that Hokkaido Television, a broadcasting company in that area, agreed to broadcast a television commercial of the newspaper to be published by the newly formed company, requested Hokkaido Television not to broadcast the television commercial. As a result, Hokkaido Television refused to broadcast the television commercial.

The JFTC decided that the conduct of Hokkaido Newspaper Press as a whole violated the Monopoly Regulation. Among the individual types of conduct, the interference with the commercial transaction between the newly formed company and Hokkaido Television clearly violated Art. 15 of the general designation. As to the issue of the area-specific version of the newspaper, the JFTC needed further fact finding to determine whether or not Hokkaido Newspaper Press violated Art. 3 or Art. 6 of the general designation. The attempt to register certain types of names for the trademark would not be covered by any articles of the general designation. In addition, the reconfirmation of existing policy adopted by Jiji would not be in violation of any articles of the JAA. As such, the JFTC had no choice but to apply the Monopoly Regulation to the conduct of Hokkaido Newspaper Press.

---

51. Hokkaido Newspaper Press, 46 SINKETUSHU 144 (FTC, 28 February 2000).

C. Controlling Conduct

1. Overview

The JAA Art. 2, para. 5 and Art. 3 prohibit conduct which controls the business activities of other firms, causing a substantial restraint of competition in the relevant market as well as exclusionary conduct. The cases concerning controlling conduct are few in number in Japan. In addition, in spite of several older cases concerning controlling conduct, decisions of these cases have been considered to be misleading. It is still unclear what policy the JFTC would take in regulating controlling conduct. That said, the book introduces one of the rare examples in this area, i.e. Noda Shoyu Case.

2. Case Law (Noda Shoyu Case)[52]

In the 1950s, despite the large number of small manufacturers of soy sauce, the majority of these producers merely produced and distributed their products in local areas. On a national level, however, there were only four producers; Noda, Yamasa, Higeta and Marukin. Among these four companies, Noda, whose trademark was 'Kikkoman' and enjoyed nation wide fame, was the leading producer with a market share of 37 per cent in the Tokyo metropolitan area. In the soy sauce industry at that time, products were clearly differentiated by grade, the highest of which was 'supreme' (*saijo*), the second grade being 'superior' (*jisaijo*), and the third grade being 'best' (*gokujo*). Different prices for each grade of products reflected such product differentiation; 'supreme' (*saijo*) products were highest in price; 'superior' (*jisaijo*) products had mid-range prices; and 'best' (*gokujo*) products were lowest in price. To consumers, price signified the grade of soy sauce and thus quality. If the price of the products were adjusted downward to the level of a lower grade, the products were regarded to have fallen from a higher grade to a lower grade. Noda's products had been considered to be 'supreme' (*saijo*) grade, as were those of Yamasa, Higeta and Marukin. Among them, however, Noda's reputation and market position was outstanding. As a result, companies other than Noda, the industry leader, found themselves in a position where they could not lower their price below Noda's price level, since doing so would lead to degradation of their products and the loss of much of their market share. Therefore, only Noda could decide the market price, with the other three producers having no choice but to follow. It could be regarded as a typical case of oligopoly and administered price in an oligopolistic market. At the time of this case, soy sauce was distributed through a two-layer distribution system, that is, wholesalers and retailers. In 1950, Noda instructed its wholesalers and retailers to raise their wholesale and retail prices respectively, thus engaging in resale price maintenance for its products. Within a few days after the price increase of

52. 8 GYOSAIREISHU 2300 (Tokyo Hi. Ct. 25 December 1957).

Noda's products, the other three producers followed it, raising their wholesale and retail price.

The JFTC intervened and found that Noda had engaged in private monopolization by controlling the price policy of its competitors and realized it through enforcing its resale price maintenance policy. It should be noted, however, that the JFTC did not challenge the price maintenance policy communicated by Noda to its wholesalers and retailers. The JFTC's challenge focused on the influence exerted by Noda on the pricing policy of its three competitors through the resale price maintenance of its products.

After the decision of the JFTC, Noda appealed to the Tokyo High Court and then to the Supreme Court, seeking the revocation of the judgment. Both courts decided that the term 'control' under Art. 2, para. 5 of the JAA was not limited to direct control and could also cover indirect control, that is, the situation where a dominant company in a relevant market engaged in the activities which, under certain condition, necessitated competitors to adopt similar conduct.

In this case, Noda applied much pressure on wholesalers and retailers to raise the price of its products. The court reasoned that, given the oligopolistic market structure and product-grading system used for soy sauce, the three competitors had no choice but to engage in resale price maintenance and keep pace with the price level set by Noda. As such, both courts upheld the JFTC's decision.

D. Unfair Inducement and Intimidation

The JAA Art. 2, para. 9, item 3 prohibits firms from unjustly inducing or coercing customers of a competitor to deal with themselves. This prohibition corresponds to the latter part of the Federal Trade Commission Act, section 5. The prohibition on unfair inducement is the regulation against misrepresentation, detail of which is provided by Art. 8 and 9 of the general designation. Art. 8 of the general designation stipulates that it is unlawful unjustly to induce customers of a competitor to deal with oneself by causing them to misunderstand that the substance of a commodity or service supplied by oneself, or terms of the transaction, or other matters relating to such transaction are much better or much favourable than the actual one or than those relating to the competitor. On the other hand, Art. 9 of the general designation forbids such an action as inducing customers of a competitor to deal with oneself by offering unjust benefits in the light of normal business practices. In addition, to supplement these regulations, the act against unjustifiable premiums and misleading representation (Law No. 134 of 1964) provides regulations against misrepresentation and unjustly inducement. The substance of the regulation is provided by Art. 4 of the act, which enumerates three types of forbidden conducts, i.e. (i) any representation by which the quality, standard or any other matter relating to the substance of a commodity or service are shown to consumers in general to be much better than the actual one or much better than that of other entrepreneurs who are in competitive relationship with the entrepreneur concerned contrary to the fact and thereby which is found likely to induce customers unjustly and to impede fair competition; (ii) any representation by which price or any other terms of transaction of a commodity or service will be misunderstood by consumers in general to be much more favourable to the consumer in general than the actual one or than those of other entrepreneurs who are in competitive relationship with the entrepreneur concerned, and thereby which is found likely to induce customers unjustly and to impede fair competition; and (iii) in addition to aforementioned two types of conducts, any representation by which any matter relating to transactions as to a commodity or service is likely to be misunderstood by consumers in general and which is designated by the JFTC as such, finding it likely to induce customers unjustly and to impede fair competition.

IV. MERGER REGULATION

A. Introduction

Concerning the merger regulation, the JAA Art. 10, para. 1, Art. 15, para. 1, Art. 15 – 2, para. 1, and Art. 16, para. 1 forbids an acquisition or holding of stock, mergers and acquisitions, transfer of business and the like that may be substantially to restrain competition in any particular field of trade (hereinafter referred to as the 'Merger Regulation').

Under the JAA, it is always necessary to examine whether or not the proposed business combination will lead to be resulting in substantially restraint of competition in any particular field of trade. Indeed, the languages of the aforementioned articles is considered to be the very ground that enables the JFTC to investigate, examine, and initiate a formal hearing, even when a submission of merger report required in the JAA, such as Art. 10, para. 2, has not been made. In addition, in Japan, inasmuch as the proposed transaction will affect a relevant market within Japan, even when one of the transaction parties locates outside of the Japanese jurisdiction, the JAA applies, whereby the JFTC can exercise its authority to block a business combination.

This book first provides the substantive case law established in Japan concerning the interpretation of 'substantially to restrain competition in any particular field of trade'. Also, this book provides an overview of the Merger Guideline.

B. Case Law

1. Toho Subaru Case

In this case, Toho reached a tentative joint administration agreement concerning the rental of two theatres with Subaru. The JFTC expressed its view that the relevant geographic market should be defined as theatres in the Yurakucho area or theatres in the Ginza area. In Yurakucho market, the total seating capacity of the eight theatres including the two theatres of Subaru comprised 90.4 per cent. In Ginza market, the seating capacity of Toho comprised 57.9 per cent of the total seating. Either market, the joint administration was expected to cause a substantial restraint of competition. In this case, the Tokyo High Court upheld the JFTC's decision on the following reason.

In terms of market definition, the Ginza area should be defined as the geographic market, based on the characteristics of theatregoers in the area. On this assumption, Toho's market share was calculated to be 50.2 per cent, whereas Subaru's market share was computed to be 7.7 per cent. As a result of the joint administration, Toho would increase its market share by 7.7 per cent. The court also stated that the condition of 'substantially to restrain competition in any particular field of trade' was the situation in which a firm could control or was likely to control the market by affecting the price, quality and quantity of goods and so on in the market, at its will, as a result of reduced competition. The Tokyo High Court held the fact that the added market share increased by only a small proportion was irrelevant in judging whether or not the agreement violated the Merger Regulation.

In conclusion, the court held that the competition in the market would be substantially restrained by the arrangement attempted by Toho.

2. Nippon Steel Corporation Case[53]

After Toho Subaru Case, the standard of 'substantially to restrain competition in any particular field of trade' was loosened, which was exemplified in Nippon Steel Corporation Case.

There were six steelmakers who engaged in large-scale iron and steel manufacturing in Japan at the time of this case. Yahataseitetsu Co. ('Yahataseitetsu') was the top manufacture with the market share of 22.1 per cent in the Japanese large-scale iron and steel manufacturing market and Fujiseitetsu Co. ('Fujiseitetsu') was the second largest manufacture with a market share of 22.4 per cent. Yahataseitetsu and Fujiseitetsu proposed to merge in 1968, and completed the deal to become Nippon Steel Corporation in 1971.

In this case, the JFTC initiated the investigations upon consultation by both parties and expressed its view in the form of an unofficial announcement that the proposed merger could be a violation of the JAA Art. 15, para. 1, pointing out the several antitrust concerns on 19 February 1969. Although both parties submitted the report in relation to their merger to the JFTC on 19 March 1969, the JFTC initiated the investigation and issued a recommendation which required both parties not to complete their merger on 7 May 1969. Although the JFTC commenced the hearing on 19 May 1969, after both parties' proposals, the consent order was issued on 30 October 1969.

---

53. Yahataseitetsu, 16 SINKETUSHU 50 (FTC, 30 October 1969).

In the consent order, the JFTC mentioned its concern regarding the condition of 'substantially to restrain competition in any particular field of trade'.

The JFTC opined that a merger would be prohibited where the market structure would be transformed into a less competitive environment than the previous structure as a result of the merger, and, that, a particular firm is likely to have a dominant position in the market, by either gaining monopoly power or the ability to determine the price, quantity, volume, and other trade terms, thereby leading to market domination. Also, the JFTC said that whether or not a firm had formed a dominant position in a market should be determined by taking into consideration such factors including the situation of the market the parties of the merger belonged to, the market share of the both parties, several factors in relation to suppliers and customers, and economical factors such as whether or not there were imports and substitutes and, whether or not it was difficult to enter the market. In addition, the JFTC ruled that even when the total market share of the parties would become high, provided that there exists competitors to the parties that could influence the price or be able to exercise the power to change the price, the conditions of 'substantially to restrain competition in any particular field of trade' was not likely to be fulfilled. In other words, the JFTC admitted the possibility to trump the presumption of illegality drawn from the market share of merged entity by the mere existence of competitors, which could hinder the merged entity's ability to exercise market power. It should be noted, however, as explained later in this book, that the JFTC made it clear that it would not adopt this concept any more in the Merger Guideline. With regard to the proposed merger, the JFTC found that the merger would be likely to cause a substantial restraint of competition in each of four submarkets, that is, (i) manufacturing rail for railways, (ii) manufacturing tin plates for can, (iii) manufacturing cast plates and (iv) manufacturing special plates. Then the JFTC took the position that the merger would not violate the Merger Regulations so long as there was at least one competitor who could hinder the merged entity's exercise of market power in each of the *above-mentioned* four submarkets as a result of the implementation of the ordered measures by the JFTC. The JFTC ordered Yahataseitetsu and Fujiseitetsu to take certain measures to create a significant competitor in the four submarkets. In the decision, the JFTC did not assess the effects on the large-scale iron market of the merger and did not order any measures affecting the large-scale iron market. In this respect, the economic analysis of this case was not sufficient.

As explained *above*, the JFTC construed that, in the Merger Regulation, 'substantially to restrain competition in any particular field of trade' shall mean the same as in the Monopoly Regulation. Due to this interpretation, the Merger Regulation has been considered as not aiming at the prevention of forming oligopolized markets which could make it easier to coordinate prices of commodities or services consciously but rather the prevention of acquiring market power.

After this case, except for one case settled in the consent order,[54] both the JFTC and the courts have not made any formal decisions concerning business

54. Hiroshimabus, 20 SINKETUSHU 282 (FTC, 7 July 1973).

combination cases. This is partly because most of the business combination cases have been dealt with in informal consultations, which have been conducted even before the filing of business combination reports to the JFTC. This way of dealing with merger cases had come to be severely criticized as being against the basic principal of the JAA. Under the Act, the substantial examination on business combination cases is supposed to be made only after official acceptance of business combination reports to the JFTC. The JFTC's practice was therefore actually contrary to the basic principles of the JAA.

3. Oji Seishi Case

From 1994, the JFTC started to release gist of factual backgrounds and antitrust concerns of merger cases in its annual report.

One of the released cases in which the JFTC reviewed the fulfilment of 'substantially to restrain competition in any particular field of trade' very closely was the merger case between Ouji Seishi Co. ('Ouji') and Kamisaki Seishi Co. ('Kamisaki'). This case was released in the JFTC's annual report of 1993 (made public in 1994).

In this case, if Ouji and Kamisaki would merge into one entity, it was expected that its market share in the Japanese filature industry would be 19.9 per cent and would be 60 per cent in two of the submarkets concerning individual filature items.

The JFTC focused on the expected market share of the merged firm in the Japanese filature industry and considered that there would not be so many differences between the merged firm and the firm in the second position in terms of market share and that there were several competitors which could hinder the merged firm from exercising market power.

Based on these findings, the JFTC determined that it would be unlikely for the merged firm to substantially restrain competition in the Japanese filature industry.

The JFTC decided, however, that it would be highly probable for the merged firm to have substantial market power given the expected market share of 60 per cent in the submarket and that the competition there would be substantially restrained. Given the concerns about the submarkets, both Ouji and Kamisaki voluntarily proposed to the JFTC that the merged firm would transfer the part of its businesses and their possession of distribution companies' stock, to a third party, so that it might not acquire excessive market power in the submarkets.

The JFTC decided that, given the proposal, the merger would not cause a substantial restraint on competition in the Japanese filature industry as well as its submarkets.

As explained *above*, the JFTC confirmed in this case that the probability that merged entities would have come to dominate a market is still indispensable. The JFTC did not mention at all, however, about the policy that would trump the presumption that the merger would cause a substantial restraint of competition by the mere existence of a competitor.

After this case, it has been said that the JFTC maintained the policy that requires the existence of the probability that merged entities would come to dominate a market as being necessary factors but that it changed the part of its policy in that it no longer allows the mere existence of competitors to trump the presumption of illegality.

C. Merger Guideline

1. Overview of the Guideline

First of all, the Merger Guideline defines the scope of transactions that are screened by the JFTC, and covers an acquisition or holding of stock, holding several directors' office concurrently, mergers and acquisitions, splitting corporations, and transferring businesses.

Second, the guideline explains how to delineate both a geographic and a product market under the JAA.

Third, the guideline details the threshold of the substantive test for the Merger Regulations.

Fourth, the guideline provides several factors to be considered in deciding whether or not the substantive test shall apply. In this regard, the guideline classifies the types of transactions into four categories, that is – horizontal mergers which would cause anti-competitive effects by themselves ('Horizontal Mergers with a Unilateral Act'), horizontal mergers which would cause anti-competitive effects through collusion or conscious parallelism ('Horizontal Mergers with a Bilateral Act'), vertical and conglomerate mergers which would cause anti-competitive effects by themselves ('Vertical Mergers with a Unilateral Act'), and vertical and conglomerate mergers which would cause anti-competitive effects through collusion or conscious parallelism ('Vertical Mergers with a Bilateral Act'). For each type of transaction mentioned *above*, the guideline introduces several factors for examination.

Also, the Merger Guideline creates a safety zone, in which the substantive test shall not apply in all four categories mentioned *above*. The first situation is where a market is not oligopolized and market share of a merged entity is less than 25 per cent. In measuring the concentration of a market, a Herfindahl-Hirschman Index ('HHI') of concentration test is used. The HHI is calculated by summing the squares of the individual market shares of all the participants. The guideline defines markets under 1,800 HHI as not highly oligopolized markets and ones under 1,000 HHI as not oligopolized. The second situation is where the market share of the merged entity is less than 10 per cent. If either of aforementioned situations should be met, the substantive test will not apply. Note that the substantive test here is to examine whether or not the condition of 'substantially to restrain competition in any particular field of trade' has been fulfilled and thus the proposed business combinations should be banned. As explained later in this book, the Merger Guideline provides several factors for the purpose of examining the substantive test.

Fifth, the guideline explains measures to lessen anti-competitive effects which may be caused by the proposed merger.

2. The Definition of Particular Field of Trade

a. The Basic Concept Concerning Particular Field of Trade

With regard to 'particular field of trade', it has been pointed out that particular field of trade should be construed as the place where transactions between suppliers and purchasers are conducted, i.e. economically speaking, 'market place'.

According to the Merger Guideline, the scope of a particular field of trade is defined in terms of traded goods and services, trading areas, stages of trade, trading partners and other factors. Therefore, the goods traded are first enumerated for all of the businesses engaged in by the company group, and the product range is defined among the goods traded, then geographic range is defined for each of the product ranges. The range of the trading partners of the company group and the range of competitors which compete for the said trading partners would be the criteria for definition of the goods range and the geographic range and other factors.

b. Product Range

According to the Merger Guideline, the rule of thumb is that products or services which have the same function and efficacy from consumers' view point will form the same range of a particular field of trade. To determine whether or not the functions and efficacy of goods traded are similar to those of other goods, it is necessary to consider, under the guideline, whether or not the other goods can be a factor that prevents price increase, or the quantity of increased priced goods will decrease, because the users can purchase the other goods as a substitute. Under the guideline, the users shall mean those to whom business activities of a company group are directed. If a company group manufactures producers' goods, the users shall mean companies that process the goods into the next level of products. If a company group manufactures consumers' goods, the users shall mean general consumers. If a company group is a distributor, the users shall mean companics in the succeeding distribution level.

For the purposc of determining the product range of a particular field of trade, this is judged from the standpoint as to whether or not the functions and efficacy of a product are similar to those of the other goods from the view point of the users (e.g. consumers). For the purpose of the *above* mentioned examination, the guideline enumerates several factors. The first factor is whether or not a product is or is possible to be employed for the same use as the product traded. To determine whether or not both products are employed for the same use, the following factors are considered: external features such as size and form, specific material characteristics such as strength, plasticity, heat-resistance and insulation, qualities such as purity, and technical features such as standards and systems. The second factor is changes of the price and quantity of the traded product at issue. The third factor is the reaction of the consumers. In this connection, for instance, even though the specific material characters of the product X and Y are different, there could be a case in which users can use either of them as raw materials to produce the product Z of the same quality. In such a case, it is considered that the product X and Y have the similar functions and efficacy. It is also considered that whether or not a user substituted product Y for X when the price of product X was increased in the past.

c. *Geographic Range*

According to the Merger Guideline, the threshold to determine whether or not particular geographic areas are in the same particular field of trade is to consider whether or not consumers in one geographic area will switch to products or services provided by suppliers in another area if prices rises. In examining consumers' responses, the guideline says that factors that should be taken into consideration include the business activities of the relevant parties and their counter parties, characteristics of products and services, transportation methods and costs, the maximum quantity of products that can be produced, and whether or not the geographic areas are sufficiently proximate such that consumers will move between areas when deciding which products or services to purchase.

3. The Several Factors with regard to the Application of the Substantive Test

a. *Horizontal Mergers with a Unilateral Act Case*

i. The Status of the Relevant Parties and Competitors

The Merger Guideline says that the market share of the relevant parties is the principal factor to consider when determining their market power and status in a market. The guideline analyzes that, if the relevant parties possess a high percentage of market share, the market share of the participants in a market will change drastically through a proposed business combination, or that there will be a large discrepancy in the market share between a combined firm and its competitors, competition in the market will be affected significantly. Further, it needs to note that if the market share position of relevant parties is high, or the market share of the combined firm will become high through the combination, competition in the market is likely to be affected significantly. It should be noted also that, in calculating market share, if relevant parties have transferred a part of their business to another firm established jointly with competitors, the jointly established firm's market share should be added to the combined firm's market share.

In addition, according to the guideline, if it is found that, before the combination, vigorous competition among the relevant parties of the combination, or the parties' actions enhanced market competition, leading to the reduction of market prices or the improvement of the quality or variety of goods, even though the combined market share of the parties or its rank is not high, the relevant business combinations will cause a large impact on the competitive environment.

Moreover, the guideline indicates that if competitors do not have sufficient productive capacities, even when relevant parties raise the price, then it is difficult for competitors to expand their sales without raising their price and anti-competitive effects are likely caused. Also, if there are no substitutes for the products or services supplied by the relevant parties, it would be easier for them to exercise market power even if there are only small differences in terms of market share among market participants.

To decide whether or not the effect of a business combination may be substantially to restrain competition, the factors including those mentioned *above* are taken into consideration in each specific case. However, in relation to market share, the guideline creates a safety zone, in which the substantive test is not likely to apply. In other words, the guideline establishes an exception to the substantive test on the assumption that under certain conditions, the possibility that the effect of horizontal business combinations may be substantially to restrain competition in a particular field of trade through unilateral conduct is usually thought to be small.

The first situation is where the market structure is not highly oligopolistic, the market share of the relevant parties after the combination is not more than 25 per cent, and there are one or more competitors whose market share is more than 10 per cent. It should be noted that the situation where the market structure is not highly oligopolistic means that the HHI after business combination is less than 1800. When it is difficult to identify the market share of all companies and to calculate the HHI accurately, estimated figures are used to decide whether the HHI is less than 1800 or not. The second situation is where the market structure is not highly oligopolistic, the market share of the company group after the combination is not more than 35 per cent, and there are two or more competitors whose market shares are more than 10 per cent. The third situation is where the increment of market share is insignificant and there are one or more competitors whose market shares are more than 10 per cent. Note that the situation where the increment of market share is insignificant means that the increase of the HHI figure by business combinations is less than 100.

ii. Imported Goods and Services

The Merger Guideline points out that it is necessary to examine whether or not there are imported goods and services equivalent to the ones supplied by the relevant parties because, given that the combined firms will have to compete with imported products and services, competition in a relevant market will not likely be affected through the proposed business combinations.

Under the guideline, in deciding whether or not the pressure from imported goods and services is sufficient, various factors should be taken into consideration such as (i) import trends, (ii) the relationship of the amount of imported goods and services to the price difference between domestic goods and imported goods and services, (iii) competitiveness of the imported goods and services with respect to price, quality etc, (iv) existence of the problems in distribution, storage facilities of import or so-called users' familiarity with domestic goods, (v) major users' experience in using the imported goods and services, (vi) likelihood of imported goods and services by leading foreign competitors, (vii) the number of such competitors and their excess capacity etc, (viii) demand and supply balance in the exporting countries, (ix) factors influencing the pricing of the imported, exported or domestic goods and services and the price difference between them, and (x) import tax system such as customs or other legislative regulations. To consider whether or not an import can be a factor which prevents the combined firm from controlling the price freely to certain extent, excess capacity of the imported goods is considered if domestic goods and the imported goods are homogenous. If these are differentiated, the degree of the substitutability between goods sold by the company group and the imported goods will be taken into consideration. Even though the current market share of the imported goods is small, if the users can increase the use of the imported goods easily when the price of domestic goods rises, the competitive pressure from the import is not negligible.

A notable case in Japan in which whether or not the expansion of imported goods was feasible at issue in a business combination case is Mitsui Sekiyu Co. and Mitsuitoatsu Kagaku Co. case. In this case, the combined firm's market share was expected to be 60 per cent in the relevant market. Despite this, the JFTC admitted that the relevant parties should merge into a single firm primarily because of the availability of imported goods. Despite the expected market share, the JFTC determined that the combined firm was not likely to exercise its market power. The JFTC stressed that because its competitors had been importing the same kinds of products, even if the combined firm decreased its production level, its competitors would be able to substitute them easily. Also, the JFTC found that competitor's importing of goods had affected prices of those kinds of products. Although the proportion of imported goods in the relevant market just before the merger was only 1.7 per cent, the JFTC noted that the proportion of imported goods had been greater when the production level of Japanese manufactures had been small. Based upon this finding, the JFTC concluded that it would not be too difficult for competitors to expand their importation levels if prices were raised. The JFTC also determined that imported goods were not inferior to domestic goods in terms of price and quality. Based upon these examinations, the JFTC concluded that the proposed merger would not cause a substantial restraint of competition.

iii. The Entry Barrier

The Merger Guideline points out that it is easier for a combined firm to dominate a market if market entry barriers are sufficiently high such that the merged entity can profitably maintain price increase above the pre-merger level. Thus, it is necessary to examine whether or not entry into a market is easy. In doing so, factors that should be taken into consideration include the minimum cost of establishing a business, the regulations to enter into the market, necessary conditions concerning geography, technology, procurement of raw materials and the possibilities that there would be potential entries from foreign nations.

iv. The Competitive Pressures from Neighbouring Markets

According to the Merger Guideline, given that there are other markets geographically adjacent to the one in question, or markets in which functionally substitutable products or services are traded, competition in those markets should be considered when applying the substantive test. The competition in those markets would make it difficult for the merged entity to exercise market power.

v. The Overall Business Competency

In addition to the *above*, the Merger Guideline notes that proper attention should be paid to changes of the overall competencies of competitors and relevant parties, including but not limited to, available technology, the ability to raise finance, and enhancement of brand image. If certain technology is available only to a combined firm, or the business combination would enhance the confidence of financial institutions in the entity, or improve the brand image of the entity to consumers, then it would be easier for the combined firm to exercise market power.

vi. The Efficiencies Achieved Through Mergers

Further, the Merger Guideline points out that any efficiencies, such as lowered prices, improved quality of good and services, and the introduction of new products generated through the proposed merger, should be considered as well. However, as far as publicized cases are concerned, there have been no cases in which the JFTC admitted proposed mergers because of such efficiencies if it was expected that the merged entity would have a large market share and the concentration of the market would be high.

Under the guideline, the efficiencies resulting from shifting production facilities formally owned separately would be viewed more favourably because they are more likely to be susceptible to verification, business combination specific (i.e. not being able to achieve other than proposed business combination), and yielding substantial pro-competitive effects, and are less likely to result in an anti-competitive reduction in output. It should be noted that the rigid relationship between efficiencies attained through business combinations and the efficiencies being passed on to consumers has not been required, while from the combined firm's view point, it would be advisable to prove the direct relationship between efficiencies and consumer's benefit. In order for cost saving to be passed on to consumers, strong competition in a market is not necessary. Based upon an economic analysis, when the combined firm faces a downward sloping curve, as virtually all real world firms do, some of the cost saving will inevitably be passed on to consumers, with the exact amount depending upon the shape of the demand curve. In connection with measuring pro-competitive effects of mergers on consumers, it is advocated to focus on the reduction of the marginal cost. With differentiated products and non-cooperative price setting, a reduction of short-run marginal cost of any product, all things being equal, causes a seller of that product to prefer selling the product at a lower price. With homogeneous products and non-cooperative quantity setting, a reduction in the short-run marginal cost of any seller, all other conditions being equal, causes sellers to increase the quality of their product.

vii. The Financial Condition

The Merger Guideline says that a business combination is not likely to create or enhance market power or to facilitate its exercise if one of the merging firms faces imminent failure causing it to exit the relevant market without the combination. Based upon this recognition, the guidelines created a safety zone, in which the substantive test shall not apply. The first situation is where the market share of a combined firm is not more than 50 per cent, and one of the relevant parties would be unable to meet its financial obligation in the near future absent the combination, and would therefore exit the relevant market. The second situation is where the market share of a merged entity is not more than 50 per cent, part of the business of a relevant party is failing and, absent the combination, the failing business would exit the relevant market.

b. Horizontal Mergers with a Bilateral Act Case

A combination may diminish competition to the extent which a combined firm may engage in coordinated interaction that, with no doubt, harms consumers. Coordinated interaction is created by actions of a group of firms that are profitable only because of the accommodating reactions of the other firms in the group. Since a combination would create the situation where coordination among competitors is more likely, this is also relevant when determining an application of the substantive test.

i. The Status of the Relevant Parties and Competitors

The Merger Guideline says that if the number of participants in a relevant market is small, competition would be affected substantially through a proposed transaction. The guideline especially notes the situation where the number of competitors decreases to the extent that it could lead to an oligopolized market structure where conscious parallelism among participants of the market is rather easy. In addition, the guideline says that if vigorous competition among relevant parties prior to the combination made the quality of products higher and prices lower before the proposed merger, then even when the market share of the relevant parties is not so high, competition will be affected significantly. Further it indicates that if the combined firm does not have sufficient productive capacities, because it is difficult to expand its market share by lowering its price, it may have an incentive to cooperate with competitors.

ii. The Competitive Situation

The Merger Guideline says that the extent of information available to firms in a market is relevant to both the ability to reach terms of coordination and to detect or punish deviations from those terms. The guideline also notes that if there are huge changes of demand, or frequent innovations of products, because it is possible to increase profit by lowering price unilaterally, the combined firm is not likely to collude with competitors.

In addition to the *above*, in determining whether or not the substantive test is satisfied, it is necessary to consider the past market share of relevant parties and changes in prices. The guideline indicates that if there are huge changes in market share or prices in the past, then it is difficult to predict competitors' behaviour, and thus the danger of collusion with competitors is decreased.

iii. The Imported Goods, Entry, and Competitive Pressures from Neighbouring Markets

The Merger Guideline indicates that if there are imported goods or much competitive pressures from neighbouring markets, or entry into a market is not difficult, it is less likely that the combined firm will collude with competitors.

iv. The Efficiencies Achieved through the Merger and the Business Situation

The Merger Guideline says that the same attention explained earlier (i.e. (a) (IV)) should be made in examining the possibilities that the combined firm would likely collude with its competitors.

c. Vertical and Conglomerate Mergers Case

The Merger Guideline does not consider, in general, that Vertical and Conglomerate Mergers will cause substantial restraint of competition because they do not decrease the number of market participants. The guideline, however, recognizes that there could be situations where competition in relevant markets will be affected significantly. Consequently it provides several factors in applying the substantive test.

With regard to the Vertical Mergers with a Unilateral Act case, the guideline provides several factors, such as the status of the relevant parties and competitors, imported goods, barriers of entry, overall competencies, efficiencies achieved through the mergers, and the business situation, about which the guidelines indicate that the same consideration should be taken as in the Horizontal Mergers with a Unilateral Act case. In relation to market share, the guideline creates a safety zone, in which the substantive test will not likely apply. The first situation is where a market is not highly oligopolized and market share of a combined firm is less than 25 per cent. The second situation is where a market is not highly oligopolized, market share of the combined firm is less than 35 per cent and there are two competitors whose market share is more than 10 per cent.

With regard to Vertical Mergers with a Bilateral Act case, the guideline also provides several factors such as the status of the relevant parties and competitors, the competitive situation, imported goods, barriers of entry, competitive pressure from neighbouring markets, the efficiencies achieved through the mergers, and the business situation, about which the guidelines indicates that the same consideration should be taken as for Horizontal Mergers with a Bilateral Act case.

d. The Measures to Lessen Anticompetitive Effects

Even when the JFTC decides that the proposed combination meets the substantive test and thus should be enjoined, it is still possible to reverse the decision by introducing several measures to eliminate the anti-competitive effects of the transaction. The guideline states that it could be useful for relevant parties to transfer part of its business to a third party so that competition in the market is increased. The guideline also suggests that competition could also be effectively maintained if the relevant parties facilitate the new entry or import of goods so that the combined firm would not acquire excessive market power. In fact, the JFTC has, on a case-by-case basis, granted conditional clearance to a proposed transaction if, for example, one or both of the parties undertake to make certain divestments or take other measures to promote competition in the relevant market. A recent example of the JFTC's policy as to remedies is its March 2002 decision in the Japan Airlines Co. and Japan Air Systems Co. consolidation. The JFTC considered that such consolidation could potentially create a substantial restraint of competition in the market for domestic air transport for passengers. As a condition to clearance and in order to alleviate competition concerns, the JFTC asked the parties to divest nine take-offs and landing slots at Tokyo's Haneda airport and take measures such as agreeing to reduce certain air fares.

V. GENERAL CONCENTRATION REGULATION

A. Overview of the General Concentration Regulation

The JAA still has a general concentration regulation that should be distinguished from the Merger Regulation. The general concentration regulation targets notorious pre-war oligopolies known as *Zaibatsu*.[55] In *Zaibatsu*, the member firms, among which the core firms are still commercial banks and trading companies, maintain close relationships through mutual transactions and mutual shareholdings. After the dissolution of *Zaibatsu* in 1947, Japanese corporate group was prohibited from having a family-held holding company or parent company which could control its member firms as its headquarters.

It should be noted that *Keiretsu* is completely different from *Zaibatsu* and particular competitive situation. The term *Keiretsu* is generally defined as a group of firms related through cross-shareholding, employee exchanges, top executive meetings, and intra-group sales and transaction. Conglomerate *Keiretsu*, referred to as 'horizontal' involves a grouping of firms that cut across a number of basic industries and include a major financial institution and trading company. Vertical *Keiretsu* consists of key manufacturing firms allied with a group of suppliers and distributors with whom it has a continuing

55. "*Zaibatsu*" refers to a certain group of renowned conglomerates, such as Mitsubishi, Mitsui and Sumitomo, that effectively controlled much of the Japanese economy before World War II.

business relationship. Vertical *Keiretsu* often is associated with conglomerate *Keiretsu*. Although in the past the JFTC opined that the JAA issues were not raised by *Keiretsu*, the Japanese government acknowledged that cross-shareholding and other aspects of Keiretsu created the impression that it did have anti-competitive effects. As such, the JFTC came to recommend that business firms, especially those in *Keiretsu* groupings, should develop and make public open procurement policies.

The late 1990s in Japan have been characterized by the so-called 'Big Bang', a general move towards both deregulation and internationalization of the economy in response to the constant global expansion of markets. In terms of the JAA and competition policy in Japan, these tendencies have induced numerous reforms, including a dramatic relaxation of the ban on holding companies. Upon an amendment to the JAA in 1998, the prohibition on incorporation of, or conversion into, a holding company was abolished to the extent that such holding company's purpose is not contrary to the stated objectives and purposes of the JAA.

B. Current Standard of the General Concentration Regulation

The JAA Art. 9 prohibits establishment of and conversion into a company which may cause excessive concentration of economic power. This concept is not intended to pertain to a simple monopoly in a distinct industry, but rather applies to a holding company which concentrates its overall economic power in certain industries, producing anti-competitive effects in such industries and creating an ensuing broad anti-competitive impact on the entire economy of Japan.

To be regulated, the 'Guidelines Concerning Companies which Constitute an Excessive Concentration on Economic Power'[56] creates the following three conditions which a holding company needs to meet.

First, the company group must fall under any one of the following three situations: (a) it has business activities whose overall scale is exceptionally large and covers a substantial number of principle fields of business; (b) it has a high degree of influence over other companies derived from trades involving funds; or (c) it occupies a substantial position in each of a substantial number of principle fields that are interrelated.

Second, it has a large influence over the national economy.

Third, it obstructs enhancement of fair and free competition.

Under the guidelines, the following cases are, in general, considered not to constitute an excessive concentration of economic power.

56. The Japanese Fair Trade Commission, *Guidelines Concerning Companies which Constitute an Excessive Concentration of Economic Power*, (2002), *available at* <http://www.jftc.go.jp/e-page/legislation/ama/Company_Concentration.pdf> (last visited 17 March 2006).

(i) When a company splits off its business sector being performed by itself to establish its subsidiaries and acquires one hundred per cent of the stock of the said subsidiaries. It should be noted that this shall apply only to cases in which one hundred per cent ownership is retained from the outset of their establishment;
(ii) When a company is a venture capital investing in those companies not listed in the Security Exchanges stipulated in Art. 2, para. 14 of the Japanese Security Exchange Act or the Over-the-Counter register book stipulated in Art. 75, para. 1 of the Act, and has capital less than JPY 500 million and the ratio of the total amount of the research and development expenditure and the costs stipulated in Art. 14, para. 1 item 5 of the Japanese Corporate Tax Ordinance with ordinary profit (the operating profit minus the revenue) arising from its fixed assets and the transfer of securities stipulated in Art. 2, para. 22 of the Corporate Tax Law is more than 3 per cent or those companies with less than one year operation history and employing 2 full time researchers or more which account more than 10 per cent of the number of its total officials and employees;
(iii) When a financial company enters another sphere of financial business different from its own by newly establishing financial companies in the said business field; and
(iv) When the total assets of the company and its subsidiaries are JPY 600 billion or less on a consolidated basis.

The holding company restriction was substantially relaxed in 1998 i.e. less companies become regulated by the General Concentration Regulation. Judging from the current situation of Japanese industry and the examples in the guidelines which is stated to cause excessive concentration of economic power, it is unlikely that the conditions provided in Art. 9 would be met by any companies.

After the amendment in 2002, Art. 9 – 2 of the JAA (restriction on total amount of stockholding by a giant non-financial company) was completely deleted. Also, Art. 11 of the Act (restriction on ratio of holding voting right by a bank or an insurance company) is expected to be deleted in the near future. The JFTC is still able to apply Art. 10 of the Act to share acquisition and shareholdings by both a bank and an insurance company regulated in Art. 10 of the Act and by large corporate group regulated in Art. 9 of the Act. The JFTC may prohibit share acquisition and shareholdings which are likely to cause substantial restraint of competition pursuant to Art. 10 of the Act.

C. Regulation of Monopolistic Situation

The JAA has general regulations to prevent the monopolistic market structure in Art. 8 – 4. Pursuant to Art. 8 – 4 of the Act, when the JFTC finds that a monopolistic situation exists, it may order the firm in that relevant market to transfer a part of his or her business or to take any other measures necessary to restore competition in the relevant market. The JFTC shall not issue such an order, however, if it finds that such measures may reduce the scale of business of the firm to such an extent that the costs required for the supply of goods or services which the firm supplies will rise sharply, undermine its financial position, or make it difficult for the firm to maintain its international competitiveness, or where other alternative measures may be taken which the JFTC finds sufficient to restore competition.

The monopolistic situation in this context shall mean circumstances in which each of the characteristics concerning the market structure and undesirable market performances explained *below* exist in any particular field of business where the aggregate total amount of prices of goods of the same description and those of any other goods having a strikingly similar function and utility thereto, which are supplied in Japan, or the total amount of prices of services of the same description which are supplied in Japan, during the latest one-year period designated by cabinet ordinance, is in excess of JPY one hundred billion. The characteristics concerning the market structure and undesirable market performances mentioned *above* are as follows: (i) where the market share of a firm in a particular field of trade exceeds one-half or where the combined share of two firms in particular fields of trade exceeds three-fourths during the said one-year period. It should be noted that, pursuant to Art. 2, para. 7 of the JAA, the market share here shall mean the ratio accounted for by the aggregate volume of the particular goods and any other goods having a similar function and utility thereto or by the volume of the services supplied by the firm to the total volume of those products in Japan; (ii) where there exists conditions which make it extremely difficult for any other firm to enter the relevant market; and (iii) where the increase in the price of the particular goods or services supplied by the firm has been remarkable or the decrease therein has been slight for a considerable period of time in light of the changes that occurred in the supply and demand, or in the cost of supplying, for such goods or services during such period, and where, in addition thereto, the firm has fallen under any one of the following requirements during said period: (a) the firm has earned a profit rate far exceeding that which is established by cabinet ordinance as the norm for the class of business designated by such cabinet ordinance to which the said entrepreneur belongs; or (b) the firm has expended a level of selling and general administrative expenses far exceeding that which is considered as the norm for the field of business to which the firm belongs.

Pursuant to Art. 8 – 4, para. 2 of the JAA, the JFTC shall, when issuing the order to restore the monopolistic market structure, take into consideration the smooth conduct of business activities by the firm and those associated with it and the stabilization of livelihood for those employed by such it, in light of the following factors:

(i) Assets, income and expenditures and other aspects of accounting;
(ii) Officers and employees;
(iii) Location of factories, work-yards, and offices and other locational conditions;
(iv) Aspects of business facilities and equipment;

(v) The substance of patent rights, trademark rights, and other intellectual property rights and other technological features;
(vi) Capacity for and situations of production and sales, etc.;
(vii) Capacity for and situations of obtaining funds and materials, etc.; and
(viii) Situations of supply and distribution of goods or services.

VI. EXEMPTIONS

A. Overview

Exemptions from the JAA are divided into explicit exemptions and implied exemptions. Explicit exemptions are explicitly provided for in the provisions of the JAA or other statutes such as the Insurance Business Act and the Air Transportation Act. Implied exemptions are implied from the purpose and the structure of the individual statutes which govern the business activities of the firms belonging to a specific regulated industry. Hereinafter this book provides a brief overview of the explicit exemptions.

B. Action of Cooperative

Actions of cooperatives are exempted from the JAA as per Art. 22 of the Act. A cooperative qualifies for the exemption when it satisfies the four prong test. First, its purpose is the mutual aid among small scale firms or consumers. Second, the participation in and withdrawal from the cooperative is made on a voluntary basis. Third, each member has equal voting right. Fourth, there is a stated limit on the distribution of profit. As an exception to the exemption, the JAA applies to the actions of the cooperative where competition in the relevant market is substantially restrained, resulting in unjust increases in price. Art. 22 allows a cooperative to do business as an enterprise like a corporation. Otherwise, the action of a cooperative as a joint sales organization or a joint purchase organization may be deemed to violate the Cartel Regulation. The actions of a cooperative as one single economic entity are regulated by the JAA in the same way that other conducts of a firm are regulated. Exclusionary conducts of a cooperative with market power in the relevant market may violate the Monopoly Regulation or the Unfair Trade Practice Regulation.

C. Resale Price Maintenance Contract

Pursuant to Art. 23, para. 1, a manufacturer is allowed to maintain the resale price of a consumer commodity designated by the JFTC. It should be noted that, currently, no commodity is designated by the JFTC under Art. 23, para. 1. Until 1992, some cosmetic products and medical products were designated. Pursuant to Art.

23, para. 4, publishing copyrighted products shall be exempted from the JAA. A publisher is allowed to maintain the resale price of copyrighted products provided for in Art. 23, para. 4. The JFTC has publicly announced that copyrighted products of Art. 23, para. 4 cover six kind of product, that is, CDs, video tapes, records, newspapers, magazines, books. As a result these are exempted from the prohibition on the resale price maintenance.

Chapter 3

Procedure of the Japanese Antimonopoly Act

I. ADMINISTRATIVE PROCEDURE

A. Japanese Fair Trade Commission

The JFTC was originally established in 1947 as an independent administrative committee modelled after the FTC in the United States. In the cabinet organization structure, the JFTC was placed under the Prime Minister's office from 1947 to 2001 and then under the Ministry of General Affairs (Public Management, Home Affairs, Posts and Telecommunication) from 2001 to 2003. From 2003, the JFTC was under the Cabinet Office.

The JFTC was originally given only the power to order an entity in violation of the JAA to cease and desist from the violation or to take other necessary measures to correct the violation. Although the JAA does provide criminal penalties for the Cartel Regulation violation and the Monopoly Regulation violation, the JFTC was not empowered to enforce the criminal articles of the Act. Instead, the JFTC was required to file an accusation of a criminal violation with the Public Prosecutor Office, which was then responsible for prosecution. The JFTC is required to impose the surcharge once it found, factually, certain types of cartels and monopolization.

The JFTC is composed of the chair person and four commissioners appointed by the Prime Minister with the consent of the Diet. The deliberation and voting requires a quorum of the chair person and at least two commissioners. Decisions are made by a majority vote. The chairperson and the commissioners exercise their authority independently and cannot be fired or have their compensation reduced without their consent. The original JAA concentrated all enforcement authority in the JFTC, including the authority of exclusive criminal accusation, providing special damage awards to injured persons. The Tokyo High Court has exclusive jurisdiction over the appeal of a JFTC's decision. It should be noted that the provisions stipulating that the Tokyo High Court has original jurisdiction over a criminal case for unreasonable restraints of trade, etc. is abolished. And district courts have jurisdiction over criminal cases for unreasonable restraint of trade, etc.

B. Administrative Procedure

1. Overview of Administrative Procedure

After a preliminary investigation, if the JFTC finds reasonable grounds for believing that a violation exists, the JFTC may initiate a formal investigation. The JFTC appoints several staff members as investigators and authorizes them to exercise the investigation. It should be noted that through the amendment in 2005, the JFCT is now able to exercise compulsory measures to investigate suspected antitrust violation cases for which criminal sanction is imposed (e.g. violation of the Cartel Regulation). Before this amendment, the JFTC was permitted to investigate antitrust cases only with the voluntary cooperation of the relevant parties. For that reason, if suspected parties refused to hand in relevant documents, the JFTC was forced to take a great deal of time to persuade the submission of them, during which time important evidence might have been destroyed. Through the amendment, upon getting a writ from the courts the JFTC can, without getting consent from the relevant parties, search for and seize evidence. Further, written statements obtained by the JFTC can now be used in court proceedings, whereas before the amendment they could not be admitted as evidence. After a formal investigation, if the JFTC does not find a violation, it closes the case. On the other hand, if the JFTC finds a violation, after the amendment in 2005, it issues elimination orders and/or surcharge orders after having provided the respondent with an opportunity to submit its opinions, etc. and initiates formal hearings upon the filing of the written request when these orders are objected to by the firm, as the recommendation system was abolished in the amendment in 2005.[1] In a formal proceeding, the adversary system is adopted and independent referees will ultimately hand down the judgment. During the formal hearing, the respondent firm may challenge the JFTC's fact finding and application of law and make proposal for corrective measures. If the JFTC finds the proposal for corrective measures is appropriate, the JFTC drops the case, ordaining the respondent firm to take the corrective measures based on the original orders.

If the JFTC finds that a violation exists at the end of the formal proceedings, the JFTC issues the formal decision ordering the respondent firm to take corrective measures. Note that through the amendment in 2005, the JFTC can render a formal

1. Before the amendment in 2005, the JFTC must first issue a recommendation which contains fact findings, allegation of violation and a cease and desist order or other corrective measures to the firm.

decision even when it is found that the respondent firm ceased the violation up to three years earlier.

If discontented with the judgment of the JFTC, the relevant parties may file litigation at the Tokyo High Court, which has exclusive jurisdiction in seeking the revocation of the judgment of the JFTC. At the Tokyo High Court, the relevant parties may plead to introduce new evidence, provided that there are reasonable grounds, either on the basis that the JFTC failed to adopt the evidence without good cause, or that it was impossible to adduce evidence at the hearing of the JFTC, and there was no gross negligence on the part of the party in failing to adduce such evidence.

The relevant parties may also file an appeal against the judgment of the Tokyo High Court with the Supreme Court for its review.

2. Comparison with the Ordinary Administrative Procedure

Under ordinary Japanese administrative procedure, when the administrative agency finds that a violation exists, before rendering an administrative order, the agency will notify the firm of the violation and of the opportunity for presenting defences. The hearing is designed to give the chance to contest the fact findings and the application of the law. The hearing is not made public. The administrative agency issues an administrative order in accordance with the notification and enforces it immediately unless it finds it necessary to reconsider its fact-findings at the hearing. If the administrative order was rendered, the firm may bring an action to revoke the order at the district court. However, even when initiating the proceedings, in order to block the enforcement of the administrative order, the firm has to apply for and be granted a preliminary injunction by the court.

On the other hand, under administrative procedure pursuant to the JAA, through the amendment in 2005, administrative orders become enforceable upon the JFTC's issuance and remain enforceable even when the relevant parties do not accept it and the JFTC is compelled to initiate a formal hearing. Along with the same line, the JFTC has become able to collect a surcharge by adding arrears of the interest rate provided by the Cabinet order if any person should fail to pay a surcharge by the designated deadline and the surcharge payment order is sustained by a decision after hearing procedure. It should be noted, however, that prior to getting a judgment, as a matter of policy, the JFTC will voluntarily prohibit the enforcement of a surcharge order. However, once a surcharge order is admitted in a judgment, the relevant parties have to pay the surcharge in addition to the interest yielded during the period between the issuance of the surcharge order and the rendering of the judgment.

3. Comparison with the United States Antitrust Law Enforcement

In the United States, the main antitrust remedy is a cease and desist order, which is rendered by a federal district court in order to prevent and restrain violation and by the FTC. The Sherman Act is basically the criminal act. All conducts in violation of section 1 or 2 are punishable as criminal. On the other hand, the Clayton Act was introduced to provide administrative procedures into antitrust enforcement for more specific conducts. Accordingly, violations of section 2, 3, 7 and 8 have never been used for criminal punishment. Also, the Federal Trade Commission Act was enacted to introduce a formal administrative proceeding. Violations of section 5 of the Federal Trade Commission Act are not crime.

In fact, criminal sanctions are limited to hard core cartels. In addition, section 4 of the Clayton Act grants that firms, whose business or property was harmed, are able to bring treble damage actions. Section 16 of the Clayton Act grants firms, who suffer or are likely to suffer injury, may seek injunctive relief in order to prevent or restrain violations. These actions are granted concerning violations of the Sherman Act and the Clayton Act and not concerning violations of section 5 of the Federal Trade Commission Act. As a result, the United States Antitrust Law enforcement heavily relied on criminal sanctions and treble damage actions.

On the other hand, the original JAA was based on the enforcement and procedure of the United States Antitrust Law. However, the developments of the JAA's enforcement have been quite different from that of the United States in that criminal sanctions have not been used so often and the private damage action has not worked until recently.

C. Investigative Authority

With respect to investigative authority, as mentioned earlier, through the Amendment in 2005, the JFCT is now able to exercise compulsory measures to investigate suspected antitrust violation cases for which criminal sanction is imposed. After the amendment, upon getting a writ from the courts the, JFTC can, without getting consent from the relevant parties, search for and seize evidence. Also, the JFTC may, when expedience is needed, with a warrant issued in advance by a judge of the district court or the summary court having jurisdiction over the location of the site to be visited, the site, person, or matters to be searched, or the matters to be seized, search for and seize evidence. In addition, the JFTC may, when necessary to investigate a criminal case and having received a warrant, seize mail, personal letters, or documents related to telegrams sent by or to criminal case suspects and stored or held by communications services personnel. If necessary, the JFTC may prohibit any person from entering or leaving the site while the questioning, inspections, retentions, visits, searches, or seizures.

Further, written statements obtained by the JFTC can now be used in court proceedings, whereas before the amendment they could not be admitted as evidence.

Instead of taking compulsory measures, and when it is necessarry to investigate antitrust violation cases, for which administrative sanction is imposed, the JFTC conduct its investigation by a traditional administrative investigation, in which the JFTC cannot exercise physical force to remove obstructions or force compliance with the order. Under a traditional administrative investigation, the JFTC may order a firm to make a report as well as to summon witness, produce documents, make expert render opinions, and enter business places of the firm as well as any other relevant places.

In investigating typical cartel cases, the investigation often starts with a surprise raid at the business places of the suspected firms. On the spot investigations are conducted to inspect office inventories such as offices, desks and file boxes. After searching the relevant evidence, the investigators order the firms to produce relevant documents as well as other items and retain them. After examining retained evidence, the investigators will order witnesses to appear at the office and make the written statements.

The JFTC announced that it would positively denounce antitrust violations as criminal cases in 1991, and the policy adopted at that time was that criminal indictments should be made when appropriate to do so. However, since the JFTC had insufficient means to investigate violations, criminal indictments were only made at a rate of one in two years. Given the introduction of compulsory measures, because there are broader possibilities for the JFTC to expose antitrust violations and thus obtain more evidence, it is expected that the number of criminal indictments will increase.

D. Formal Proceedings and Formal Decision

1. Overview of the Formal Proceedings

Formal proceedings at the JFTC are based on those of the FTC in the United States. Considering the administrative procedure against antitrust violation cases, the formal proceedings at the JFTC could be regarded as equivalent to the proceedings at the district court in the two respects. First, in the formal proceeding, an adversary system and a trial type hearing is adopted. Second, the procedure of the formal hearing is, in principle, subject to the Japanese Civil Procedure Act.

If dissatisfied with an administrative order, the firm may request the JFTC to initiate hearing procedures. In such a case, the JFTC shall commence the formal proceeding without delay. Formal proceedings are divided into three stages, that is, (i) pleading stage, (ii) trial stage, and (iii) closing stage.

During the pleading stage, investigators of the JFTC make an opening statement and the respondent firms make a reply statement. Also, at this stage, issues to be discussed in the trial stage are specified and the burden of proof for each issue is allocated in accordance with the JAA. Further, each party will request an examination of evidence, scope and method of which will be determined by referees of the formal proceeding.

During the trial stage, the permitted evidence is examined. Documentary evidence is presented and an oral testimony of the witnesses is conducted. Most of the evidence submitted by investigators of the JFTC is documentary evidence obtained from the on-spot-investigations and the written statements taken in interviews. Not only direct evidence but also circumstantial evidence is admissible, although its relevancy to the subject at issue is examined.

During the closing stage, both investigators and respondent firms make closing statement. A nominated administrative referee presides over the formal proceeding. It should be noted that under the JAA, although the commission may preside over the formal proceedings, this has not been done recently. Five referees are appointed primarily from the JFTC's staff members. At the end of the formal proceedings, the administrative referees render the final decision.

2. Development of the Case Law

a. *Newspaper Publishing Company Distribution Contract Case*[2]

With respect to the nature of the formal proceeding, the Tokyo High Court judgment of Newspaper Publishing Company Distribution Contract Case was the main precedent which established that the nature of the formal proceedings were equivalent to normal administrative procedures in a civil law country. The Tokyo High Court decision on Toshiba Chemical Case reversed the rationale of Newspaper Publishing Company Distribution Contract Case and is the current binding precedent which established that the nature of the formal proceedings were equivalent to the formal proceedings in the United States style independent administrative commission.

In Newspaper Publishing Company Distribution Contract Case, the administrative judge was lawfully assigned to be the administrative judge of the case. Later, he was promoted to be the Director General for the Investigation Division, whose duties included directing and supervising the investigators of the case and trying the case. But after he was promoted for Director General, he continued to preside over the formal proceedings and drafted the final decision on the case.

In the case, the Tokyo High Court found that the administrative judge was in the position of performing contradictory duties of presiding and judging the case independently and fairly as well as trying the case in directing the investigators. The Tokyo High Court concluded that the conduct of the administrative judge did not violate the Act under the following reasoning. The court said that the formal proceedings do not adopt the adversary system and there were no violation of the JAA in the aforementioned conduct, because the JFTC played the role of both the public prosecutor and judge. As a result, under this rationale, the JFTC and the respondent firms are two disputing parties in the structure of the formal hearing.

b. *Toshiba Chemical Case*

In the Toshiba Chemical Case, the JFTC initiated the formal proceedings against Toshiba Chemical, rendering a complaint stating that Toshiba Chemical and seven

2. 4 GYOSAIREISHU 609 (Tokyo Hi, Ct. 9 March 1953).

other manufacturers conspired to fix the price for their products and issued a formal decision finding that Toshiba Chemical joined the conspiracy. In the case, Toshiba Chemical did not accept the recommendation, although the seven other cartel members accepted the recommendations and recommendation decisions were rendered on them. In this case, the commissioner joined the deliberations and voted on the formal decision. But he also used to be the Director General for the Investigation Division, and was in charge of the investigation of the case, although he was not the investigator. In addition, he was actually well informed of the case and made an elaborate comment on the case in front of the attorneys of Toshiba Chemical when handing over the copy of the recommendation. In this case, the Tokyo High Court revoked the decision and reminded the case to the JFTC for further review, holding that the participation of the former Director General in the formal decision process violated the Act on the following reasoning. The Tokyo High Court ruled that the formal proceedings under the JAA were different from normal administrative proceedings. Also, it added that formal proceedings were conducted in accordance with the principles of due process because the formal proceedings under the Act adopted the adversary system and had the same function as district courts. Actually, the formal proceedings are the precondition in order for the Tokyo High Court to review the JFTC's decisions.

Therefore, the JFTC is supposed to serve as a neutral judge and needs to be fair and without prejudice in order to perform its duty. In this respect, a commissioner shall be disqualified from the participation in the deliberation when involved in what might cast doubt about its fairness, due to social position, economic interest or personal relationships.

In this case, the administrative judge's participation in the process of formal decision makings was not only unnecessary in order to satisfy the attendance requirement but also may harm the fairness of the JFTC. Based on this finding, the Tokyo High Court concluded that the administrative judge's involvement in the formal decisions violated a fundamental principle of the procedure, which made it necessary to revoke the decision regardless as to whether or not it actually affected the decision.

E. Administrative Warning

By definition, a firm does not need to comply with administrative warnings by the JFTC. In other words, theoretically, a firm should not be disadvantaged by the JFTC for not following administrative warnings. In some cases, however, the JFTC indicates that it will conduct further investigation if a firm does not comply with a warning by taking corrective measures. An administrative warning is often welcomed by firms in cartel cases because they escape liability for paying a surcharge. A warning means to request a firm to take corrective measures voluntarily. A warning is issued when there is still a probability that a violation exists and the JFTC is not able to collect enough evidence to prove the violation. A warning has played an important role in the enforcement of the JAA. However, it lacks transparency. Moreover, there is no way to contest with an administrative warning under the Act. They are the very reason why the case law has not developed in this area.

F. Surcharge Order

1. Surcharge Order

A Surcharge is a unique type of administrative fine.

The surcharge system was introduced in 1977. At the time, neither the criminal sanctions nor damage award system worked very well. When a cartel was found, elimination orders were issued to cartel participants. As a result, cartel participants were able to keep undue profit earned during the period in which they formed cartels. It was emphasized at the time of its introduction that the surcharge was intended to disgorge undue profits from cartel participants.

However, a surcharge is clearly an administrative sanction design to deter certain types of cartels because the amount of the surcharge differs from the actual amount of the profit for cartel participants. The JFTC issues a surcharge order to cartel participants to pay certain amounts of fines to the national treasury in addition to issuing an elimination order.

The amount of a surcharge does not take into account any aggravating or mitigating factors in terms of the culpability of the violator. Surcharges are a very rigid administrative fine in their application. Its rigidity may come from the argument that a discretionary administrative fine may be against the double jeopardy rule in the Japanese Constitution which prohibits imposing sanction twice for a single conduct. That said, currently it is understood that the surcharge system has the function of not only disgorging undue profit but also penalizing cartels. The Tokyo High Court said the surcharge is an administrative sanction for the purpose of both ensuring social fairness by disgorging undue profits from cartel participants and ensuring the effectiveness of bans on cartels by punishing illegal conduct.[3]

Except for a reduction or exemption through an application of the Leniency Program and coordination with criminal penalties, the basic equation to calculate the amount of the surcharge is to multiply the profit received from the sales of products or services relating to cartels which the cartel members were involved during the cartel period by a certain percentage provided by the Act. After the introduction of the surcharge, although Japanese industries criticized it as a mere criminal sanction on forming cartels under the guise of an administrative order, it has contributed to the deterrence for violating the Cartel Regulation, and has helped to change the prevailing attitudes of industry so that the realization that forming cartels is illegal has become prevalent. After its introduction, the number of cartel cases brought by the JFTC clearly decreased, although this is also due to the careful fact finding practice adopted by the JFTC.

---

3. 46 KOKEISHU 108 (Tokyo Hi. Ct. 21 May 1993).

Through the Amendment to the JAA in 2005, several significant reforms have been made to the surcharge.

The first significant reform is that the principal percentage to calculate the amount of the surcharge which will primarily be applied to manufactures was increased from 6 per cent to 10 per cent. This is intended to have the double effect of deterrence and of making the Leniency Program more attractive to ongoing Cartel Regulation violators. This takes into consideration the criticism that 6 per cent is not enough to deter antitrust violations. The increase in the principal percentage to 10 per cent is based upon data showing that the average profit that members of cartels have enjoyed for the last ten years is more than 8 per cent. From 1993 to 2003, it was reported that approximately 10 per cent of all companies that violated the JAA re-offended, as compared to a rate of approximately 3 per cent in the European Union over the same period. This statistic gave the very ground to increase the percentage in calculating the surcharge.

Other than the principal percentage, percentages to be applied to small and medium-sized manufactures, wholesalers, and retailers are also increased, summarized as follows;

Manufacturers, etc.	Large-sized enterprises: 6% → 10% Small and Medium-sized enterprises: 3% → 4%
Wholesalers	Large-sized enterprises: 1% → 2% Small and Medium-sized enterprises: 1% (no change)
Retailers	Large-sized enterprises: 2% → 3% Small and Medium-sized enterprises: 1% → 1.2%

As a further penalty, the principal percentage shall be 15 per cent in the case where violators have been issued with another surcharge order over the past ten years. On the other hand, relevant parties that obtained a surcharge order can still enjoy a 20 per cent reduction of amount payable when three conditions have been satisfied: first, they ceased their violations within two years from commencement; second, they ceased their violations more than a month before an inspection by the JFTC; and third, they have not been issued with a surcharge order for the last ten years.

The second significant reform is that the scope of the surcharge order was broadened. Before the amendment, a surcharge order was issued only when finding cartels concerning price or limiting the volume of products or services to affect the price. Through the amendment, however, cartels having the purpose of restricting the counter parties that cartel members may transact with or of defining the market share of each cartel member, or certain kinds of private monopolizations which aim to achieve the same result as the *above* said cartels, may now be issued with surcharge orders. In sum, after the amendment, the scope has been broadened to include unreasonable restraints of trade (cartels) restraining the price of goods or services and those which may affect the price of goods or services by substantially restraining the volume of supply or purchase, market share, or customers or suppliers, and private monopolization through controlling the business activities of other enterprises which restrain the price of their goods or services or which may affect the price of their goods or services by substantially restraining the volume of their supply, market share or customers.

The third significant reform is that, through the amendment, a surcharge order remains enforceable even when the relevant parties do not accept it and the JFTC is compelled to initiate a formal hearing. Also, the JFTC has become able to collect a surcharge by adding arrears of the interest rate provided by the Cabinet order if any person should fail to pay a surcharge by the designated deadline and the surcharge payment order is sustained by a decision after a hearing procedure. Along the same line, the recommendation system was abolished through the amendment. It should be noted, however, that prior to getting a judgment, as a matter of policy the JFTC will voluntarily prohibit the enforcement of a surcharge order. However, once a surcharge order is admitted in a judgment, the relevant parties have to pay the surcharge in addition to the interest yielded during the period between the issuance of the surcharge order and the rendering of the judgment.

2. Leniency Program

a. The Overview of the Leniency Program

Through the Amendment in 2005, the Leniency Program was introduced for the first time in the JAA's history.

Under the program, violators of the Cartel Regulation may be able to enjoy a reduction or exemption of the surcharge when they voluntarily report their violations and submit relevant documents.

A reduction or exemption will be made as follows:

The cartel member which first reports its violation prior to an inspection by the JFTC can enjoy an exemption from the surcharge; the second cartel member to report its violation prior to an inspection by the JFTC can enjoy a 50 per cent reduction of the surcharge; the third cartel member to report its violation prior to an inspection can enjoy a 30 per cent reduction of the surcharge; and a business which reports its violation after an inspection by the JFTC may enjoy a 30 per cent reduction of the surcharge.

First applicant before initiation of investigation	Total immunity
Second applicant before initiation of investigation	50% reduction
Third applicant before initiation of investigation	30% reduction
An applicant after initiation of investigation	30% reduction

It is expected in Japan that the Leniency Program will not only increase the number of successful exposures of cartel cases, but also give cartel members enough incentive to cease their violations voluntarily.

Before the amendment, it was very hard to pull out of cartels because of the double risk - that is, the risk of losing much of their business opportunities, and the risk of facing a large surcharge order. Under the Leniency Program, it has become possible to pull out of cartels without paying any surcharge.

However the following cartel members do not qualify to enjoy the benefit provided by the Program: cartel members who make false reports to the JFTC; cartel members who, after informing the JFTC of their violations, refuse to cooperate with the JFTC or make a false report; and cartel members who compel other members to participate in their cartels, or prevent other members from reporting their violations.

With regard to 'false reports', this refers to the situation where it is obvious that cartel members have purposely concealed or distorted the facts so as to evade responsibilities arising from their violations. Therefore, it should be noted that a mere mistake of information will not prevent the party from taking advantage of the Leniency Program.

With regard to compelling members to participate or preventing cartel members from reporting the cartel, it has been confirmed through discussion at the upper house of the Japanese Diet that this refers to the use of intimidations or physical force. Thus, it should be noted that even when a member of a cartel organizes or coordinates meetings, it may still be able to apply for the Leniency Program.

Before the introduction of the Leniency Program it was pointed out that if cartel members who enjoy the benefit of the Leniency Program still potentially face criminal charges, there is little incentive for them to discontinue their cartels. Actually, the Leniency Program only purports to offer leniency with respect to the surcharge and does not offer express immunity from criminal prosecution. This aspect differs from that of the United States which is primarily directed at offering violators a way to avoid criminal indictment. Consequently, the JFTC announced that it would not recommend that criminal charges be brought by the prosecutor's office against those who violate the Cartel Regulation if a violator first reports the violation to the JFTC prior to an inspection, although this is expected to be done on a case-by-case basis. In addition, as discussions in the Japanese Diet make clear, the Public Prosecutors Office will respect the decision of the JFTC, so that criminal charges will not be brought against violators of the Cartel Regulation if the JFTC does not recommend such an action. Also, the Japanese Ministry of Justice issued a statement that the Public Prosecutors Office would give due considerations to decision made by the JFTC. This is to ensure that the Leniency Program can function properly. Therefore, in order to avoid criminal charges being brought against them, it is expected that members of cartels will have enough incentive to apply for the Leniency Program.

With regard to the private action, the Leniency Program is not expected to provide a bar to the private enforcement. The private claims pursuant to the JAA Art. 25 may not be initiated unless and until the JFTC renders a final and conclusive order. Even when the applicant for the Leniency Program enjoys immunity, as the JFTC may order an elimination order, it would be compelled to expose itself to the risk of subsequent private action pursuant to Art. 25 of the Act. Nonetheless, in Japan, it is considered that the aforementioned private enforcement actions might not be a significant disincentive to apply for the Leniency Program for the following reasons. First, the JAA does not allow for class action or treble damages claim. As such, the amount to be sought in private actions has not been an incentive to cartel members so as not to engage in cartel activities. Second, the number of private action in Japan is much less than that of the United States, because courts in Japan adopt the strict view in finding causation between antitrust violations and damages. This fact-finding trend has deterred bringing private actions in antitrust violation cases.

b. How to Apply for the Leniency Program

When applying for the Leniency Program, the first thing to do is to contact the JFTC to see if there are other cartel members that have already made an application for the Leniency Program. At this stage, anonymous contact will suffice, meaning that the JFTC can be contacted through legal counsel without disclosing the name of his or her client.

In a case where an inspection by the JFTC has not been initiated, should there be less than three members who have already applied for the program, the next thing to do is to reveal the company's name and submit a simple format report ('Simple Report') regarding the violation via fax to secure the company's provisional position regarding the order in which each company reports its violation for the purpose of the Leniency Program. In this regard, the only permitted way to submitting Simple Report as a Leniency application to the JFTC is fax, which purportedly determine the precise date and time of each application, thus avoiding the problem of determining which company applied first.

Once the JFTC receives a Simple Report, the provisional order is secured. In other words, the Simple Report is used to give him a marker position, so that the first company who submits the report is qualified as the first applicant, and is afforded roughly 15 business days before submitting the detailed report ('Detailed Report') as well as necessary materials and documents.

After obtaining the aforementioned report via fax, the JFTC will request the business to submit a Detailed Report together with the necessary materials and documents. Pursuant to the request by the JFTC, the business must submit a detailed report regarding the violation.

In cases where the JFTC has already initiated its investigation, another kind of report is used. This report is almost identical to the Detailed Report described *above* in its content and must be submitted via fax.

The information obtained at the time of a Leniency application under the report is used by the JFTC to start an investigation on a matter.

Any information obtained by the JFTC by using the compulsory power under the JAA cannot be used for other purposes than the enforcement of the Act. It is expected, however, that the JFTC will share the information with the Public Prosecutors Office. This only happens when the JFTC files a criminal accusation regarding specific cases. Also, there could be the situation where the JFTC's disposition is contested by the respondent companies, and the case moves to the hearing stage. If other cartel participants are contesting the JFTC's disposition at the hearing, it might be necessary for the JFTC to use the information submitted or any materials and documents provided by the Leniency applicants. Note that although theoretically it could be possible for the JFTC to submit the report filed by a Leniency applicant, this is rather rare. This is because under ordinary circumstances, investigators will take depositions by interviewing with directors and employees of involved companies including the applicant company after the start of investigation activities. The depositions taken by investigators may expose the Leniency applicant to far greater financial risk than any written report.

The level or standard of disclosure of the facts shall be sufficient to initiate an investigation, not less than that, but not more than that. The information is used by the JFTC to judge whether or not the applicant shall be afforded a Leniency status of immunity, or reduction of penalty. The information obtained through a Leniency application need not be sufficient for proving a violation. The JFTC can and will produce necessary evidence later in its pursuits of investigation activities.

Those reports must be submitted under the name of a company representative, or its attorney. It must have a company seal or attorney's seal to show its authenticity. After the officer in charge of a Leniency application at the JFTC examines the Detailed Report, the JFTC will issue a notice or a letter to the company telling them that the Leniency application is properly processed and it has qualified as the first, second or third applicant. This status is guaranteed so long as the company does not fall under any one of the disqualification requirements stipulated under the JAA Art. 7 – 2, para. 12, namely, where the applicant submitted a report containing false information, the applicant does not submit additional information even if he is so requested by the JFTC, or where the applicant forced other entrepreneurs to engage in cartels and bid riggings or tried to block other entrepreneurs from casing such illegal conducts. If the first applicant falls under any one of the disqualification requirements after obtaining immunity status, this does not change the status of the second and the third applicant.

G. Judicial Review

Fact-findings of the JFTC's decision supported by substantial evidence are binding on court. 'Supported by substantial evidence' shall mean that courts find that a reasonable person would reach the same findings based on the same facts. Courts examine the case record of formal proceedings and determine whether or not the fact-findings at the JFTC are supported by substantial evidence. The court may accept new evidence upon request for examination of new evidence by both parties when the JFTC failed to introduce the evidence in the formal proceedings or when producing the evidence is impossible for the parties. Courts will remand the case to the JFTC for further review when they find that new evidence needs to be examined.

The court may revoke the JFTC's decision when they find that the decision falls under one of the following two situations. First, the facts on which the decision is based are not supported by substantial evidence. Second, the decision violates the Japanese Constitution or other laws. Among recently revoked decisions, the decision on Tokyo Seimaiki Case was revoked under the first condition and the decision on Toshiba Chemical Case was revoked under the second condition.

The court may remand the case to the JFTC for further proceedings, stating the reasons when it revokes the decision. In an exceptional case where the court find that a different violation does exist or a violation does not exist, the court revokes the decision or enters the new decision by itself.

The firms in respect to which the JFTC's decisions are made have standing to appeal the decision to the Tokyo High Court pursuant to the JAA. The firms are able to dispute whether or not the fact findings are supported by substantial evidence and whether or not the decision violates the Japanese Constitution or other laws.

H. Provisional Injunction

The JFTC may make an application to the Tokyo High Court for ordering an alleged violator to take provisional measures when it finds that it is necessary to stop possible violations of an alleged violator in order to maintain the status quo. The court may order provisional measures against an alleged violator upon the application of the JFTC when it finds that it is necessary to take into account the possibility of the violation and irreparable harm caused by the conduct which is alleged to be in violation of the JAA. The court may determine appropriate measures on a case-by-case basis.

II. MERGER REGULATION REVIEW PROCEDURE

A. Report Obligations

Mergers, business transfers and corporate splits may, depending on whether or not they exceed certain monetary asset or turnover thresholds, be subject to a prior notification requirement and a 30 – day waiting period, although it should be noted that, generally speaking, no notification is required for transactions which amount to internal re-organizations of companies within a group.

Share acquisitions, depending on whether or not they exceed certain monetary asset or turnover as well as shareholding thresholds, may be subject to a post-facto notification requirement (30 days after the relevant share acquisition). Further, as explained earlier in this book, there are additional restrictions that apply to acquiring or holding stock which results in the creation of a company with excessive concentration of economic power as well as restrictions on shareholdings of financial institutions. The *above* restrictions also apply to foreign companies.

For mergers, generally speaking, a monetary asset or turnover threshold of JPY 10 billion and JPY 1 billion is used. The asset and turnover threshold will be met when, on the basis of the most recent audited financial statements, a company whose total assets, i.e. based on the latest balance sheet, the sum of the total amount of assets of the said company, subsidiaries in Japan of the said company (i.e. companies in which the said company holds more than 50 per cent of the total voting rights of all stockholders), and a company in Japan which holds more than 50 per cent of the total voting rights of all stockholders of the said company (or for non-Japanese companies, domestic sales, i.e. the sales in the profit and loss statement made together with the latest balance sheet of the non-Japanese company's business offices in Japan, including its Japanese subsidiary offices) exceed JPY 10 billion and a company whose total assets (or for non-Japanese companies, domestic sales) exceed JPY 1 billion, merge. In the case of a merger between two non-Japanese companies, a filing will only be required if both of the two non-Japanese companies have either a Japanese business office or subsidiary and the requirements described *above* are met.

For business transfers, the assets or turnover threshold will be met when an acquiring company (including a non-Japanese company), whose total assets exceed JPY 10 billion, acquires: (i) all of the business of a Japanese company whose assets on a non-consolidated basis exceed JPY 1 billion; and (ii) a substantial part of a Japanese company's business, or all or a substantial part of the fixed assets of a Japanese company's business, in each case the turnover (i.e. the sales in the profit and loss statement made together with the latest balance sheet) from which exceeds JPY 1 billion.

For a corporate split, the threshold is based on assets and turnover. A corporate split is similar to a business transfer in that assets and liabilities are transferred, while it differs in that assets and liabilities are comprehensively transferred as an organizational transfer and therefore, no individual consent is necessary. For a corporate split, the basic threshold is the same as for a business transfer.

There are two types of corporate split that are subject to the filing requirement. Under the first type, which consists of jointly establishing a new company by corporate split, the threshold will be met when total assets (for a Japanese company which intends to transfer a whole part of its business), turnover of the business being transferred (for a Japanese company which intends to transfer a substantial part of its business) or domestic sales (for non-Japanese companies), of one entity exceed JPY 10 billion and the total assets, turnover of the business being transferred or domestic sales, of another entity exceed JPY 1 billion. Under the second type of corporate split, which consists of transferring a business to an existing company by corporate split, the threshold will be met when the transferring entity's total assets, turnover of the business being transferred or domestic sales (for non-Japanese companies), exceed either JPY 10 billion or JPY 1 billion and the total assets or domestic sales (for non-Japanese companies) of the receiving company exceed JPY 1 billion or JPY 10 billion.

For share acquisitions, the threshold is based both on assets or turnover, and shareholding. First, the threshold is met if the assets of the acquiring company (including a non-Japanese company) on a non-consolidated basis exceed JPY 2 billion and the total assets of the said acquiring company exceed JPY 10 billion, and the acquiring company either acquires (or obtains control over) shares of a Japanese company whose assets on a non-consolidated basis exceed JPY 1 billion, or a non-Japanese company whose Domestic Sales exceed JPY 1 billion. Second, the threshold is also met if the shareholding ratio after such acquisition exceeds 10, 25 or 50 per cent (so that an acquisition that increases a shareholding from 9 to 11 per cent requires a filing, but an acquisition that increases a shareholding from 11 to 24 per cent does not require one).

In the case of a merger or corporate split, both companies intending to effect a merger or corporate split are jointly responsible for the filing. In the case of a business transfer, the receiving company is responsible for the filing. In the case of a share acquisition, the acquiring party is responsible for making the post-facto filing. There are no filing fees.

In terms of timing, where a prior-notification is needed, the standard 30 – day waiting period will apply, during which the JFTC may request additional information in the form of reports, data, etc. In certain cases the JFTC may shorten the 30 – day waiting period (for example because at the informal consultation stage it indicated that the case raises no competition concerns) but may also extend the period by taking actions (including having the parties take corrective measures) within the longer period of either 120 days from the date of receipt of the initial notification or 90 days from the date of the receipt of the additional report.

B. Report Obligations of Foreign Companies

Reporting obligations of foreign companies were introduced in 1999. Concerning mergers between foreign companies, they have to make a prior notification when (i) the amount of annual Japanese sales, which include the sale of a Japanese branch and sales of a Japanese branch's subsidiaries, of one merging company exceeds JYP 10 billion, and (ii) the amount of annual Japanese sales of the other merging company exceeds JPY 1 billion. In terms of acquisition of foreign assets, the acquiring company (whether or not it is a Japanese company or a foreign company) has to make a prior notification when (i) the amount of total asset of the acquiring company exceeds JPY 10 billion, and (ii) all the acquired company's asset will be transferred, (iii) the amount of annual Japanese sales of the acquired business exceeds JPY 1 billion. In terms of acquisition of shares of a foreign company, the acquiring company (whether or not it is a Japanese company or a foreign company) has to file a report at the time when the acquired shares reach 15 per cent, 25 per cent, and 50 per cent of outstanding shares of the acquired company when (i) the account of asset owned solely by the acquiring company exceeds JPY 2 billion, (ii) the amount of total assets of the acquiring company exceeds JPY 10 billion and, (iii) the amount of annual Japanese sales of the acquired business exceeds JPY 1 billion.

C. Informal Consultation

Qualifying transactions are usually submitted to the JFTC under the voluntary informal consultation procedure prior to the formal statutory filing of a proposed transaction under the JAA. Using the informal prior consultation procedure presents the advantage that as a general rule the JFTC will make up its mind about a particular case at this early stage and will almost always keep that opinion in the formal consultation procedure.

Within 30 days of the notification for informal consultation, the JFTC will indicate either that the proposed transaction does not raise the JAA issues, or that a further detailed examination is necessary. In the latter case, the JFTC will explain to the notifying party the issues of concern on the basis of specific products or services markets as well as geographic markets. If the notifying company decides to proceed (rather than withdraw its application), its application will be made public and the JFTC will commence its detailed investigation of the matter, including through contacts with competitors, retailers and end users. The JFTC will also receive opinions from the public for a period of 30 days after disclosure of the proposed transaction. At this stage of the procedure the notifying party has an opportunity to make amendments to the proposal in order to address the JFTC's issues of concern.

The JFTC will then issue its informal decision within 90 days after receipt of the necessary documents and information and will inform the notifying party of the result of its examination including the reasoning behind its decision.

If the JFTC indicates to the notifying company that informal approval of its proposed transaction is unlikely to be given, the notifying company may decide to withdraw the submission if it believes that the possibility of ultimately securing approval under the statutory procedure is small. If the JFTC concludes that the proposed transaction poses competition problems, and the applicant has offered some remedies to resolve the problem, the JFTC will provide its answer taking into account the notifying parties' offer.

If the JFTC stated that there are no competition issues, either at the end of the 30 days documentary examination or at the end of the detailed examination, the parties can file the official statutory notification on the basis that an unconditional approval will be obtained, provided that there is no material change of circumstance.

III. CRIMINAL PROCEDURE

The Cartel Regulation and the Monopoly Regulation violations can give rise to criminal liability. However, in practice, criminal sanctions for Cartel Regulation violations are generally limited to hard core cartels, typically, bid riggings. The JFTC has exclusive authority for bringing a criminal accusation against the violators to the Public Prosecutor General. The prosecutor's office cannot make an indictment without the criminal accusation of the JFTC. Usually, the Tokyo High Prosecutors Office, to which the Public Prosecutor General transfers the case, together with the assistance of the District Public Prosecutors Office, conducts a criminal investigation after the receipt of the accusation and brings a public charge to courts if the prosecutor believes that its evidence is sufficient to prove a violation beyond reasonable doubt.

Prior to 1989, there had been only 6 criminal prosecutions under the JAA, of which three were brought in 1949 and one was brought in 1969. There really were no significant criminal antitrust prosecutions in Japan, however, until the two oil cartel cases brought in 1974 against the Petroleum Industry Federation and the major Japanese oil companies and their officers for output restrictions and price fixing. Convictions obtained in one of these prosecutions were affirmed by the Supreme Court.

In 1991, the JFTC published its policy, which stated that it would bring criminal accusation more actively. The JFTC announced that it would make a criminal accusation against cartels when they were considered to affect national economy and when cartel participants committed the violation intentionally and repeatedly. Also, in 1991, the Public Prosecutors Office and the JFTC established a pre-accusation consultation meeting, the 'Committee on Matters Concerning Criminal Accusation'.

After the introduction of the *above-mentioned* policy, the first antitrust criminal case was brought in 1991 against eight polyvinyl chloride stretch film manufacturers and fifteen of their executives. The defendants were convicted after trial in 1993. The companies were fined between JPY 6 and 8 million; the executives received prison terms of six month to a year, all suspended for two years. The second criminal case grew out of the Tokyo District Public Prosecutors investigation of major printing firms for bid rigging contracts for privacy seals used by the Social Insurance Agency. Following the Public Prosecutor's successful investigation and prosecution under the Japanese Criminal Code of the individuals involved in the bid rigging, the JFTC referred the case to the Public Prosecutor for criminal prosecution under the JAA. The third case was made in 1995 against the nine electrical equipment manufacturers who had engaged in bid rigging in the installation of electrical equipment for the Japanese Sewage Works Agency.

In spite of the several successful cases introduced *above*, from 1991 until 2004, the overall trend of antitrust criminal cases in Japan was that the JFTC brought one criminal accusation in every two years to the Public Prosecutor General, of which all criminal accusations resulted in criminal indictments. Also, all criminal cases in which judgments were rendered resulted in criminal sanctions.

Before the amendment to the JAA in 2005, the JFTC was admitted to exercise traditional administrative investigative authority, which had been a sufficient method to collect the evidence to meet the 'preponderance of evidence' standard of proof only when it could secure the voluntary cooperation of the suspected firms. Through the amendment, upon getting a writ from the courts the JFTC can, without getting consent from relevant parties, search for and seize evidence. Further, written statements obtained by the JFTC can now be used in court proceedings, whereas before the amendment they could not be admitted as evidence.

There have been some Cartel Regulation violation cases which had affected relevant markets not only in Japan but also in the United States. As such, the United States and Japan entered into an agreement in 1999 concerning cooperation on anticompetitive activities, allowing the DOJ and the JFTC to investigate and take action against international cartels operating in both countries. Pursuant to this agreement, the DOJ and the JFTC are able to share information. Similarly, the European Commission and Japan have entered into a cooperation agreement, effective since 9 August 2003. The agreement requires the JFTC and the European Commission to notify each other of significant enforcement operations and to cooperate in investigations.

Once the DOJ initiates criminal investigations against a Japanese company, the company usually learns of a DOJ criminal investigation of its alleged anticompetitive activities when a subpoena is served on its subsidiary in the United States. The DOJ will have commenced its criminal investigation by convening a grand jury, consisting of 23 individuals, and the grand jury issues the subpoenas allowing the DOJ to gather evidence in its investigation. In practice, the subpoena is frequently quite detailed and shows that the DOJ already possesses substantial factual information about the alleged international cartel. Even though the subpoena has geographic limitations and is generally not binding on the Japanese headquarters, the Japanese company must often move quickly to determine its and its subsidiary's legal position in order to decide whether it should 'get on line' with the DOJ and apply for the Leniency Program in the United States.[4] It should be noted, as far

4. Under the Leniency Program in the United States, complete immunity from federal criminal prosecution and therefore from fines and imprisonment can be granted when: (i) no DOJ investigation has been commenced; (ii) the company is the "first through the door"; (iii) the company has ceased to be involved in the anticompetitive conduct; (iv) the company offers full and

as a criminal investigation initiated in the United Stated is concerned, that as soon as it is aware of the DOJ's investigation, it is necessary to commence its own rapid and thorough investigation to decide whether or not it should apply for the Leniency Program in the United States. The key objective of the initial internal investigation will be to determine the facts regarding the alleged cartel, the company's legal position and whether or not to seek the Leniency Program. The internal investigation should ideally be complete as soon as possible within one month of receiving the subpoena. Also, it is necessary to interview employees in the subsidiary and directors and other managers in Japan responsible for international operations and to review all potentially relevant documents.

IV. CIVIL PROCEDURE

A. Damage Award

1. Damage Award based on the Japanese Civil Code Art. 709

The Japanese Civil Code Art. 709 provides that an injured person may recover damages from the person who cause injury by proving (i) his/her intent or

---

ongoing cooperation with the DOJ; (v) the company publicly admits its wrongdoing; (vi) the company compensates customers to the extent possible; and (vii) the company was not a leader of the conspiracy and did not coerce others to participate in the conspiracy. Leniency in the form of a reduction in fines is relevant when the DOJ has already commenced an investigation, and is therefore the basis on which most applications are made under the DOJ's Leniency Program. In general, the requirements (iii) through (vii) above must still be met. Because complete immunity applications can be made only before the DOJ commences an investigation, it is much more common to apply and qualify for leniency rather than immunity (since the issuance of a subpoena means that the DOJ has already commenced investigations). The company's internal investigation may have revealed a conflict between the company and the key implicated individuals (*e.g.* the company wants to pursue a Leniency application, but one executive implicated in the alleged conspiracy will not support the application because he or she faces personal criminal responsibility. In this case, the individual naturally has a right to pursue his or her own interests and retain separate legal counsel. While providing independent advice in the best interests of the individual, it is often desirable for that lawyer to cooperate with counsel for the company to achieve the best possible result for both the company and the individual(s) concerned. To date, a Japanese person has served jail time in the United States for antitrust violations in 2004. Also, executives from Canada, Germany, Switzerland and Sweden have served jail terms in the United States for violations of the Sherman Act as part of negotiated corporate Leniency agreements. Thus far, several Japanese executives have been indicted by the DOJ for antitrust violations. In each case, these individuals have declined to appear and have thus, in effect, avoided formal punishment. Nonetheless, Japanese executives who are "no shows" in response to DOJ indictments remain "wanted" by the United Sates Government and cannot enter United States territory at any time for any reason without risking arrest. This raises difficult issues about whether or not the company may pay the fine on behalf of its indicted executive. In general, if the company does pay the fine for the individual, Japanese shareholders may bring shareholder derivative action against the company.

negligence, (ii) unlawful conduct, (iii) causation between the unlawful conduct and the injury, and (iv) injury and damage. A person that suffers harm from conduct in violation of the JAA may recover actual damage from the violators by proving the aforementioned four elements just like persons who suffer damages due to other administrative law violations. Furthermore, whether or not each antitrust violation satisfies the aforementioned elements is determined on a case-by-case basis.

After a formal judgment is rendered by the JFTC, the existence of a violation for each article of the JAA is presumed in civil court proceedings from fact-finding process. However, it is not conclusive because civil proceedings are separate procedure from administrative proceedings.

2. Damages Award based on the Japanese Antimonopoly Act Art. 25

The special damages award system was introduced for violation of the JAA Art. 3 and 19 in 1947 and are different damages award based on the general tort clause of the Japanese Civil Code Art. 709. According to the JAA Art. 25 and 26, a firm whose interest was injured by conducts in violation of the JAA Art. 3 and 19, for which the JFTC has rendered a decision and became final, may recover actual damages from a violator in an expedient way. This special damages award system has the following four special characteristics when compared to the damage award system pursuant to the Japanese Civil Code Art. 709. First, the relevant firm may not escape liability by proving the non-existence of intent or negligence concerning the conduct for which the JFTC found violation of the JAA. In other words, the firm shall bear strict liability. Second, injured firms may claim damages and bring a damage action after the JFTC's decision becomes final and conclusive. The statute of limitations period is extended to 3 years after the JFTC's decision becomes final and conclusive. Third, the court is to request the opinion of the JFTC on the amount of damage caused by conducts violating the JAA. The opinion of the JFTC could possibly include causation between the violation in question and injury as well as the amount of damages. Fourth, the Tokyo High Court has exclusive jurisdiction for the action.

Under the special damages award system, a damages award is expected to be given in an expedient way for primary violation of the JAA Art. 3 and 19 for which the JFTC's decision is rendered and becomes conclusive. Special damages were intended to deter violation of the JAA by making the proof of the liability and amount of the damages much easier for injured firms. The damages award is, however, a single damages and is not treble damages or a punitive damages. The Allied Occupation Forces unsuccessfully introduced the treble damages award into the JAA. Treble damages awards and punitive damage award were regarded as fundamentally in opposition to the Japanese legal system. Under the Japanese legal system, it was difficult for injured firms to recover more than actual damages.

3. Relationship Between the Two Damages Actions

The special damages award system was introduced on the assumption that damage caused by conduct in violation of the JAA cannot recovered through the Japanese Civil Code Art. 709 as a general torts claim. Case law soon established, however, that an actual damages award could be granted pursuant to the Japanese Civil code Art. 709 against all violations of the JAA regardless of whether or not the JFTC's decision has been made. This case law made the special awards system redundant except for the extension of 3 years of the statute of limitation, i.e. 3 years statute of limitation does not apply to the special damages award system.

Concerning strict liability, every conduct deemed in violation of the JAA Art. 3 and 19 for which the JFTC's decision was rendered has satisfied the intent or negligence requirement of the Japanese Civil Code Art. 709. Opinions as to the amount of damages given by the JFTC were expected to assist the injured firm. However, the JFTC conducts an investigation to prove violations, not to find the amount of damage incurred by the injured parties. As a result, it is very unlikely for the JFTC to be able to opine the exact amount of damage and produce relevant evidence. Since the special awards system is almost redundant except for the extension of the statute of limitation, it would be one good idea to integrate the special damages award system into a damage award based on the Japanese Civil Code Art. 709 for which the JFTC's decision has been rendered and becomes final. Also, in that case, provisions should be added such as extending the terms of the statute of limitation, shifting the burden of proof, and imposing on the court the duty to request the opinions of the JFTC as to the amount of damages.

This concern, how to coordinate two similar actions effectively, was realized in the civil actions made concerning Water Meter Bid Rigging Case.[5]

In this case, a damages action pursuant to the Japanese Civil Code Art. 709 was brought by local residents at the Tokyo District Court and then a damage action based on the JAA Art. 25 was brought by the local government at the Tokyo High Court. Since both actions actually co-existed, the Tokyo District Court decided to stay the whole proceedings by the presiding judge's order. It is the current practices for one of the courts to suspend its proceedings when both actions are pending.

That said, there are few damage actions seeking compensation due to violation of the JAA brought to the Japanese courts. This could be because of firms' inability to gather sufficient evidence to bring actions and prove the conducts in violation of the JAA. Also, strict fact-finding adopted by Japanese courts might be another reason preventing firms from bringing actions.

5. The JFTC referred this case to the Public Prosecutor's office to initiate the criminal prosecution. The Tokyo High Court found that the defendants were criminally liable. *See* 50 KOHKEISHU 181 (Tokyo. Hi. Ct. 24 December 1997).

4. Development of the Damages Action

Until the latter half of the 1990s, it had been said that private antitrust actions had been virtually non-existent in Japan, creating a contrast to that of the United States, where more private actions have been brought than public cases.

a. Damages Awarded on Lost Profit Basis

Since the latter half of the 1990s, the damages award system began to work. For example, Osaka High Court held in 1993 that a tie-in arrangement of replacement parts of its own elevator or a parent company's elevator with maintenance service for the elevator was in violation of the general designation Art. 10.[6]

In this case, Toshiba Elevator implemented a tie-in arrangement and intentionally refused or delayed supply of spare parts to the independent maintenance service providers. The court found that Toshiba Elevator was liable for implementing the tie-in arrangement and ordered Toshiba Elevator to pay a damages award to the independent maintenance service providers. This is the very first case in which a damages award was conclusively granted for a violation of the JAA.

The Tokyo District Court decision on National Toy Gun Association Case was the second case in which a damage award was granted for a violation of the JAA. In this case, the Toy Gun Association, whose members were all toy gun manufactures except Dejikon Denshi, organized wholesalers into three associations for the purpose of promoting a safety standard for toy guns. When Dejikon Denshi began to market more powerful toy gun exceeding the safety standard, the Toy Gun Association urged its members and associations of wholesalers to request retailers not to deal in the new toy gun of Dejikon Denshi. The Tokyo District Court held that the Association and its president were liable for the conduct which was in violation of the JAA Art. 8, para. 1, item 1 and ordered them to pay damages to Dejikon Denshi.

In these cases, the damages awards were granted pursuant to the Japanese Civil Code Art. 709 and the amount of damage was calculated based on a traditional lost profit basis.

b. Damage Award on Overcharge Basis

Subsequent to the price fixing case on petroleum products, consumers brought two damages actions, one of which was based on the JAA Art. 25,[7] and another of which was based on the Japanese Civil Code Art. 709.[8] The Supreme Court

6. *Toshiba Elevator Technos K.K. v. Kousei Denki Yugengaisha*, 833 HANREITIMES 62 (Osaka Hi. Ct. 30 July 1993).
7. 43 MINSHU 1259 (Supp. Ct. 8 December 1989).
8. 41 MINSHU 785 (Supp. Ct. 2 July 1987).

rejected to grant a damage awards based upon both the JAA Art. 25 and the Japanese Civil Code Art. 709 and denied recovery of damages, finding that neither the damage amount nor causation, were proved. This was because at the time of price fixing, prices were increasing rapidly due to the OPEC's oil cartels. The increase of the petroleum related products could have exceeded the fixed price had the cartels not been formed. However, the Supreme Court granted standing for the consumer in this case. Moreover, the Supreme Court's decision indicated that the difference between the actual purchase price and pre-cartel retail price might be recovered as damages in ordinary business circumstances, which gave the wrong impression that the amount of damage could be proved easily in the case of indirect purchasers.

Under the United States Antitrust Law, the direct-indirect purchaser doctrine has been established based on the passing-on theory. According to the doctrine, the direct purchaser is able to recover all the damages calculated on an overcharge basis. On the other hand, the indirect purchaser does not have standing and is not able to recover any damages. The core reasoning is that it is almost impossible for the court to find the exact amount of damage for either the direct purchaser or the indirect purchaser when the product at issue reaches the indirect purchaser through a chain of distribution. This reasoning would apply to cases in Japan in that it would be almost impossible for an indirect purchaser to prove the amount of damage in cartel cases. The Supreme Court should have exercised caution more carefully in rendering these decisions.

c. Damage Award in Bid Rigging Case

Since around 2000, district court's decisions which granted damages awards to local governments in bid rigging cases began to emerge, although all the cases were appealed to high courts. In these cases, local residents have brought damage actions against participants of bid riggings on behalf of local governments pursuant to Art. 242, para. 2. of the Local Government Administrative Procedure Act after the JFTC rendered its decision. Most of the courts found that the amount of damages was 5–10 per cent of the contract price of the work that the winning bidders had done.

In 1998, the Japanese Civil Procedure Act Art. 248 became effective, which allowed courts to determine the amount of damage in cases where a plaintiff suffered injuries due to a defendant's conduct and it is extremely difficult for a plaintiff to produce evidence to prove the amount of damage due to the nature of the injury. In bid rigging cases, local governments are always compelled to suffer injuries because the contract price is always higher than the competitive price. In addition, producing evidence concerning the amount of damage is extremely difficult in bid rigging case because individual work has unique characteristics and proving the competitive price is almost impossible. As such, there is good foundation for courts to apply the Japanese Civil Procedure Act Art. 248 in bid rigging cases.

B. Injunctive Relief

The use of injunctive relief by firms was introduced in 2001. A firm whose interest is seriously injured or is likely to be injured by conducts in violation of the JAA Art. 19 or Art. 8, para. 1, item 5 may seek to suspend the conduct of the relevant firm. A firm whose interest is seriously injured or likely to be injured may bring an action seeking the aforementioned injunctive relief against the relevant firm at the district court. The court is to notify the JFTC of the filing of the action and may request the opinion of the JFTC.

Under the Japanese Civil Procedure Act, a plaintiff does not have sufficient means to collect evidence to prove violation of the JAA Art. 19. After the amendment to the Act in 2001, it is increasingly clear that it is very difficult for a plaintiff to prove a violation of the JAA Art. 19 without the additional ability to collect evidence retained by a defendant. The lack of evidence gathering capability of a plaintiff is one of the main impediments in using injunctive relief effectively in Japan.

C. Voidance of Contract

Under the Japanese Civil Code, whether or not conduct violating the JAA should be deemed null and void is determined by courts on a case-by-case basis. In so doing, Japanese courts often take into account such factors as the purpose of the prohibition of conduct at issue, the degree of illegality of conduct, to what extent conducts harmed the competition in the relevant market, the need to protect third parties involved in the transaction, and the need for ensuring safe trade.

When a clause which is in violation of the JAA is separable from the entire contract, the clause, rather than the entire contract, shall become null and void. Under the Japanese Civil Code, the contract is deemed void at the time of conclusion if the contract is held to be void by the court. This means that the voidance shall take effect retroactively, making it possible for anyone to seek the restoration of the original state as a result of the voidance. This is true even when not only both parties but also any third parties have already performed their duties. Under the Japanese legal system, voidance of a contract has serious effects on transactions, so courts are very cautious in holding that unlawful conduct is void. For the same reason, courts are very careful in voiding contracts which are in violation of the JAA.

By contrast, in the United States, contracts violating the United States Antitrust Law shall become unenforceable. The unenforceability of an unlawful contract does work as a defence when parties bring actions seeking performance of the contact, although voluntary performance is deemed valid. As a result, in the United States, injunctive relief is a more effective remedy than an unenforceability defence.

V. INTERNATIONAL ENFORCEMENT

A. Extraterritorial Application of the Japanese Antimonopoly Act

1. International Rule Concerning Subject Matter Jurisdiction

Whether or not the JAA should apply to conduct outside of the Japanese jurisdiction is a jurisdictional issue.

In the United States, the Supreme Court reconfirmed the effect doctrine as a jurisdictional principle of the Sherman Act and the DOJ has actively applied the Act to conducts outside of the United States. Under the effect doctrine, the broad extraterritorial application of the law could be granted and the jurisdiction can be established when conduct has a direct, substantial and reasonably foreseeable effects on markets of the country.

In Japan, the jurisdictional issues are divided into three different aspects, that is, subject matter jurisdiction, personal jurisdiction and procedural jurisdiction. Subject matter jurisdiction covers the extent to which the JAA is applied to conducts outside of Japanese territory. Personal jurisdiction covers the extent to which foreign firms, the JFTC could duly initiate the proceedings in Japan, on the assumption that the subject matter jurisdiction has been established. Procedural jurisdiction discusses how the documents are duly served.

With regard to the subject matter jurisdiction of the JAA, the objective territorial doctrine has been supported by the majority of scholars. Under the objective territorial doctrine, the JAA has jurisdiction over conduct formed outside the territory but performed inside the territory.

Personal jurisdiction is granted over foreign firms that engage in the conduct for which subject matter jurisdiction has been granted, as long as the foreign firms have some connection with the Japanese market. Furthermore, there is a very influential view in Japan which says that under Japanese law, personal jurisdiction is automatically granted to firms which engage in conduct for which subject matter jurisdiction has been granted.

The JFTC would be allowed to apply the JAA to agreements which are intended to be performed and actually performed inside Japanese territory such as sole distributorship agreements and licensing agreements, even if the agreement is signed outside of Japan. As a result, the JFTC can apply the JAA to those agreements and order foreign firms to take corrective measures.

2. Case Law (Triple Transportation Fare Case)[9]

The formal decision on Triple Transportation Fare Case is still the leading precedent concerning the jurisdictional reach of the JAA.

9. 19 SINKETUSHU 57 (FTC, 18 August 1972).

The Japan-Europe route sea cargo transportation conference, whose members were mostly sea cargo operators of routes between Japan and Europe, decided in their London general meeting that they would give favourable fares to sea cargo owners who agree to enter into additional exclusive contracts with them. The member operators implemented the new fare policy in the member countries. Japanese and foreign operators negotiated with cargo owners and concluded additional agreement with cargo owners inside the Japanese territory.

In this case, the JFTC issued a formal decision that concluded that additional exclusive contracts in Japan violated the JAA Art. 19. In the decision, the JFTC made it clear that the JAA was not applied to the agreements in the London meeting but applied to the conducts within Japanese territory. The JFTC was considered to accept the territorial doctrine in determining the jurisdictional reach of the JAA. Moreover, the JFTC cancelled its decision to initiate the formal proceedings against foreign operators because the written complaint was not served lawfully to them. Although the written complaints were sent to local representatives of the foreign operators, the JFTC found that they did not have the authority to receive the documents for the foreign operators. The JFTC decided, however, that the documents could be served lawfully when a foreign firm accepted the JFTC's jurisdiction by replying complaints or when a representative was proved to have authority to receive the documents on behalf of a company.

When the decision was made, the objective territorial doctrine, which requires that a main implementation action occur inside Japanese territory, was widely accepted among scholars as a principle for the extraterritorial application of the JAA. The JFTC could have decided that a whole range of conducts form making the agreements in London to concluding the additional exclusive contracts violated the JAA Art. 3 or Art. 19. From this analysis, the JFTC has been considered to take a restricted view concerning the extraterritorial application of the JAA.

3. The Amendment to the Japanese Antimonopoly Act in 2002

Until 2002, the JAA did not have any procedures for serving documents directly on a foreign company. Under case law, the JFTC had to serve relevant documents to the Japanese branch office or subsidiary of the foreign company, which needed to be regarded as a sales place or office in order to bring the foreign company into its jurisdiction. As an exception, the JFTC could duly initiate formal proceedings against a foreign company consenting to such practices, or when the foreign company joined the procedures voluntarily by making a reply statement or appointing a representative of the case.

As a result of the amendment to the JAA in 2002, the JFTC is able to directly reach a foreign company over which the JFTC has subject matter jurisdiction as well as personal jurisdiction through the following methods. First, service of process may be made on the foreign company through Japanese representatives in the foreign country such as the Japanese Ambassador. Second, if the *above* method is not made within a certain period, service of process is able to be made by publication. In this case, copies of the documents are to be sent to the foreign company by mail in order to make the parties aware of the proceedings initiated in Japan.

After the amendment in 2002, if the JFTC finds that a violation exists after a formal investigation, it may initiate formal proceedings against a foreign firm over which the JFTC has personal jurisdiction. Also, the JFTC can issue a formal decision and/or issue a surcharge order against the foreign company when it finds that a violation exists based on evidence presented in the formal proceedings. Furthermore, a surcharge order to a foreign company is enforceable in Japan if it has assets in Japanese territory.

However, service of process by sending registered mail directly to a foreign company has not been introduced because such a method might violate the sovereignty of the foreign country without an international treaty.

B. Special Regulation on International Transactions Based on Art. 6

1. Overview

The JAA Art. 6 was originally intended to prohibit Japanese firms from participating in international cartels. Even at the time of introduction, however, it was considered to be a violation of international public law for the JFTC to apply the JAA to cartels which had no effect to the Japanese market.

Through the amendment to the JAA in 1953, the notification requirement was created in Art. 6, para. 2, which made it necessary to report certain types of international agreements. Since the JAA Art. 6, para. 2 was deleted in 1997 and notification system was completely abolished, Art. 6 has been losing its significance.

Art. 6 provides that no firms may enter into an international agreement or an international contract which contains such matters that constitute unreasonable restraint of trade or unfair trade practices. At the time of its introduction, there were two merits to creating Art. 6.

First, with regard to the prohibition of an international agreement which contains such matters that constitute unreasonable restraint of trade under the JAA, it could be possible for the JFTC to regulate the international agreement earlier than the Cartel Regulation, because it was interpreted that Art. 6 permitted that the JFTC prohibited an international cartel agreement when it was entered into. On the other hand, at the time of introduction, the prevailing view considered that the Cartel Regulation violation occurred only when actual implementation or actual anticompetitive effects accompanied the agreement. The Supreme Court of Japan adopted, however, the *quasi per se* rule against hard core cartels, so that cartel agreement would be a violation at the time of its formation. Due to this decision, Art. 6 lost the aforementioned significance in prohibiting international agreements containing unreasonable restraint of trade.

Second, with respect to the prohibition of international contracts which contain terms that constitute unfair trade practices, the prohibition pursuant to Art. 6 was considered to have merit, so that the JFTC would be able to regulate conducts even when they were not covered by the Unfair Trade Practice Regulation. However, this view was on the presumption that the Cartel Regulation did not cover vertical restraint such as distribution contracts and licensing contracts. Since it was considered that the Unfair Trade Practice Regulation prohibited firms from employing unfair trade practice, and, did not provide any regulations to firms with whom such conducts were employed, vertical restraints could be covered by Art. 6. In the context of international contracts, when a foreign firm employs unfair trade practices against Japanese firms and the JFTC does not exercise jurisdiction over the foreign firm because it cannot serve notice on it, the JFTC cannot apply the Unfair Trade Practice Regulation to neither foreign firms nor Japanese counterparties. However, the JFTC can apply Art. 6 to the international contracts by holding that the international contacts is a violation of Art. 6 and order the Japanese firm to take corrective measures in the decision. It should be noted that the Tokyo High Court decision on Seal Bid Rigging Case[10] made it clear that the Cartel Regulation covered vertical restraints such as international license contracts, international distribution contracts and international joint venture contacts within the jurisdiction of the JAA. The rationale of this decision means that the JFTC can render an elimination order against both parties of a vertical restraint contract and that all international agreements containing unreasonable restraint of trade could be covered by the Cartel Regulation regardless of whether or not the restraint was horizontal or vertical. As the decision of Seal Bid Rigging Case made clear, Art. 6 lost its aforementioned significance in prohibiting international agreements.

According to recent cases, it is the practice of the JFTC to apply Art. 3 or Art. 19 so long as the international agreements at issue could be covered by either of them.

Taking into consideration the basic structure of the JAA, it is not necessary to have provisions such as Art. 6. On the contrary, since Art. 6 might be a potential obstacle against extraterritorial application of the JAA, it should be deleted immediately.

The JFTC now executed bilateral treaties for enforcement and cooperation with both the United States and the European Union. There are five basic components to each of these treaties: (i) the parties shall notify each other if the enforcement of one signatory's competition laws will affect another signatory's interest; (ii) the parties will support the regulatory authorities of their co-signatories that are responsible for competition law by, among other things, cooperating in an investigation; (iii) the parties will coordinate enforcement activities in connection with cases that involve the regulatory authorities of both signatories to ensure efficiency and consistency across regimes; (iv) if anticompetitive activity within

10. 46 KOHKEISHU 322 (Tokyo Hi. Ct. 14 December 1993).

the territory of one signatory affects another signatory, the former may request the latter enforce its competition law; and (v) the competition authorities in each signatory shall carefully consider the interests of the other signatory. These treaties between and among Japan, the United States and the European Union hold considerable significance in the maintenance of a cooperative international regime that makes the JFTC's extraterritorial jurisdiction possible. They also provide substantial cooperation in the area of investigation, prosecution and sanction. It should be noted that only the JFTC can demand that the Public Prosecutor General conduct a criminal investigation. A future challenge in this area would be the development of a treaty regarding enforcement cooperation that will further enhance international ties by means such as sharing information in connection with company secrets.

2. Case Law

a. Amano Case[11]

In this case, a distribution agreement between Amano Pharmaceutical K.K. ('Amano') and Novo Indistri S.A. ('Novo') was at issue. Both parties entered into the agreement, whereby Novo gave Amano the exclusive right to distribute its product in Japan. Three kinds of restrictions were included in the agreement. The first was the provision which required Amano to maintain certain resale price levels for the product in Japan. The second restriction prohibited Amano from dealing with competing products during the term of the contract and for a period of three year after the contract expired. The third restriction banned Amano from manufacturing competing products during the term of the contract and thereafter, presumably for an indefinite period.

Two years after this contract was signed, Amano reported the contract to the JFTC, which decided that the three restrictions contained in the agreement were in violation of the JAA Art. 6. The JFTC issued the formal recommendation to Amano to delete the three requirements from the agreement. Subsequently, the JFTC rendered a recommendation decision, ordering Amano to delete the exclusive dealing provision and the provision prohibiting Amano from producing competing products. The recommendation order did not refer to the provision as to the resale price maintenance because, between the time the recommendation was accepted by Amano and the JFTC issued the recommendation decision, the provision in question was cancelled and the resale price maintenance became moot. Novo, a foreign company and not the subject of the JFTC's recommendation order, filed a lawsuit at the Tokyo High Court seeking to quash the JFTC's order. Presumably, Novo's intent was to have the JFTC's order revoked and to sue Amano for breach of contract.

11. Amano, 16 SINKETUSHU 134 (FTC, 12 June 1970).

The issue in question at the Tokyo High Court case involved the question as to Novo's standing to apply for a court order to quash the recommendation order of the JFTC. Under the Japanese Administrative Litigation Procedure Act, a party bringing a suit to quash an administrative order must prove that his interest has been adversary affected by the order. Without considering the merit of Novo's claim, the Tokyo High Court held that Novo had no standing to sue. The court stated that, given any JFTC's recommendation decision which held a contract unlawful, it did not automatically follow that the contract was null and void as a matter of private laws. Therefore, the court concluded that the JFTC's decision did not necessarily deprive Novo of the right to sue Amano and, Novo's legal interest was not adversary affected by the JFTC's decision. Although Novo appealed to the Supreme Court, it handed down the decision denying Novo's standing to sue. The Supreme Court stated that since the recommendation decision was made by the JFTC on the basis of Amano's acceptance of the recommendation, it was only binding on Amano and Novo, whereas third parties were not bound by it as far as the recommendation was concerned. The court held that Amano, if it was sued by Novo for breach of contract, could not raise the JFTC's decision in its defence and Novo's potential appellant was not adversely affected by the JFTC's recommendation decision.

The rationale employed by the Supreme Court to justify its denial of Novo's standing in this case was based on very complicate reasoning, whereas the conclusion was very clear; foreign parties to an international contract which may violate the JAA Art. 6 do not have standing to bring an action at a Japanese court to quash the JFTC's decisions. This decision represents a narrow interpretation of the standing of private parties to challenge administrative orders in Japan.

The decision has been criticized by commentators as overly harsh and restrictive. In Novo case, if Novo did not have standing to sue, no other party could possibly bring a suit. Amano could not bring a motion to quash the decision since Amano accepted the JFTC's recommendation and would be stopped from taking such legal actions. The standing of someone who is not a party to the contract in question would be even more unlikely. It should also be mentioned that this decision gave Amano an undue advantage over the foreign party. In fact, Amano had nothing to lose by accepting the JFTC's recommendation and subsequent decision. It would serve Amano's best interest to delete the provision in the contract imposing unwanted conditions on Amano at the detriment of Novo.

As a result of this case's ruling, foreign parties to international contracts have little recourse when the JFTC invokes of the JAA Art. 6 against their Japanese partners as far as judicial review of the JFTC's order is concerned. Any injustice which might be caused to foreign parties to international contracts stems from the very nature of the aforementioned interpretation as it applies to international contracts involving unfair business practices. The method of imposing a legal prohibition on the party bearing the burden of a restrictive provision is inherently conductive to abuse by the domestic party.

b. *Komatsu Case*[12]

Although this case was terminated before the final decision was made, it raised a number of important legal issues.

Involved in this case was a joint venture between a Japanese power shovel manufacturer, Komatsu Manufacturing K.K. ('Komatsu') and a United States power shovel manufacture, Bucyrus Erie Company ('Bucyrus'). Komatsu was in need of certain technology to manufacture power shovel and approached Bucyrus. Instead of licensing its technology, however, Bucyrus preferred entering into a joint venture agreement with Komatsu. As such, the joint venture agreement was entered into by Komatsu, Bucyrus, and Mitsui Bussan, in which Komatsu would own 40 per cent, Bucyrus 40 per cent, and Mitsui 20 per cent of the outstanding stocks of the newly established joint venture company known as Komatsu-Bucyrus Company K.K. ('KB'). Bucyrus licensed its technology to KB and KB commissioned Komatsu, its parent company, as the subcontractor, to produce power shovels using the licensed technology. When power shovels were manufactured by Komatsu, they were transferred to KB and KB sold them to Komatsu, which in turn distributed them to customers. KB was in fact merely a paper company which had to pay royalties to Bucyrus for the licensed technology. However, in accordance with the financial arrangements, it was Komatsu which paid the royalties. This arrangement was approved by the Japanese government under the Foreign Investment Act.

The licensing agreement between Bucyrus and KB was subject to cancellation by advance notice by either party. In fact, however, KB was in no position to cancel. While a unanimous resolution of KB's board of directors was required to propose the cancellation of the agreement, Bucyrus was represented on the KB's board and unless Bucyrus directors agreed, a cancellation was impossible. Komatsu grew dissatisfied with this arrangement because it had to keep paying the royalties until Bucyrus chose to cancel the contract.

Komatsu filed a complaint with the JFTC arguing that the joint venture agreement amounted to a unilateral incensing agreement between Komatsu and Bucyrus and Bucyrus had imposed unreasonable royalty payments and cancellation conditions on its Japanese partners. The complaint charged that such agreement infringed the JAA Art. 6.

The JFTC learned its lesson in Amano Case and this time it initiated an open administrative hearing in which both Komatsu and Bucyrus were named respondents. Administrative hearings were held a number of times. Meanwhile, negotiation between Komatsu and Bucyrus continued and finally they reached an agreement. The JFTC thereupon terminated the administrative proceeding and the case was dropped.

Although the conclusion of this case was anti-climatic, some important legal points were raised. First, there was the service of process on the foreign respondent.

12. Komatsu, 28 SINKETUSHU 79 (FTC, 26 October 1981).

The complaint by the JFTC did not state where the complaint was served on Bucyrus, however, the JFTC must have located a Bucyrus office in Japan. Second, the JFTC proceeded against the foreign enterprise as well as the domestic party. This is a much better approach than that taken in the Amano Case, since the foreign respondent is given a chance to argue its case in an open hearing and should a ruling be made against it, there would be no question that it would have standing to challenge the JFTC's decision at the Tokyo High Court.

Third, the agreement at issue was approved by the Japanese government under the Foreign Investment Act. It was made clear an approval under the Foreign Investment Act did not provide any immunity from the JAA. In fact, there was a provision in the act to the effect that an approval under the act would not affect the power of the JFTC in any way. Although the Foreign Investment Act no longer exists, a similar question might arise concerning measures taken under the Foreign Exchange and Foreign Trade Control Act which also contains a provision that approval under such act does not affect the power of the JFTC to challenge enterprises.

Chapter 4

Importance of Compliance Program under the Japanese Antimonopoly Act

In practice, under the JAA, it is imperative to design an antitrust compliance program that can deter firms' anticompetitive activities.

Under the JAA, a sound antitrust compliance program should have two principal objectives: prevention and detection. The true benefit of compliance programs is to prevent the commission of the JAA violations, not to enable firms that commit such violations to escape punishment for them. This should be true for the company as well. Every first and primary objective in their compliance program should be to prevent wrongdoing. A second important objective of a compliance program is to detect wrongdoing as early as possible, while the damages are still small. Early detection of the JAA violation will give a company a head start in the race for minimizing anticipated damages. In Japan, it has been rather a rare case where an employee who committed JAA violations was acting solely for his own benefit and not the firms' benefit. This trend clearly shows how important it is to demonstrate in an effective compliance program that JAA violations will never benefit firms. A strong compliance program may help any firms in Japan and those affecting Japanese market to avoid being challenged and to incurring huge damages due to antitrust enforcements, so long as the firms take aggressive steps to discipline the wrongdoers and ensure that future violations do not occur.

There are several essential factors which enable compliance program to function well in light of the JAA:

(i) Clearly established compliance standards;
(ii) Assigning overall responsibility to oversee compliance through firms;
(iii) Exercising due care not to delegate responsibility to employees who have a propensity to engage in illegal conduct;

(iv) Taking reasonable steps to communicate standards and procedures effectively to all employees;
(v) Taking reasonable steps to achieve compliance with standards;
(vi) Consistent enforcement of standards through appropriate disciplinary mechanisms; and
(vii) Taking reasonable steps when an offence occurs to respond and to present future violations.

In order for a compliance program to be truly effective, it must be customized to fit the firm's business, organization, personnel, and culture.

It should be noted, with regard to the element of 'effective communication', that every compliance program should include a clear statement of the firms' commitment to comply with the JAA, accompanied by a set of practical do's and don'ts written in plain languages so that everybody in the firms can understand them. A policy statement is, however, only the beginning. Under the JAA, firms should develop active training programs that include in-person instruction by knowledgeable counsel. The in-person training sessions can be supplemented by video and Internet training tools, but these are no replacements for some personal instruction. The instruction should be as practical as possible, including case studies drawn from the firms' actual experiences. The instruction should also include education as to the consequences of JAA violations, both for the firms and for the individual employees.

With regard to the essential element of 'steps to achieve compliance', it should also be noted that while training is important, it is not sufficient to assure compliance with the JAA. To achieve that goal, firms must have a proactive law department that is dedicated to practicing preventive law. It is critical that the firms' lawyers regularly attend management meetings and regularly visit the firms' facilities so that employees know whom to call if they have a question or a problem. It is also critical that the lawyers gain the respect of their clients by responding quickly to questions with sound legal advice that takes full account of the practical business issues the clients face. Firms also need to have in place and to publicize a reporting system so that employees know whom to report possible misconduct. In spite of the fact that many Japanese companies have been reluctant to develop these systems, thus accumulating small practical examples, it would be one idea to establish ombudsmen and hot lines for this purpose. It would be another idea to require employees to report possible wrongdoing to the law department. Whatever system is in place, it should assure employees seeking to report misconduct confidentiality and protection from retaliation. Finally, a company should conduct regular antitrust audits, preferably unannounced, to monitor compliance. These audits can be kept informal, but should include a review of both paper and computer files (especially e-mails) of employees with competitive decision-making authority or sales and marketing responsibilities. It is important also to interview employees about their business and their contacts with competitors.

With regard to the element of 'consistent standard', under the real practice of the JAA, it is absolutely critical that firms establish a record of consistently disciplining employees who disregard the firms' compliance policy or who fail to report misconduct by others. In so doing, the firms should discipline senior managers who failed adequately to supervise or who created a climate of disrespect for antitrust principles in their organizations, even if they did not have actual knowledge of the particular wrongdoing.

In addition to the *above* and more important than any of the aforementioned elements, under the JAA, it is indispensable to take reasonable steps to respond to violations. This includes initiating an immediate investigation and reporting promptly to the JFTC. In addition to disciplining the employees responsible, it would be also necessary to take steps to make restitution to its customers, either through settling the private damage actions or through commercial arrangements directly with the customers. If JAA violations should occur, it is also necessary to re-examine compliance programs in order to learn from its mistakes and to make whatever modifications are necessary to ensure that future violations do not occur. In so doing, it should be noted, in light of Japanese industrial culture, that nothing is more important than senior managements' commitment and leadership to compliance with the JAA. In Japanese companies, a culture of competition begins at the very top of the company. Respect for the JAA is a necessary, but not sufficient, condition to achieve this goal. Senior managements must be vocal in making that commitment known to employees. In addition to strong, positive leadership, it is important also that a company have sound incentive structures in place. There should be strong negative incentives against violating the JAA and strong positive incentives for reporting and deterring violations.

In counselling especially Japanese clients and conducting antitrust audits in light of the JAA, there are several common red flags to look for.

First, it is necessary to see, when firms are members of trade associations, whether or not the positions of attendees at trade association meetings match the ostensible purpose of the meeting, whether or not the association is gathering detailed industry data, especially specific transaction data or forward-looking pricing and output data, whether or not meetings are attended by counsel and whether or not there is an agenda for the meetings and a record of what was discussed.

Second, it is necessary to see firms' market shares to examine if they are more stable than they would be expected to be in a competitive market. Market shares that are stable over a long period of time are a strong indicator of the JAA violations.

Third, it is necessary to see whether or not firms' executives have been receiving calls at home or from callers giving fictitious names or refusing to identify themselves. When conducting audits, therefore, it is necessary to talk not only to the executives, but to their assistants.

Fourth, it is necessary to see whether or not there are unexplained price increases and copies of competitor price announcements in the firms' files. If anything is found, it is always necessary to look for where they came from.

[STRICTLY CONFIDENTIAL]

Compliance Manual on the Japanese Antimonopoly Act NISHIFUKA International Inc.[1]

APRIL 2006

1. Note that Nishifuka International Inc. is a fictitious company, mentioned in this book solely for the purpose of introducing the sample compliance manual under the Japanese Antimonopoly Act.

Compliance Manual of the Japanese Antimonopoly Act Nishifuka International Inc.

PREFACE

It is Nishifuka's policy to strictly comply with all applicable laws.

This includes in particular compliance with antitrust and competition laws as being in force both on a national and a supranational level, e.g. in the European Union (hereafter 'Competition Laws').

The objective of Competition Laws is to preserve a free economy by assuring competition in the market place. Real competition only works if each company determines its strategies and policies, e.g. price policy, without any involvement (discussions, exchange of information etc.) of competitors, i.e. anyone who offers in the same market products and/or services which, from the customer's point of view, may serve the same purpose.

Therefore, as a general rule, any discussion or agreement with competitors, distributors, suppliers etc. in whatever form, with the object or effect to prevent, restrict or distort competition, is in violation of Competition Laws and this manual. Major violations, such as price fixing or pre-determining the winner of a project, are against the customers' interests, as customers may have to pay higher prices or may not have the desired choice of products or services.

Competition Laws are complex and their violation may result in serious consequences both for Nishifuka and for employees involved, such as huge fines imposed by antitrust authorities (e.g. the European Commission may impose a maximum fine of 10 per cent of the annual world-wide turnover of involved companies/groups), possibly civil lawsuits resulting in substantial damage claims from customers (e.g. class actions in the US), disciplinary sanctions for involved employees and in some jurisdictions (particularly in the US) even criminal sanctions against such employees.

Therefore, this manual is designed to provide employees a basic understanding of Competition Laws and their application to Nishifuka's business.

Not knowing that a specific conduct is illegal, is not accepted as an excuse or a defence. This means, that you are strongly advised: to seek legal advice from your internal or external lawyer or legal department, if you are unsure about the conduct in any such situations; to assure compliance with this manual by clear instructions and thorough training.

I. OUTLINE OF THE JAPANESE ANTIMONOPOLY ACT

> The management policy of the Company is 'creditworthy and fair management', and it is a responsibility of the Company to comply with the Japanese Antimonopoly Act which aims to promote 'free and fair competition' at markets.

1. *Japanese Antimonopoly Act*

'Law Concerning Prohibition of Private Monopolization and Maintenance of Fair Trade' (Law No. 54 of 1947, hereinafter, the 'Antimonopoly Act') is an important law which aims to promote 'free and fair competition' in the market, and to thereby stimulate the creative initiative of entrepreneurs and to protect the interests of consumers in general. As described *below*, the Antimonopoly Act prohibits an entrepreneur from engaging in (1) the restraint of 'free and fair competition' by consulting with other entrepreneurs, (2) the unjustly maintenance of its monopolistic position or the unjust exclusion of other competitors, or (3) the distorting of any competition by using any of the 16 types of unfair trade practices.

2. *No Cartel*

Among the three prohibited conducts mentioned *above*, the conduct referred to in item (1) is called 'unreasonable restraint of trade (cartel)', which means 'to mutually restrict business activities by making cooperative decisions concerning sales price, sales volume, consolidation of manufacturing facilities and restriction of business partners among competitors, thereby causing substantial restricting of the competition in any field of trade'. This unreasonable restraint of trade includes conducts such as 'bid rigging', 'price cartel', 'market segmentation cartel', 'transaction terms cartel', 'cartel on supply restriction', 'trading partner restriction cartel', and others.

Even if the competitors are only exchanging information, this shall be illegal under the Antimonopoly Act as cartel practices if any 'implicit understanding' or common intention is formed among the companies by such exchange. Particularly, the Company should avoid exchanging information relating to price.

The Japanese Fair Trade Commission puts utmost effort in strictly regulating these cartel practices. Since there are quite a number of manufacturers, any person should be very careful with respect to this matter upon contacting other competitors.

3. *Prohibition of Private Monopolization*

The conduct stated in (2) *above* is called 'private monopolization', which means that the entrepreneurs 'exclude or control the business activities of other entrepreneurs, thereby causing, contrary to the public interest, a substantial restraint of competition in any particular field of trade'. Specifically, this means any conduct by a company with high market share which prevents the participation of new entrants or restrain the business activities of other competitors by using unjust means (in many cases, but not limited to, any means that violate the Act) in order to increase or maintain its market share.

4. Prohibition of Unfair Trade Practices

'Unfair Trade Practices' described in (3) *above* means 16 types of conduct designated by the Japanese Fair Trade Commission which may inhibit fair trade (efficient competition). These types of conduct are prohibited as preliminary acts of aforementioned cartel or private monopolization.

(i) Concerted refusal to deal
(ii) Other refusal to deal
(iii) Discriminatory pricing
(iv) Discriminatory treatment of transaction terms, etc.
(v) Discriminatory treatment in a trade association
(vi) Unjust low price sales
(vii) Unjust high price purchasing
(viii) Deceptive customer inducement
(ix) Customer inducement by unjust benefits
(x) Tie-in sales, etc.
(xi) Dealing on exclusive terms
(xii) Resale price maintenance
(xiii) Dealing on restrictive terms
(xiv) Abuse of dominant bargaining position
(xv) Interference with a competitor's transaction
(xvi) Interference with internal operation of a competitor's company

[Laws, etc.]
Articles 3 and 19 of the Antimonopoly Act
Unfair Trade Practices (Fair Trade Commission Notification No. 15 of 1982)

[Punishment]

(1) Punishment (in case of private monopolization and unreasonable restraint of trade (Cartel))
  (i) Performer: penal servitude for not more than three (3) years or by a fine of not more than five (5) million yen (Article 89 of the Antimonopoly Law)
  (ii) Corporate Representative: a fine of not more than five (5) million yen (Article 95 – 2 of the Antimonopoly Law)
  (iii) Corporation: a fine of not more than five hundred (500) million yen (Article 95 of the Antimonopoly Law)
(2) Order of Elimination Measures (in all cases, Articles 7 and 20 of the Antimonopoly Act)
(3) Surcharges (in case of unreasonable restraint of trade (Cartel), Article 7 – 2 of the Antimonopoly Act)
(4) Other Claims for Damages from Victims (civil liability)

[For reference]
Legal Department

II. Relations with Competitors

A. Unreasonable Restraint of Trade (Cartel)

1. The competitors shall not make any arrangement concerning sales price, or hold any discussions which may lead to such arrangement.
2. The competitors shall not make any arrangement concerning purchase price, or hold any discussions which may lead to such arrangement.
3. The competitors shall not make any arrangement or hold discussions concerning production volume, sales volume, trading partner, sales territory, type/quality/standard, etc. of products, establishment of new facilities and operation restriction.

1. The cartel practices such as 'price cartel', 'market segmentation cartel', 'supply restriction cartel', and 'bid rigging' as mentioned *above* are handled under the *quasi per se* illegal principle, and basically, arguments which claim that the conduct was intended to prevent any price decrease by avoiding unnecessary competition or to fairly allocate the total demand are not acceptable.

2. Even when there are no express decisions, if there was an implicit understanding or common intention concerning the sales and purchase price among the competitors, and as a result, the competition at the markets was substantially restricted, then it shall be concluded to be illegal. With respect to the maintenance of price, determining the minimum sales price, rate of price increase or decrease, or setting up the rebates, commissions, etc. and other factors that are substantial components of pricing (including matters regarding contributions to retailers and contracts with artists) shall constitute a price cartel.

3. Other than directly restricting the production volume and sales volume, indirect restriction of volumes such as the conduct of restricting the purchase volume of raw materials and operation of facilities shall also constitute a cartel on supply restriction.

4. In the case where the same matters are on the verge of being agreed in a trade association, the Company's employee should firmly declare that no consent can be made due to the possibility of violating the Antimonopoly Act. After leaving the place of discussion, return to the Company immediately to submit a report in writing to the superior concerning this incident. Failure to do so may result in the Company being considered to have agreed to the matter.

[Laws, etc.]
Article 3 of the Antimonopoly Act (Unreasonable Restraint of Trade)

[For reference]
Legal Department

B. Sole Distributorship Contracts Between Competitors and Interference of Parallel Imports

> 1. In case of executing sole distributorship contract [exclusive contract] between certain entrepreneurs, consult with the Legal Department.
> 2. Any interference of parallel import by other entrepreneurs is forbidden.

1. If any sole distributorship contract is executed between competitors, it may eliminate competition between the two parties, or help reinforce the market status of the entrepreneur, which becomes the sole distributor. Thus, depending on the products covered under the contract or the entrepreneur's market status which serves as the sole distributor, the contract may violate the Antimonopoly Act. It should be noted that parallel import shall mean that in the case of a sole import distributorship contract, a product covered by the contract is imported by a third party by way of channels other than that arranged between the contracting parties, on the assumption that the imported product is a genuine product which does not infringe trademark rights.

2. The sole distributor or supplier may not conduct the following conduct to maintain the price of products covered by the contract, since it shall be illegal:

(1) In case where a parallel importer makes an offer to purchase to the supplier's overseas trading partner, to cause such overseas trading partner not to sell the products to the parallel importer;
(2) To induce a supplier's overseas trading partner to cease selling any product to the parallel importer, by means such as tracing the supply channel of parallel import goods by checking their serial number and the like and notifying the same to the supplier or its overseas trading partner;
(3) To induce the wholesaler or the trading partner, not to sell the product to a retailer that is handling parallel import goods;
(4) To cause the entrepreneur which is handling parallel import goods to cease and desist in handling them, while alleging, without adequate reasons, that they are counterfeit;
(5) To corner the parallel import goods sold by the retailer;
(6) In the case where it is extremely difficult for any party other than the sole distributor or its distributors to repair the parallel import goods or obtain necessary repair parts, to refuse the repair work or the supply of repair parts or induce the distributors to refuse such repair work or supply of repair parts solely due to the fact that these parallel import goods are not being handled by its own company; or
(7) To induce magazines, newspapers and other media, which are its trading partners, not to carry advertisements on the parallel import goods or in

any manner obstruct the advertising activities of the parallel import goods.

[Laws, etc.]
Article 19 of the Antimonopoly Act, Article 13 and 15 of the general designation

[For reference]
Legal Department

C. Activities of Trade Association

> The trade associations may not engage in the following conduct:
>
> 1. To substantially restrain competition in any particular field of trade;
> 2. To execute international agreements or international contracts which contain such matters that constitute unreasonable restraint of trade or unfair trade practices;
> 3. To limit the number of constituent entrepreneurs;
> 4. To unjustly restrict the functions or activities of constituent entrepreneurs; and
> 5. To cause the entrepreneurs to engage in any unfair trade practices.

1. 'Trade association' shall refer to any association which was organized with its principal purpose to enhance the common business interests of the entrepreneurs. The trade associations which Nishifuka belongs to in Japan are as follows:

- Better Bread Study Association in Akasaka
- Japan Music Software Association
- Software Distribution Study Group Roppongi

2. 'Guidelines Concerning the Activities of Trade Associations' was set forth by the Japanese Fair Trade Commission effective October 1995.

3. In the case where the *above* matters are on the verge of being agreed to within the trade association, Nishifuka's employee **shall firmly declare** that no consent can be made due to the possibility of violating the Antimonopoly Act. After leaving the place of discussion, return to the company immediately to submit a report in writing to the superior concerning this incident. Failure to do so may result in Nishifuka being considered to have failed to take necessary measures to prevent or improve the plan or conduct which may be violating the Antimonopoly Act, and thereby Nishifuka, which is a member of the trade association, may also become subject to punishment.

[Laws, etc.]
Article 8 of the Antimonopoly Law

[Punishment]

(1) Punishment (in case of *above* paragraphs 1. to 4.)

(i) Performer:

(in case of 1): penal servitude for not more than three (3) years or by a fine of not more than five (5) million yen (Article 89 of the Antimonopoly Act)

(in cases 2 to 4): penal servitude of not more than two (2) years or by a fine of not more than three (3) million yen (Article 90 of the Antimonopoly Act)

(ii) Corporate Representative:

(in case of 1): a fine of not more than five (5) million yen (Article 95 – 3 of the Antimonopoly Act)

(in cases 2 to 4): a fine of not more than three (3) million yen (Article 95 – 3 of the Antimonopoly Act)

(iii) Corporation:

(in case of 1): a fine of not more than five hundred (500) million yen (Article 95 of the Antimonopoly Act)

(in cases 2 to 4): a fine of not more than three (3) million yen (Article 95 of the Antimonopoly Act)

(2) Order of Elimination Measures (in all cases, Article 8 – 2 of the Antimonopoly Act)

(3) Surcharges (in cases 1 and 2, Article 8 – 3 and Article 7 – 2 of the Antimonopoly Act)

(4) Other Claims for Damages from Victims (civil liability)

[For reference]
Legal Department

III. Sales Relations (Unfair Trade Practices)

A. Concerted or Independent Refusals to Deal

1. No refusal or restriction shall be imposed concertedly with competitors or trading partners, concerning deals with a certain entrepreneur or new entrant. 2. No unjust refusal or restriction on any deals with trading partners shall be made.

1. Basically, since Nishifuka has the freedom of choice to decide its trading partners, it shall not be problematic under the Antimonopoly Act even if Nishifuka decides not to deal with a certain trading partner under its own judgment. Provided,

however, that Nishifuka may not refuse to deal with a trading partner which did not comply with the means that were intended to maintain the resale price, to violating the Antimonopoly Act such as imposing restrictions on trade practices or achieve unjust purposes (independent refusal to deal), and Nishifuka may also not refuse to deal with a particular trading partner in concert among competitors or with entrepreneurs and distributors.

2. Concerted or independent refusal to deal not only includes conduct by which Nishifuka personally refuses to deal with the counterparty, but also the conduct instructing other competitors or trading partners such as wholesalers or retailers to refuse to deal with such counter party. Particularly, since various entrepreneurs are involved in such concerted refusal to deal, Nishifuka's employee should be aware that such conduct is likely to be illegal in principle.

3. Refusal to deal is likely to occur in cases where the counterparty continues to offer cheap sales prices, the counterparty newly enters into the business industry, or the counterparty obtains an abundant trading volume through a franchise system.

[Laws, etc.]
Article 19 of the Antimonopoly Act, Article 1 and 2 of the general designation

[For reference]
Legal Department

B. Discriminatory Pricing or Discriminatory Treatment

1. No payment of rebates shall be made which have the function of restricting the business activities of the trading partners.
2. No unjust discrimination of price or transaction terms shall be done depending on the territory or trading partners.
3. In the case where any discrimination shall be set forth for any rebates, trading price, transaction terms determined by Nishifuka for each trading partner, Nishifuka's employee should inform the Legal Department in advance. This is because although the discrimination based on justified reasons are allowed, such as discrimination in accordance with annual or monthly volume, or discrimination in accordance with the level of achievement of a campaign, determining the validity of the discrimination is difficult.

1. If the price discrimination by rebate, discriminatory price, discriminatory treatment of transaction terms, etc., are based on reasonable cause such as to reflect the difference of sales volume, in the case where the cost differences depending on the territory, or rebates are set forth in accordance with the level of achievement of a campaign, the discrimination shall be considered to be under justified reasons in principle. However, the provision of rebates, discriminatory pricing and

discriminatory treatment of transaction terms which may become the means to maintain the sales price, treatment of products by competitors and trading partners, shall thereby restrict the business activities of the distributors. Thus, such conduct may be illegal.

2. Since these are difficult matters to consider when determining validity, the Company's employee should make a determination through the Legal Department at all times.

[Laws, etc.]
Article 19 of the Antimonopoly Act, Article 3 and 4 of the general designation

[For reference]
Legal Department

C. Unjust Low Price Sales

The products of the Company may not be sold continuously at a price excessively below the manufacturing cost which the Company incurred, for the purpose of winning the competition against other competitors.

1. In general, it shall be considered to be an unjust low price sales when a party sells a product at a price (1) excessively below the cost incurred in supplying the product (manufacturing cost and general management fee), (2) the sale is carried out continuously (generally for more than one (1) or two (2) months), and (3) the sales may cause difficulties to the business activities of other entrepreneurs.

2. However, unjust low price sales may be permitted in cases where it is conducted in order to reduce the products in stock, or to compete with competitors who are also cutting price. In the case where Nishifuka needs to sell the products at a price below the manufacturing cost, Nishifuka's employee must contact the Legal Department, since determining whether or not such low prices sales are permissible is difficult.

3. It is generally believed that it is extremely difficult for the Japanese Fair Trade Commission to prove this violation of the Act for manufacturers, since verifying the manufacturing cost is difficult if the concerned party is a manufacturer. Therefore, many of the violation matters related to this paragraph shall mostly be the retailers, since verifying the purchase price is relatively easy.

[Laws, etc.]
Article 19 of the Antimonopoly Law, Article 6 of the general designation

[For reference]
Legal Department

D. Deceptive Customer Inducement (Premiums and Representations Act)

Upon selling the Company's product, no advertisements, etc. shall be made which use expressions that may cause the customers to misunderstand that the product is much better than the actual product or the competitors' product, or advertisements which may cause the consumers to misunderstand that the Company's product is much more favourable than those of other entrepreneurs.

1. Act Against Unjustifiable Premiums and Misleading Representations (Act No. 134 of 1962, hereinafter the 'Premiums and Representations Act') is a special act under the Antimonopoly Act with the purpose of securing fair competition and protect the interests of consumers in general by preventing inducement of customers by unjustifiable means. This Act prohibits the 'misrepresentation' and 'excessive provision of premiums' which may cause consumers to misunderstand.

2. Any advertisements using expressions indicating that a product is much more favourable than the actual one and cause consumers to inadvertently purchase a product thinking it is another product are called 'deceptive customer inducements' and are prohibited.

3. For example, even if the expression 'best-selling product' is true, there would be less danger to cause any misunderstandings such as by using a 'note' to add objective expressions such as 'amount of sales for the previous month according to the Better Bread Study Association in Akasaka's survey'.

[Laws, etc.]
Article 19 of the Antimonopoly Act, Article 8 of the general designation, Article 4 of the Premiums and Representations Act

[For reference]
Legal Department

E. Customer Inducement Under Unjust Interests (Premiums and Representations Act)

Upon selling the Company's products, as a rule, the following rules should be complied with when offering premiums. Provided, however, contact the Legal Department for reference since there are exceptions regarding this matter.

1. 10 per cent Rule

The value of a premium offered to all consumers in general shall be within ten (10) per cent of the transaction (sales price) value included in the premium offer, and which is found reasonable in light of normal business practices.

2. 20 Times Rule

The maximum value of the premiums offered by lotteries or prize competitions shall not exceed 20 times of the value of the transaction (sales price) in connection with the lotteries or prize competition (when the price involved in the transaction exceeds JPY 100,000, the maximum value shall be JPY 100,000). Also, the aggregate of the premiums offered by lotteries or prize competitions in one scheme shall not exceed two (2) per cent of the estimated total value of transactions in connection with the lotteries or prize competitions in that scheme.

3. Paragraphs 1 and 2 *above* are regarded as different schemes, and therefore, it is possible to conduct the two schemes in parallel form.

[Laws, etc.]

Article 19 of the Antimonopoly Act, Article 9 of the general designation, Article 3 of the Premiums and Representations Act

Restriction on Premium Offers to General Consumers (Japanese Fair Trade Commission Notification No. 5 of 1977, Japanese Fair Trade Commission Notification No. 2 of 1996 (revised)), Restriction on Premium Offers by Lotteries or Prize Competition (Japanese Fair Trade Commission Notification No. 3 of 1977, Japanese Fair Trade Commission Notification No. 1 of 1996, as amended)

[For reference]

Legal Department

F. Tie-In Sales

Upon selling the Company's products to distributors, no enforcement of any tie-in sales, which only allows the sale a product of the Company together with another certain product, shall be taken.

From the consumer and retailer's point of view, if they are forced to purchase a product which they do not want when purchasing their target product, the enforcement of such purchase may infringe the freedom of choice concerning the products held by the consumer or the retailer. Thus, the conduct is prohibited under the Antimonopoly Act as tie-in sales.

[Laws, etc.]

Article 19 of the Antimonopoly Law, Article 10 of the general designation

[For reference]

Legal Department

G. Dealing on Exclusive Terms and Dealing on Restrictive Terms (Vertical Non-Price Restraints)

1. No restrictions shall be imposed on trading partners such as wholesalers and retailers regarding handling of competing products.
2. No assignment of a specific territory shall be made which causes the trading partners to restrict sales outside the territory.
3. To cause wholesalers to specify the trading partner to which the products are being sold, to cause the wholesalers to restrict the supply to retailers who deal with certain wholesalers, or, to impose a restriction by instructing the wholesalers not to sell the products is not allowed.
4. No restriction of sales methods shall be made such as (1) restricting the retailers concerning the prices presented at stores and on fliers, etc., or prohibiting the retailers from producing advertisements which expressly indicate the price, or, (2) causing advertising media such as magazines and newspapers to refuse to publish advertisements of bargain sales or which expressly indicate the price.
5. No restriction shall be imposed on the sales price of the retailers by means of restricting the sales methods.
6. Restrictions on handling competing products, sales territories, trading partners and sales practices may be permitted depending on the circumstances. Thus, with regard to applying the restrictions on the matters stated *above*, consult the Legal Department in advance.

1. Other than the conduct explained *above*, even if the conduct is not directly related to the handling of competing products, restriction of sales territories, dealing with competitors, and restriction of sales methods, similar discriminating conducts which sets a low price or offers large amount of rebates to trading partners, such as wholesalers and retailers who agree to such restrictions, or which gives financial disadvantages to trading partners which do not accept Nishifuka's request, may be problematic under the Antimonopoly Act.

2. In the case where the restriction on the handling of competing products and sales territories is imposed by an 'influential manufacturer in a market', and if the restriction may result in making it difficult for new entrants or existing competitors to easily secure alternative distribution channels, or may cause the price of such competing product to be maintained, then such restriction shall be deemed illegal under the Antimonopoly Act. Whether a manufacturer is an 'influential manufacturer in a market', shall be in the first instance judged by the market share of the manufacturer, that is, whether or not it has no less than 10 per cent of the market share or its position is within the top three in the market.

3. There are many conducts which fall under the conduct described in article 13 of the general designation (Dealing on Restrictive Terms).

[Laws, etc.]
Article 19 of the Antimonopoly Act, Article 2, 11, 13 of the general designation

[For reference]
Legal Department

H. Resale Price Maintenance

1. No restriction on wholesale price or retail price of the distributors shall be imposed.
2. Nishifuka's employee shall not cause the distributor to sell at the price indicated by Nishifuka under a written or oral agreement between the trading partner.
3. In the case where any artificial means, such as imposing or suggesting to impose economic disadvantage if sales are not made at Nishifuka's indicated price, Nishifuka's employees shall not cause the distributors to sell at the indicated price.
4. The following acts may not be conducted:
   (i) Collecting sales price reports, patrolling retail establishments, conducting price supervision by sales persons dispatched to shops, examining ledgers or records of retailers, and others in order to ascertain whether sales are being made at Nishifuka's indicated price;
   (ii) Identifying price-cutting distributors by making use of secret marks and requesting wholesalers who supplied goods to such distributors not to sell them;
   (iii) Buying goods from price-cutting distributors and requesting such distributors or wholesalers who supplied them to buy the goods or pay the cost of their purchases;
   (iv) Transmitting complaints to price-cutting distributors from nearby distributors with regard to low-price sales, and causing the price-cutting distributors to end such sales.

1. Since it is one of the most basic matters for an entrepreneur to determine its own sales price in accordance with the business conditions, any activities which may restrict the free pricing power of the counterparty (complete discretion concerning the sales price) shall not be allowed. In particular, the restrictive activities may not be conducted against small wholesalers or retailers. This is due to the fact that small distributors are more unlikely to be able to resist Nishifuka's request.

2. Resale price maintenance is considered the *quasi per se* illegal under the Antimonopoly Act, and if any of the restrictive conduct is identified, the conduct shall be immediately detected.

3. Exemption of Resale Price Maintenance

Although any resale price maintenance is basically illegal under the Antimonopoly Act, such provisions of the Antimonopoly Act do not apply to the 'products designated by the Japanese Fair Trade Commission (resale designated products)' and 'copyrighted works' (Article 23 of the Antimonopoly Law). As of June 2003, all designations for the resale designated products have been cancelled, and resale price maintenance may be conducted only with regard to the 'copyrighted works' (interpreted and managed by the Japanese Fair Trade Commission that the copyrighted works refer to six (6) items: books, magazines, newspapers, records, audio cassette tapes and audio CDs).

With respect to records, audio cassette tapes and audio CDs related to such products, the Company has adopted the following voluntary rules in response to the Japanese Fair Trade Commission's request to improve the negative effects of the distribution systems and business practices under the current resale price maintenance system: (1) flexible operation of the resale price maintenance system such as limited resale (a method by which to limit the term of resale to six months, one year, two years, etc. after publication; (2) diversified pricing such as through the introduction of various discount systems; (3) securement of independent usage and condition of the resale price maintenance by entrepreneurs; (4) securement of sales promotion methods by the retailer to consumers, such as distribution of coupons; (5) diversification of distribution routes such as utilization of mail-order sales and direct sales, as well as diversification of pricing in accordance thereof; or (6) facilitation and rationalization of distribution and clarification of trading relations.

[Laws, etc.]

Article 19 of the Antimonopoly Law, Article 12 of the general designation (Concerning exemptions: Article 23 of the Antimonopoly Act)

'Status of Discussions and Opinions Concerning the Revision of Resale System for Copyrighted Works' (prepared by the Japanese Fair Trade Commission as of 7 December 2000), and 'Engagements in Flexible Operation of Resale System for Audio CDs, etc. (as of 31 October 2002)' (submitted to the Japanese Fair Trade Commission from the Recording Industry Association of Japan on 26 December 2002)

[For reference]

Legal Department

I. Abuse of Dominant Bargaining Position

1. In the case where Nishifuka is in a dominant position relative to its counterparty regarding the continuous business relationship between such counterparty, Nishifuka may not, by making use of that position, unjustly coerce the counterparty to purchase Nishifuka's products in light of normal business practices.

> 2. In the case where Nishifuka is in a dominant position relative to its counterparty regarding the continuous business relationship between such counterparty, Nishifuka may not, by making use of that position, cause the counterparty to provide money, service and any other economic interests (including collection of contributions, or request for dispatch of employees).

1. In the 'abuse of dominant bargaining position' section under the Antimonopoly Act, (i) any party in a dominant bargaining position over its counterparty (ii) is prohibited to unjustly abuse such position. This is a kind of so-called basket provision (general provision), and it is believed to be difficult to identify the abuse as provided for in the Antimonopoly Act.

2. Therefore, coercion of a counterparty to engage in certain actions may be deemed illegal under the Antimonopoly Act. Such conducts include: coercion to engage in campaigns by manufacturers, coercion to purchase the unmarketable products in the manufacturer's stock, contributions to increase profits on the balance sheet at the end of terms which are unrelated to sales of products, etc. Conducting such actions may definitely result in the counterparty filing a notification to the Japanese Fair Trade Commission.

[Laws, etc.]
Article 19 of the Antimonopoly Law, Article 14 of the general designation

[For reference]
Legal Department

IV. Purchase Relations (Unfair Trade Practices)

A. Concerted or Independent Refusals to Deal

No refusal to deal with, or causing other party to deal with, new entrant competitors or existing competitors (1) by agreement between competitors, (2) concertedly with the entrepreneurs and its trading partners, or (3) by refusal to deal by a trade association shall be made. In addition, although a single entrepreneur basically has the freedom of choice to decide its trading partners, Nishifuka may not refuse to deal with a party with the objective to engage in conduct that is in breach of the Antimonopoly Act.

B. Discriminatory Pricing or Discriminatory Treatment

No unjust discriminatory treatment shall be made to the trading partners with respect to the purchase price or transaction terms.

C. Unjust High Price Purchasing

> No unjust high price purchase of any product or service shall be made, which shall cause difficulties to the business activities of other entrepreneurs.

To unjustly purchase any product or service at a high price in order to exclude other competitors is prohibited under the Antimonopoly Act for similar reasons as are described in regard to unjust low price sales.

[Laws, etc.]
Article 19 of the Antimonopoly Law, Article 7 of the general designation

[For reference]
Legal Department

D. Dealing on Exclusive Terms and Dealing on Restrictive Terms (Vertical Non-Price Restraints)

> 1. No terms shall be imposed on the trading partners, such as raw material suppliers and component manufacturers, that they shall not deal with Nishifuka's competitors.
> 2. Upon purchasing the products of the trading partners, no dealings that set terms to purchase Nishifuka's products (reciprocal dealings) shall be conducted.
> 3. Since there are cases where these restrictions shall not always be illegal, consult the Legal Department in advance upon conducting these restrictions.

1. The restriction of trade with competitors shall be deemed illegal under the Antimonopoly Act in the case where the restrictions imposed by an 'influential entrepreneur in a markets' result in reducing business opportunities of competitors or making it difficult for such competitors to easily find alternative trading partners. 'Influential entrepreneur in a market' shall be in the first instance judged by the market share of the entrepreneur, that is, whether it has no less than 10 per cent market share or its position is within the top three in the market.

2. With respect to reciprocal dealings, this shall be deemed illegal under the Antimonopoly Act in cases where the influential entrepreneur in the market forces other parties to purchase its own products, and such obligation results in reducing the business opportunities of entrepreneurs other than the trading partners which can purchase the products, or the competitors of the *above mentioned* influential entrepreneur, or makes it difficult for these parties to easily find alternative trading partners. Depending on the form of transactions or the position in the market, the reciprocal dealings may be judged as tie-in sales (article 10 of the general

designation) or abuse of dominant bargaining position (article 14 of the general designation).

3. Other than the *above*, any conduct such as establishing counteracting pricing to maintain continuous business relations shall constitute dealing on restrictive terms. There are many types of conduct that falls under the conduct described in article 13 of the general designation (Dealing on Restrictive Terms).

[Laws, etc.]
Article 19 of the Antimonopoly Act, Article 2, 11, 13 of the general designation

[For reference]
Legal Department

E. Abuse of Dominant Bargaining Position

No conduct shall be performed which, by using its dominant bargaining position on the strength of continuous transaction relationships, renders unjust disadvantage in light of normal business practices to its trading partners concerning conditions or implementation of transactions. The decision on whether or not Nishifuka is 'in a dominant bargaining position' is a difficult task, since it shall be comprehensively decided by considering its position in the market, the possibility of change of its trading partners, supply and demand of products, etc. However, the following conducts (which are related to reciprocal dealing) shall not be performed:

(1) For the person in charge of purchasing to request the trading partner (counterparty) to purchase Nishifuka's products;
(2) To make an organized or intentional request to another party to purchase Nishifuka's products;
(3) To request any party with no intention to purchase Nishifuka's products to purchase the same; or
(4) To request other party to purchase Nishifuka's products while insinuating that the transaction relationship may be affected in the future if they are not purchased.

F. Compliance with the Subcontract Act

1. Act Against Delay in Payment of Subcontract Proceeds, Etc. to Subcontractors (Act No. 120 of 1956, hereinafter, the 'Subcontract Act') aims to protect the interests of the subcontractors, and thereby contributing to the wholesome development of the national economy. Under this Act, entrepreneurs who hold more than a certain amount of capital or equity ('parental entrepreneur') may not, upon giving manufacturing commission or repairing commission to entrepreneurs holding less than a certain amount of capital or equity, delay payment of subcontract proceeds, unjustly fix a

low amount of subcontract proceeds, or refuse to receive work or return the products without any reasonable cause, etc.

2. Upon giving manufacturing commission or repairing commission to subcontractors with respect to Nishifuka's products, Nishifuka shall comply with the Subcontract Act.

V. Other Regulations Under the Antimonopoly Act

Other than the *above*, Nishifuka shall comply with the provisions under the Antimonopoly Act concerning the restrictions on stockholding, interlocking directorates, mergers and acquisition of business, necessary notifications and reports.

[Translation]

Act Concerning Prohibition of Private Monopolization and Maintenance of Fair Trade (Act No. 54 of 14 April 1947)

TABLE OF CONTENTS

Chapter I
General Provisions

Art. 1 *[Purpose]*

This Act, by prohibiting private monopolization, unreasonable restraint of trade and unfair trade practices, by preventing excessive concentration of economic power and by eliminating unreasonable restraint of production, sale, price, technology and the like, and all other unjust restriction of business activities through combinations, agreements and otherwise, aims to promote free and fair competition, to stimulate the creative initiative of entrepreneurs, to encourage business activities of enterprises, to heighten the level of employment and people's real income, and thereby to promote the democratic and wholesome development of the national economy as well as to assure the interests of consumers in general.

Art. 2 *[Definitions]*

(1) The term 'entrepreneur' as used in this Act shall mean a person, who carries on a commercial, industrial, financial or any other business. Any officer, employee, agent, or any other person who acts for the benefit of any entrepreneur shall be deemed to be an entrepreneur in regard to the application of the provisions of the following paragraph and of Chapter III of the Act.

(2) The term 'trade association' as used in this Act shall mean any combination or federation of combinations of two or more entrepreneurs having as its principal purpose the furtherance of their common business interest as entrepreneurs and includes one taking either of the following forms: Provided, That a combination or federation of combinations of two or more entrepreneurs, whose stock or other paid-up capital is owned by the constituent entrepreneurs, and whose principal purpose is to operate and which is actually operating a commercial, industrial, financial or any other business for profit shall not be included:

(i) Any association incorporated or not incorporated of which two or more entrepreneurs are members (including any position similar thereto);
(ii) Any foundation with or without juridical personality of which two or more entrepreneurs control the appointment or dismissal of directors or managers, the execution or continuation of business activities;
(iii) Any association of which two or more entrepreneurs are members, or any contractual combination of two or more entrepreneurs.

(3) The term 'officer' as used in this Act shall mean a director, a partner with unlimited liabilities and executive power, an auditor, or any person with a similar position, a manager, or other employee in change of business of the main or branch office.

(4) The term 'competition' as used in this Act shall mean a situation in which two or more entrepreneurs do or may, within the normal scope of their business activities and without undertaking any significant change in their business facilities or kinds of business activities, engage in any act prescribed in the following items.

- (i) Supplying the same or similar goods or services to the same consumers or users;
- (ii) Receiving supplies of the same or similar goods or services from the same supplier.

(5) The term 'private monopolization' as used in this Act shall mean such business activities, by which any entrepreneur, individually or by combination or conspiracy with other entrepreneurs, or by any other manner, excludes or controls the business activities of other entrepreneurs, thereby causing, contrary to the public interest, a substantial restraint of competition in any particular field of trade.

(6) The term 'unreasonable restraint of trade' as used in this Act shall mean such business activities, by which any entrepreneur, by contract, agreement or any other concerted actions, irrespective of its names, with other entrepreneurs, mutually restrict or conduct their business activities in such a manner as to fix, maintain, or increase prices, or to limit production, technology, products, facilities, or transaction counterparties, thereby causing, contrary to the public interest, a substantial restraint of competition in any particular field of trade.

(7) The term 'monopolistic situation' as used in this Act shall mean circumstances in which each of the following market structures and undesirable market performances exist in any particular field of business where the aggregate total amount of prices (this term refers to the prices of the goods concerned less a sum equivalent to the amount of taxes levied directly on such goods) of goods of the same description (including goods capable of being supplied without making any significant change to their business facilities or kinds of business activities; hereinafter in this paragraph referred to as 'particular goods') and those of any other goods having a strikingly similar function and utility thereto, which are supplied in Japan (excluding those exported) or the total amount of prices (this term refers to the prices of the services concerned less a sum equivalent to the amount of taxes levied on the recipient of such services with respect thereto) of services of the same description which are supplied in Japan, during the latest one-year period designated by cabinet ordinance, is in excess of hundred billion yen:

- (i) Where the share of a field of business (this refers to the ratio accounted for by the aggregate volume [in cases where calculation in terms of volume is not appropriate, volume shall be represented in terms of aggregate total amount of prices; the same shall apply hereinafter in this item] of the particular goods and any other goods having a strikingly similar function and utility thereto or by the volume of the services, which are supplied by the entrepreneur or entrepreneurs concerned, to the total volume of those supplied in Japan [excluding those exported]; the same shall apply hereinafter in this item) of an entrepreneur exceeds one-half or where the combined share of a field of business of two entrepreneurs exceeds three-fourths during the said one-year period;

(ii) Where there exist conditions which make it extremely difficult for any other entrepreneur to be newly engaged in the said particular field of business;

(iii) Where the increase in the price of the particular goods or services supplied by the entrepreneur concerned has been remarkable or the decrease therein has been slight for a considerable period of time in the light of the changes that occurred in the supply and demand, or in the cost of supplying, for such goods or services during such period, and where, in addition thereto, the said entrepreneur has fallen under any one of the following requirements during said period:

(a) That the entrepreneur has earned a profit rate far exceeding that which is established by cabinet ordinance as the norm for the class of business designated by such cabinet ordinance to which the said entrepreneur belongs; or

(b) That the entrepreneur has expended a level of selling and general administrative expenses far exceeding that which is considered as the norm for the field of business to which the entrepreneur belongs.

(8) In the event any change has occurred in the economic conditions resulting in a drastic change in domestic industrial shipments and wholesale prices, the amount of prices as prescribed in the preceding paragraph may be revised by virtue of cabinet ordinance to reflect such change.

(9) The term 'unfair trade practices' as used in this Act shall mean any act coming under any one of following items, which tends to impede fair competition and which is designated by the Fair Trade Commission as such:

(i) Unjustly discriminating against other entrepreneurs;
(ii) Dealing at unjust prices;
(iii) Unjustly inducing or coercing customers of a competitor to deal with oneself;
(iv) Dealing with another party on such terms as will restrict unjustly the business activities of the said party;
(v) Dealing with another party by unjust use of one's bargaining position;
(vi) Unjustly interfering with a transaction between an entrepreneur who competes in Japan with oneself or the company of which oneself is a

stockholder or an officer and another transaction counterparty; or, in case such entrepreneur is a company, unjustly inducing, instigating, or coercing a stockholder or an officer of such company to act against the interests of such company.

(10) The term 'subsidiaries' as used in this Act shall mean other companies in Japan of which more than fifty per cent of total voting rights (excluding voting rights related to the kinds of stock or shares of partnership as provided for in Article 211–2(iv) of the Commercial Code [Law No. 48 of 1899], but including voting rights related to the stock or shares of partnership deemed to have the voting rights under the provision of paragraph (v) of the same article; the same meaning shall apply to Chapter IV) of all stock holders (including shares of all partners; hereinafter the same) is held by a company.

Chapter II
Private Monopolization and Unreasonable Restraint of Trade

Art. 3 *[Prohibition of Private Monopolization or Unreasonable Restraint of Trade]*

No entrepreneur shall effect private monopolization or unreasonable restraint of trade.

Art. 4 *[Prohibition of Particular Concerted Practices]*

Deleted. (Law No. 259 of 1953)

Art. 5 *[Prohibition of Private Control Organization]*

Deleted. (Law No. 259 of 1953)

Art. 6 *[Prohibition of Particular International Agreements or Contracts, Filing Requirement]*

No entrepreneur shall enter into an international agreement or an international contract which contains such matters as constitute unreasonable restraint of trade or unfair trade practices.

Art. 7 *[Elimination Measures]*

(1) In case there exists any act in violation of the provisions of Article 3 or the preceding article, the Fair Trade Commission may, in accordance with the procedures as provided for in Division II of Chapter VIII, order the entrepreneur concerned to cease and desist from such acts, to transfer a part of his business, or to take any other measures necessary to eliminate such acts in violation of the said provisions.

(2) The Fair Trade Commission may, when it finds it particularly necessary, even when an act in violation of the provisions of Article 3, or the preceding Article has already ceased to exist, order the entrepreneurs concerned, in accordance with the procedures as provided for in Division II of Chapter VIII, to take measures to publicize that the said act has been discontinued and order any other measures necessary to ensure elimination of the said act: Provided, That the foregoing shall not apply to cases where three years have elapsed since the date of discontinuation of the said act.

Art. 7–2 *[Surcharges]*

(1) In case any entrepreneur effects an unreasonable restraint of trade or enters into an international agreement or an international contract containing such matters as constitute an unreasonable restraint of trade, and this falls within the purview of any of the items set out *below* in this paragraph, the Fair Trade Commission shall order the said entrepreneur, in accordance with the procedures as provided for in Division II of Chapter VIII, to pay to the Treasury a surcharge of an amount equivalent to an amount arrived at by multiplying the sales amount of such goods or services (in the case that the implementation of such conduct is related to the receipt of goods or services provided, the purchase price computed in accordance with the method prescribed by cabinet ordinance for the said goods or services) computed in accordance with the method prescribed by cabinet ordinance, for the period from the date on which the entrepreneur was engaged in the business activities as implementation of such conduct to the date on which the entrepreneur ceased to engage in the business activities as implementation of such conduct (in case such period exceeds three years, the period shall be for three years retroactively from the date on which the entrepreneur ceased to engage in the business activities as implementation of such conduct; hereinafter referred to as 'period of such implementation') by ten per cent (or by three per cent for retail or by two per cent for wholesale business): Provided, That in case the amount thus computed falls below one million yen, the Commission shall not order the payment of such a surcharge.

(i) Pertaining to prices of goods or services;
(ii) Substantially restraining any of the following with respect to goods or services and thereby affecting their prices:
   (a) Supply or purchase volume;
   (b) Market share;
   (c) Transaction counterparties.

(2) The provisions of the preceding paragraph shall apply mutatis mutandis to cases in which an entrepreneur, through private monopolization (limited to that arising from the control of the business activities of other entrepreneurs), has acted in any way that falls within the purview of any of the items *below* with respect to goods or services supplied by the said other entrepreneurs (hereinafter referred to as 'controlled entrepreneurs' in the is paragraph). In such cases, 'sales amount of such goods or services (in the case that the implementation of such conduct is related to the receipt of goods or services provided, the purchase price computed in accordance with the method prescribed by cabinet ordinance for the said goods or services) computed in accordance with the method prescribed by cabinet ordinance' in the preceding paragraph shall be read as 'the sales amount computed in accordance with the method prescribed by cabinet ordinance of such goods or services supplied by the said entrepreneur to controlled entrepreneurs (including goods or services necessary for supply by the said controlled entrepreneurs of the

said goods or services in any particular field of trade related to the conduct concerned) and of such goods or services supplied by the said entrepreneur (excluding those supplied to the said controlled entrepreneurs) in any particular field of trade', and '(or by three per cent for retail or by two per cent for wholesale business)' shall be read as '(or by three per cent in the case that the said entrepreneur engages in retail business or by two per cent for in the case that the said entrepreneur engages in wholesale business)'.

(i) Pertaining to their prices;
(ii) Substantially restraining any of the following and thereby affecting their prices:
(a) Supply volume;
(b) Market share;
(c) Transaction counterparties.

(3) The term 'market share' prescribed in the preceding two paragraphs shall mean the ratio accounted for by the aggregate volume of the said goods or services that one or two or more entrepreneurs supply or receive supply of to the total volume of the said goods or services supplied in any particular field of trade within defined period, or the ratio accounted for by the aggregate total amount of prices of the said goods or services that one or two or more entrepreneurs supply or receive supply of to the total amount of prices of the said goods or services supplied in any particular field of trade within defined period.

(4) In the case of paragraph (1), the term 'ten per cent' appearing in that paragraph shall read 'four per cent,' the term 'three per cent' shall read 'one point two per cent,' and the term 'two per cent' shall read 'one per cent' if the said entrepreneur falls under any one of the following items:

(i) Any company or subscription is not more than three hundred million yen and any company or individual whose regular employees number is not more than three hundred persons, whose main activity is to engage in businesses related to manufacturing, construction, transportation, and other industries (excluding the industries stipulated in items (ii) through (iv) inclusive of this item and the industries stipulated by cabinet ordinance pursuant to item (v) of this paragraph);
(ii) Any company or subscription is not more than one hundred million yen and any company or individual whose payroll employees number is not more than one hundred persons, whose main activity is to engage in businesses related to wholesale trade (excluding the industries stipulated by cabinet ordinance pursuant to item (v) of this paragraph);
(iii) Any company or subscription is not more than fifty million yen and any company or individual whose payroll employees number is not more than one hundred persons, whose main activity is to engage in businesses

related to service (excluding the industries stipulated by cabinet ordinance pursuant to item (v) of this paragraph);

(iv) Any company or subscription is not more than fifty million yen and any company or individual whose payroll employees number is not more than fifty persons, whose main activity is to engage in businesses related to retail trade (excluding the industries stipulated by cabinet ordinance pursuant to the following item);

(v) Any company or subscription is not more than that specified by cabinet ordinance for the industry the company engages in and any company or individual whose payroll employees number no more than that specified by cabinet ordinance for that industry, whose main activity is to engage in businesses related to the industry specified by such cabinet ordinance;

(vi) Any cooperative association and other association established, based on special laws, with the main objective of cooperation in the conduct of business (including association federations), any association of a scale corresponding to that provided in the items (i) through (v) for the individual industry in the preceding items as provided in cabinet ordinance.

(5) In the case an entrepreneur is ordered to pay a surcharge as provided in paragraph (1), the term 'ten per cent' in paragraph (1) shall read 'eight per cent,' the term 'three per cent' in paragraph (1) shall read 'two point four per cent', the term 'two per cent' in paragraph (1) shall read 'one point six per cent', the term 'four per cent' in paragraph (4) shall read 'three point two per cent', the term 'one point two per cent' in paragraph (4) shall read 'one per cent', and the term 'one per cent' in paragraph (4) shall read 'zero point eight per cent' if the said entrepreneur ceases to commit the said violative act by the day one month prior to the day when the measures mentioned in Article 47(1)(iv) or the measures as provided for in Article 102 (1) were first implemented (hereinafter referred to in this article as 'investigation start date') in relation to the said violative act (if the said measures are not implemented, the day one month prior to the day the said entrepreneur received the notification regarding the said violative act [referred to in paragraph (6) and in paragraph (7) as 'advance notification'] in accordance with the provisions of Article 49 (5) applicable mutatis mutandis under Article 50 (6)) (applied only in cases where the period of implementation of the violative act is less than two years, except for cases that fall under the following paragraph).

(6) In the case an entrepreneur is ordered to pay a surcharge as provided in paragraph (1) (including cases applicable mutatis mutandis under paragraph (2); the same shall apply hereinafter in this paragraph), the term 'ten per cent' in paragraph (1) shall read 'fifteen per cent', the term 'three per cent' in paragraph (1) shall read 'four point five per cent', the term 'two per cent' in paragraph (1) shall read 'three per cent', the term 'four per cent' in paragraph (4) shall read 'six per cent', the term 'one point two per cent' in paragraph (4) shall read 'one point eight per cent', and the term 'one per cent' in paragraph (4) shall read 'one point five per cent' if the said entrepreneur falls under any one of the following items:

(i) Within ten years counting retroactively from the investigation start date, the entrepreneur received an order pursuant to the provisions of paragraph (1) (applied only in cases where the said order is final and conclusive; the same shall apply in the following item), a notification pursuant to the provisions of paragraph (13) or (16), or a decision pursuant to the provisions of Article 51 (2);

(ii) Within ten years counting retroactively from the day on which the entrepreneur received advance notification regarding the said violative act in the case that the measures mentioned in Article 47 (1)(iv) or provided for in Article 102 (1) were not implemented, the said entrepreneur received an order pursuant to the provisions of Article 7–2 (1), a notification pursuant to the provisions of Article 7–2 (13) or (16), or a decision pursuant to the provisions of Article 51 (2).

(7) Notwithstanding the provisions of paragraph (1), the Fair Trade Commission shall not order the said entrepreneur to pay the surcharge if the entrepreneur falls under both of the following items:

(i) The entrepreneur is the first among the entrepreneurs that committed the violative act to individually submit reports and documents regarding the facts of said violative act to the Fair Trade Commission as provided in the Rules of the Fair Trade Commission (excluding cases where the said reports and documents are submitted on or after the investigation start date [the day on which the entrepreneur received advance notification regarding the said violative act in the case that the measures mentioned in Article 47 (1)(iv) or provided for in Article 102 (1) were not implemented; the same shall apply in the following item and paragraph] in relation to the said violative act);

(ii) The entrepreneur did not commit further acts on or after the investigation start date in connection with violation under investigation.

(8) In the case of paragraph (1), the Fair Trade Commission shall reduce the said surcharge by the amount calculated by multiplying by fifty per cent the surcharge calculated in accordance with the provisions of paragraph (1) or (4) through (6) inclusive in the case that the entrepreneur falls under items (i) and (iii) of this paragraph and by the amount calculated by multiplying by thirty per cent the surcharge calculated in accordance with the provisions of paragraph (1) or (4) through (6) inclusive in the case that the entrepreneur falls under items (ii) and (iii) of this paragraph:

(i) The entrepreneur is among the entrepreneurs that committed the violative act to individually submit reports and documents regarding the facts of said violative act to the Fair Trade Commission as provided in the Rules of the Fair Trade Commission (excluding cases where the said reports and documents are submitted on or after the investigation start date in relation to the said violative act);

(ii) The entrepreneur is the third among the entrepreneurs that committed the violative act to individually submit reports and documents regarding the facts of said violative act to the Fair Trade Commission as provided in the Rules of the Fair Trade Commission (excluding cases where the said reports and documents are submitted on or after the investigation start date in relation to the said violative act);

(iii) The entrepreneur is not the one that committed the said violative act on or after the investigation start date in regard to the said violative act.

(9) In the case of paragraph (1), the Fair Trade Commission shall reduce the said surcharge by the amount calculated by multiplying by thirty per cent the surcharge calculated in accordance with the provisions of paragraph (1) or (4) through (6) inclusive in the case that the entrepreneur that committed the said violative act falls under both of the following items if the number of entrepreneurs who submitted reports and documents regarding the said violative act pursuant to the provisions of (7)(i) or (8)(i) or (ii) is fewer than three (only applicable if the sum of the number of entrepreneurs who submitted reports and documents pursuant to the provisions of (7)(i) or (8)(i) or (ii) and the number of entrepreneurs who submitted reports and documents pursuant to the provisions of item (i) *below* is three or fewer):

(i) The entrepreneur, in accordance to the Rules of the Fair Trade Commission, individually submitted reports and documents of the facts regarding the said violative act (excluding materials related to the facts already ascertained by the Fair Trade Commission under the measures mentioned in Article 47(1) (i) through (iv) inclusive or provided for in Article 102(1) or other means) to the Fair Trade Commission by the deadline set in the Rules of the Fair Trade Commission after the investigation start date for the case of the said violative act;

(ii) The entrepreneur is someone other than the entrepreneurs that committed the said violative act on or after the day when the reports and documents in the preceding paragraph were submitted.

(10) When the Fair Trade Commission receives the submission of reports and documents pursuant to the provisions of paragraph (7)(i), (8)(i) or (ii), or (9)(i), the Fair Trade Commission promptly shall notify the entrepreneur that submitted the said reports and documents of that fact in writing.

(11) Prior to issuing an order pursuant to the provisions of paragraph (1) or a notification pursuant to the provisions of paragraph (13) to an entrepreneur who falls under any one of the provisions of paragraph (7) through (9) inclusive, the Fair Trade Commission can additionally request the said entrepreneur to submit reports or documents related to the facts of the said violative act.

(12) If it is deemed that a fact that falls under any one of the following items exists, these provisions shall not apply, notwithstanding the provisions of paragraph (7) through (9) inclusive, for the period until the Fair Trade Commission issues an order pursuant to the provisions of paragraph (1) or a notification pursuant to the provisions of paragraph (13) to entrepreneurs that submitted reports and documents pursuant to the provisions of paragraph (7)(i), (8)(i) or (ii), or (9)(i):

- (i) The report or documents submitted by the said entrepreneur contained false information;
- (ii) In the case of paragraph (11), the said entrepreneur fails to submit the requested reports or documents or submits false reports or documents;
- (iii) In the case related to the violative act committed by the said entrepreneur, the said entrepreneur coerced another entrepreneur to commit the violative act stipulated in paragraph (1) or blocked another entrepreneur from ceasing to commit the said violative act.

(13) If the Fair Trade Commission has decided not to order the payment of a surcharge pursuant to the provisions of paragraph (7), the Commission shall notify the said entrepreneur of this in writing at the time of issuing an surcharge payment order to an entrepreneur other than the said entrepreneur regarding the case related to the violative act committed by the entrepreneur that falls under the provisions of paragraph (7) (by the deadline stipulated in the Rules of the Fair Trade Commission in the case that the Fair Trade Commission does not issue an order pursuant to the provisions of paragraph (1); the same shall apply in paragraph (16)).

(14) In the case of paragraph (1) (including cases applicable mutatis mutandis under paragraph (2); the same shall apply hereinafter in this paragraph and in paragraphs (17) and (18)), the Fair Trade Commission shall, if there is a final and conclusive court ruling regarding the same case stipulating that the said entrepreneur be subject to a fine, set the surcharge as the amount calculated in accordance with the provisions of paragraph (1), (4) through (6) inclusive, (8), or (9) minus the amount equivalent to one-half of the said fine, instead of simply the amount calculated in accordance with the provisions of paragraph (1), (4) through (6) inclusive, (8), or (9): Provided, That the foregoing shall not apply if the surcharge amount calculated in accordance with the provisions of paragraph (1), (4) through (6) inclusive, (8), or (9) does not exceed the sum equivalent to one-half of the amount of the said fine, or if the surcharge is less than one million yen after the said deduction.

(15) In the proviso in the preceding paragraph, the Fair Trade Commission shall not order payment of the surcharge.

(16) In the case that the Fair Trade Commission does not order payment of the surcharge pursuant to the provisions of the preceding paragraph, the Commission shall issue a written notification to the fined entrepreneur when the Commission

issues the order pursuant to the provisions of paragraph (1) (including cases applicable mutatis mutandis under paragraph (2)) to an entrepreneur other than the said entrepreneur regarding the case related to the violative act pursuant to paragraphs (1) and (2). The notification shall inform the said entrepreneur both that he or she shall not be ordered to pay the surcharge and that another entrepreneur shall be ordered to pay the surcharge.

(17) Any entrepreneur who has received an order under the provisions of paragraph (1) shall pay the surcharge calculated in accordance with the provisions of paragraph (1), (4) through (6) inclusive, (8), (9), or (14).

(18) In case the amount of surcharge calculated in accordance with the provisions of paragraph (1), (4) through (6) inclusive, (8), (9), or (14) contains a fraction less than ten thousand yen, such fraction shall be disregarded.

(19) In the case that the entrepreneur who has committed a violative act stipulated in the provisions of paragraph (1) or (2) is a company and if such company has ceased to exist through a merger with another company, the violative act committed by the said company shall be considered as a violative act committed by the company continuing after or established as a result of the merger and the order pursuant to the provisions of paragraph (1) (including cases applicable mutatis mutandis under paragraph (2)), the notification pursuant to the provisions of paragraph (13) and paragraph (16), and the decision pursuant to the provisions of Article 51(2) received by said company (hereinafter referred to as 'order, etc.' in this paragraph) shall be considered as an order, etc. received by the company continuing after or established as a result of the merger, and the provisions of the preceding paragraphs shall apply thereto.

(20) In the case of the preceding paragraph, matters necessary for the application of the provisions of paragraphs (7) through (9) inclusive shall be prescribed by cabinet ordinance.

(21) After three years has elapsed from the date on which the violative act ended, the Fair Trade Commission cannot order the entrepreneur to pay a surcharge for said violative act.

Chapter III
Trade Associations

Art. 8 *[Prohibited Acts of a Trade Association, Filing Requirement]*

(1) No trade association shall engage in any acts which come under any one of the following items:

(i) Substantially restraining competition in any particular field of trade;
(ii) Entering into an international agreement or an international contract as provided for in Article 6;
(iii) Limiting the present or future number of entrepreneurs in any particular field of business;
(iv) Unjustly restricting the functions or activities of the constituent entrepreneurs (meaning an entrepreneur who is a member of the trade association; hereinafter the same);
(v) Causing entrepreneurs to employ such acts as constitute unfair trade practices.

(2) Every trade association shall, when formed, in accordance with the Rules of the Fair Trade Commission, file a report thereof with the Commission within thirty days as from the date of its formation. However, the trade associations stipulated in items (i), (ii), and (iii) are not required to file a report.

(i) Trade associations established under the provisions of special laws and stipulated by cabinet ordinance as falling under (a) and (b):
  (a) Trade associations that are not at risk of committing one of the acts stipulated in the items of the preceding paragraph in light of the purposes, business, and activities defined in this Act;
  (b) Trade associations whose purpose is mutual aid among small-scale entrepreneurs or consumers or whose purpose is the sound development of them.
(ii) Trade associations whose purpose is mutual aid among small-scale entrepreneurs provided by cabinet ordinance as those that are not at risk of committing one of the acts stipulated in the items of the preceding paragraph;
(iii) Clearinghouses designated in the provisions of the Bills Act (Act No. 20 of 1932) or the Check Act (Act No. 57 of 1933).

(3) When any change has occurred to the matters reported under the preceding paragraph, the trade association concerned shall, in accordance with the Rules of

the Fair Trade Commission, file a declaration thereof with the Commission, within two months after the end of the business year during which such change occurred (excluding trade associations stipulated in the items of paragraph (2)).

(4) Every trade association shall, when dissolved, in accordance with the Rules of the Fair Trade Commission, file a report thereof with the Commission, within thirty days after the date of its dissolution (excluding trade associations stipulated in the items of paragraph (2)).

Art. 8–2 *[Elimination Measures Against Prohibited Acts of Trade Associations]*

(1) When there exists any act in violation of the provisions of paragraph (1) of the preceding article, the Fair Trade Commission may, in accordance with the procedures as provided for in Division II of Chapter VIII, order the trade association concerned to cease and desist from such act, to dissolve the said association, or to take any other measures necessary to eliminate the said act.

(2) The provisions of Article 7 (2) shall apply mutatis mutandis to any act in violation of provisions of Article 8 (1).

(3) In ordering a trade association to take any of the measures set forth in paragraph (1) or Article 7 (2) applicable mutatis mutandis under the provisions of the preceding paragraph, the Fair Trade Commission may, when it finds it particularly necessary, also order, in accordance with the procedures as provided for in Division II of Chapter VIII, an officer, manager, or constituent entrepreneur (including the said entrepreneur when the officer, employee, agent, or any other person acting for the benefit of the entrepreneur is a constituent entrepreneur; the same shall apply in Article 26 (1) and Article 59 (2)) of the said association to take measures necessary to ensure the measures provided for in paragraph (1) *above* or Article 7 (2) applicable mutatis mutandis under the provisions of thc preceding paragraph.

Art. 8–3 *[Surcharges Against Constituent Entrepreneurs]*

The provisions of Article 7–2 (1), (3) through (5) inclusive, (7) through (13) inclusive, (17), (18), and (21) shall apply mutatis mutandis to cases where an act is committed in violation of the provisions of Article 8 (1)(i) (applying only to those entrepreneurs who commits an act which constitutes unreasonable restraint of trade) or Article 8 (1)(ii) (applying only to those entrepreneurs who is a party to an international agreement or an international contract which contains such matters as constitute unreasonable restraint of trade). In this case, the following shall apply: The term 'entrepreneur' appearing in Article 7–2 (1) shall be read as 'trade association'; and the term 'said entrepreneur' appearing therein shall be read as 'the constituent entrepreneur of the said trade association (including the said entrepreneur when the officer, employee, agent, or any other person acting for the benefit of the entrepreneur is a constituent entrepreneur; hereinafter referred to in this Article as 'specified entrepreneur')'. The term 'said entrepreneur' appearing in Article 7–2 (4) shall be read as 'said specified entrepreneur'. The term 'entrepreneur' appearing in Article 7–2 (5) shall be read as 'specified entrepreneur'; the term 'ceases to commit' appearing therein shall be read as 'ceases the business activities that involve the commitment of'; and the term 'implementation of the violative act is less than two years, except for cases that fall under the following paragraph' shall be read as 'implementation of the business activities that involve the commitment of the violative act is less than two years'. The term 'entrepreneur' appearing in Article 7–2 (7) shall be read as 'specified entrepreneur'; and the term 'entrepreneurs that committed the violative act' appearing therein shall be read as 'specified entrepreneurs of the trade association that committed the violative act'; and the term 'that committed' appearing therein shall be read as 'that performed the business activities that involved the commitment of'. The term 'entrepreneur' appearing in Article 7–2 (8) shall be read as 'specified entrepreneur'; the term 'paragraph (1) or (4) through (6) inclusive' appearing therein shall be read as 'paragraph (1), (4), or (5)'; the term 'entrepreneurs that committed the violative act' appearing therein shall be read as 'specified entrepreneurs of the trade association that committed the violative act'; and the term 'that committed' appearing therein shall be read as 'that performed the business activities that involved the commitment of'. The term 'entrepreneur' appearing in Article 7–2 (9) shall be read as 'specified entrepreneur'; the term 'entrepreneur that committed the said violative act' appearing therein shall be read as 'specified entrepreneur of the trade association that committed the said violative act'; and the term 'paragraph (1) or (4) through (6) inclusive' appearing therein shall be read as 'paragraph (1), (4), or (5)'; and the term 'that committed' appearing therein shall be read as 'that performed the business activities that involved the commitment of'. The term 'entrepreneur' appearing in Article 7–2 (10) and (11) shall be read as 'specified entrepreneur'. The term 'entrepreneurs that submitted' appearing in Article 7–2 (12) shall be read as 'specified entrepreneurs that submitted'; the term 'submitted by the said entrepreneur' appearing therein shall be read as 'submitted by the said specified entrepreneur'; the term ', the said entrepreneur' appearing therein shall be read as ', the said specified entrepreneur'; the term 'committed by the said entrepreneur' appearing therein shall be read as 'committed by the said trade association'; the term 'another entrepreneur' appearing therein shall be read as 'another specified entrepreneur'; the term 'commit the violative act stipulated in paragraph (1)' appearing therein shall be read as 'conduct the business activities that involved the commitment of the said violative act'; and the term 'ceasing to commit' appearing therein shall be read as 'ceasing the business activities that involved the commitment of'. The term 'entrepreneur' appearing in Article 7–2 (13) shall be read as 'specified entrepreneur'; and the term 'violative act committed' appearing therein shall be read as 'reports submitted pursuant to the provisions of paragraph (7)(i)'. The term '(4) through (6) inclusive, (8), (9), or (14)' appearing in Article 7–2 (17) and (18) shall be read as '(4), (5), (8), or (9)'.

Chapter III-II
Monopolistic Situations

Art. 8–4 *[Measures Against a Monopolistic Situation]*

(1) When a monopolistic situation exists, the Fair Trade Commission may order the entrepreneur concerned, in accordance with the procedures provided for in Division II of Chapter VIII, to transfer a part of his or her business or to take any other measures necessary to restore competition with respect to such goods or services: Provided, That the foregoing shall not apply to cases where the Commission finds that such measures may reduce the scale of business of the said entrepreneur to such an extent that the costs required for the supply of goods or services which such entrepreneur supplies will rise sharply, undermine its financial position, and make it difficult for the entrepreneur to maintain its international competitiveness, or where other alternative measures may be taken which the Commission finds sufficient to restore competition with respect to such goods or services.

(2) In issuing an order prescribed in the preceding paragraph, the Fair Trade Commission shall give consideration, based on the items prescribed in each of the following paragraphs, to the smooth conduct of business activities by the entrepreneurs concerned, and those associated with them and the stabilization of livelihood for those employed by such entrepreneurs:

(i) Assets, income and expenditures and other aspects of accounting;
(ii) Officers and employees;
(iii) Location of factories, work yards, and offices and other locational conditions;
(iv) Aspects of business facilities and equipment;
(v) The substance of patent rights, trademark rights, and other intellectual property rights and other technological features;
(vi) Capacity for and situations of production and sales, etc.;
(vii) Capacity for and situations of obtaining funds and materials, etc.;
(viii) Situations of supply and distribution of goods or services.

Chapter IV
Stockholdings, Interlocking Directorates, Mergers, Divisions, and Acquisitions of Business

Art. 9 *[Prohibition of Establishment of a Company Which May Cause Excessive Concentration of Economic Power, Filing Requirement]*

(1) Any company, which may cause excessive concentration of economic power, by means of holding of the stock (including shares of partnership; hereinafter the same) of other companies in Japan shall not be established.

(2) A company (including a foreign company; hereinafter the same) shall not cause excessive concentration of economic power in Japan by acquiring or holding the stock of other companies in Japan.

(3) The term 'excessive concentration of economic power' in the preceding two paragraphs shall mean a situation in which the extreme largeness of a company and its subsidiaries and other companies in Japan whose overall business scale over a significant number of fields of business are controlled by the company by means of holding of stock, the remarkably large influence of the said companies on other entrepreneurs due to transactions relating to finance or the occupancy of influential positions over a significant number of mutually related fields of business by the said companies, has a large effect on the national economy and impedes the promotion of free and fair competition.

(4) Any other company in Japan of which more than fifty per cent of total voting rights of all stockholders is held by a company and any one or more subsidiaries of the said company, or by any one or more subsidiaries of a company, shall be regarded as a subsidiary of the said company; provisions stipulated in this article shall be applied to any such companies as subsidiaries of the said company.

(5) Any company fitting any of the descriptions presented in the following paragraphs, when the sum total (concerning assets of the companies in Japan), summed according to the procedure specified by the Rules of the Fair Trade Commission, of its total assets (calculated in accordance with the procedure specified by the Rules of the Fair Trade Commission; hereinafter the same in this paragraph) and that of its subsidiaries, is greater than the amount so provided for by cabinet ordinance and not lower than the amount listed in each of the following paragraphs, shall submit, in accordance with the Rules of the Fair Trade Commission, a report on the

business of the said company and its subsidiaries to the Fair Trade Commission within three months from the end of each business year: Provided, That this shall not apply if the said company is a subsidiary of another company.

(i) A company of which the total acquisition value (or other price if it is so listed in the latest balance sheet) of the stock of any subsidiary constitutes more than fifty per cent of the value of the total assets of the said company (referred to as 'holding company' in the following paragraph): Six hundred billion yen
(ii) A company that is engaged in banking, insurance, or securities businesses (excluding those classified as a holding company and stock broking business): Eight trillion yen
(iii) A company other than those listed in the preceding two paragraphs: Two trillion yen

(6) A company that corresponds to any of the descriptions prescribed in the preceding paragraph when it is newly established shall, in accordance with the Rules of the Fair Trade Commission, file a report with the Commission to that effect within thirty days from the date of its establishment.

Art. 10 *[Prohibition of Particular Stockholding by a Company, Filing Requirement]*

(1) No company shall acquire or hold stock of any other companies where the effect of such acquisition or holding of stock may be substantially to restrain competition in any particular field of trade, or shall acquire or hold stock of other companies through unfair trade practices.

(2) Every company whose assets (meaning total amount of the assets according to the latest balance sheet; hereinafter the same) exceed the amount, not less than two billion yen, as provided for by cabinet ordinance, as well as the sum of the total amount of assets of the said company, subsidiaries of the said company, and a company in Japan which holds more than fifty per cent of the total voting rights of all stockholders of the said company (hereinafter 'total assets'), exceeds the amount (this company is called 'stockholding company' in this article), not less than ten billion yen, as provided for by cabinet ordinance, in case that it acquires or holds the stock (including the stock held in the form of trust property of pecuniary or security trust of which it is a trustor or beneficiary and can exercise its voting rights or where such trustor or beneficiary can issue instructions regarding the exercise of such voting rights) of other companies in Japan whose total amount of assets exceeds the amount, not less than one billion yen, as provided for by cabinet ordinance (hereinafter in this article 'issuing company'), so that the ratio of shares acquired or held by the stockholding company to the total outstanding stock of the issuing company is to exceed the ratio, not less than ten per cent, as provided for by cabinet ordinance (in the case that more than one value is provided, each

numerical value as provided for by cabinet ordinance), shall submit, in accordance with the Rules of the Fair Trade Commission, a report on such stock within thirty days as from the date of exceeding: Provided, That the foregoing shall not apply to cases where the issuing company establishes the acquired company and the former acquires all of the outstanding stock of the latter concurrently with the establishment, cases where a company engaging in banking or insurance business acquires or holds stock of other companies in Japan (excluding those engaged in banking or insurance business or those as provided for in the Rules of Fair Trade Commission; the same shall apply in paragraphs (1) and (2) of the next article), or cases where a company engaging in securities acquires or holds stock in the course of its business.

(3) The provisions of the preceding paragraph shall apply mutatis mutandis in cases where the stockholding company acquires or holds the stock of a foreign company whose net sales in the profit and loss statement which is made with the latest balance sheet of its business offices in Japan (including the business offices of its subsidiaries) (hereinafter 'domestic sales') exceeds the amount, not less than one billion yen, as provided for by cabinet ordinance.

Art. 11 *[Restriction on Rate of Holding Voting Rights by a Bank or an Insurance Company]*

(1) No company engaged in the banking or insurance business shall acquire or hold voting rights of other companies in Japan if by doing so it holds in excess of five per cent (ten per cent in the case of an insurance company; the same in paragraph (2)) of the total voting rights of all stockholders: Provided, That the foregoing shall not apply to such cases where authorization of the Fair Trade Commission is obtained in advance in accordance with the Rules of the Fair Trade Commission, or to such cases falling under any one of the following items:

(i) If voting rights are acquired or held by acquiring or holding of stock as a result of the enforcement of lien, pledge, mortgage, or of payment in kind;
(ii) If the ratio of the voting rights of the possessed stock of other companies in Japan to total voting rights of all stockholders increases as a result of other companies' acquisition of their own stock;
(iii) If voting rights are acquired or held by acquiring or holding the stock in the form of trust property related to pecuniary or security trust;
(iv) If voting rights are acquired or held because stock as property of partnership is acquired or held by becoming a limited partner in an investment-purpose limited partnership for small and medium-sized enterprises, etc. (referred to as 'limited partner' hereinafter in this item): Provided, That this shall not apply to cases where the limited partner can exercise its voting rights, cases where the limited partner can instruct a partner with unlimited liability in the investment-purpose limited partnership for small and medium-sized enterprises, etc.,

regarding the exercise of such voting rights, and cases where the limited partner holds the said voting rights in excess of the period as provided for by cabinet ordinance from the date when the said voting rights were held;

(v) If voting rights are acquired or held because stock as property of partnership is acquired or held by becoming a partner in a partnership (limited to partnerships that entrust one or more partners with the execution of business) that was constituted by a partnership contract as provided for in Article 667 (1) of the Civil Code (Law No. 89 of 1896) covering operation of investment business in companies (excluding the partners entrusted with the execution of business; referred to hereinafter in this item as 'non-executive partner'): Provided, That this shall not apply to cases where the non-executive partner can exercise its voting rights, cases where the non-executive partner can instruct the partner entrusted with the execution of business regarding the exercise of such voting rights, and cases where the non-executive partner holds the said voting rights in excess of the period as provided for by the cabinet ordinance referred to in the preceding item from the date when the said voting rights were held;

(vi) If, in addition to the cases listed in each of the preceding items, acquisition or holding of voting rights falls under any of the cases for which it is stipulated by the Rules of the Fair Trade Commission that there is no likelihood that such act will restrain the business activities of other companies in Japan.

(2) Any company, in the cases of items (i) through (iii) inclusive and (v) of the preceding paragraph (in the case of item (iii) of the preceding paragraph, cases where the trustor or the beneficiary can exercise its voting rights or the trustor or beneficiary can instruct the trustee regarding the exercise of such voting rights are excluded), that attempts to hold the voting rights of another company in Japan over a period of one year from the date of such acquisition in excess of five per cent of total voting rights of all stockholders' outstanding stock shall, in accordance with the Rules of the Fair Trade Commission, obtain authorization in advance from the Commission. The authorization of the Fair Trade Commission in such cases shall, except for the case stipulated in item (iii) of the same paragraph, be granted on the condition that the company engaged in banking or insurance business promptly disposes of the said voting rights.

(3) When the Fair Trade Commission grants authorization under the provisions of the two preceding paragraphs, it shall, in advance, consult with the Prime Minister.

(4) The affairs of the Prime Minister stipulated in the proceeding paragraph shall be delegated to the Commissioner of the Financial Services Agency.

Art. 12 *[Restriction on Acquisition of Corporate Bonds]*

Deleted. (Law No. 214 of 1948)

Art. 13 *[Prohibition of Particular Interlocking Directorates, Filing Requirement]*

(1) Neither an officer nor an employee (meaning in this article a person other than officers in the regular employment of a company) of a company shall hold at the same time a position as an officer in another company wherever the effect of such an interlocking directorate may be substantially to restrain competition in any particular field of trade.

(2) No company shall coerce another company in competition with it in Japan through unfair trade practices, to admit one of its officers concurrently to the position of officer or employee of the latter company or companies, or to admit its employee, concurrently to the position of officer of such company or companies.

Art. 14 *[Prohibition of Particular Stockholding by a Person Other Than a Company, Filing Requirement]*

No person other than a company shall acquire or hold stock of another company whenever the effect of such acquisition or holding of stock may be substantially to restrain competition in any particular field of trade, or shall acquire or hold stock of a company in Japan through unfair trade practices.

Art. 15 *[Prohibition of Particular Mergers, Filing Requirement]*

(1) No company shall effect a merger coming under any one of the following items:

(i) Where the effect of a merger may be substantially to restrain competition in any particular field of trade;
(ii) Where unfair trade practices have been employed in the course of the merger.

(2) Every company in Japan, which intends to become a party to a merger (hereinafter in this article 'merging company') shall, in accordance with the Rules of the Fair Trade Commission, file a declaration with the Commission, in case that the total assets of one company exceeds the amount, stipulated by cabinet ordinance, which is not less than ten billion yen, and that the total assets of one of the other companies exceed the amount, stipulated by cabinet ordinance, which is not less than one billion yen: Provided, That the foregoing shall not apply to such cases falling under any one of the following items:

(i) Any one of the merging companies holds more than fifty per cent of the total voting rights of all stockholders of each of the other merging companies;
(ii) More than fifty per cent of the total voting rights of all stockholders of each of the merging companies are held by one company.

(3) The provisions of the previous paragraph shall apply mutatis mutandis to any foreign company that intends to become a party to merger. In such cases, 'total assets' in this paragraph shall be read as domestic sales'.

(4) No company which filed a declaration, in accordance with paragraph (2) (including cases applicable mutatis mutandis under paragraph (3)), shall effect a merger until the expiration of the thirty-day waiting period from the date of acceptance of the said declaration: Provided, That the Fair Trade Commission may, when it finds it necessary, shorten the said period.

(5) The Fair Trade Commission shall, where it intends to order necessary measures regarding the merger in question pursuant to the provisions of Article 17–2 (1), notify the merging companies pursuant to the provisions of Article 49 (5) before the expiration of the thirty-day waiting period provided for in the preceding paragraph, or of any shortened period under the proviso thereof (in case that the Fair Trade Commission required one or more companies among the merging companies to submit necessary reports, information, or documents in accordance with the provisions of the Rules of the Fair Trade Commission [hereinafter in this paragraph 'reports, etc.'] before the expiration of the period, the Commission shall notify the merging companies either during the one hundred twenty days from the date of acceptance of the declaration provided for in the preceding paragraph or during the ninety days from the date of acceptance of all the reports, etc., whichever is later): Provided, That the foregoing shall not apply to such cases falling under any one of the following items:

(i) Important matters, in light of paragraph (1), are not carried out by the deadline by which they should have been carried out according to the plan regarding the merger filed in accordance with paragraph (2) (including cases applicable mutatis mutandis under paragraph (3); the same shall apply in the following item);
(ii) There has been a false statement with respect to important matters in the plan regarding the merger filed in accordance with the provisions of paragraph (2).

(6) In cases falling under the provisions of item (i) of the previous paragraph, the Fair Trade Commission shall send a notification as provided in the previous paragraph within one year from the deadline in item (i) if it contemplates ordering necessary measures relating to the said merger pursuant to the provisions of Article 17–2 (1).

Art. 15–2 *[Prohibition of Particular Divisions, Filing Requirement]*

(1) No company shall effect a joint establishment division (meaning establishment division that one company effects jointly with another company; hereinafter the same) or acquisition division under any one of the following items:

(i) Where the effect of a joint establishment division or acquisition division may be substantially to restrain competition in a particular field of trade;
(ii) Where unfair trade practices have been employed in the course of the joint establishment division or acquisition division.

(2) Every company in Japan which intends to become a party to a joint establishment division shall, in accordance with the Rules of the Fair Trade Commission, file in advance a plan with the Commission regarding the joint establishment division, if any one of the following applies:

(i) The total assets of one of the companies which intends to become a party to the joint establishment division (limited to companies that intend to have the company established through the joint establishment division acquire all of their business [hereinafter in this item 'total alienation company']) exceed the amount stipulated by cabinet ordinance, which is not less than ten billion yen, and the total assets of another one of the companies (limited to total alienation companies) exceed the amount, stipulated by cabinet ordinance, which is not less than one billion yen;
(ii) The total assets of one of the companies which intends to become a party to a joint establishment division (limited to total alienation companies) exceed the amount, stipulated by cabinet ordinance, which is not less than ten billion yen, and net sales of the said acquisition in the profit and loss statement which is made with the latest balance sheet of another one of the companies (limited to the company that intends to have the company established through the joint establishment division acquire a substantial part of its business [hereinafter in this item 'substantial part alienation company']) exceed the amount, stipulated by cabinet ordinance, which is not less than one billion yen;
(iii) The total assets of one of the companies which intends to become a party to a joint establishment division (limited to total alienation companies) exceed the amount, stipulated by cabinet ordinance, which is not less than one billion yen, and the net sales in the profit and loss statement which is made with the latest balance sheet of the alienated part of another one of the companies (limited to substantial part alienation companies) exceed the amount, stipulated by cabinet ordinance, which is not less than ten billion yen (excluding cases that fall under the previous item);

(iv) The net sales in the profit and loss statement which is made with the latest balance sheet of the alienated part of one of the companies (limited to substantial part alienation companies) exceed the amount, stipulated by cabinet ordinance, which is not less than ten billion yen, and the net sales of the said acquisition in the profit and loss statement which is made with the latest balance sheet of another one of the companies (limited to substantial part alienation companies) exceed the amount, stipulated by cabinet ordinance, which is not less than one billion yen.

(3) Every company in Japan, which intends to become a party to an acquisition division, shall, in accordance with the Rules of the Fair Trade Commission, file in advance a plan with the Commission regarding the acquisition division, if any one of the following items applies:

(i) The total assets of one of the companies which intends to effect an acquisition division (limited to companies that intend to alienate all of their business through the division [hereinafter in this item 'total alienation company']) exceed the amount, stipulated by cabinet ordinance, which is not less than ten billion yen, and the total assets of the company which intends to succeed to the business through the division exceed the amount, stipulated by cabinet ordinance, which is not less than one billion yen;
(ii) The total assets of one of the companies which intends to effect an acquisition division (limited to total alienation companies) exceed the amount, stipulated by cabinet ordinance, which is not less than one billion yen, and the total assets of the company which intends to succeed to the business through the division exceed the amount, stipulated by cabinet ordinance, which is not less than ten billion yen (excluding a case that falls under the previous item);
(iii) The net sales in the profit and loss statement which is made with the latest balance sheet of the divided part of another one of the companies (limited to companies that intend to alienate a substantial part of their business through the division [hereinafter in this item 'substantial part alienation company']) exceed the amount, stipulated by cabinet ordinance, which is not less than ten billion yen, and the total assets of the company which intends to succeed to the business through the division exceed the amount, stipulated by cabinet ordinance, which is not less than one billion yen;
(iv) The net sales in the profit and loss statement which is made with the latest balance sheet of the divided part of one of the companies (limited to substantial part alienation companies) exceed the amount, stipulated by cabinet ordinance, which is not less than one billion yen, and the total assets of the company which intends to succeed to the business through the division exceed the amount, stipulated by cabinet ordinance, which is not less than ten billion yen.

(4) The provisions of the preceding two paragraphs shall not apply to such cases falling under any one of the following items:

(i) Of the companies which intend to become a party to a joint establishment division or an acquisition division, any one company holds more than fifty per cent of the total voting rights of all stockholders of every other company;
(ii) More than fifty per cent of the total voting rights of all stockholders of every company which intends to become a party to a joint establishment division or an acquisition division are held by one company.

(5) The provisions of the preceding three paragraphs shall apply mutatis mutandis to any foreign company which intends to become a party to a joint establishment division or an acquisition division. In such cases, 'total assets' and 'net sales in the profit and loss statement which is made with the latest balance sheet' in paragraphs (2) and (3) shall be read as 'domestic sales'.

(6) The provisions of paragraphs (4) through (6) inclusive of the preceding article shall apply mutatis mutandis to the restriction of joint establishment divisions and acquisition divisions concerning the notification under paragraphs (2) and (3) (including cases applicable mutatis mutandis under the preceding paragraph) and the orders made by the Fair Trade Commission pursuant to the provisions of Article 17–2 (1). In such cases, the term 'merger' appearing in paragraphs (4) and (6) of the preceding article shall be read as 'joint establishment division or acquisition division'; the term 'regarding the merger' appearing in paragraph (5) of the preceding article shall be read as 'regarding the joint establishment division or acquisition division'; and the term 'merging companies' appearing therein shall be read as 'companies which intend to become parties to a joint establishment division or an acquisition division'.

Art. 16 *[Prohibition of Particular Acquisitions of Business, etc., Filing Requirement]*

(1) No company shall take action coming under any one of the following where the effect of such action may be substantially to restrain competition in any particular field of trade, or shall take such action through unfair trade practices:

(i) Acquiring the whole or a substantial part of the business of another company;
(ii) Acquiring the whole or a substantial part of the fixed assets used for the business of another company;
(iii) Taking on lease of the whole or a substantial part of the business of another company;

(iv) Undertaking the management of the whole or a substantial part of the business of another company;

(v) Entering into a contract which provides for a joint profit and loss account for business with another company.

(2) Any company, whose total assets exceed the amount, provided for by cabinet ordinance, not less than ten billion yen and that falls under any of the following items (in paragraph (4) referred to as 'acquiring company'), shall file, in advance, to the Fair Trade Commission in accordance with the Rules of the Fair Trade Commission, a plan for acquisition of a business or the fixed assets used in the business (hereinafter in this article as 'business, etc.').

(i) Acquiring the whole business of another company in Japan whose total assets exceed the amount, provided for by cabinet ordinance, not less than one billion yen;

(ii) Where the company acquires a substantial part of the business or all or a substantial part of the fixed assets for the business of another company in Japan, and the net sales of the said acquisition in the profit and loss statement which is made with the latest balance sheet of the acquiring business, exceed the amount, provided for by cabinet ordinance, not less than one billion yen.

(3) The provisions of the preceding paragraph shall not apply to an act of a company coming under any one of the following items:

(i) Either the company acquiring the business, etc. or the company transferring the business, etc. concerned holds more than fifty per cent of the total voting rights of all stockholders of every other company;

(ii) More than fifty per cent of the total voting rights of all stockholders of both the company acquiring the business, etc. and the company transferring the business, etc. concerned, are owned by the same company.

(4) The provisions of the preceding two paragraphs shall apply mutatis mutandis to the acquiring company which acquires the business, etc. of other foreign companies. In such cases, the term 'total assets' appearing in paragraph (2)(i) and the term 'net sales of the said acquisition in the profit and loss statement which is made with the latest balance sheet' appearing in paragraph (2)(ii) shall be read as 'domestic sales'.

(5) The provisions of Article 15 (4) through (6) inclusive shall apply mutatis mutandis to the restriction of acquisition of business, etc. related to the declaration pursuant to Article 15 (2) (including cases applicable mutatis mutandis under the preceding paragraph) and the orders made by the Fair Trade Commission pursuant

to the provisions of Article 17–2 (1). In such case, the term 'merger' appearing in Article 15 (4) and (6) shall be read as 'acquisition of a business or the fixed assets used in the business'; the term 'regarding the merger' appearing in Article 15 (5) shall be read as 'regarding the acquisition of a business or the fixed assets used in the business'; and the terms 'one or more companies among the merging companies' and 'the merging companies' appearing therein shall be read as 'the company that intends to acquire the business or the fixed assets used in the business'.

Art. 17 [Prohibition of Evasion]

No acts in whatever form or manner shall be committed to evade such prohibitions or restrictions as provided for by Articles 9 through 16 inclusive. Art. 17–2 [Elimination measures against unlawful acts relating to a company, etc.] (1) Where there exists any act in violation of the provisions of Article 10 (1), Article 11 (1), Article 15 (1), Article 15–2 (1), Article 16 (1), or the preceding article, the Fair Trade Commission may, in accordance with the procedures provided for in Division II of Chapter VIII, order the entrepreneur concerned to dispose of all or some of his or her stocks, to transfer a part of his or her business, or to take any other measures necessary to eliminate such acts in violation of the said provisions.

(2) Where there exists any act in violation of the provisions of Article 9 (1) or (2), Article 13, Article 14, or the preceding article, the Fair Trade Commission may, in accordance with the procedures provided for in Division II of Chapter VIII, order the person violating such provisions to dispose of all or some of his or her stocks, to resign from his or her position as an officer of the company, or to take any other measures necessary to eliminate such acts in violation of the said provisions.

Art. 18 [Measures Against an Illegal Merger]

(1) The Fair Trade Commission may, in cases where companies have merged in violation of the provisions of Article 15 (2) (including cases applicable mutatis mutandis under Article 15 (3)) and Article 15 (4), bring a lawsuit to have the said establishment or merger declared null and void.

(2) The preceding paragraph shall apply mutatis mutandis to cases where companies have effected a joint establishment division or acquisition division in violation of the provisions of Article 15–2 (2) and (3) (including cases where these provisions are applied mutatis mutandis under Article 15–2 (5)) and Article 15 (4) which are applied mutatis under Article 15–2 (6). In such cases, 'the said establishment or merger' in the preceding paragraph shall be read as 'the said joint establishment division or acquisition division'.

Chapter V
Unfair Trade Practices

Art. 19 *[Prohibition of Unfair Trade Practices]*

No entrepreneur shall employ unfair trade practices.

Art. 20 *[Measures Against Unfair Trade Practices]*

(1) When there exists any act in violation of the preceding article, the Fair Trade Commission may, in accordance with the procedures provided for in Division II of Chapter VIII, order the entrepreneur concerned to cease and desist from the said act, to delete the clauses concerned from the contract, and to take any other measures necessary to eliminate the said act.

(2) The provisions of Article 7 (2) shall apply mutatis mutandis to an act in violation of the preceding article.

Chapter VI
Exemptions

Art. 21 *[Acts Under Intellectual Property Rights]*

The provisions of this Act shall not apply to such acts recognizable as the exercise of rights under the Copyright Act, the Patent Act, the Utility Model Act, the Design Act, or the Trademark Act.

Art. 22 *[Acts of Associations]*

The provisions of this Act shall not apply to such acts of an association (including a federation of associations) which conforms to the requirements stipulated in each of the following items and which has been formed in accordance with the provisions of a separate law: Provided, That the foregoing shall not apply to such cases where unfair trade practices are employed, or where competition in any particular field of trade is substantially restrained, resulting in unjust rise of prices:

(i) The purpose of the association shall be mutual aid among small-scale entrepreneurs or consumers;
(ii) The association shall be voluntarily formed; and the participation in and withdrawal from the association shall be voluntary;
(iii) Each member shall possess equal voting rights; and
(iv) If distribution of profits among members is contemplated, the limits shall be stipulated by law or cabinet ordinance, or in the articles of association.

Art. 23 *[Resale Price Maintenance Contracts]*

(1) The provisions of this Act shall not apply to legitimate acts performed by an entrepreneur who produces or sells a commodity, the uniform quality of which is easily identifiable and which is designated by the Fair Trade Commission, with another entrepreneur who buys such commodity, in order to fix and maintain the resale price thereof (this term means hereinafter the price at which the latter entrepreneur or a third entrepreneur who purchases from him or her sells such commodity): Provided, That the foregoing shall not apply if the said act tends to be grossly injurious to the interest of consumers in general, or if it is done against the will of the entrepreneur who produces the said commodity by an entrepreneur whose business is to sell the said commodity.

(2) The Fair Trade Commission shall not designate a commodity under the provisions of the preceding paragraph unless it comes under each of the following items:

(i) The commodity shall be for the daily use by the consumers in general; and
(ii) Free competition shall exist with respect to the commodity.

(3) The designation of a commodity under the provisions of paragraph (1) *above* shall be made by an official announcement.

(4) Legitimate acts performed by an entrepreneur whose business is to publish copyrighted works or by an entrepreneur whose business is to sell such published works, in order to fix and maintain with another entrepreneur who buys such works the resale price thereof, shall be exempted from the application of the provisions of this Act.

(5) Organizations formed in accordance with the provisions of any one of the following Acts shall not be included in the term 'another entrepreneur' who buys commodities or copyrighted works provided for in paragraph (1) or the preceding paragraph: Provided, That the foregoing provisions shall, in the case of the organizations formed under the provisions of any one of the Acts mentioned in items (viii) and (viii–ii) hereunder, only apply to cases where a business cooperative, a minor business cooperative, a federation of cooperatives, a commercial and industrial association, or a federation of commercial and industrial associations purchases such commodity as provided for in paragraph (2) *above* or copyrighted works as provided for in paragraph (4) *above*, for the consumption of persons directly or indirectly constituting the said business cooperative, federation of cooperatives, commercial and industrial associations, or a federation of commercial and industrial associations:

(i) National Public Service Act;
(ii) Agricultural Cooperatives Act;
(iii) National Public Service, etc., Mutual Aid Association Act;
(iii–ii) Local Public Service, etc., Mutual Aid Association Act;
(iv) Consumer Cooperatives Act;
(v) Fisheries Cooperatives Act;
(vi) Public Corporation, etc. Labor Relations Act;
(vii) Labor Unions Act;
(viii) Small and Medium-Sized Enterprise, etc., Cooperatives Act;
(viii–ii) Small and Medium-Sized Enterprises Organization Act;
(ix) Local Public Service Act;
(x) Forestry Cooperatives Act;
(xi) Local Public Enterprise Labor Relations Act.

(6) When an entrepreneur as stipulated in paragraph (1) *above* has fixed the resale price under the said paragraph and has entered into contract for the purpose of

maintaining it, the entrepreneur shall, in accordance with provisions of the Rules of the Fair Trade Commission, file a declaration thereon with the Fair Trade Commission within thirty days from the date of the conclusion of the said contract: Provided, That the foregoing shall not apply if the Fair Trade Commission stipulates otherwise in its Rules.

Chapter VII
Injunctions and Damages

Art. 24 *[Injunction Rights]*

A person, whose interests are infringed or likely to be infringed by an act in violation of Article 8 (1)(v) or Article 19 and who is thereby suffering or likely to suffer serious damages, is entitled to demand the suspension or prevention of such infringements from an entrepreneur or a trade association that infringes or is likely to infringe such interests.

Art. 25 *[Absolute Liability]*

(1) Any entrepreneur that has committed an act in violation of Articles 3, 6, or 19 (entrepreneurs whose act has violated Article 6 are limited to those who have effected unreasonable restraint of trade or employed unfair trade practices in the international agreement or contract concerned) and any trade association that has committed an act in violation of Article 8 (1) shall be liable to indemnify the person injured.

(2) No entrepreneur or trade association may be exempted from the liability prescribed in the preceding paragraph by proving non-existence of willfulness or negligence on its part.

Art. 26 *[Restriction on Exercise of the Right to Claim for Damages in Court, Prescription]*

(1) The right to claim for damages in the preceding article may not be exercised in court until the cease and desist order pursuant to the provision of Article 49 (1) (in the case that no such order is issued, the payment order pursuant to Article 50 (1) [excluding those issued against an entrepreneur that is a constituent member of a trade association that commits an act in violation of the provision of Article 8 (1)(i) or (ii)]) or the decision pursuant to the provisions of Article 66 (4) has become final and conclusive.

(2) The right under the preceding paragraph shall become extinct by prescription upon expiration of three years from the date on which the cease and desist order or the payment order or decision in the said paragraph became final and conclusive.

Chapter VIII
Fair Trade Commission

DIVISION I ORGANIZATION AND POWER

Art. 27 *[Duty and Position]*

(1) The Fair Trade Commission shall be established in order to achieve the purposes of Article 1 of this Act based on the provisions of Article 49 (3) of the Cabinet Office Establishment Law (Law No. 89 of 1999).

(2) The Fair Trade Commission shall be administratively attached to the Prime Minister. Art. 27–2. [Affairs under the jurisdiction of the Fair Trade Commission] To perform the duties in paragraph (1) of the preceding Article, the Fair Trade Commission shall be responsible for the following matters:

(i) Matters relating to regulation on private monopolization;
(ii) Matters relating to regulation on unreasonable restraint of trade;
(iii) Matters relating to regulation on unfair trade practices;
(iv) Matters relating to regulation on monopolistic situations;
(v) Matters relating to international cooperation about affairs under the jurisdiction of the Fair Trade Commission;
(vi) Business which is assigned to the Fair Trade Commission based on a law (including an order based on a law), in addition to those stipulated in any one of the preceding items.

Art. 28 *[Independence]*

The chairman and the commissioners of the Fair Trade Commission perform their duties independently.

Art. 29 *[Organization, Appointment of Chairman and Commissioners and their Status]*

(1) The Fair Trade Commission shall be composed of a chairman and four commissioners.

(2) The chairman and the commissioners shall be appointed by the Prime Minister with the consent of both Houses of the Diet from among persons whose age is thirty-five or more and who are experts in law or economics.

(3) The appointment or dismissal of the chairman shall be attested to by the Emperor.

(4) The chairman and the commissioners shall be public service officials.

Art. 30 *[Term of Office for Chairman and Commissioners]*

(1) The term of office for the chairman and the commissioners shall be five years: Provided, That the term of office for the chairman and the commissioners appointed to fill a vacancy shall be the remainder of the term of office of his or her predecessor.

(2) The chairman and the commissioners may be reappointed.

(3) The chairman and the commissioners shall retire from the office upon reaching the age of seventy.

(4) If the term of office for the chairman or the commissioners expires, or a vacancy occurs at the time when the consent of both Houses of the Diet is unobtainable because the Diet is not in session or the House of Representatives is dissolved, the Prime Minister may appoint the chairman or a commissioner from among such persons having qualifications as provided for in paragraph (2) of the preceding article. In this case, the subsequent approval of both Houses shall be obtained at the earliest session of the Diet after the appointment.

Art. 31 *[Guarantee of Status of Chairman and Commissioners]*

The chairman or a commissioner may not, against his or her will, be removed from office during his or her term of office, except in cases falling under any one of the following items:

(i) When he or she has been adjudicated as incompetent, quasi-incompetent, or in bankruptcy;
(ii) When he or she has been dismissed by way of disciplinary punishment;
(iii) When he or she has been punished for violation of this Act;
(iv) When he or she has been sentenced to imprisonment or heavier penalty;
(v) When the Fair Trade Commission has decided that he or she is incapable of executing his or her duties on account of physical or mental breakdown;
(vi) When the subsequent approval of both Houses of the Diet could not be obtained in the case of paragraph (4) of the preceding article.

Art. 32 *[Dismissal of Chairman or Commissioners]*

In the case of items (i) or (iii) through (vi) inclusive of the preceding article, the Prime Minister shall dismiss the chairman or the commissioner concerned from office.

Art. 33 *[Chairman]*

(1) The chairman shall preside over the affairs of the Fair Trade Commission and shall represent it.

(2) The Fair Trade Commission shall choose in advance a commissioner from among the commissioners who acts on behalf of the chairman in case he or she cannot execute the chairman duties.

Art. 34 *[Quorum and Voting]*

(1) Meetings of the Fair Trade Commission shall not be declared open, and a decision shall not be made without the attendance of the chairman and two or more commissioners.

(2) All decisions of the Fair Trade Commission shall be made by majority vote of the attending commissioners. In case the votes are evenly divided, the chairman shall have the power to decide.

(3) The decision of the Fair Trade Commission under the provisions of Article 31 (v) shall, irrespective of the provisions of the preceding paragraph, be made with the unanimous concurrence of all commissioners or the chairman except for the commissioner or chairman concerned.

(4) For the purpose of applying the provisions of paragraph (1) *above*, in case the chairman cannot execute the chairman duties, the commissioner chosen to act on behalf of the chairman pursuant to paragraph (2) of the preceding article shall be deemed to be the chairman.

Art. 35 *[Secretariat]*

(1) A general secretariat shall be established at the Fair Trade Commission for the discharge of its affairs.

(2) The general secretariat shall have a secretary general.

(3) The secretary general shall preside over the affairs of general secretariat (excluding those affairs which the Fair Trade Commission decides to designate hearing examiners to conduct in accordance with the provisions of Article 56 (1)).

(4) The general secretariat shall be composed of the secretariat and bureaus.

(5) The provisions of Article 17 (2) through (8) inclusive of the Cabinet Office Establishment Law shall apply mutatis mutandis to the establishment of the

secretariat and bureaus in the preceding paragraph, the scope of the affairs under its jurisdiction, and the internal organization.

(6) The secretariat and bureaus established based on the provisions of paragraph (4) shall not exceed three in number.

(7) Hearing examiners shall be posted at the general secretariat to conduct all or part of the hearing procedures (excluding the rendering of a decision).

(8) The number of hearing examiners shall be stipulated by cabinet ordinance.

(9) Hearing examiners shall be selected by the Fair Trade Commission from among the staff members of the general secretariat who have been found to have the necessary knowledge and experience in law and economics to conduct the hearing procedures and to be capable of making a fair judgment.

(10) A public prosecutor and a private attorney practicing at the time of the appointment or a person qualified to be an attorney at law shall be among the staff members of the general secretariat.

(11) The duties of the public prosecutor who is a staff member under the preceding paragraph shall be limited to matters relating to cases in violation of the provisions of this Act.

Art. 35–2 *[Local Offices]*

(1) Local offices shall be maintained at necessary locations as local organizations of the general secretariat of the Fair Trade Commission.

(2) The name, location, and territorial jurisdiction of each local office under the preceding paragraph shall be provided for by cabinet ordinance.

(3) Branches may be maintained at necessary locations under local offices in order to conduct some of the affairs of the local offices.

(4) The name, location, and territorial jurisdiction of each branch under the preceding paragraph shall be provided for by Cabinet Office ordinance.

Art. 35–3 *[Administration of Staff Members]*

With regard to the appointment, dismissal, disciplinary measures, and other matters relating to the administration of staff members of the general secretariat, the provisions of the National Public Service Law (Law No. 120 of 1947) shall apply.

Art. 36 *[Salaries of Chairman and Commissioners]*

(1) The salaries of the chairman and the commissioners shall be provided for separately.

(2) The salaries of the chairman and the commissioners shall not be reduced in amount against their will while they are in office.

Art. 37 *[Prohibition of Certain Activities of Chairman, Commissioners, and Staff Members]*

The chairman, commissioners, and such staff members of the Fair Trade Commission as may be stipulated by cabinet ordinance shall not engage in any of the following activities while they are in office:

(i) Become a member of the Diet or of the legislative assembly of a local public authority, or actively engage in political activities;
(ii) Hold any other remunerative position except as permitted by the Prime Minister; or
(iii) Engage in commerce or any other business for pecuniary gain.

Art. 38 *[Prohibition of Expression of Opinion]*

The chairman, commissioners and other staff members of the Fair Trade Commission shall not express their views outside the Fair Trade Commission on the existence or non-existence of facts or application of law with regard to a case: Provided, That the foregoing shall not apply to cases provided for in this Act or cases where the chairman, commissioner, or staff member gives a presentation on his or her research on this Act.

Art. 39 *[Duty to Preserve Trade Secrets]*

The chairman, commissioners, and other staff members of the Fair Trade Commission, or any person who once held such position, shall not divulge or make surreptitious use of trade secrets of entrepreneurs which came to their knowledge in the course of their duties.

Art. 40 *[Compulsory Powers of Inquiry]*

The Fair Trade Commission may, if necessary for the performance of its functions, order government agencies, juridical persons established by a special law or an order, entrepreneurs, or organizations of entrepreneurs, or their personnel to appear before the Commission, or may require them to submit necessary reports, information, or documents.

Art. 41 *[Entrustment of Research and Surveys]*

The Fair Trade Commission may, if necessary for the performance of its functions, entrust government agencies, juridical persons established by a special law or an order, schools, entrepreneurs, organizations of entrepreneurs, experts, or others to carry out necessary research and surveys.

Art. 42 *[Public Hearings]*

The Fair Trade Commission may, if necessary for the performance of its duties, hold public hearings to obtain views of the public.

Art. 43 *[Publication of Appropriate Matters]*

The Fair Trade Commission may, in order to ensure proper enforcement of this Act, make public any appropriate matters with the exception of trade secrets of entrepreneurs.

Art. 44 *[Reports to the Diet, Submission of Opinions]*

(1) The Fair Trade Commission shall submit to the Diet, through the Prime Minister, an annual report on the enforcement of this Act.

(2) The Fair Trade Commission may submit to the Diet, through the Prime Minister, its views on matters necessary to attain the purpose of this Act.

DIVISION II PROCEDURES

Art. 45 *[Report and Detection of Violation]*

(1) Any person may, when he or she considers that a fact in violation of this Act exists, report the said fact to the Fair Trade Commission and ask for the appropriate measures to be taken.

(2) The Fair Trade Commission, upon receipt of such report as provided for in the preceding paragraph, shall make necessary investigation with respect to the case.

(3) Where any report submitted under the provisions of paragraph (1) *above* specifies in writing any fact or facts in accordance with the Rules of the Fair Trade Commission, and when the Commission decides to take, or not to take, appropriate measures with respect to the case referred to in the report, the Fair Trade Commission shall promptly notify that effect to the person who made such report.

(4) The Fair Trade Commission may, when it considers that a violation of this Act or a monopolistic situation exists, take appropriate measures on its own authority.

Art. 46 *[Procedures for Measures Against a Monopolistic Situation]*

(1) The Fair Trade Commission shall, if it considers that there exists a fact which falls under the purview of a monopolistic situation, and if it decides to take a measure set forth in paragraph (4) of the preceding article, make a notice of such action to the competent minister having jurisdiction over the business in which the entrepreneur concerned is engaged.

(2) In case a notice under the provisions of the preceding paragraph has been issued, the minister may present to the Commission his or her view regarding the existence or the absence of such a monopolistic situation and his or her view regarding other alternative measures which he or she feels would be sufficient to restore competition as provided for in the proviso to Article 8–4 (1).

Art. 47 *[Compulsory Measures for Investigation]*

(1) The Fair Trade Commission may, in order to conduct the necessary investigation with regard to a case of violation, take the following measures:

(i) Ordering persons concerned with a case, or witnesses to appear for interrogating, hearing their views or collecting reports from them;
(ii) Ordering experts to appear to have them give expert testimony;
(iii) Ordering persons holding accounting books, documents, and other matters to submit the same, or retaining such submitted matters at the Fair Trade Commission;
(iv) Entering any place of business of the persons concerned with a case, or other necessary sites and inspecting conditions of business operation and property, accounting books, documents, and other matters.

(2) The Fair Trade Commission may, when it finds it proper, designate, in accordance with the provisions of cabinet ordinance, investigators from among the staff members of the Fair Trade Commission and have them take the measures provided for in the preceding paragraph.

(3) Where an inspection is to be conducted by the staff members in accordance with the provisions of the preceding paragraph, they shall be required to carry their identification cards and to show it to the persons concerned.

(4) The authority to take action pursuant to the provision of paragraph (1) *above* shall not be construed as one granted for criminal investigation.

Art. 48 *[Investigation Record]*

The Fair Trade Commission shall, when it has conducted the necessary investigation of a case of violation, keep an investigation record of the main points thereof, and when it has taken any measures as provided for in paragraph (1) of the preceding article, it shall set out the date of implementation of the measures and the result thereof.

Art. 49 *[Order to the Violator to Take Elimination Measures]*

(1) An order issued pursuant to the provisions of Article 7 (1) or (2) (including cases applicable mutatis mutandis under Article 8–2 (2) or Article 20 (2)), Article 8–2 (1) or (3), Article 17–2 or Article 20 (1) (hereinafter referred to as 'cease and desist order') shall be rendered in writing, and the written order shall indicate the measures necessary to eliminate the violation or to ensure that the violation is eliminated and the facts found by and the application of law thereto made by the Fair Trade Commission, and the chairman and the commissioners participating in the voting in accordance with the provisions of Article 69 (1) shall sign it and affix their seal thereto.

(2) An order to take elimination measures shall become valid by serving to the addressee a certified copy of such order to take elimination measures.

(3) The Fair Trade Commission shall, when it intends to issue an order to take elimination measures, give in advance to the person who is to be the addressee for the said order an opportunity to present his or her views and to submit evidence in support thereof.

(4) At the time of presenting his or her views or submitting evidence pursuant to the preceding paragraph, the person who is to be the addressee for the said order may appoint an agent (limited to an attorney at law, a law firm, or a person approved as appropriate by the Fair Trade Commission; hereinafter the same in Article 52 (1), Article 57, Article 59, Article 60, and Article 63).

(5) The Fair Trade Commission shall, when offering an opportunity to present views and to submit evidence in support thereof pursuant to the provisions of paragraph (3), set a deadline that ensures an appropriate period for the presentation of views and the submission of evidence in support thereof and notify the person who is to be the addressee for the order to take elimination measures in writing of the following matters:

(i) Tentative content of the order to take elimination measures;
(ii) The facts found by and the application of law thereto made by the Fair Trade Commission; and

(iii) The opportunity to present his or her views and to submit evidence in support thereof to the Fair Trade Commission and the deadline thereof regarding the matters in the two preceding items.

(6) If any person is dissatisfied with the order to take elimination measures, he or she may request, in accordance with the Rules of the Fair Trade Commission and within sixty days from the date on which the certified copy of such order was served (in the event of force majeure or other unavoidable reason why the request was not made by the deadline, within one week calculated from the day after the day when the reason ceased to be valid), the Fair Trade Commission to initiate hearing procedures on the said order.

(7) If there is no request provided in the preceding paragraph within the period provided in the paragraph, the order to take elimination measures shall become final and conclusive.

Art. 50 *[Procedures for Surcharges]*

(1) An order issued pursuant to the provisions of Article 7–2 (1) (including cases applicable mutatis mutandis under Article 7–2 (2) or Article 8–3) (hereinafter referred to as 'payment order') shall be rendered in writing, and the written surcharge payment order shall state the amount of the surcharge to be paid, the basis of calculation of such amount, the violative act related to such surcharge, and the deadline for payment, and the chairman and the commissioners participating in the voting in accordance with the provisions of Article 69 (1) shall sign it and affix their seal thereto.

(2) A payment order shall become valid by serving to the addressee a certified copy of such surcharge payment order.

(3) The deadline for payment of such surcharge as prescribed in paragraph (1) shall fall on a day three months after the day on which the certified copy of such payment order is issued.

(4) If any person is dissatisfied with the payment order, he or she may request, in accordance with the Rules of the Fair Trade Commission and within sixty days from the date on which the certified copy of such order was served (in the event of disaster or other unavoidable reason why the request was not made by the deadline, within one week calculated from the day after the day when the reason ceased to be valid), the Commission to initiate hearing procedures on the said order.

(5) If there is no request provided in the preceding paragraph within the period provided in that paragraph, the payment order shall become final and conclusive.

(6) The provisions of paragraphs (3) through (5) inclusive of the preceding article, are applicable mutatis mutandis regarding the payment order. In this case, the term 'Tentative content of the order to take elimination measures' appearing in Article 49 (5)(i) shall be read as 'Amount of the surcharge intended to be ordered for payment'; the term 'The facts found by and the application of law thereto made by the Fair Trade Commission' appearing in Article 49 (5)(ii) shall be read as 'The basis of calculation of such amount and the violative act related to such surcharge'.

Art. 51 *[Surcharge Reductions in Case of Fine]*

(1) After the Fair Trade Commission has issued a payment order pursuant to the provisions of Article 7–2 (1) (including cases applicable mutatis mutandis under Article 7–2 (2)), the Fair Trade Commission shall, if there is a final and conclusive court ruling that imposes a fine on the person that received the said payment order, modify, by a decision, the amount of the surcharge in the said payment order to an amount that is reduced by an amount equivalent to one-half of the fine ordered in the said court ruling: Provided, That this shall not apply if the amount of the surcharge related to the said payment order does not exceed the sum equivalent to one-half of the said fine or the amount after the said modification is less than one million yen.

(2) In the case of the proviso in the preceding paragraph (if the amount of the surcharge related to the said payment order does not exceed the sum equivalent to one-half of the said fine or the amount after the said modification is less than one million yen), the Fair Trade Commission shall revoke the said payment order by a decision.

(3) In the case of paragraph (1), the Fair Trade Commission shall, if the hearing procedures related to the said payment order are not completed, modify, notwithstanding the provisions of the paragraph (1), the amount of the surcharge in the said payment order by reducing the amount decided through the said hearing procedures by an amount equivalent to one-half of the fine pursuant to paragraph (1) by a decision regarding the request for hearings related to the said payment order.

(4) In the case of the three preceding paragraphs, the Fair Trade Commission shall promptly refund in pecuniary form any amount already paid based on the pre-modification or pre-revocation payment order (excluding any arrearage charge pursuant to Article 70–9 (3)) if there is some portion that should be refunded.

Art. 52 *[Commencement of Hearing]*

(1) Any person requesting hearings pursuant to the provisions of Article 49 (6) or Article 50 (4) (hereinafter referred to as 'hearing request') shall submit

to the Fair Trade Commission a request that states the matters in the following items:

(i) the name or title and address or domicile of the person making the hearing request or his or her agent;
(ii) order related to the hearing request; and
(iii) purpose and reason for the hearing request.

(2) The purpose provided in item (iii) of the previous paragraph shall clearly state the scope of the request for revocation or modification of the order, and the claim (in the case of an order to take elimination measures, the claim against the facts that led to the order; in the case of a payment order, the claim against the basis of calculation of the surcharge) against cease and desist order or payment order (referred to as 'original administrative measures' in paragraph 5, Article 58, Article 59 (1), Article 66 (3) and (4), and Article 70–8) shall be clarified in the reason provided in the same item.

(3) In the case that a hearing request has been submitted, the Fair Trade Commission shall initiate hearings regarding the order related to the said hearing request without delay, except for cases that fall under Article 66 (1).

(4) The hearing request may be withdrawn in writing at any point up to the date of the final hearing.

(5) After hearing procedures have been initiated pursuant to the provisions of Article 55 (3), the original administrative measures become final and conclusive when there is a request to withdraw hearing procedures.

Art. 53 *[Initiation of Hearing Procedures]*

(1) The Fair Trade Commission may, in cases where a monopolistic situation (excluding cases provided for in the proviso to Article 8–4 (1); the same shall apply in Article 67 (1)) exists, initiate hearing procedures on the said case if the Commission finds that it would be in the public interest to initiate hearing procedures on the case.

(2) The Fair Trade Commission shall, when it intends to initiate hearing procedures on a case related to the provisions of the previous paragraph, consult with the competent minister having jurisdiction over the business in which such entrepreneur is engaged.

Art. 54 *[Suspension of Execution of Order]*

(1) The Fair Trade Commission may suspend the execution of all or part of a cease and desist order if it deems it necessary in the case where a hearing request is submitted in relation to the said order to take elimination measures.

(2) In the case of the suspension of execution pursuant to the provisions of the preceding paragraph, the Fair Trade Commission shall, if it deems that the suspension of the said execution would possibly make it difficult to ensure competition in the market or otherwise deems it necessary, revoke the suspension of the said execution.

Art. 55 *[Complaints, Initiation of Hearing Procedures]*

(1) The Fair Trade Commission shall, when it initiates hearing procedures pursuant to the provisions of Article 52 (3), send a notification of hearing procedures to the person who submitted the hearing request.

(2) The complaint pursuant to the provisions of Article 53 (1) shall be made in writing and shall state the outline of the case and the name or title of the addressee of the measures pursuant to Article 8–4 (1), and the chairman and the commissioners participating in the voting of the decision to issue the complaint shall sign it and affix their seal thereto.

(3) The hearing procedures shall be initiated by sending a notification of hearing procedures to the person who submitted the hearing request in paragraph (1) or serving a certified copy of the complaint upon the addressee in the preceding paragraph.

(4) The person who submitted the hearing request in paragraph (1) or the addressee in paragraph (2) (hereinafter referred to as 'respondent') shall be ordered to appear in the hearing room on the date of the hearings.

(5) The date of the hearings shall be fixed on the day thirty days from the date of issue of the notification of hearing procedures or the date of issue of the certified copy of the order of hearing procedures: Provided, That the foregoing shall not apply when the consent of the respondent is obtained.

(6) The person who received the certified copy of the complaint pursuant to paragraph (2) shall submit an answer without delay to the Fair Trade Commission.

Art. 56 *[Designation of Hearing Examiners and Entrusted Proceedings]*

(1) The Fair Trade Commission may, after initiating the hearing procedures, designate hearing examiners for each case and entrust them to conduct all or part of the subsequent hearing procedures (excluding the decision; the same in the following paragraph, Article 63, and Article 64) in addition to entrusting them with the research and surveys pursuant to the provisions of Article 41 and the performance of the compulsory measures for investigation under each item of Article 47 (1) in accordance with the Rules of the Fair Trade Commission: Provided, That no person

who has performed duties as an investigator of the said case or who has been involved in the investigation of the said case in another way may be designated as a hearing examiner.

(2) The hearing examiners designated pursuant to the provisions of the preceding paragraph (in the case that more than one hearing examiner has been designated, the person nominated from among them) shall supervise the affairs related to the hearing procedures they are entrusted with by the Fair Trade Commission based on the provisions of that paragraph in accordance with the Rules of the Fair Trade Commission.

Art. 57 *[Non-appearance of Respondents]*

The Fair Trade Commission or the hearing examiners may conduct the hearings even if the respondent or his or her agent fails to appear on the date of the said hearings without a justifiable cause.

Art. 58 *[Powers of Investigators at Hearings]*

(1) An investigator designated in accordance with the provisions of Article 47 (2) may attend hearings, make a claim about the facts that led to the original administrative measures, the application of law thereto, and the suitability of the original administrative measures (in the case the hearings concern a case related to Article 8–4 (1), a fact which falls under the purview of a monopolistic situation), offer evidence, and perform other necessary acts.

(2) In the case of the preceding paragraph, an investigator may make such a claim when a modification (limited to modifications within the scope prescribed by the Rules of the Fair Trade Commission) is deemed necessary regarding the facts that led to the original administrative measures and the application of law thereto (in the case the hearings concern a case related to Article 8–4 (1), a fact which falls under the purview of a monopolistic situation): Provided, That this shall not apply in the case that it would harm the interests of the respondent.

Art. 59 *[Respondent's Defense]*

(1) A respondent or his or her agent may, at hearings, state the reason why the original administrative measures or the measures being ordered pursuant to the provisions of Article 8–4 (1) by the Fair Trade Commission in regard to the said case are unfair; may submit supporting evidence therefore; may request the Fair Trade Commission to interrogate necessary witnesses, order expert witnesses to testify, order holders of accounting books, documents, and other matters to submit them, or enter the necessary sites and inspect the conditions of business and property, accounting books, and other matters, or entrust research and surveys; or may interrogate witnesses or expert witnesses who are required to attend the hearings by

order of the Fair Trade Commission; or may question those entrusted to perform research and surveys.

(2) A respondent (except when the respondent is a constituent entrepreneur of a trade association that has committed an act in violation to Article 8 (1)(i) or (ii); the same in the following paragraph) or his or her agent may not, in the hearings related to the payment order, claim the nonexistence of the violative act related to the said payment order (in the case of item (iii), limited to that portion of the violative act found by the Commission) in the case that any one of the following items applies:

- (i) the order to take elimination measures regarding the violative act related to the payment order pursuant to Article 49 (7) has become final and conclusive;
- (ii) the respondent or his or her agent has withdrawn the hearing request regarding the order to take elimination measures regarding the violative act related to the payment order; or
- (iii) all or part of the violative act is found true by the Commission in the decision regarding the order to take elimination measures regarding the violative act related to the payment order.

Art. 60 *[Disclosure of Reasons for Non-Acceptance of Evidence]*

If the Fair Trade Commission or hearing examiner does not accept the evidence introduced by the investigator, the respondent, or his or her agent, the Commission or hearing examiner shall state the reason for not having accepted such evidence.

Art. 61 *[Hearings Records]*

(1) All hearings shall be made public: Provided, That when it is found necessary to protect the trade secrets of an entrepreneur, or necessary to the public interest, hearings shall not be made public.

(2) Records of the hearings shall be created in accordance with the Rules of the Fair Trade Commission.

Art. 62 *[Qualifications for Witness, Right to Refuse Testimony, Oath, etc.]*

(1) The provisions of Articles 143 through 147 inclusive, Article 149, Articles 154 through 156 inclusive, Article 165, and Article 166 of the Code of Criminal Procedure (Law No. 131 of 1948) shall apply mutatis mutandis to the procedures by which the Fair Trade Commission or hearing examiners, in the course of hearings, interrogate witnesses, or order expert witnesses to give an expert testimony.

(2) In such cases provided for in the preceding paragraph, the terms 'court', 'question', and 'defendant' shall be read as 'the Fair Trade Commission or hearing examiners', 'interrogate', and 'respondent', respectively.

Art. 63 *[Opportunity to State the Case Directly to the Commission]*

In cases where the Fair Trade Commission has entrusted hearing examiners to conduct all or part of the hearing procedures pursuant to the provisions of Article 56 (1), the Commission shall, if the respondent or his or her agent so requests, give the respondent or his or her agent an opportunity to state their views directly to the Commission: Provided, That this shall not apply to cases in which the hearing procedures regarding a payment order have been initiated pursuant to the provision of Article 52 (3) and the said violation has been found by the Commission in a decision related to the order to take elimination measures regarding the violative act related to the said payment order.

Art. 64 *[Merging and Separation of Hearing Procedures]*

The Fair Trade Commission or the hearing examiners may, when deemed appropriate, merge or separate the hearing procedures on its or their own authority.

Art. 65 *[Consent Decision]*

After the Fair Trade Commission has determined to initiate hearing procedures under the provisions of Article 53 (1) regarding a case pursuant to Article 8–4 (1), the Commission may, when the respondent, admitting the finding of facts and the application of law stated in the complaint, submits to the Commission a written statement setting forth his or her acceptance of the decision without resorting to subsequent hearing procedures and files a plan setting forth concrete measures which he or she proposes voluntarily to take in order to restore competition with respect to the goods or services involved in the monopolistic situation, render a decision in line with the concrete measures stated in such plan without conducting subsequent hearing procedures if the Commission finds it appropriate.

Art. 66 *[Decision After Hearing]*

(1) The Fair Trade Commission shall, if the hearing request is made after the legal period had elapsed or is otherwise unlawful, reject the said request by a decision.

(2) The Fair Trade Commission shall, if the hearing request is groundless, dismiss the said request by a decision after the hearing procedures have been completed.

(3) The Fair Trade Commission shall, if the hearing request has sufficient grounds, revoke or modify all or part of the original administrative measures by a decision after the hearing procedures have been completed.

(4) In the case of revocation of all or part of the original administrative measures pursuant to the provisions of the preceding paragraph, the Fair Trade Commission shall, when it finds that an act in violation the provisions of Article 3, Article 6, Article 8 (1), Article 9 (1) or (2), Article 10 (1), Article 11 (1), Article 13, Article 14, Article 15 (1), Article 15–2 (1), Article 16 (1), Article 17, or Article 19 existed prior to the issuance of the original administrative measures but that the violative act had already ceased to exist at the time of issuance of the said original administrative measures, make these facts clear by an administrative decision.

Art. 67 *[Formal Decision]*

(1) The Fair Trade Commission shall, when it finds after the hearing procedures have been completed that a monopolistic situation exists, order the respondent by a decision to take such measures as provided for in Article 8–4 (1).

(2) The Fair Trade Commission shall, when it finds, after the hearing procedures have been completed, that a monopolistic situation did not exist prior to the serving of the complaint, or that a monopolistic situation existed prior to the issuance of the complaint, but the said monopolistic situation has already ceased to exist, or that a monopolistic situation exists and falls under the proviso to Article 8–4 (1), make clear the said fact by a decision.

Art. 68 *[Findings Based on Evidence]*

In rendering a decision pursuant to the provisions of Article 66 (2) through (4) inclusive and the preceding article, the Fair Trade Commission shall, except in the case of facts not contested by the respondent or known publicly, find the facts in question based on the evidence examined at the hearing procedures.

Art. 69 *[Meetings for Decision]*

(1) Orders to take elimination measures, payment orders, and decisions shall be made by a meeting of the chairman and the commissioners.

(2) The provisions of Article 34 (1), (2), and (4) shall apply mutatis mutandis to such meetings as provided for in the preceding paragraph.

(3) For a decision ordering the respondent to take the measures provided for in Article 8–4 (1), the decision shall be supported by three or more people present at the meeting of the chairman and the commissioners, notwithstanding the provisions of Article 34 (2) which are applied mutatis mutandis under the preceding paragraph.

Art. 70 *[Closed Meetings]*

Meetings of the Fair Trade Commission shall not be open to the public.

Art. 70–2 *[Form of Decision]*

(1) Decisions shall be rendered in writing; and the written decisions shall show the facts found by and the application of law thereto made by the Fair Trade Commission and, in the case of decisions under Article 66 (3) regarding payment orders, the basis of calculating the surcharge; and the chairman and the commissioners participating in the voting shall sign it and affix their seals thereto.

(2) A dissenting opinion may be stated in a written decision.

(3) A decision shall take effect by serving the certified copy of the written decision upon the respondent or other addressee.

(4) No decision ordering the respondent to take measures provided for in Article 8–4 (1) may be enforced unless and until such decision becomes final and conclusive.

Art. 70–3 *[Interventions of Interested Third Parties]*

The Fair Trade Commission may, if it finds it necessary, cause, on its own authority, a third person interested in the results of the decision, to be a party to the hearing procedures: Provided, That it shall in advance interrogate the respondent and the said third party.

Art. 70–4 *[Interventions of a Government Agency or Public Organization]*

Any government agency or public organization interested in a case may, if it finds it necessary in the public interest, be a party to the hearing procedures with the approval of the Fair Trade Commission.

Art. 70–5 *[Opinions of a Government Agency or Public Organization]*

Any government agency or public organization interested in a case may, in order to protect the public interest, express its views to the Fair Trade Commission.

Art. 70–6 *[Stay of Execution of FTC's Order by Deposit]*

(1) When the Fair Trade Commission has issued an order to take elimination measures, the respondent may stay the execution of the said order by depositing such bonds or securities (including book-entry transfer corporate bonds, etc. provided in Article 129 (1) of the Law Concerning Book-Entry Transfer of Corporate Bonds, etc. [Law No. 75 of 2001]; same in paragraph (1) of the following article and Article 70–14) as the court may fix until the said order to take elimination measures becomes final and conclusive.

(2) The court ruling under the provisions of the preceding paragraph shall be made in accordance with the Law of Procedure in Non-Contentious Matters (Law No. 14 of 1898).

Art. 70–7 *[Forfeitures of Deposit]*

(1) In a case where a respondent has made the deposit in accordance with the provisions of paragraph (1) of the preceding article and the order to take elimination measures in question has become final and conclusive, the court may, upon petition of the Fair Trade Commission, forfeit the whole or a part of such bonds or securities deposited.

(2) The provisions of paragraph (2) of the preceding article shall apply mutatis mutandis to the court ruling under the provisions of the preceding paragraph.

Art. 70–8 *[Compulsory Measures for Investigation After Decision]*

After issuing an order to take elimination measures (limited to those orders that have become final and conclusive under the provisions of Article 49 (7) or Article 52 (5)), or a decision (excluding decisions that revoke all original administrative measures) rendered in accordance with the provisions of Article 66 (1) through (3) inclusive, or a decision rendered in accordance with the provisions of Article 65 or Article 67 (1), the Fair Trade Commission may, if it considers it particularly necessary, take the measures necessary or may cause its staff members to take the measures necessary to ascertain whether the measures ordered to be taken or maintained in that order or decision are being so taken or maintained in accordance with the provisions of Article 47.

Art. 70–9 *[A Reminder for Payment of Surcharge and Measures Against Delinquency]*

(1) If any person fails to pay a surcharge by the designated deadline, the Fair Trade Commission shall press such person to pay the surcharge by serving a written reminder specifying a deadline thereof.

(2) Notwithstanding the provisions of the preceding paragraph, the Fair Trade Commission shall, if a hearing request regarding the payment order has been submitted (excluding cases where the said hearing request is rejected pursuant to the provisions of Article 66 (1); the same shall apply in the following paragraph), promptly press, after a decision on the said hearing request has been made, such person to pay the surcharge related to the said payment order and the arrearage charge, if there is an arrearage charge pursuant to the following paragraph, by serving a written reminder specifying a deadline thereof, excluding cases where the said payment order is revoked in its entirety pursuant to the provisions of Article 66 (3): Provided, That the foregoing shall not apply to cases where the

said surcharge and arrearage charge are paid in their entirety by the date when a certified copy of the written decision in regard to the hearing request regarding the said payment order was served.

(3) In cases where the person fails to pay the surcharge by the deadline, the Fair Trade Commission may collect an arrearage charge computed at a rate of fourteen point five per cent per annum (if a hearing request regarding the payment order related to the said surcharge has been submitted, the rate specified by cabinet ordinance, but not exceeding seven point twenty-five per cent per annum up to and including the date a certified copy of the written decision regarding the hearing request is served) of the amount of such surcharge for the number of days intervening between the day after the deadline and the day of payment: Provided, That the foregoing shall not apply to cases where the arrearage charge involved is less than one thousand yen.

(4) In case the amount of an arrearage charge, computed in accordance with the provisions of the preceding paragraph, contains a fraction of less than one hundred yen, such fraction shall be disregarded.

(5) In the case that a person upon whom a reminder has been served under the provisions of paragraphs (1) or (2) fails to pay the overdue surcharge by the designated date, the Fair Trade Commission may collect such surcharge based on the example of the national tax delinquency procedures.

(6) The claim on a defaulted surcharge prescribed in the preceding paragraph shall have a lien next to those of national and local taxes, and the prescription on such claim shall be the same as that on national tax.

Art. 70–10 *[Refund]*

(1) In the case that all or part of a payment order is revoked pursuant to the provisions of Article 66 (3), the Fair Trade Commission shall promptly refund in pecuniary form any amount already paid based on the pre-revocation payment order that should be refunded.

(2) In the case of refunds in the preceding paragraph, the Fair Trade Commission shall add to the amount that should be refunded the amount computed at a rate specified by cabinet ordinance, but not exceeding seven point twenty-five per cent per annum, of the amount of the refund for the number of days intervening between the day after the day the said amount was paid and the day the decision was made to pay the refund.

(3) The provisions in the proviso to paragraph (3) and paragraph (4) of the preceding article shall apply mutatis mutandis to amounts added pursuant to the preceding paragraph.

Art. 70–11 [Rejection of Application for Authorization, etc.]

(1) The Fair Trade Commission shall, when an application for authorization under the provisions of Article 11 (1) or (2) has been filed, reject it by a decision if the Commission finds the said application to be groundless.

(2) The provisions of Article 45 (2) shall apply mutatis mutandis to the application for authorization in the preceding paragraph.

Art. 70–12 [Revocation or Modification of Authorization, Approval or Decision]

(1) In cases where authorization pursuant to Article 11 (1) or (2) has been granted, the Fair Trade Commission may, when it finds that the facts required for the said authorization have ceased to exist or have changed, revoke or modify such authorization by a decision after hearing procedures. In such case, the Fair Trade Commission may initiate hearing procedures on its own authority.

(2) The Fair Trade Commission may, when it finds that maintenance of an order to take elimination measures or a decision pursuant to the provisions of Article 65 or Article 67 (1) is inappropriate due to changes in economic conditions or other reasons, revoke or modify it by a decision: Provided, That the foregoing shall not apply if the interests of the respondent may be injured thereby.

Art. 70–13 [Urgent Injunction]

(1) The court may, upon petition of the Fair Trade Commission, when it finds the matter to be one of urgent necessity, order the person doing an act suspected of violation of the provisions of Article 3, Article 6, Article 8 (1), Article 9 (1) or (2), Article 10 (1), Article 11 (1), Article 13, Article 14, Article 15 (1), Article 15–2 (1), Article 16 (1), Article 17, or Article 19 to suspend from the said act, the exercise of voting rights, or the execution of duties as an officer in a company, or may revoke or modify such order.

(2) The provisions of Article 70–6 (2) shall apply mutatis mutandis to the court ruling under the provisions of the preceding paragraph.

Art. 70–14 [Stay of Urgent Injunction]

(1) The execution of an urgent injunction under the provisions of the paragraph (1) of the preceding article may be stayed by depositing such bond or securities as the court may fix.

(2) The provisions of Article 70–7 shall apply mutatis mutandis to forfeiture of the bond or securities deposited under the provisions of the preceding paragraph.

Art. 70–15 [Access to Records]

Any interested person may, after the hearing procedures have been initiated, request the Fair Trade Commission for permission to peruse or copy the records of the case in question, or may ask the Fair Trade Commission for a certified copy of the order to take elimination measures, the surcharge payment order, the complaint, or the written decision, or an abridged copy thereof.

Art. 70–16 [Documents to be Served]

Documents to be served shall be determined, in addition to those as stipulated by this Act, by the Rules of the Fair Trade Commission.

Art. 70–17 [Service of Documents]

With regard to the service of documents, the provisions of Article 99, Article 101, Article 103, Article 105, Article 106, Article 108, and Article 109 of the Code of Civil Procedure (Law No. 109 of 1996) shall apply mutatis mutandis. In this case, the terms 'marshal' in Article 99 (1) of the Code shall be read as 'staff members of the Fair Trade Commission', 'chief judge' in Article 108 of the Code and 'court' in Article 109 of the Code shall be read as 'the Fair Trade Commission'.

Art. 70–18 [Service by Public Notification]

(1) The Fair Trade Commission can serve by public notification in the following cases:

(i) When the address, domicile, or other place of contact of the person that is to receive the service is unknown;
(ii) With regard to service to be made in foreign countries, when the provisions of Article 108 of the Code of Civil Procedure applied mutatis mutandis in the preceding article cannot be applied, or when it is recognized that service cannot be made based on the said provisions; or
(iii) When documents certifying the service are not received after the passage of six months from the date when a foreign competent authority was commissioned to serve under the provisions of Article 108 of the Code of Civil Procedure applied mutatis mutandis in the preceding article.

(2) Service by public notification shall be made through posting on the notice board of the Fair Trade Commission that the documents to be served shall be furnished any time to the person that is to receive the service.

(3) Service by public notification shall take effect after the passage of two weeks from the date when posting started under the provisions of the preceding paragraph.

(4) Regarding service by public notification to be made in foreign countries, the time period stated in the preceding paragraph shall be six weeks.

Art. 70–19 [Notification of Measures by Electronic Information Processing System]

(1) Notifications of administrative measures as provided for in Article 2 (vii) of the Law Concerning Use of Information and Telecommunications Technology in Administrative Procedure (Law No. 151 of 2002) and are to be served pursuant to the provisions of this Law and the Rules of the Fair Trade Commission, may not be served using an electronic information processing system ('electronic information processing system' as defined in Article 4 (1) of the Law Concerning Use of Information and Telecommunications Technology in Administrative Procedure; the same shall apply hereinafter in this article) if the recipient of the said notification of measures has given no indication via the method stipulated in the Rules of the Fair Trade Commission about receiving the service, notwithstanding the provisions of that article.

(2) The staff members of the Fair Trade Commission shall, when performing affairs related to the notification of measures provided for in the preceding paragraph using an electronic information processing system, record matters related to the service under the provisions of Article 109 of the Code of Civil Procedure which applies mutatis mutandis under Article 70–17 in a file stored in a computer (including input and output devices) used by the Fair Trade Commission via an electronic information processing system instead of preparing and submitting a hard copy document that states those matters.

Art. 70–20 [Matters to be Provided for by Cabinet Ordinance]

Necessary matters with respect to procedures for investigations and hearings of the Fair Trade Commission, any other matters relating to the disposal of cases, as well as those with respect to deposits pursuant to Article 70–6 (1) and Article 70–14 (1) shall be provided for by cabinet ordinance except for such matters as are provided for in this Act.

Art. 70–21 [Exemption to Administrative Procedures Law]

The provisions of Chapter II and Chapter III of the Administrative Procedures Law (Law No. 88 of 1993) shall not apply to cease and desist orders, payment orders, and measures relating to applications for authorization under Article 70–11 (1) by the Fair Trade Commission or to decisions or any other measures (including the measures effected by investigators under the provisions of Article 47 (2) and by hearing examiners under the provisions of Article 56 (1)) that have been rendered under the provisions of this Division.

Art. 70–22 *[Special Provisions for Appeals]*

Orders to take elimination measures and payment orders as well as decisions and any other measures (including the measures effected by investigators under the provisions of Article 47 (2) and by hearing examiners under the provisions of Article 56 (1)) that have been rendered by the Fair Trade Commission under the provisions of this Division shall not be appealed under the Administrative Complaint Review Act (Act No. 160 of 1962).

DIVISION III MISCELLANEOUS PROVISIONS

Art. 71 *[Procedures for Designation of Unfair Trade Practices in a Specific Field of Business]*

The Fair Trade Commission shall, when it designates specific trade practices in a specific field of business in accordance with the provisions of Article 2 (9), first hear the views of entrepreneurs operating in the same line of business as that of the entrepreneurs who employ the said specific trade practices, and hold a public hearing to obtain the views of the public and thereupon shall make the designation after due consideration of the views presented.

Art. 72 *[Designation of Unfair Trade Practices by Means of Official Announcement]*

Designation under the provisions of Article 2 (9) shall be made by official announcement.

Art. 73 *[Public Hearing on a Monopolistic Situation]*

In case the Fair Trade Commission contemplates initiating hearing procedures pursuant to the provisions of Article 53 (1), the Commission shall hold a public hearing to obtain the views of the public.

Art. 74 *[Accusation, Report on Non-Prosecution]*

(1) The Fair Trade Commission shall, when it is convinced after an investigation conducted according to the procedures stipulated in Chapter XII that a criminal offense has taken place, file an accusation with the Public Prosecutor General.

(2) In addition to the provisions of the preceding paragraph, the Fair Trade Commission shall, when it considers that a crime violating the provisions of this Act exists, file an accusation with the Public Prosecutor General.

(3) The Public Prosecutor General shall, when he or she has taken measures not to prosecute in a case which is the subject of an accusation under the provisions of the preceding two paragraphs, without delay submit to the Prime Minister through the Minister of Justice a written report stating the said fact and reasons thereof.

Art. 75 *[Compensation for Witnesses or Expert Witness]*

Witnesses or expert witnesses who have been ordered to appear or to give expert testimony in a hearings in accordance with the provisions of Article 47 (1)(i) or (ii), Article 47 (2), or Article 56 (1), may claim a traveling allowance and fees as provided for by cabinet ordinance.

Art. 76 *[Rule-making Powers of the Fair Trade Commission]*

(1) The Fair Trade Commission may establish rules with respect to its internal disciplines, procedures for disposing cases and filing reports, applications for authorization or approval, and other matters.

(2) In establishing rules with respect to procedures for disposing cases pursuant to the preceding paragraph, the Fair Trade Commission shall keep in mind the assurance of the availability of the said procedures, including ensuring sufficient opportunity for a respondent to state his or her claims and present evidence, etc.

Chapter IX
Lawsuits

Art. 77 *[Filing of a Suit to Quash a Decision]*

(1) A suit to quash a decision of the Fair Trade Commission shall be filed within thirty days (three months in case of the decision under the provisions of Article 8–4 (1)) from the date on which the decision became effective.

(2) The time period stated in the preceding paragraph shall be peremptory.

(3) No suits may be brought regarding matters about which a hearing request may be made unless the suit concerns a decision.

Art. 78 *[Defendant in Protest Suits on the Decision of the Fair Trade Commission]*

The Fair Trade Commission shall be the defendant in suits lodged under Article 3 (1) of the Administrative Case Litigation Law (Law No. 139 of 1962) to appeal a decision made by the Fair Trade Commission.

Art. 79 *[Transmission of Records]*

The court shall, upon receipt of a suit, request the Fair Trade Commission without delay, to transmit the records of the case concerned (including interrogation records of persons concerned in the case, witnesses, and expert witnesses, records of the hearings, and any other matters that may be used as evidence in court).

Art. 80 *[Binding Authority of the Fair Trade Commission's Findings]*

(1) Findings of fact made by the Fair Trade Commission shall, if established by substantial evidence, be binding upon the court in regard to the suit provided for in Article 77 (1).

(2) Whether such substantial evidence as provided for in the preceding paragraph exists or not shall be determined by the court.

Art. 81 *[Offering of New Evidence, Reference Back of the Case to the Fair Trade Commission]*

(1) A party may plead to the court for offer to introduce new evidence relevant to the case:

Provided, that any such offer to introduce new evidence relating to the facts found by the Fair Trade Commission shall have as its reason any one of the following items:

(i) Where the Fair Trade Commission failed to adopt the evidence without good cause; or
(ii) Where it was impossible to adduce evidence at the hearings of the Fair Trade Commission, and there was no gross negligence on the part of the party in failing to adduce such evidence.

(2) In the cases prescribed in the proviso to the preceding paragraph, the onus shall be on the party concerned to show either of the reasons provided for in the items of the preceding paragraph.

(3) When the court finds there is a reason for offer to introduce new evidence under the proviso to paragraph (1) and it is necessary to examine such evidence, it shall refer the case back to the Fair Trade Commission and order it to take appropriate measures after examining such evidence.

Art. 82 *[Quashing Decisions]*

(1) The court may quash a decision of the Fair Trade Commission if the decision falls under any one of the following items:

(i) If the facts on which the decision is based are not established by substantial evidence, or
(ii) If the decision violates the Constitution or other laws or orders.

(2) The Fair Trade Commission shall, when the judgment regarding the quashing of the decision (limited to decisions pursuant to Article 66) becomes final and conclusive, render another decision regarding the hearing request in accordance with the spirit of the judgment.

Art. 83 *[Reference Back of a Decision]*

The court may, when it finds it necessary for further hearings to be conducted in a case where it shall quash a decision of the Fair Trade Commission (limited to decisions pursuant to Article 67 and Article 70–12 (1)), refer the case back to the Fair Trade Commission giving the reasons thereof.

Art. 83–2 *[Security Against Filing for the Unfair Purpose]*

(1) When a suit to demand the suspension or prevention of infringement pursuant to the provisions of Article 24 has been filed, the court may, upon motion, order the plaintiff to furnish adequate security at the petition of the defendant.

(2) In order to lodge a petition pursuant to the preceding paragraph, the fact that the suit in said paragraph has been filed for an unfair purpose (meaning the purpose of acquiring wrongful profits, inflicting injury on another person, or other unfair purpose) shall be established by prima-facie evidence.

Art. 83–3 *[Notification to the Commission on Injunction Suit]*

(1) When a suit to demand the suspension or prevention of infringements mentioned in Article 24 has been filed, the court shall notify the Fair Trade Commission to that effect.

(2) When a suit mentioned in the preceding paragraph has been filed, the court may request the opinion of the Fair Trade Commission with respect to the application of this Act or other matters necessary.

(3) When a suit mentioned in paragraph (1) has been filed, the Fair Trade Commission may, with the permission of the court, state an opinion on the application of this Act for the case or other matters necessary.

Art. 84 *[Request for the Fair Trade Commission's Opinion on Amount of Damages]*

(1) When a suit for indemnification of damages under the provisions of Article 25 has been filed, the court shall, without delay, request the opinion of the Fair Trade Commission with respect to the amount of damages caused by such violations as provided for in the said article.

(2) If a counter claim for indemnification of damages under the provisions of Article 25 is made in court proceedings for the purpose of offsetting the other claim, the provisions of the preceding paragraph shall apply mutatis mutandis.

Art. 84–2 *[Jurisdiction of Injunction Suit]*

(1) With respect to a suit to demand the suspension or prevention of infringements mentioned in Article 24, in cases where the courts mentioned in the following items have jurisdiction over the said suit in accordance with the provisions of Article 4 and Article 5 of the Code of Civil Procedure, the suit can also be brought before the court determined in any of the said items:

(i) A district court located within the jurisdiction of the Tokyo High Court (excluding the Tokyo District Court), the Osaka District Court, the Nagoya District Court, the Hiroshima District Court, the Fukuoka District Court, the Sendai District Court, the Sapporo District Court, the Takamatsu District Court, or the Tokyo District Court
(ii) A district court located within the jurisdiction of the Osaka High Court (excluding the Osaka District Court), the Tokyo District Court, or the Osaka District Court
(iii) A district court located within the jurisdiction of the Nagoya High Court (excluding the Nagoya District Court), the Tokyo District Court, or the Nagoya District Court
(iv) A district court located within the jurisdiction of the Hiroshima High Court (excluding the Hiroshima District Court), the Tokyo District Court, or the Hiroshima District Court
(v) A district court located within the jurisdiction of the Fukuoka High Court (excluding the Fukuoka District Court), the Tokyo District Court, or the Fukuoka District Court
(vi) A district court located within the jurisdiction of the Sendai High Court (excluding the Sendai District Court), the Tokyo District Court, or the Sendai District Court
(vii) A district court located within the jurisdiction of the Sapporo High Court (excluding the Sapporo District Court), the Tokyo District Court, or the Sapporo District Court
(viii) A district court located within the jurisdiction of the Takamatsu High Court (excluding the Takamatsu District Court), the Tokyo District Court, or the Takamatsu District Court

(2) With respect to the application of the provisions of Article 7 of the Code of Civil Procedure to cases where several claims are made by one suit, including a claim under Article 24 of this Act, the words 'from Article 4 through Article 6 inclusive (excluding Article 6 (3))' appearing in Article 7 of the Code of Civil Procedure shall read as 'from Article 4 through Article 6 inclusive (excluding Article 6 (3)) of this Code and Article 84–2 (1) of the Act Concerning Prohibition of Private Monopolization and Maintenance of Fair Trade'.

Art. 84–3 [Jurisdiction of District Courts]

Original jurisdiction over any suit concerning offenses as provided for in Articles 89 through Article 91 inclusive shall lie in the district court.

Art. 84–4 [Special Cased on Jurisdiction of District Courts]

In cases involving offenses pursuant to the preceding article, when the courts listed in the items of Article 84–2 (1) of this Act have jurisdiction pursuant to the provisions of Article 2 of the Code of Criminal Procedure, the courts in the said items also may have jurisdiction over such cases.

Art. 85 [Original Jurisdiction]

Original jurisdiction over any suit coming under any one of the following items shall lie in the Tokyo High Court:

(i) Protest suits (excluding suits under Article 3 (5) through (7) inclusive of the Administrative Case Litigation Law) under Article 3 (1) of the Administrative Case Litigation Law regarding decisions made by the Fair Trade Commission; and
(ii) Suits concerning indemnification of damages under the provisions of Article 25.

Art. 86 [Exclusive Jurisdiction of the Tokyo High Court]

Any case stipulated in Article 70–6 (1), Article 70–7 (1) (including cases applicable mutatis mutandis under Article 70–14 (2)), Article 70–13 (1), Article 97, and Article 98 shall be under the exclusive jurisdiction of the Tokyo High Court.

Art. 87 [Special Panel in the Tokyo High Court]

(1) A panel of judges invested with the jurisdiction to hear exclusively the suit provided for in Article 85 and such cases as stipulated in the preceding article shall be established within the Tokyo High Court.

(2) The number of judges in the panel under the preceding paragraph shall be five.

Art. 87–2 [Transfer of Injunction Suit]

The court may, in cases where a suit to demand the suspension or prevention of infringements mentioned in Article 24 has been filed, and the same or the same type of suits pursuant to Article 24 have been pending in another court, when the court thinks it proper in consideration of circumstances such as the addresses or domiciles of the parties and witnesses to be examined, the commonality of issues or evidence, transfer, by petition or on its own authority, the suit in whole or in part to the other court concerned or the courts having jurisdiction on the said suit under the provisions of Article 84–2 (1).

Art. 88 [Special Provisions for Suits Relating to FTC Decisions]

With respect to protest suits under Article 3 (1) of the Administrative Case Litigation Law regarding decisions of the Fair Trade Commission, the provisions of Article 6 of the Act Concerning the Authority of the Minister of Justice over Suits in Which Interests of State Are Involved (Law No. 194 of 1947) shall not apply.

Chapter X
Miscellaneous Provisions

Art. 88–2 *[Interim Measures]*

In case a cabinet ordinance or the Rules of the Fair Trade Commission is instituted, amended, or repealed in accordance with the provisions of this Act, necessary interim measures (including those relating to penal provisions) may be provided for by virtue of such cabinet ordinance or Rules of the Fair Trade Commission to the extent deemed reasonably necessary as a consequence of such institution, amendment, or repeal.

Chapter XI
Penal Provisions

Art. 89 *[Penalties Against Private Monopolization or Unreasonable Restraint of Trade, or Substantial Restraint of Competition by a Trade Association]*

(1) Any person committing any one of the following offenses shall be punished by penal servitude of not more than three years or by a fine of not more than five million yen:

(i) Any person who, in violation of the provisions of Article 3, effected private monopolization or unreasonable restraint of trade; or
(ii) Any person who, in violation of the provisions of Article 8 (1)(i), effected substantial restraint of competition in any particular field of trade.

(2) Any attempted offense falling under the preceding paragraph shall be punished.

Art. 90 *[Penalties Against Prohibited International Agreements or Contracts, Prohibited Acts of Trade Association, or Non-Observance of Final and Conclusive Decision]*

Any person committing any one of the following offenses shall be punished by penal servitude of not more than two years or by a fine of not more than three million yen:

(i) Any person who, in violation of the provisions of Article 6 or Article 8 (1)(ii), entered into an international agreement or an international contract which contains such matters as constitute unreasonable restraint of trade;
(ii) Any person who violated the provisions of Article 8 (1)(iii) or (iv); or
(iii) Any person who fails to comply with an order to take elimination measures or a decision as provided for in Article 65 or Article 67 (1), after it has become final and conclusive.

Art. 91 *[Penalties Against Prohibited Stockholding or Interlocking Directorates, etc.]*

Any person committing any one of the following offenses shall be punished by penal servitude of not more than one year or by a fine of not more than two million yen:

(i) Any person who, in violation of the provisions of the first part of Article 10 (1), acquired or held stock;
(ii) Any person who, in violation of the provisions of Article 11 (1), acquired or held stock; or who, in violation of the provisions of paragraph (2) of the said article, held stock;
(iii) Any person who, in violation of the provisions of Article 13 (1), held concurrently positions as an officer of a company;
(iv) Any person who, in violation of the provisions of the first part of Article 14, acquired or held stock; or
(v) Any person who, in violation of the provisions of Article 17, committed such prohibitions or restrictions prescribed in the items *above*.

Art. 91–2 *[Penalties Against Failure to File Reports, etc.]*

Any person committing any one of the following offenses shall be punished by a fine of not more than two million yen:

(i) Any person who, in violation of the provisions of Article 8 (2) through (4) inclusive, failed to file a declaration or filed a false declaration;
(ii) Any person who, in violation of the provisions of Article 9 (5), failed to file a report or filed a false report;
(iii) Any person who, in violation of the provisions of Article 9 (6) failed to file a declaration or filed a false declaration;
(iv) Any person who, in violation of the provisions of Article 10 (2), (including cases applicable mutatis mutandis under Article 10 (3)) failed to submit a report or filed a false report;
(v) Any person who, in violation of the provisions of Article 15 (2) (including cases applicable mutatis mutandis under Article 15 (3)) failed to file a declaration or filed a false declaration;
(vi) Any person who, in violation of the provisions of Article 15 (4), effected registration of establishment of a company by merger or the registration of change in the previously registered entry;
(vii) Any person who, in violation of the provisions of Article 15–2 (2) and (3) (including cases applicable mutatis mutandis under Article 15–2 (5)) failed to file a declaration or filed a false declaration;
(viii) Any person who, in violation of the provisions of Article 15 (4) that are applied mutatis mutandis in Article 15–2 (6), effected registration of

establishment of a company by joint establishment division or registration of change by acquisition division;

(ix) Any person who, in violation of the provisions of Article 16 (2) (including cases applicable mutatis mutandis under Article 16 (4)) failed to file a declaration or filed a false declaration;

(x) Any person who, in violation of the provisions of Article 15 (4) which are applied mutatis mutandis in Article 16 (5), carried out an act coming under Article 16 (1)(i) or (ii); or

(xi) Any person who, in violation of the provisions of Article 23 (6), failed to file a (i) declaration or filed a false declaration.

Art. 92 *[Concurrent Punishment]*

Any person committing any one of the offenses stipulated in Article 89 through Article 91 inclusive may, according to the circumstances, be punished by both penal servitude and a fine.

Art. 92–2 *[Penalties Against Perjury]*

(1) Where any witness or expert witness who under oath, in accordance with the provisions of Article 54 or Article 166 of the Code of Criminal Procedure which are applied mutatis mutandis in Article 62 of this Act, made a false statement or expert testimony, he or she shall be punished by penal servitude from not less than three months to not more than ten years.

(2) Where a person committing an offense under the preceding paragraph confesses his or her crime prior to the termination of the hearing procedures and before the discovery of such crime, the penalty for such offense may be commuted or remitted.

Art. 93 *[Penalties Against Divulging Secrets]*

Any person who violated the provisions of Article 39 shall be punished by penal servitude of not more than one year or by a fine of not more than one hundred thousand yen.

Art. 94 *[Penalties Against Interference With Inspection, etc.]*

Any person who falls under any one of the following items shall be punished by penal servitude of not more than one year or by a fine of not more than three million yen:

(i) Any person concerned with a case or any witness who, in violation of the measures issued to him or her under the provisions of Article 47 (1)(i) or (2) or Article 56 (1), fails to appear or to give a statement, or gives a false statement, or fails to submit a report, or submits a false report;

(ii) Any expert witness who, in violation of the measures issued to him or her under the provisions of Article 47 (1)(ii) or (2) or Article 56 (1), fails to appear or to give expert testimony, or gives a false expert testimony;

(iii) Any holder of the matters who, in violation of the measures issued to him or her under the provisions of Article 47 (1)(iii) or (2) or Article 56 (1), fails to submit the same; or

(iv) Any person who refuses, obstructs, or evades the inspection as provided for in Article 47 (1)(iv) or (2) or Article 56 (1).

Art. 94–2 *[Penalties Against Non-Compliance With Compulsory Measures]*

Any person who falls under any one of the following items shall be punished by a fine of not more than two hundred thousand yen:

(i) Any person who, in violation of such measures as provided for in Article 40, fails to appear or to submit a report, information, or documents, or submits a false report, information, or documents; or

(ii) Any witness or expert witness who, in violation of the order issued to him or her under the provisions of Article 154 or Article 166 of the Code of Criminal Procedure which are applied mutatis mutandis in Article 62 of this Act, refuses to take the oath.

Art. 95 *[Double Punishment]*

(1) When a representative of a juridical person, or an agent, an employee, or any other person in the service of a juridical person or of an individual has, with regard to the business or property of the said juridical person or individual, committed a violation as provided for in any of the following items, the said juridical person or the said individual shall be punished by such fine as provided for in the said items in addition to the punishment of the offender.

(i) Article 89: Fine of not more than five hundred million yen.

(ii) Article 90 (iii) (excluding cases of violations of orders pursuant to Article 7 (1) or Article 8–2 (1) or (3) [limited to segments ordering the party to cease and desist from the act in violation of the provisions of Article 3 or Article 8 (1) (i)]): Fine of not more than three hundred million yen.

(iii) Article 90 (i), (ii), or (iii) (limited to cases of violations of orders pursuant to Article 7 (1) or Article 8–2 (1) or (3) [limited to segments ordering the party to cease and desist from the act in violation of the provisions of

Article 3 or Article 8 (1)(i)]), Article 91 (excluding (iii)), Article 91–2, or Article 94: Fine as provided for in the relevant Article.

(2) Where a representative, a manager, an agent, an employee, or any other person in the service of a non-juridical organization has, with regard to the business or property of the said organization, committed a violative act as provided for in any of the following items, the said non-juridical organization shall be punished by such fine as provided for in the said item in addition to the punishment to the offender.

(i) Article 89: Fine of not more than five hundred million yen.
(ii) Article 90 (iii) (excluding cases of violations of orders pursuant to Article 7 (1) or Article 8–2 (1) or (3) [limited to segments ordering the party to cease and desist from the act in violation of the provisions of Article 3 or Article 8 (1)(i)]): Fine of not more than three hundred million yen.
(iii) Article 90 (i), (ii), or (iii) (limited to cases of violations of orders pursuant to Article 7 (1) or Article 8–2 (1) or (3) [limited to segments ordering the party to cease and desist from the act in violation of the provisions of Article 3 or Article 8 (1)(i)]), Article 91 (iv) or
(iv) (limited to segments related to (iv)), Article 91–2 (i), or Article 94 : Fine as provided for in the relevant Articles.

(3) In the case of the preceding paragraph, the representative or manager shall represent the said organization in related acts of procedure and the provisions of the Code of Criminal Procedure related to acts of procedure where the juridical person is the defendant or the suspect shall apply.

Art. 95–2 *[Punishment of Representatives of Juridical Persons Who Failed to Prevent Violation]*

In case of a violation of Article 89 (1)(i), Article 90 (i) or (iii), or Article 91 (excluding (iii)), the representative of a juridical person (excluding those who come under a trade association in case of violation of Article 90 (i) or (iii)) who failed to take necessary measures to prevent such violation while knowing of the existence of such a plan or who failed to take necessary measures to rectify such violation while knowing of the existence of such violation, shall also be punished by such fine as provided for in the relevant Articles.

Art. 95–3 *[Punishment of Directors, etc. of Trade Associations Who Failed to Prevent Violation]*

(1) Where a violation of Article 89 (1)(ii) or Article 90 was committed, a director or any other officer or a manager of a trade association or its constituent entrepreneurs (including, in the case where the officer, employee, agent, or other person who

committed the act for the benefit of the entrepreneur was a constituent entrepreneur, the said entrepreneur) who failed to take necessary measures to prevent such violation while knowing of the existence of such a plan or who failed to take necessary measures to rectify such violation while knowing of the existence of such violation, shall also be punished by such fine as provided for in the relevant Articles.

(2) Where a director or any other officer or a manager of a trade association or its constituent entrepreneurs as prescribed in the preceding paragraph is a juridical person or any other organization, the provision of the said paragraph shall apply to such director or any other officer or a manager of the said organization.

Art. 95–4 *[Dissolution of Trade Associations]*

(1) The court may, when it considers that sufficient grounds exist, issue a sentence, simultaneously with the pronouncement of penalties as provided for in Article 89 (1)(ii) or Article 90, declaring a trade association to be dissolved.

(2) When the dissolution has been sentenced in accordance with the provisions of the preceding paragraph, the trade association shall be dissolved by such sentence, notwithstanding the provisions of any other law or order, articles of association, or any other stipulations.

Art. 96 *[Exclusive Accusation by the Fair Trade Commission]*

(1) Any offense under Article 89 through Article 91 inclusive shall be considered only after an accusation of the Fair Trade Commission has been filed.

(2) The accusation under the preceding paragraph shall be made in writing.

(3) The Fair Trade Commission, in filing the accusation under paragraph (1) may, when it considers it appropriate that the sentence under paragraph (1) of the preceding Article or Article 100 (1)(i) should be made with respect to an offense under the accusation, state the said effect in the said accusation.

(4) The accusation under paragraph (1) shall not be withdrawn after public prosecution has been instituted.

Art. 97 *[Administrative Fines for Contraventions of Decisions]*

Any person who has violated an order to take elimination measures shall be liable to an administrative fine of not more than five hundred thousand yen: Provided, That the foregoing shall not apply when the said act shall be punished under the penal provisions.

Art. 98 *[Administrative Fines for Disobeying Urgent Injunction]*

Any person who has disobeyed a ruling of the court under the provisions of Article 70–13 (1), shall be liable to an administrative fine of not more than three hundred thousand yen.

Art. 99

Deleted. (Law No. 214 of 1949)

Art. 100 *[Revocation of Patent Rights or Patent Licenses and Exclusion from Government Contacts]*

(1) The court may, in a case coming under Article 89 or Article 90, according to circumstances, issue the following sentences simultaneously with the pronouncement of penalties: Provided, that the sentence under item (i) hereunder shall be made only when the said patent right, or exclusive or non-exclusive license for a patented invention belongs to the offender:

- (i) That the patent under patent right or the exclusive or non-exclusive license for the patented invention to which the offense relates shall be revoked; or
- (ii) That the offender shall be barred from becoming a party to a contract with the government for a period of not less than six months and not more than three years after the date when the judgment became final and conclusive.

(2) When a judgment with a sentence as provided for in item (i) of the preceding paragraph becomes final and conclusive, the court shall transmit the certified copy thereof to the Director-General of the Patent Office.

(3) Thc Director-General of the Patent Office shall upon receipt of the certified copy of the judgment under the provisions of the preceding paragraph, revoke the patent right, or the exclusive or non-exclusive license for the patented invention.

Chapter XII
Compulsory Investigation of Criminal Cases

Art. 101 *[Questioning, Inspection, Retention, and Report]*

(1) When necessary to investigate a criminal case (cases related to offences in Article 89 through Article 91 inclusive; the same shall apply hereinafter in this chapter), the staff members of the Fair Trade Commission (limited to the staff designated by the Fair Trade Commission; hereinafter referred to in this chapter as 'FTC staff members') may request criminal case suspects or witnesses (hereinafter referred to in this paragraph as 'criminal case suspects and others') to appear in the Fair Trade Commission, may question criminal case suspects and others, may inspect matters held or abandoned by offence suspects and others, or may retain matters voluntarily submitted or abandoned by criminal case suspects and others.

(2) FTC staff members may, in their investigation of a criminal case, inquire at national and local government offices or public or private organizations and request them to submit a report regarding the necessary matters.

Art. 102 *[Visit, Search and Seizure]*

(1) FTC staff members may, when necessary to investigate a criminal case, visit, search, or seize with a warrant issued in advance by a judge of the district court or the summary court having jurisdiction over the location of the Fair Trade Commission [Note: the Tokyo District Court and the Tokyo Summary Court].

(2) FTC staff members may, when expedience is needed in the case of the previous paragraph, take the measures in the preceding paragraph with a warrant issued in advance by a judge of the district court or the summary court having jurisdiction over the location of the site to be visited; the site, person, or matters to be searched; or the matters to be seized.

(3) FTC staff members shall, when requesting a warrant provided for in paragraph (1) or (2) (hereinafter referred to in this Chapter as 'warrant'), submit documents that confirm the existence of a criminal case.

(4) In the case of a request provided for in the preceding paragraph, the judge of the district court or the summary court shall issue to the FTC staff member a warrant with the judge's signature and seal affixed and the following information written: the site to be visited; the site, person, or matters to be searched; or the matters to be

seized; the position and name of the person making the request; the warrant's period of validity, the fact that the visit, search, or seizure cannot be commenced after the warrant's period of validity has expired and the warrant must be returned after the warrant's period of validity has expired; and the warrant's date of issue; the name of the court issuing the warrant. In such cases, the name of the criminal case suspect and the facts of the criminal case shall, if known, be written.

(5) FTC staff members may grant the warrant to another FTC staff member and have that person perform the visit, search, or seizure.

Art. 103 *[Seizure of Mail]*

(1) FTC staff members may, when necessary to investigate a criminal case and having received a warrant, seize mail, personal letters, or documents related to telegrams sent by or to criminal case suspects and stored or held by communications services personnel based on legal provisions.

(2) FTC staff members may, having received a warrant, seize mail, personal letters, or documents related to telegrams that do not fall under the provisions of the preceding paragraph and are stored or held by communications services personnel based on legal provisions if there are sufficient grounds to suspect the items are related to a criminal case.

(3) In the case that measures in the *above* two paragraphs have been taken, FTC staff members shall notify the sender or recipient of the items to that effect: Provided, That the foregoing shall not apply if the investigation of the criminal case may possibly be impeded by such notification.

Art. 104 *[Limitation on Visit, Search, and Seizure after the Sunset]*

(1) No visit, search, or seizure may be performed between sunset and sunrise unless it is specified on the warrant that such a measure may be performed at night.

(2) Visits, searches, or seizes that commence before sunset may, when deemed necessary, extend beyond sunset.

Art. 105 *[Presentation of Warrant]*

Warrants for visits, searches, or seizures shall be presented to those against whom such measures are to be performed.

Art. 106 *[Carrying and Presentation of Identification Card]*

FTC staff members shall, when performing questioning, inspections, retentions, visits, searches, or seizures pursuant to the provisions of this chapter, carry identification cards that indicates their identity and show them upon request by a person concerned.

Art. 107 [Unlocking, Opening and Any Other Necessary Measures]

(1) FTC staff members may, when necessary to perform a visit, search, or seizure, open locks, break open the seal on mail, and take other necessary measures.

(2) The measures in the preceding paragraph may be taken in relation to matters retained or seized.

Art. 108 [Prohibition on Entry]

FTC staff members may prohibit any person from entering or leaving the site while the questioning, inspections, retentions, visits, searches, or seizures pursuant to the provisions of this chapter are being conducted.

Art. 109 [Presence of Witness]

(1) FTC staff members shall, when performing visits, searches, or seizures of a person's domicile or a person's guarded residence, building, or other site, have the owner, the building superintendent (including the representative or agent of the owner or building superintendent or other person who can stand in for the owner or superintendent), an employee of the owner or building superintendent, or the owner or superintendent's relative who is of legal age and also living in that domicile or residence witness the visit, search, or seizure.

(2) If it is not possible, in the case of the preceding paragraph, to have a person stipulated in that paragraph witness the visit, search, or seizure, the FTC staff member shall have a neighbor who is of legal age or a local police officer or local government employee witness the visit, search, or seizure.

(3) Any body search of a girl or woman shall be performed with the witness of another woman who is of legal age: Provided, that the foregoing shall not apply when expedience is needed.

Art. 110 [Assistance of Police]

FTC staff members may, when necessary in the performance of a visit, search, or seizure, request the assistance of police officers.

Art. 111 [Record of Criminal Investigation]

FTC staff members, when performing questioning, inspections, retentions, visits, searches, or seizures pursuant to the provisions of this chapter, shall prepare an investigation record that states the date the investigative actions were taken and their findings, shall show it to the person who was questioned or the person who witnessed the investigative actions, and shall, along with the person who was questioned or the person who witnessed the investigative actions, sign the investigation report and affix their seal thereto: Provided, That, if the person who was questioned or the person who witnessed the investigative actions does not sign the investigation report and affix his or her seal thereto or is unable to do so, it is sufficient to append a note to that effect to the investigation report.

Art. 112 *[Inventory of Retention and Seizure]*

FTC staff members shall, when retaining or seizing matters, draft an inventory of the matters retained or seized and issue a certified copy of the list to the owners or holders of the matters retained or seized or a person who can stand in for the owners or holders.

Art. 113 *[Storage of Matters Retained and Seized]*

Regarding matters retained or seized that are hard to transport or store, FTC staff members may, with the consent of the owners or holders of the matters or other person that the FTC staff member deems appropriate, receive a trust receipt from that person and have that person store the matters.

Art. 114 *[Returning of Matters Retained and Seized]*

(1) The Fair Trade Commission shall, after the matters retained or seized no longer need to be held in custody, return the matters to the persons to whom they should be returned.

(2) The Fair Trade Commission shall, in the case that it cannot return the matters retained or seized in accordance with the preceding paragraph because it does not know the address or domicile of the person to whom the matters should be returned or because of another reason, make an announcement to that effect.

(3) The matters retained or seized in relation to the announcement in the preceding paragraph shall, if there is no request for return of the matters six months after the date of the announcement, belong to the Treasury.

Art. 115 *[Report of the Fair Trade Commission]*

FTC staff members shall, after completing the investigation of the criminal case, report to the Fair Trade Commission the results of the investigation.

Art. 116 [Obligation to Hand Over Matters Retained and Seized in Case of Accusation]

(1) The Fair Trade Commission shall, if there are matters retained or seized, take over possession of the matters as well as the inventory of such matters in the case that an accusation is made pursuant to the provisions of Article 74 (1) as a result of the investigation of the criminal case.

(2) In the case that the matters retained or seized in the preceding paragraph are stored under the provisions of Article 113, the Fair Trade Commission shall take over the matters with the trust receipt provided for in that Article and notify that to the person storing the matters provided for in that Article.

(3) When matters retained or seized are taken over pursuant to the provisions of the preceding two paragraphs, the said matters shall be deemed as seized under the provisions of the Code of Criminal Procedure.

Art. 117 [Non Application of the Administrative Procedures Law]

The provisions of Chapter 2 through Chapter 4 inclusive of the Administrative Procedures Law do not apply to measures and administrative guidance implemented by the Fair Trade Commission or FTC staff members based on the provisions of this chapter.

Art. 118 [Limitation of Appeal]

Measures taken by the Fair Trade Commission or FTC staff members based on the provisions of this chapter may not be appealed under the Administrative Complaint Review Act.

[Translation]

Designation of Unfair Trade Practices June 18, 1982

Fair Trade Commission Notification No. 15 of 1982

In accordance with the provisions of Article 2 (9) of Act Concerning Prohibition of Private Monopoly and Maintenance of Fair Trade (Law No. 54 of 1947), Unfair Trade Practices (Fair Trade Commission Notification No. 11 of 1953) shall be totally amended as follows and put into force on 1 September 1982.

UNFAIR TRADE PRACTICES

(Concerted Refusal To Deal)

1. Without proper justification, taking an act specified in one of the following paragraphs concertedly with another entrepreneur who is in a competitive relationship with oneself (hereinafter, referred to as a 'competitor'):

- (i) Refusing to deal with a certain entrepreneur or restricting the quantity or substance of a commodity or service involved in the transaction with a certain entrepreneur; or
- (ii) Causing another entrepreneur to take an act which comes under the preceding paragraph.

(Other Refusal to Deal)

2. Unjustly refusing to deal, or restricting the quantity or substance of a commodity or service involved in the transaction with a certain entrepreneur, or causing another entrepreneur to take any act which comes under one of these categories.

(Discriminatory Pricing)

3. Unjustly supplying or accepting a commodity or service at prices which discriminate between regions or between the other parties.

(Discriminatory Treatment on Transaction Terms, etc.)

4. Unjustly affording favourable or unfavourable treatment to a certain entrepreneur in regard to the terms or execution of a transaction.

(Discriminatory Treatment in a Trade Association, etc.)

5. Unjustly excluding a specific entrepreneur from a trade association or from a concerted activity, or unjustly discriminating against a specific entrepreneur in a trade association or a concerted activity, thereby causing difficulties in the business activities of the said entrepreneur.

(Unjust Low Price Sales)

6. Without proper justification, supplying a commodity or service continuously at a price which is excessively below cost incurred in the said supply, or otherwise unjustly supplying a commodity or service at a low price, thereby tending to cause difficulties to the business activities of other entrepreneurs.

(Unjust High Price Purchasing)

7. Unjustly purchasing a commodity or service at a high price, thereby tending to cause difficulties to the business activities of other entrepreneurs.

(Deceptive Customer Inducement)

8. Unjustly inducing customers of a competitor to deal with oneself by causing them to misunderstand that the substance of a commodity or service supplied by oneself, or terms of the transaction, or other matters relating to such transaction are much better or much favourable than the actual one or than those relating to the competitor.

(Customer Inducement by Unjust Benefits)

9. Inducing customers of a competitor to deal with oneself by offering unjust benefits in the light of normal business practices.

(Tie-in Sales, etc.)

10. Unjustly causing the other party to purchase a commodity or service from oneself or from an entrepreneur designated by oneself by tying it to the supply of another commodity or service, or otherwise coercing the said party to deal with oneself or with an entrepreneur designated by oneself.

(Dealing on Exclusive Terms)

11. Unjustly dealing with the other party on condition that the said party shall not deal with a competitor, thereby tending to reduce transaction opportunities for the said competitor.

(Resale Price Restriction)

12. Supplying a commodity to the other party who purchases the said commodity from oneself while imposing, without proper justification, one of the restrictive terms specified below:

(i) Causing the said party to maintain the selling price of the commodity that one has determined, or otherwise restricting the said party's free decision on selling price of the commodity; or
(ii) Having the said party cause an entrepreneur who purchases the commodity from the said party to maintain the selling price of the commodity that one has determined, or otherwise causing the said party to restrict the said entrepreneurs' free decision on selling price of the commodity.

(Dealing on Restrictive Terms)

13. Other than any act coming under the preceding two paragraphs, dealing with the other party on conditions which unjustly restrict any transaction between the said party and his other transacting party or other business activities of the said party.

(Abuse of Dominant Bargaining Position)

14. Taking any act specified in one of the following paragraphs, unjustly in the light of the normal business practices by making use of one's dominant bargaining position over the other party:

(i) Causing the said party in continuous transaction to purchase a commodity or service other than the one involved in the said transaction;
(ii) Causing the said party in continuous transaction to provide for oneself money, service or other economic benefits;

(iii) Setting or changing transaction terms in a way disadvantageous to the said party;
(iv) In addition to any act coming under the preceding three paragraphs, imposing a disadvantage on the said party regarding terms or execution of transaction; or
(v) Causing a company which is one's other transacting party to follow one's direction in advance, or to get one's approval, regarding the appointment of officers of the said company (meaning those as defined by Paragraph 3 of Article 2 of the Act Concerning Prohibition of Private Monopoly and Maintenance of Fair Trade).

(Interference with a Competitor's Transaction)

15. Unjustly interfering with a transaction between another entrepreneur who is in a domestic competitive relationship with oneself or with the company of which one is a stockholder or an officer and its other party to such transaction, by preventing the formation of a contract, or by inducing the breach of a contract, or by any other means whatsoever.

(Interference with Internal Operation of a competing company)

16. Unjustly inducing, abetting, or coercing a stockholder or an officer of a company which is in a domestic competitive relationship with oneself or with a company of which one is a stockholder or an officer, to take an act disadvantageous to such company by the exercise of voting rights, transfer of stock, divulgence of secrets, or any other means whatsoever.

[Translation]

Rules on Hearing by the Fair Trade Commission

Fair Trade Commission Rule No.8 of 2005

Table of Contents

Chapter I
General Rules

Art. 1 [Purpose and Definition]

(1) The proceedings of hearings of the Fair Trade Commission (hereinafter referred to as 'Commission') shall follow these Rules and the Act Concerning Prohibition of Private Monopolization and Maintenance of Fair Trade (Law No. 54 of 1947. Hereinafter referred to as 'the Act') Including where the Act is applied in Article 95–4 of the Fishery Industry Cooperative Association Law (Law No. 242 of 1948), and Article 108 of the Law on Cooperative Association of Small and Medium Enterprises (Law No. 181 of 1949), the Act against Unjustifiable Premium and Misleading Representation (Law No. 34 of 1962); provided, however, that the hearing procedure stipulated in Article 53 (1) and Article 70–12 (1) of the Act and Article 12 (6) of the Act against Unjustifiable Premium and Misleading Representation shall be carried out as otherwise stipulated.

(2) The terms used in these Rules that are the same as those used in the Act shall have the same meaning as the terms used in the Act.

Art. 2 [Computation of Period]

(1) The computation of period shall be made according to the provisions of the Civil Code (Law No. 89 of 1896) concerning period.

(2) If the last day of a period falls on any of the days mentioned in the items of Paragraph 1 of Article 1 of the Law for Closed Days of the National Administrative Organs (Law No. 91 of 1988), the period shall expire at a day following the said last day.

Art. 3 [Language]

The Japanese language shall be used in the hearing procedure.

Art. 4 [Method for Official Notice]

The Commission may insert the official notice into an official gazette or newspaper. With respect to the official notice to be served in a foreign country, the Commission may notify that the official notice was served instead of inserting it into the official gazette or newspapers.

Art. 5 [Preparation of Documents]

(1) Unless otherwise specially stipulated, any document to be prepared for the proceeding of hearing procedure shall be dated, signed and sealed.

(2) When the document mentioned in the preceding paragraph is a duplicate to be made by the Commission, the official who made the duplicate shall note that the duplicate does not differ from its original in a place contiguous to the concerned statement, shall sign and seal the duplicate, and shall impress a seal across it and the contiguous leaf or take similar action.

Art. 6 [Correction of Documents]

No character shall be altered in preparing documents for the proceedings of a hearing. If any character is added, deleted or shown in the margin of a page, a seal shall be impressed on it for confirmation. In this case, any deleted character shall remain legible.

Art. 7 [Submission of Documents by Facsimile]

(1) The documents to be submitted for the hearing, excluding the following documents, may be submitted using facsimile.

(i) Documents to be submitted based on measures that were taken by the hearing examiner pursuant to the provision of Article 56 (1) of the Act, as mentioned in each item of Article 47 (1) of the Act,
(ii) Written request for hearing and document for withdrawing the request,
(iii) Written motion for objection pursuant to the provision of Article 35 (1) of the Act,
(iv) Written motion for objection pursuant to the provision of Article 75 of the Act, and
(v) Documents proving authorization or the authority of the representative necessary for the hearing and other documents proving important matters for the hearing.

(2) When a document is submitted using facsimile, the document shall be deemed to have been submitted to the Commission or the hearing examiner when the Commission receives it.

(3) The Commission or the hearing examiner may, when he or she deems necessary in the case mentioned in the preceding paragraph, have the person who submitted the document submit the original document used for transmission.

Art. 8 [Submission of Information written in Document Submitted to the Hearing Examiner by Electromagnetic Devices]

The hearing examiner may, when he or she deems it necessary, and the investigator, the respondent or the respondent's representative has the Electromagnetic Files (the term 'Electromagnetic File' shall mean a record prepared by means of an electronic method, a magnetic method or any other method that is not perceivable by human senses and is used for information processing by computers) recorded the contents of the document which have been submitted or intended to be submitted to the hearing examiner, seek the investigator, the respondent or the respondent's representative to submit the information recorded in the Electromagnetic Files by Electromagnetic Devices (the term 'Electromagnetic Devices' shall mean such device using an electronic information processing system or utilizing any other information and communications technology) determined by the hearing examiner.

Chapter II
Initiation of Hearing Procedure

Art. 9 [Written Request for Hearing]

(1) The hearing requests pursuant to the provisions of Article 49 (6) or Article 50 (4) of the Act shall be submitted to the Commission by a written request for hearing stipulated in the provisions of Article 52 (1) of the Act.

(2) The written request for hearing pursuant to the provisions of Article 52 (1) of the Act shall be made in Form No.1, and include the claim on the reason for the hearing request as concretely as possible, and shall contain the important facts related to the claim and the evidences for each matters to prove.

(3) The Commission may, when it deems that the hearing request does not follow the provisions of Article 52 (1) and (2) of the Act and can be revised, seek to correct it, with a considerable period of time. In this case, the Commission may correct them on its own authority if the defects are minor.

Art. 10 [Withdrawal of Hearing Request]

Withdrawal of hearing request pursuant to the provision of Article 52 (4) of the Act shall be made in Form No.2.

Art. 11 [Initiation of Hearing]

A notification of hearing procedure pursuant to the provision of Article 55 (1) of the Act shall include following matters.

(i) Indication of original administrative measures,
(ii) A Number of the case, and
(iii) That the respondent or the respondent's representative is requested to appear on the date of the hearing.

Chapter III
Designation of Hearing Examiner, Persons in Hearings

Art. 12 [Designation of the Hearing Examiners]

(1) The Commission shall, when having opened a hearing it had decided to designate hearing examiners for each case and entrust them to conduct all or part of the hearing procedures for the concerned case pursuant to the provision of Article 56 (1) of the Act, inform the respondent or the respondent's representative of the name of the hearing examiner.

(2) When the scope and extent of the hearing procedure to be carried out by the hearing examiner is limited in the case of preceding paragraph, the Commission shall report the name of the hearing examiner mentioned in the preceding paragraph as well as the scope and extent of the hearing procedure to be carried out by the hearing examiner to the respondent or the respondent's representative.

(3) When more than one hearing examiner is carrying out the hearing procedure in the case of Paragraph 1, the Commission shall nominate one of the hearing examiners as a person who shall supervise the affairs related to the hearing procedures, and inform the respondent or the respondent's representative of thereof.

(4) In the case of preceding paragraph, unless otherwise provided for in this Rules, the measures which is made by hearing examiner of the hearing procedure in the said case is issued by the committee consisting of the hearing examiners. In this case, resolutions of the committee consisting of the hearing examiners shall be carried by a majority.

Art. 13 [Hearing Examiner's Power]

(1) Hearing examiners shall exercise the power vested with the Commission with respect to hearings pursuant to the provision of Article 56 of the Act and this Regulation.

(2) Hearing examiners shall execute their duties fairly, expeditiously, and independently.

Art. 14 [Officials]

(1) The Commission shall have its officials perform tasks related to hearings.

(2) The officials mentioned in the preceding paragraph (hereinafter referred to as 'Officials') shall perform such tasks as the preparation, custody, service and delivery of records or other documents and as notification under the provisions of this regulation at hearings pursuant to the instructions of the person who was nominated as a person who shall supervise the affairs related to the hearing procedures under the Article 12 (3) (In the case the designated hearing examiner under the provision of Article 56 (1) of the Act is one, the hearing examiner carry out, hereinafter referred to as 'chief hearing examiner').

Art. 15 [Representative]

The powers of a representative who is an attorney or a corporation of attorneys shall be verified in writing.

(2) The name of a bar association to which the representative belongs, and the address of his office, shall be given in the statement mentioned in the preceding paragraph, and the scope and extent of his authority shall be clearly indicated thereon.

(3) When the representative is a corporation of attorneys, the name of the attorney who is in charge of the case in question as a member of the corporation, the name of the bar association to which the attorney belongs, and the scope and extent of tasks (work) that each attorney can perform shall be stated clearly in the document mentioned in Paragraph 1.

(4) The respondent shall, when intending to obtain approval for the appointment of a person other than an attorney or a corporation of attorneys as the respondent's representative, submit to the hearing examiner a statement in which the name, address and occupation of said person, and the person's relationship with the respondent, and such other matters sufficient for determining whether or not said person is eligible to act as representative are stated.

(5) Document that clearly shows the authority and scope of authority of the representative shall be attached to the statement mentioned in the preceding paragraph.

(6) In the case that the statement mentioned in the paragraph (4) is submitted, when the hearing examiner decided to approve or disapprove the applied person as the respondent's representative, the hearing examiner shall inform the respondent and the investigator thereof.

(7) The respondent shall, if the representative's authority had been expired, notify the hearing examiner thereof in writing without delay.

Art. 16 [Intervention]

(1) The Commission may, when it interrogates a respondent or a third party pursuant to the provision of the proviso to Article 70–3 of the Act, do so in writing.

(2) The Commission may have the hearing examiner conduct questioning as mentioned in the preceding paragraph. In this case, the hearing examiner who conducts questioning shall submit a report on the results of the questioning to the Commission.

(3) The Commission shall, where it rules out permission for a third party to intervene as a party, notify the respondent and the third party (hereinafter referred to as 'Intervener') to that effect.

Art. 17 [Acts of Intervenor]

Intervenors may make factual and legal statements at hearings, or call for evidence, or perform other necessary acts.

Art. 18 [Realization of Proper and Prompt Hearing]

(1) The hearing examiner shall, set a target aiming to terminate a hearing procedure within two years as prompt as possible, and make efforts toward achieving this target by operating fulfilling procedures.

(2) The hearing examiner, the investigator and the respondent or the respondent's representative shall attempt to carry out systematically hearing procedures for realization of proper and prompt hearings.

Chapter IV
Date of Hearing and Preparation

Art. 19 [Designation of Hearing Date]

(1) The hearing dates shall be designated by the hearing examiner.

(2) Notice of a hearing date served to the investigator and the respondent or the respondent's representative shall include notifications of the date and venue to appear, and other necessary matters; provided, however, that such notice may be made orally to those attending or appearing on the hearing date.

(3) The hearing examiner may, when deemed necessary, change the hearing date.

(4) The hearing examiner shall, when he or she has changed the hearing date, notice the effect to the investigator, the respondent and the respondent's representative immediately.

Art. 20 [Hearing court]

(1) Hearings shall be held at the Commission's hearing court. However, the hearing examiner may, as deemed necessary, designate a suitable venue for hearings in that date.

(2) The hearing examiner shall, when designate a suitable venue for hearings of a given case in the hearing date pursuant to the provision of the proviso to preceding paragraph, forthwith notify the investigator and the respondent or the respondent's representative thereof.

Art. 21 [Attendance at Hearings]

(1) Hearings on a fixed hearing date shall be held in the presence of the hearing examiner, Officials and investigators.

(2) The respondent or the respondent's representative shall appear on the hearing date.

Art. 22 [Notification of Non-Appearance of Respondent or Respondent's Representative]

If unable to appear on the hearing date, the respondent or the respondent's representative shall notify the hearing examiner thereof without delay, together with a clear reason.

Art. 23 [Application for Closed Hearing]

(1) Application for a closed hearing shall be made by clearly stating the scope and extent of closed hearing, the grounds for the closed hearing and the period.

(2) The hearing examiner shall, when the hearing is held behind closed [locked] doors, make a statement to that effect and provide grounds.

Art. 24 [Opening Procedure]

(1) The respondent or the respondent's representative shall state the purpose and reason for the hearing request mentioned in the written request for hearing at the opening of the hearing procedure.

(2) The investigator shall, following the statement of the respondent or the respondent's representative pursuant to the preceding paragraph, make a claim about contains of the original administrative measures, the facts that led to the original administrative measures, the application of law thereto, and the suitability of the original administrative measures in accordance with a preliminary pleading (the document which mentions the matter intended to be stated in the date of hearing).

(3) The certified copy of the cease and desist order or the surcharge payment order related to the hearing request shall be attached to the preliminary pleading mentioned in the preceding paragraph.

Art. 25 [Fiction of statement]

When neither the respondent nor the respondent's representative fails to appear on the hearing date, hearing examiner may interpret that the matter written in the hearing request or the preparation document submitted by the respondent or the respondent's representative is stated in the hearing date.

Art. 26 [Examination of Evidence]

(1) Hearing Examiner may conduct the examination of evidence upon its own motion or upon application.

(2) The examination of evidence shall be commenced in accordance with the procedure prescribed in the next chapter.

(3) The examination of evidence shall be conducted on the hearing date unless otherwise provided for in this Rules.

Art. 27 [Last Disclosure of Opinion]

(1) Upon completion of the examination of evidence, the investigator may state his opinion about facts that led to the original administrative measures, the application of law thereto, and the suitability of the original administrative measures.

(2) The respondent or the respondent's representative shall be given an opportunity to state opinions at the end.

(3) When the respondent or the respondent's representative fails to appear without due cause on the date mentioned in the preceding paragraph, the hearing procedure may be completed without giving another opportunity to the respondent or the respondent's representative to state opinions.

Art. 28 [Change Claim by Investigator]

(1) The investigator may change the claim on the fact that led to the original administrative measures and the application of law thereto pursuant to the provision of Article 58 (2) of the Act within the scope and extent not to be lost the identity of the case.

(2) The investigator may not do the change, when the change mentioned in the proceeding paragraph brings remarkable delay in the hearing procedure.

(3) The hearing examiner shall, when the investigator did the change mentioned in the paragraph 1, consider not to cause substantial disadvantages for respondent's method for defence by the change.

(4) The hearing examiner shall, when he or she does not approve the change mentioned in paragraph 1, by investigator, clarify thereof and the reason on the hearing date.

Art. 29 [Maintenance of Order]

The chief hearing examiner may command any matter necessary or take measures for the maintenance of order in the hearing court.

Art. 30 [Limitations of Argument]

The chief hearing examiner may reject any question or statement by the investigator, the respondent or the respondent's representative, when the said question or statement merely constitutes repetition of earlier questions or statements, or is irrelevant to the matter of the case, or the chief hearing examiner deems it particularly necessary.

Art. 31 [Explanation and Questions]

(1) The chief hearing examiner may question the investigator, the respondent or the respondent's representative or urge them to testify on any factual and legal matter to clarify the case on the hearing date or on dates other than the hearing date.

(2) Hearing examiners other than the chief hearing examiner may take the measures mentioned in the preceding paragraph by notifying the chief hearing examiner thereof.

(3) The investigator, the respondent, the respondent's representative may, when he or she is unable to understand a statement made by the other party, ask the chief hearing examiner to put a question to the other party, or directly question the other party with the consent of the chief hearing examiner on the hearing date or dates other than the hearing date.

(4) The chief hearing examiner or the hearing examiner other than the chief hearing examiner shall, when he or she took measures pursuant to the provision of Paragraph 1 or 2 for a matter that may cause a major change in the method for prosecution or defence on dates other than the hearing date, notify the other party of the details thereof.

Art. 32 [Consolidation and Separation of Hearing]

(1) The hearing examiner shall, when consolidate or separate hearings, inform the investigator and the respondent or the respondent's representative thereof pursuant to the provision of Article 64 of the Act.

(2) The consolidation of hearings may be implemented even before the first hearing date.

Art. 33 [Termination and Reopening of Hearing]

(1) The hearing examiner may, when deemed appropriate, terminate hearings, or reopen hearings that have been terminated, upon its own motion or upon application.

(2) The hearing examiner shall, when reopen hearings pursuant to the provision of the preceding paragraph, inform the investigator and the respondent or the respondent's representative thereof.

Art. 34 [Motion for Objection to the Hearing Examiner]

(1) The investigator, or the respondent or the respondent's representative may, if he or she is dissatisfied with measures (excluding measures mentioned in each item of

Article 47 (1) of the Act that was taken by the hearing examiner pursuant to the provision of Article 56 (1) of the Act) relating to the hearing taken by the hearing examiner, make a motion for objection to the Committee consists of hearing examiners without delay (In the case the designated hearing examiner under the provision of article 56 (1) of the Act is one, the hearing examiner carries out: the same shall apply hereinafter in this article.) .

(2) The Committee consists of hearing examiners in the preceding paragraph shall, when deemed the motion for objection reasonable, withdraw, cancel, or change the measures against which the motion for objection was made.

(3) The Committee consists of hearing examiners in the preceding paragraph 1 shall clarify the reason, in case the committee have rejected the motion for objection.

Art. 35 [Motion for Objection to the Commission]

(1) A person subject to one of the measures mentioned in the items of Article 47 (1) of the Act that was taken by the hearing examiners pursuant to of Article 56 (1) of the Act, if he or she is dissatisfied with the measures make a motion for objection to the Commission in writing the grounds for the motion, within one week of the date of being subject to the measure.

(2) The Commission shall, if it recognizes that there are the grounds for the motion for objection, order the hearing examiner to withdraw, cancel, or change the action against which the motion for objection was made, and notify the petitioner thereof.

(3) The Commission shall, if it has rejected a motion for objection, give notice to the petitioner to that effect. In the case, the reasons for the rejection shall be given.

Art. 36 [Preparatory Pleading]

(1) Claims on the hearing date shall be prepared by preparatory pleadings.

(2) The Preparatory pleadings shall be submitted to the hearing examiner, with an appropriate period necessary for other party to prepare for the matters mentioned in the preparatory pleadings.

Art. 37 [Period of Submission of Preparatory Pleading etc]

The chief hearing examiner may fix the period to submit preparatory pleadings or to apply for evidences.

Art. 38 [Preparatory Proceedings]

(1) The hearing examiner may, if deemed appropriate, carry out preparatory proceedings by requesting the attendance of the investigator and the respondent or the respondent's representative, to arrange points of dispute and evidence. In this case, he or she may, if deemed necessary, have the investigator, the respondent or the respondent's representative submits the preparatory pleadings or other documents to substitute for or supplement the above method.

(2) The hearing examiner may conduct examination of documents (including other materials as mentioned in Article 50) in the date of Preparatory Proceedings.

(3) The hearing examiner may permit the person who is recognized as appropriate to hear the Preparatory Proceedings on the date. However the hearing examiner shall permit the person who has been applied by the respondent or the respondent's representative to hear the proceedings, except that the hearing examiner deems the fear of impediment to the proceedings exists.

(4) The hearing examiner may, when the respondent or the respondent's representative lives in a distant place or he or she finds it proper, conduct the proceedings on the date of Preparatory Proceedings by means which enable the hearing examiner, the investigator and the respondent or the respondent's representative to communicate simultaneously by transmission and reception of voice. In this case, the respondent or the respondent's representative who participated in the Preparatory Proceedings without appearing on the date shall be deemed to attend the date.

(5) The hearing examiner shall, when the Preparatory Proceedings is conducted by means which enable the hearing examiner, the investigator and the respondent or the respondent's representative to communicate simultaneously by transmission and reception of voice pursuant to the provisions of the preceding paragraph, confirm the people who speak and the places for a call.

(6) The investigator and the respondent or the respondent's representative shall state the result of the preparatory proceeding at the hearing date.

Chapter V
Evidence

DIVISION I APPLICATION FOR EVIDENCE, RULING ON EXAMINATION OF EVIDENCE

Art. 39 [Order of Application for Evidence]

(1) The investigator shall apply for evidence deemed necessary for hearing the case at the start of the examination of the evidence.

(2) The respondent or the respondent's representative may apply for evidence that is deemed necessary for hearing the case after the application mentioned in the preceding paragraph.

Art. 40 [Written Application for Evidence]

Application for evidence shall be made by stating in writing the evidence and the matters the evidence is intended to prove.

Art. 41 [Application for the Interrogation of Witnesses]

(1) An application for the interrogation of witnesses shall be made by clearly stating the name, address and occupation of the witnesses, the matters to be covered in the interrogation and the need for the interrogation.

(2) An application for interrogation of the respondent himself or herself shall be made by clearly stating the name, address, the matters to be covered in the interrogation and the need for the interrogation.

Art. 42 [Application for Inspection]

An application for examination of evidence by means of an inspection shall be made by stating the purpose and necessity thereof.

Art. 43 [Application for Expert Proof]

An application for expert proof shall be made by clearly stating the matters about which an expert will be testifying and the need for the expert proof.

Art. 44 [Expert Testimony]

The chief hearing examiner shall, when he or she has instructed an expert to provide expert testimony in accordance with provision of Article 47 (1) (ii) of the Act pursuant to the provision of Article 56 (1) of the Act, have him or her report the process and result thereof by a written statement.

Art. 45 [Application for the Examination of Documents]

(1) An application for the examination of documents shall be made by submitting the relevant documents, or by applying for submitting from the person in possession of the documents.

(2) An application for the examination of documents through the submission of the documents shall be made by clearly stating the title of the documents and the purpose of proof, except where these are clearly stated in the documents.

(3) A submission of documents may, if approval has been obtained from the chief hearing examiner, be achieved by means of copies of the documents in lieu of the originals.

Art. 46 [Application for Order for Submission of Documents and Other Materials]

(1) An application for the order for the submission of documents and other materials shall be made by the document clearly stating the following information.

(i) The representation of the documents and other materials,
(ii) The purpose of the documents,
(iii) The party in possession of the documents and other materials,
(iv) The facts to be proved, and
(v) the reason and necessity for the application

(2) The hearing examiner shall, if he or she recognizes that there are ground for the application, order the possessor to submit the documents and other materials (hereinafter referred to as 'document, etc.' in this article.).

(3) The hearing examiner may, when deemed necessary, retain the submitted document, etc.

Art. 47 [Return, or Temporary Return, of Retained Materials]

Any retained material that is deemed to be unnecessary shall be returned without waiting for the closure of the case.

(2) Any retained material may be temporarily returned upon the request of its owner or the person who provided it.

Art. 48 [Documents Submitted Voluntarily]

The hearing examiner shall, when he or she deemed necessary when receiving documents and other materials provided voluntarily, request the provider of the documents to submit a document indicating the party in possession, holder of the submitted materials, the name, occupation and address of the party providing the materials, the kind of the submitted materials, and the date of provision.

Art. 49 [Attachment of Translations]

In the case a document written in foreign language is submitted for application for the examination of documents, the applicant shall attach a translation of a part of the document for examination.

Art. 50 [Apply Mutatis Mutandis for other Materials]

The provisions concerning documents shall be applied mutatis mutandis to drawings, pictures, recordings, videocassette tapes and other materials except documents to represent the information.

Art. 51 [Ruling on Examination of Evidence]

(1) When an application for evidence has been made, the investigator and the respondent or the respondent's representative may state their own opinion about the acceptance or rejection of the evidence.

(2) The hearing examiner may not accept evidence that was applied by the investigator and the respondent or the respondent's representative, when deemed unnecessary. In this case, the reason for rejecting the evidence shall be indicated.

(3) The hearing examiner may, when an examination of the evidence poses an obstacle of indefinite duration, forgo the examination.

DIVISION II – INTERROGATION

Art. 52 [Timing for Submission of Documents and Other Materials used for Interrogation]

Documents to be used in the questioning of witnesses, experts and the respondent, excluding documents used as evidence to argue the reliability of the statement of witnesses, experts and the respondent, shall be submitted well in advance of the start date for questioning witnesses, experts and the respondent. However, when it is not possible to submit the originals of the documents, a copy of the documents may be submitted.

Art. 53 [Subpoenas]

(1) Subpoenas issued to witnesses shall include the following information, and shall be served under the signature and seal of the chief hearing examiner.

(i) Date, time and place that the witness is to appear,
(ii) A Number of the case,
(iii) Matters to be covered in the interrogation,
(iv) Legal penalty for a failure to appear, and
(v) Any other pertinent matters.

(2) The provision of the preceding paragraph shall be applied *mutatis mutandis* to subpoenas issued to experts or to the respondent himself or herself.

(3) If a witness, expert or the respondent himself or herself is in court during the hearing, he or she may, notwithstanding the preceding two paragraphs, be immediately interrogated, or be caused to give expert witness.

Art. 54 [Separate Interrogation]

(1) A witness, expert, or the respondent himself or herself shall be interrogated separately.

(2) The chief hearing examiner, if other witnesses or experts who are to be subsequently interrogated are in court during the hearing, shall instruct them to leave the room. However, this shall not apply if it is deemed necessary for the witnesses or experts to remain.

Art. 55 [Identification]

The chief hearing examiner shall first check the identification of witnesses, experts and the respondent himself or herself.

Art. 56 [Oath]

(1) An oath shall be taken prior to interrogation.

(2) The oath shall be in the form of a statement.

(3) The oath for witnesses shall be such a statement that he or she hereby swears to tell the truth, the whole truth and nothing but the truth.

(4) The oath for experts shall be such a statement that he or she hereby swears to provide expert testimony in a conscientious and faithful manner.

(5) The chief hearing examiner shall cause a witness or expert to read the oath aloud, and to sign and seal it.

(6) When a witness or expert cannot sign an oath as mentioned in the preceding paragraph, another person shall sign on behalf of the witness or expert. When a witness or expert cannot seal an oath, he or she shall be fingerprinted. However, where another person signs an oath on behalf of a witness or expert, the person shall state the reason in the oath and sign and seal it.

(7) The oath shall be administered solemnly, with everybody in the court standing.

(8) Notwithstanding the provisions of the three preceding paragraphs, the oath by the expert may be administered by a submission of a written oath to the hearing examiner. In this case, an explanation of the purpose of the oath and a notification of the punishment in false proof by the chief hearing examiner are conducted by sending a document which contains these items, to the expert.

Art. 57 [Warning]

The chief hearing examiner shall notify a witness or expert who has taken an oath prior to interrogation that a false statement or expert testimony shall be punished pursuant to the provisions of Article 92–2 of the Act, and that the refusal to provide a statement or expert testimony without justifiable reason shall be punished pursuant to the provisions of Article 94 of the Act.

Art. 58 [Interpreter]

(1) When a person not versed in the Japanese language make a statement, an interpreter shall interpret his or her statement into Japanese.

(2) In the case of the preceding paragraph, the interpreter shall make an oath. In this case, the provisions of Article 56 (except Paragraph 3 and 8) shall be applied *mutatis mutandis* to the oath of the interpreter.

Art. 59 [Procedure for Interrogating Witnesses]

(1) The investigator and the respondent or the respondent's representative may, upon notifying the chief hearing examiner, interrogate witnesses, experts and the respondent himself or herself. In this case, when the questioning of witnesses, experts or the respondent himself or herself has commenced subject to a request made by the investigator or the respondent or the respondent's representative, the person who made the request shall first interrogate them.

(2) The hearing examiner may interrogate the witnesses, experts or the respondent himself after the completion of the interrogation as mentioned in the preceding paragraph.

(3) The chief hearing examiner may, when deemed appropriate, change the order of interrogation as mentioned in the preceding two paragraphs, after listening to the opinions of the investigator and the respondent or the respondent's representative.

(4) The chief hearing examiner may at any time, when deemed necessary, interrogate the witnesses, experts or the respondent himself in addition to the interrogation pursuant to Paragraph 2.

(5) The hearing examiner other than the chief hearing examiner may, upon notifying the chief hearing examiner, interrogate the witnesses, experts or the respondent himself.

(6) Witness and experts may not make statements based on documents unless they have the approval of the chief hearing examiner.

Art. 60 [Restrictions on Questions]

(1) Questions shall be asked in a particular and specific manner as possible.

(2) The investigator and the respondent or the respondent's representative shall not ask the following questions. However, this restriction shall not apply to the questions mentioned in Items 2 to 5 if there is a justifiable reason.

(i) Questions to insult or embarrass witnesses, experts or the respondent,
(ii) Leading questions,
(iii) Questions that are same as a question that has an already been asked,
(iv) Questions irrelevant to the points of dispute, and
(v) Questions requesting the statement of an opinion.

(3) The chief hearing examiner may, when a question conflicts with the provisions of the preceding paragraph, limit the question on its own motion or on application.

Art. 61 [Confrontation]

The chief hearing examiner may, when he or she deems necessary, instruct the witness, the expert, and respondent to confront mutually.

Art. 62 [Expert Witness]

The provision of the interrogation of the witness shall apply to the interrogation of the expert witness.

Art. 63 [Interrogation by Transmission and Reception of Pictures and Voice]

(1) In the case of a interrogation of a witnesses, a experts or a respondent, when the witnesses, the experts or the respondent lives in distant place, or if the hearing examiner finds it proper, the interrogation may be conducted by means which enable persons at a distance to communicate, being able to mutually recognize the state of the other by transmission and reception of pictures and voice.

(2) In the case of the interrogation of witnesses or experts pursuant to the provision of the preceding paragraph, the interrogation may be conducted, listening to the opinions of the investigator and the respondent or the respondent's representative, by means which have the respondent or the respondent's representative appear in the hearing court, and have witnesses or experts appear to the local office of Fair Trade Commission where the device necessary to the interrogation was established.

(3) In the case of the interrogation of respondent pursuant to the provision of Paragraph 1, the interrogation may be conducted, listening to the opinions of the investigator, the respondent or the respondent's representative, by means which have the respondent appear in the local office of Fair Trade Commission where the device necessary to the interrogation was established.

(4) Facsimile may be used for the presentation of a copy of documents or other procedures necessary for interrogation.

(5) When the interrogation pursuant to the provision of Paragraph 1 of the preceding article has been conducted, the record shall be stated that effect, the local office of the Fair Trade Commission where the witness, the experts or the respondent have appeared.

DIVISION III EXAMINATION OF EVIDENCE EXCEPT HEARING DATE

Art. 64 [Examination of Evidence except Hearing Date]

(1) The hearing examiner may, when deemed necessary, conduct the examination of evidence except for hearing date. In this case, the hearing examiner shall afford the investigator and the respondent or the respondent's representative an opportunity to observe the examination of evidence.

(2) The chief hearing examiner may, when deemed necessary, have a hearing examiner who is not a chief hearing examiner conduct the examination of evidence pursuant to the provision of Paragraph 1. In this case, the chief hearing examiner shall notify the investigator and the respondent or the respondent's representative, of the name of the hearing examiner who conducts the examination of evidence.

Chapter VI
Protocol for Hearings

Art. 65 [Protocol for Hearings]

(1) Officials shall prepare a record for every hearing date. This record shall include the following information, and shall be signed and sealed by officials. The record shall bear the seal of the hearing examiner as confirmation.

(i) Date of the hearing and place,
(ii) Name and official title of the hearing examiner, officials, the investigator who attended the hearings and name of the respondent or the respondent's representative, the stenographer and the interpreter attending the hearings,
(iii) If the respondent or the respondent's representative does not appear, a statement to that effect and the reason thereof,
(iv) If the hearing is closed to the public, a statement to that effect and the reason thereof,
(v) The name of witnesses and experts interrogated, and if they did not take an oath, a statement to that effect, and the reason thereof,
(vi) Application for examination of evidence or other applications,
(vii) A summary of statements made by the investigator or the respondent or the respondent's representative on facts and law, as well as a summary of statements and the interrogation of witnesses, experts or the respondent (or a reference to stenographic records or documents as a substitute for the summaries),
(viii) The title of the documents and other materials examined,
(ix) Rulings of the hearing examiner, and other matters, and,
(x) Matters ordered for inclusion by the chief hearing examiner.

(2) Officials may, when the chief hearing examiner has permitted, record a witness's, an expert's or the respondent's statement on a tape or videocassette tape (including articles on which certain matters can be recorded by corresponding methods) as substitute for a record.

(3) The investigator or the respondent or the respondent's representative may motion for objection concerning the accuracy of the record. When the objection is motioned, Officials shall record that effect.

(4) The hearing examiner shall, when he or she deems the objection pursuant to the preceding paragraph reasonable, order a change of the matters related with

the objection in the record, and notify the investigator and the respondent or the respondent's representative, of that effect.

Art. 66 [Record of Retention]

(1) The hearing examiner shall, when he or she has retained any material provided in accordance with the provision of Article 47 (1) (iii) of the Act pursuant to the provision of Article 56 (1) of the Act, prepare a record for such retention. In this case, the hearing examiner may have Officials prepare it.

(2) The record mentioned in the preceding paragraph shall incorporate the number of the case, the name, occupation and address of the owner of the retained materials and the person who provided the retained materials, and the date and place of retention, and, the record shall be signed and sealed by the hearing examiner or Officials, and which shall be confirmed with the seal of the hearing examiner.

(3) A list showing the nature of the retained materials shall be attached to the record mentioned in Paragraph 1.

(4) A copy of the list shall be made available upon the request of the owner of the retained materials or a person who provided the retained materials.

Art. 67 [Record of Examination of Evidence except Hearing Date]

(1) Officials shall, when the examination of evidence except hearing date pursuant to the provision of Article 64 is conducted, prepare a record. The results of examination of evidence and other necessary matters shall be stated in the record which shall be signed and sealed by the officials in charge of the hearing administration, and which shall be confirmed with the seal of the hearing examiner.

(2) The record mentioned in the preceding paragraph shall be presented on hearing date.

(3) The provisions of Article 65 (2)–(4) shall apply *mutatis mutandis* to the record mentioned in Paragraph 1.

Art. 68 [Record of Preparatory Proceeding]

(1) When preparatory proceedings were carried out, Officials shall prepare a record. The results of proceedings and other necessary matters of each date shall be stated in the record which shall be signed and sealed by the officials in charge of the hearing administration, and which shall be confirmed with the seal of the hearing examiner.

(2) Officials shall, when the procedure mentioned in Article 38 (4) was done, mention that effect and the linked telephone number in the record. In this case, Officials may record the linked place in addition to the linked number.

(3) The provisions of Article 65 (3) (4) shall apply *mutatis mutandis* to the record mentioned in Paragraph 1.

Art. 69 [Citations in the Protocol]

In the record mentioned from Articles 65 through the preceding article, a reference to documents, photographs and other materials as deemed proper by the chief hearing examiner may be made a part of the record as an attachment thereto.

Art. 70 [Stenographic Records]

(1) The chief hearing examiner may, when deemed necessary, have stenographer attend the hearing date to stenograph a statement.

(2) The stenographer attending the hearings shall prepare a stenographic record, and shall submit it to the hearing examiner after signing and sealing the record.

(3) The hearing examiner shall confirm the stenographic record mentioned in the preceding paragraph and affix his seal.

Chapter VII
Hearing Procedures by the Fair Trade Commission

Art. 71 [Hearing Procedure by the Commission]

(1) When the Commission conducts hearings, the Commission may not do without the presence of the chairman and two or more commissioners.

(2) With respect the application of the provision of the preceding paragraph, when the chairman is unable to fulfil his function, a person who shall represent the chairman as stipulated in Article 33 (2) of the Act shall be deemed the chairman.

Art. 72 [Apply Mutatis Mutandis of the Provisions of Hearing Procedure by the Hearing Examiner]

The provisions of hearing procedure by the hearing examiner (excluding the provision concerning preliminary decision) shall apply *mutatis mutandis* to the hearing procedures by the Commission.

Chapter VIII
Decision

Art. 73 [Preliminary Decision]

The hearing examiner shall, after the completion of hearings, make a preliminary decision without delay. The hearing examiner shall submit it to the Commission together with the record of the case, and serve a copy of it on the investigator and the respondent or the respondent's representative.

Art. 74 [Matters Stated in Preliminary Decision]

(1) The hearing examiner shall, when he or she considers it reasonable to make a decision pursuant to the provisions of the Article 66 of the Act, state a content of the order, facts, evidences, and application of laws and ordinances (and basis of calculation of the surcharge, when it is considered reasonable to make a decision mentioned in Article 66 (3) of the Act concerned the order for payment) in preliminary decision. However when he or she renders the decision pursuant to the provision of the Article 66 (1), he or she may not state evidences.

(2) The hearing examiner shall sign and seal the preliminary decision.

(3) When a hearing examiner is unable to sign and seal the preliminary decision due to a problem, another hearing examiner shall sign and seal the preliminary decision by noting the reason thereof.

Art. 75 [Motion for Objection against the Preliminary Decision]

The investigator or the respondent or the respondent's representative may make a motion for objection to the Commission in writing within two weeks of the date of receiving a copy of the preliminary decision.

Art. 76 [Proposed Statement]

(1) The respondent or the respondent's representative shall, if he or she intends to make a proposal of statement in accordance with the provisions of Article 63 of the Act, submit to the Commission a document stating the intent and a summary of the statement within the period mentioned in the preceding article.

(2) If the proposal of statement pursuant to the preceding paragraph has been made, the Commission shall, without delay following the expiry of the period mentioned

in the preceding paragraph, designate a date for hearing the statement. The Commission shall also serve a written notice to the respondent or the respondent's representative that indicates the date, time, place and other necessary information.

Art. 77 [Holding a Hearing of the Statement]

(1) If unable to appear on the date for the hearing of the statement, the respondent or the respondent's representative shall notify the chairman thereof without delay, together with a clear reason.

(2) The chairman may, who deemed necessary, change the date for the hearing of the statement.

(3) The chairman presides the hearing of the statement on the date for the hearing of the statement.

(4) The respondent or the respondent's representative shall, at the hearing of the statement, make a statement based on the document submitted pursuant to the provision of Paragraph 1 of the preceding article.

(5) For the hearing of statement, the officials shall prepare a record stating a summary of the stated opinion and other necessary matters and sign and seal. The chairman shall seal the summary.

(6) When the respondent or the respondent's representative fails to appear on the date for the hearing of the statement without due reason, the proposal for the statement shall be deemed to be withdrawn.

(7) The provisions of Article 71 shall be applied to the hearing of the statement.

Art. 78 [Decision Based on Preliminary Decision]

(1) After the period mentioned in Article 75 has expired (and after an opportunity is provided to make a statement if a proposal of statement was made in accordance with the provisions of Article 63 of the Act), the Commission may forthwith render a decision having the same content as that of the preliminary decision, if the preliminary decision is deemed appropriate. The decision may be rendered after examining the preliminary decision on the basis of the record of the case submitted in accordance with the provisions of Article 73, the written motion for objection submitted in accordance with the provisions of Article 75 and the hearing of statement made in accordance with the provision of the preceding article.

(2) As a result of the examination mentioned in the preceding paragraph, the Commission may, if it deems that the objection or the statement is supported by reason, or otherwise deems necessary, render a decision that differs from the

preliminary decision. Alternatively, the Commission may hold hearings by itself in respect to the case, or may order the hearing examiner to reopen the hearings with instructions on points needing further examination.

Art. 79 [Reopening of Hearings]

The Commission shall, when it has ruled that it will hold the hearings by itself or that it will order the hearing examiner to reopen the hearings in accordance with the provision of Paragraph 2 of the preceding article, prepare a written ruling and serve its copy on the respondent or the respondent's representative.

Art. 80 [Decisions]

(1) If a decision is rendered pursuant to the provisions of Article 66 of the Act, the text of the order and the evidence shall be stated in the decision, in addition to the matters provided in Article 70–2 (1) of the Act, however, if a decision is rendered pursuant to the provision of Article 66 (1) of the act, the evidence may not be stated (in the decision).

(2) A certified copy of the decision shall be served on the respondent or the respondent's representative.

Art. 81 [Decision relating to corrections]

(1) When there is a clear error, including a transcript error, in the decision, the Commission may make a decision to correct the error upon its own motion or upon application.

(2) A motion for an objection against the decision for correction may be made in writing to the Commission within two weeks of the date a certified copy of the decision was served.

(3) The Commission shall, if it turns down a motion for objection as mentioned in the preceding paragraph, notify the applicant thereof.

Art. 82 [Hearings for Cases Held in Remand]

(1) If the case has been held in remand in accordance with the provisions of Article 81 (3) of the Act, the Commission shall forthwith set a hearing date.

(2) The Commission may, when deemed appropriate, have the hearing examiner preside over hearings to be held after the case has been held in remand as mentioned in the preceding paragraph *above*.

[For Information] Provision Deleted

Chapter V
Decision

DIVISION I CONSENT DECISION

Art. 81 [Application for Consent Decision]

(1) The respondent may, at any time after the decision on the initiation of the hearing, apply for a consent decision as stipulated in Article 53–3 of the Act.

(2) During the hearing by the hearing examiner, the application mentioned in the preceding paragraph shall be made through the hearing examiner.

(3) The hearing examiner shall submit to the Commission the application mentioned in the preceding paragraph together with his opinion.

[Translation]

Rules On Administrative Investigation by the Fair Trade Commission

Fair Trade Commission Rule No.5 of 2005

Table of Contents

Chapter I
General Rules

Art. 1 [Purpose and Definition]

(1) The investigation procedures of the Fair Trade Commission (hereinafter referred to as 'the Commission') shall follow these Rules and the Act Concerning Prohibition of Private Monopolization and Maintenance of Fair Trade (Act No.54 of 1947). (Including where the Act is applied in Article 95–4 of the Fishery Industry Cooperative Association Law (Act No.242 of 1948), and Article 108 of the Law on Cooperative Association of Small and Medium Enterprises (Act No.181 of 1949). Hereinafter referred to as 'the Act'.), the Act against Unjustifiable Premium and Misleading Representation (Act No.34 of 1962) as well as the Cabinet Ordinance concerning Designation of Investigator as stipulated in Article 47 (2) of the Act Concerning Prohibition of Private Monopolization and Maintenance of Fair Trade (Cabinet Ordinance No.264 of 1953. Hereinafter referred to as 'the Cabinet Ordinance Concerning Designation of Investigator'); provided, however, that the procedures on reporting and submission of materials regarding immunity from or reduction of surcharges shall be carried out as otherwise stipulated.

(2) The terms used in these Rules that are the same as those used in the Act shall have the same meaning as the terms used in the Act.

Art. 2 [Computation of Period]

(1) The computation of period shall be made according to the provisions concerning period of the Civil Code (Act No.89 of 1896).

(2) If the last day of a period falls on any of the days indicated in the items of 1 (1) of the Law for Closed Days of the National Administrative Organs (Act No.91 of 1988), the period shall expire at the next day of the said last day.

Art. 3 [Language]

(1) The Japanese language shall be used in the investigation procedures.

(2) When a person not versed in the Japanese language is required to make a statement, an interpreter shall be used to interpret.

Art. 4 [Method for Service by Public Notification]

The Commission may insert service by public notification into an official gazette or newspaper. With respect to the public notification to be served in a foreign country, the Commission may notify that the public notification was served instead of inserting it into the official gazette or newspapers.

Art. 5 [Preparation of Document]

(1) Unless otherwise specially stipulated, any document to be prepared for the investigation procedures shall be dated, signed and sealed.

(2) When the document stipulated in the preceding Paragraph is a duplicate to be made by the Commission, the official who made the duplicate shall note that the duplicate does not differ from its original in a place contiguous to the concerned statement, shall sign and seal the duplicate, and shall impress a seal across it and the contiguous leaf or take similar action.

Art. 6 [Correction of Document]

No character shall be altered in preparing documents for the investigation procedures. If any character is added, deleted or, entered in the margin of a page, a seal shall be impressed on it for confirmation. In this case, any deleted character shall remain legible.

Chapter II
Investigation Procedures

DIVISION I GENERAL PROCESS

Art. 7 [Initiation of Investigation Procedure]

(1) The Director General of the Investigation Bureau of the General Secretariat shall, upon coming into contact with the incipient facts of a case, report to the Commission with any connection concerning whether it is necessary to proceed with an investigation.

(2) In making the report stipulated in the preceding Paragraph, the following matters shall be clarified as possible:

(i) Incipiency
(ii) Synopsis of the facts of the case
(iii) Applicable provisions of the Act

(3) In the case of Paragraph 1, the Commission shall, with respect to a case that the Commission acknowledges as requiring the action stipulated in Article 47 (1) of the Act, designate an investigator and assign him to investigate the said case pursuant to Article 47 (2) of the Act and the Cabinet Ordinance concerning Designation of Investigator.

Art. 8 [Identification Card]

The form of the identification card stipulated in Article 47 (3) of the Act shall be as shown in the separated form.

Art. 9 [Measures Taken by Investigator]

(1) The investigator shall, when taking the measures as provided for in Article 47 (1) of the Act pursuant to the provision of Article 47 (2) of the Act, take measures by serving the document indicated in each of following items, according to the classification indicated in each of the items.

(i) In the case of ordering persons concerned with a case or witnesses to appear for interrogating them; a writ of appearance
(ii) In the case of hearing to present their opinions or collecting reports from the persons indicated in the preceding Item; a writ of report

(iii) In the case of ordering experts to appear for giving expert testimony; a writ of expert testimony
(iv) In the case of ordering persons holding accounting books, documents, and other materials to submit the said materials; a writ of submission

(2) The documents described in the preceding Paragraph shall include the following matters, and each leaf of the documents shall bear a seal stamped across both it and the contiguous leaf.

(i) Title of the case
(ii) Name of the party to be served
(iii) Requested matters
(iv) In the case of a writ of appearance or a writ of submission, date and place of appearance and submission
(v) Penal provisions of the Act in the event of default

(3) A writ of submission shall include the materials to be ordered to submit or shall attach the list of the articles of them.

Art. 10 [Preparation of Record]

(1) The staff members of the Commission shall, when preparing the record as provided for in this Division for the case pursuant to the provisions of Article 48 of the Act, enter the date of preparation and the name of the bureau, put signs and seals in the record.

(2) In the case of preparing the record stipulated in the preceding Paragraph, when any character is added, deleted, or shown on the margin of a page, the number of characters shall be entered in the record.

(3) Where documents, photographs, and such other materials to be deemed appropriate may be cited and attached to the record stipulated in Paragraph 1 for regarding as parts of the record.

(4) Each leaf of the record stipulated in Paragraph 1 shall bear a seal stamped across it and the contiguous leaf.

Art. 11 [Record of Interrogation]

(1) The investigator shall, when having interrogated persons concerned with a case or witnesses in accordance with the provision of Article 47 (1) (i) of the Act pursuant to the provision of Article 47 (2) of the Act, prepare the record of interrogation, read it to the deponent or have the deponent peruse it, and ask the deponent if there is no mistake in the record. If the deponent makes a motion for any addition or deletion, the deponent's statement shall be entered in the record.

(2) When the deponent makes a motion that there is no mistake in the record stipulated in the preceding Paragraph, the investigator may ask to sign and seal the record.

(3) In the case of the preceding Paragraph, when the deponent is unable to sign, another person shall sign on behalf of the deponent. When the deponent is unable to seal, the deponent shall be fingerprinted. However, where another person signs on behalf of the deponent, the said person shall state the reason in the record and sign and seal it.

(4) In the case of Paragraph 2, where the deponent refuses to sign and seal the record, that effect shall be entered in the record.

Art. 12 [Special Rules when Interrogating Via an Interpreter]

(1) The investigator shall, when interrogating a person concerned with a case or witness via an interpreter, enter the fact and effect that the investigator read the record to the person via the interpreter in the record of interrogation.

(2) The investigator may ask the interpreter to sign and seal the record stipulated in the preceding Paragraph.

Art. 13 [Record of Statement]

(1) In the case where a person concerned with a case or a witness makes a voluntary statement, when the staff member of the Commission deems it necessary, a record of statement that shall record the statement shall be prepared.

(2) The provisions of the preceding two Articles shall be applied to the record stipulated in the preceding Paragraph.

Art. 14 [Expert Testimony]

The investigator shall, when he has ordered an expert to give expert testimony in accordance with the provision of Article 47 (1) (ii) of the Act pursuant to the provision of Article 47 (2) of the Act, have the expert report the process and result thereof with a written statement.

Art. 15 [Record of Retention]

(1) The investigator shall, when he has retained any submissions in accordance with the provision of Article 47 (1) (iii) of the Act pursuant to the provision of Article 47 (2) of the Act, prepare a record of retention.

(2) The record stipulated in the preceding Paragraph shall incorporate the title of the case, the name, occupation and address or workplace of the owner and the person who provided the retained materials, and the date and place of retention.

(3) The record stipulated in Paragraph 1 shall attach a list of the articles of the retained materials.

Art. 16 [Notice on Retained Materials, and Others]

(1) The investigator shall, when he has retained any submissions in accordance with the provision of Article 47 (1) (iii) of the Act pursuant to the provision of Article 47 (2) of the Act, notify in writing that he retained the said materials to the person who provide the materials.

(2) The documents stipulated in the preceding Paragraph shall attach a copy of the list stipulated in Paragraph 3 of the preceding Article.

(3) A copy of the list stipulated in Paragraph 3 of the preceding Article shall, when the owner of the retained materials request, be issued.

Art. 17 [Return or Temporary Return of Retained Materials]

(1) Any retained material that no longer needs to be held in custody shall be returned without waiting for the closure of the case.

(2) Any retained material may be temporarily returned upon the request of its owner or the person who provided it.

Art. 18 [Peruse and Copy of the Materials to be Ordered to Submit]

(1) A person, who was ordered to submit accounting books, documents, and other materials in accordance with the provision of Article 47 (1) (iii) of the Act, may peruse or copy the said materials. However, where perusing and copying the materials may be to provide a particular trouble in the investigation of a case, the foregoing shall not apply.

(2) In the case of perusing or copying pursuant to the provision of the preceding Paragraph, the investigator shall designate the date and time, place, and method with taking into consideration the opinion of person who was ordered to submit the said materials.

Art. 19 [Documents Submitted Voluntarily]

In the case of receiving books, documents, and other materials that are provided voluntarily by parties concerned or witnesses, when the staff members of the

Commission shall, when he deems it necessary, request the persons concerned with a case or the witnesses for submitting a document stating a list of the submissions, the date of providing the materials, and the name, occupation, and address of the owner and person who provided them.

Art. 20 [Notice of Alleged Fact and Others]

The investigator shall, when carrying out an inspection in accordance with the provision of Article 47 (1) (iv) of the Act pursuant to the provision of Article 47 (2) of the Act, make available the document stating the following matters for concerned persons.

(i) Title of a case
(ii) Main point of the alleged fact violating the provision of the Act
(iii) Applicable provisions of the Act

Art. 21 [Record of Inspection]

(1) The investigator shall, when having carried out an inspection in accordance with the provision of Article 47 (1) (iv) of the Act pursuant to the provision of Article 47 (2) of the Act, prepare a record of inspection.

(2) The record stipulated in the preceding Paragraph shall include the title of a case, the purpose, date and time, and place of an inspection, the name and occupation of persons who were presented at the inspection, and the results of the inspection.

Art. 22 [Motion for Objection Against Measures Taken by Investigator]

(1) Any person, who was subject to the measures as provided for in any items of Article 47 (1) of the Act, which was taken by the investigator pursuant to the provision of Article 47 (2) of the Act, may make a motion for objection to the Commission within one week from the day subject to the measure by a document stating the grounds, when being dissatisfied with the said measure.

(2) The Commission shall, when recognizing that there are grounds for the motion for objection, order the investigator to withdraw, cancel, or change the measure against which the motion for objection was made, and notify thereof to the petitioner.

(3) The Commission shall, when having rejected the motion for objection, notify thereof to the petitioner. In this case, the reasons for the rejection shall be given.

Art. 23 [Report of Investigation Result]

(1) The Director General of the Investigation Bureau of the General Secretariat shall, when closing the investigation of a case, promptly make a report on the results to the Commission.

(2) In the case of the preceding Paragraph, a report on a case where the investigator took the measures as provided for in Article 47 (1) of the Act pursuant to the provision of Article 47 (2) of the Act shall be made with clarifying the following matters:

(i) Incipiency
(ii) Investigational process
(iii) Synopsis of the facts of the case
(iv) Applicable provisions of the Act
(v) Opinion of the investigator

DIVISION II THE CEASE AND DESIST ORDER

Art. 24 [Notice Before the Cease and Desist Order]

(1) When notifying pursuant to the provision of Article 49 (5) of the Act, a document stating the matters indicated in the following items shall be served to the person who is to be the addressee for the cease and desist order.

(i) Tentative content of the cease and desist order
(ii) The facts found by the Commission and the application of law thereto
(iii) The opportunity to present his or her opinions in writing and to submit evidence in support thereof to the Commission and the deadline therefore regarding the matters indicated in the two preceding Items

(2) The Commission may, when recognizing that there is justifiable reason, extend the deadline stipulated in Item 3 of the preceding Paragraph upon its own motion or upon application.

Art. 25 [Explanation Before the Cease and Desist Order]

When a person, who received the service of the document stipulated in Paragraph 1 of the preceding Article, or a representative appointed in accordance with the provision of Article 49 (4) of the Act, makes a motion, and when there are other necessities, the investigator shall explain the matter indicated in Paragraph 1 (1) and (2) of the preceding Article to the person who received the service of the said document and his representative. In this case, the investigator shall explain the evidence necessary for establishing the foundation for the facts findings of the Commission regarding the person to be explained.

Art. 26 [Formality of Statement of Opinion and Others]

(1) A person served with a document stipulated in Article 24 (1) may state opinions in writing and provide evidence with respect to the matters indicated in 24 (1) (i) and (ii) to the Commission by the designated deadline. In this case, when a deposition is provided as evidence, it shall be done with a document signed and sealed by a deponent.

(2) When providing the evidence pursuant to the provision of the preceding Paragraph, the matter to be proved shall be clarified.

(3) Without prejudice to the provision of Paragraph 1, the Commission may, when recognizing that there is the particular necessity, have the person state his or her opinion orally. In this case, the Commission shall designate a staff member who hears the opinion, and notify of the date and time, and place of stating to the person who is about to state the opinion.

(4) The Commission shall, when notifying in accordance with the provision of preceding Paragraph, in advance, hear the opinion on the date and time, and place from the person who is about to the state opinion.

Art. 27 [Statement of Opinion by Representative, and Others]

(1) In the case where the person served with a document stipulated in Article 24 (1) appoint an representative at the time of presenting his opinions or submitting evidence in accordance with Article 49 (3) of the Act, when the representative is a attorney at law or a law firm, the representative shall verify the authority in writing.

(2) The document stipulated in the preceding Paragraph shall clearly indicate the title of a bar association and an office to which the representative belongs, and the scope and extent of authority of representative.

(3) Where a representative is a law firm, the name of a attorney at law who is in charge of the case in question as a member of the said corporation, the title of a bar association to which the attorney at law belongs, and the scope and extent of tasks (work) that each attorney at law can perform shall be stated clearly in the document stipulated in Paragraph 1.

(4) The person served with a document stipulated in Article 24 (1) shall, when intending to obtain approval for the appointment of a person other than a attorney at law or a law firm as an representative at the time of presenting his or her opinion or

submitting evidence in accordance with Article 49 (3) of the Act, submit to the Commission a document stating the name, address, and occupation of the person, and the relationship with the person served with a document stipulated in Article 24 (1) and others which are sufficient for determining whether or not the said person is eligible to act as an representative.

(5) The document stipulated in the preceding Paragraph, requesting approval for the appointment of a person other than a attorney at law or a law firm as the representative, shall attach a letter that clearly indicates the authority of the representative and the scope and extent of it shall be attached.

(6) In the case of receiving the submission of the document stipulated in Paragraph 4, requesting approval for the appointment of a person other than a attorney at law or a law firm as the representative, the Commission shall, when deciding to give or not to give the approval, file a notice the person who requested the approval stipulated in Paragraph 4 thereof.

(7) The person who served with a document stipulated in Article 24 (1) shall, where the authority of a representative lapsed, file a notice with the Commission thereof in writing without delay.

Art. 28 [Service of the Written Cease and Desist Order]

(1) The certified copy of the written cease and desist order shall be served to the addressee or representative.

(2) When serving the certified copy of the written cease and desist order, a written notification stating that the hearing procedure on the said cease and desist order may be requested shall de attached to it.

DIVISION III PAYMENT ORDER OF SURCHARGE

Art. 29 [Notice Before Payment Order, and Others]

The provisions of Articles 24 to 28 shall apply mutatis mutandis to the payment order of surcharge. In this case, the term 'Article 49 (5) of the Act' in Article 24 (1) shall be read as 'Article 49 (5) applicable mutatis mutandis under Article 50 (6) ', and 'the addressee for the cease and desist order' shall be read as 'the addressee for the payment order' and 'Tentative content of the cease and desist order' in Article 24 (1) (i) shall be read as 'Amount of surcharge intended to order to pay', and 'The facts found by the Commission and the application of law thereto' in Article 24 (1) (ii) shall be read as 'The basis of calculation of such amount and the violative act related to surcharge ', and 'Paragraph 1 of the preceding Article' in Article 25 and 'Article 24 (1)' in Article 26 (1) and Article 27 (1), (4) and (7) shall be read as

'Article 24 (1) applicable mutatis mutandis under Article 29', and 'Article 49 (4) of the Act ' in Article 25 shall be read as 'Article 49 (4) of the Act applicable mutatis mutandis under Article 50 (6) ', and 'the facts finding of the Commission' in Article 25 shall be read as 'the basis of calculation of such amount or the violative act related to such surcharge', and 'Article 49 (3) of the Act ' in Article 27 (1) and (4) shall be read as 'Article 49 (3) of the Act applicable mutatis mutandis under Article 50 (6) ', and 'the certified copy of the written cease and desist order ' in Paragraph 1 of the preceding Article shall be read as 'the certified copy of the written surcharge payment order', and 'When serving the certified copy of the written cease and desist order, a written notification stating that the hearing procedure on the said cease and desist order' in Paragraph 2 of the same Article shall be read as 'When serving the certified copy of the written surcharge payment order, a written notification stating that the hearing procedure on the said payment order'.

Art. 30 [Time of Notifying to Entrepreneurs Who aren't Ordered Pay Surcharge]

The time stipulated in the Rules of the Commission as provided for in Article 7–2 (13) of the Act (including cases applicable mutatis mutandis under Article 8–3 of the Act) and Article 7–2 (16) of the Act is the time when notifying entrepreneur other than the said entrepreneur of not giving the order pursuant to Article 7–2 (1) (including cases applicable mutatis mutandis under Article 7–2 (2) or Article 8–3).

Chapter III
Supplementary Rules

Art. 31 [Notice to Reporting Person]

(1) The notice pursuant to the provisions of Article 45 (3) of the Act shall be given, where the report pursuant to Article 45 (1) was made by a document stating the matters indicated in each of the following items:

(i) Name or title and address of a reporting person
(ii) Name or title of a person who commits or has committed an act considered a violation of the provisions of the Act
(iii) Details of the activity, time, place and other facts of an act considered a violation of the provisions of the Act

(2) The notification stipulated in the preceding Paragraph shall be filed, where a report including the matters indicated in each item of the preceding Paragraph, which is transmitted using an electronic information processing organization, is indicated clearly in documents by using computers including their peripheral devices and other equipment used by the Commission.

(3) The notification stipulated in Paragraph 1 shall, in cases indicated in each of the following items, be filed by a document stating thereof. However, where the notification stipulated in any of the following items is filed for cases regarding a similar report, no subsequent notice shall be served.

(i) When the ccase and desist order was issued for the said case
(ii) When the order for payment was issued for the said case
(iii) When measures for elimination were taken for the said case in accordance with the provision of Article 6 (1) of the Act against Unjustifiable Premiums and Misleading Representations
(iv) When any of the measures indicated in the preceding items were not taken for the said case

(4) In the documents stipulated in the preceding Paragraph, any matters deemed appropriate may be stated in addition to the matters to be stated pursuant to the provisions of the preceding Paragraph.

Art. 32 [Submission of Documents by Facsimile]

(1) The documents to be submitted in the investigation procedures may be submitted by transmitting in facsimile, excluding the following documents:

(i) Documents to be submitted pursuant to the measures indicated in each item of Article 47 (1) of the Act
(ii) Written opinion and evidence on the notice before the cease and desist order
(iii) Written opinion and evidence on the notice before the order for payment
(iv) Documents proving authorization or the authority of the representative necessary for stating opinion before the cease and desist order or the order for payment
(v) Written motion for objection against measures taken by the investigator

(2) When a document is submitted by using facsimile, the document shall be deemed to have been submitted to the Commission at the time when the Commission receives it.

(3) The chairman or the investigator may, when recognizing there is necessary in the case as provided for in the preceding Paragraph, have the submitting person submit the original document used for transmission.

Art. 33 [Decision for Corrections]

(1) When there is a clear error, including a transcript error, in the written cease and desist order or the written surcharge payment order, the Commission may make a decision to correct the error upon its own motion or upon application.

(2) A motion for an objection against the decision for correction may be made in writing to the Commission within two weeks of the date when the certified copy of the written decision was received.

(3) The Commission shall, when having turned down a motion for objection stipulated in the preceding Paragraph, notify the petitioner thereof.

Art. 34 [Suspend the Execution of Cease and Desist Order, and Others]

(1) The Commission shall, when having suspended the execution of all or parts of the cease and desist order pursuant to the provision of Article 54 (1) of the Act, notify the person who requested the hearing procedure thereof.

(2) The Commission shall, when revoking the suspension of the execution pursuant to the provision of Article 54 (2), notify the person who requested the hearing procedure thereof with reason.

[Translation]

Rules on Compulsory Investigation of Criminal Cases by the Fair Trade Commission

Fair Trade Commission Rule No.6 of 2005

The rules on compulsory investigation of criminal cases by the Fair Trade Commission shall be established pursuant to the provision of Article 76(1) of the Act Concerning Prohibition of Private Monopolization and Maintenance of Fair Trade (Act No. 54 of 1947) as follows:

RULES ON COMPULSORY INVESTIGATION OF CRIMINAL CASES BY THE FAIR TRADE COMMISSION

Art. 1 [Purpose of the Rules]

The proceedings of Compulsory Investigation of Criminal Cases by staff members (hereinafter referred to as "staff members for criminal investigation") designated by the Fair Trade Commission (hereinafter referred to as "the Commission"), as provided for in Article 101(1) of the Act Concerning Prohibition of Private Monopolization and Maintenance of Fair Trade (hereinafter referred to as "the Act"), shall follow the Rules as well as the Act.

Art. 2 [Designation of the staff members for Compulsory Investigation of Criminal Cases]

The designation by the Commission as provided for in Article 101(1), shall be made only for the staff members in the Criminal Investigation Department, the Investigation Bureau of the General Secretariat.

Art. 3 [Identification Card]

The form of identification card stipulated in Article 106 of the Act shall be as shown in the separated Form.

Art. 4 [Initiation of Criminal Investigation]

The Director General of the Investigation Bureau of the General Secretariat shall, upon coming into contact with the incipient facts of a criminal case, report to the Commission.
2. In making the report mentioned in the preceding paragraph, the following matters shall be stated as clearly as possible:

(i) Incipiency
(ii) Synopsis of the facts of the case
(iii) Applicable provisions of the Act

3. The Commission shall, with respect to a case that the Commission acknowledges as necessary in the case of Paragraph 1, assign the staff members for criminal investigation to investigate the said case.
4. The Investigator shall, when the contacted facts in the case which he took the measures as provided for in Article 47(1) of the Act pursuant to the provision of Article 47(2) of the Act is considered to be the incipiency of a criminal case, immediately report to the Director General of the Investigation Bureau of the General Secretariat and follow his instructions, and shall not report on the facts directly to the staff members for criminal investigation.

Art. 5 [Reported Matters after Investigation]

In the case of making the report pursuant to Article 115 of the Act, following matters shall be clearly stated.

(i) Incipiency
(ii) Investigational process
(iii) Synopsis of the facts of the case
(iv) Applicable provisions of the Act
(v) Opinion of the staff members for criminal investigation

[Translation]

Rules on Reporting and Submission of Materials Regarding Immunity from or Reduction of Surcharges by the Fair Trade Commission

Fair Trade Commission Rule No.7 of 2005

Art. 1 [Reporting the Summary of Violative Act Prior to the Investigation Starting Date]

(1) An entrepreneur, who is about to report and submit materials pursuant to the provisions of Article 7–2 (7) (i), 7–2 (8) (i), or 7–2 (8) (ii) of the Act Concerning Prohibition of Private Monopolization and Maintenance of Fair Trade (hereinafter referred to as 'the Act') (including cases where these articles shall apply *mutatis mutandis* to Article 8–3 of the Act; hereinafter the same), shall submit a written report using the Form No.1 to the Fair Trade Commission (hereinafter referred to as 'the Commission') by transmitting it in facsimile.

(2) The fax number for the submission of a written report as provided for in the preceding Paragraph shall be 03–3581–5599. [Note: The fax number from outside Japan shall be +81–3–3581–5599.]

(3) Where a written report as provided for in Paragraph (1) is submitted by transmitting it in facsimile, it shall be deemed to be submitted to the Commission at the time when the Commission receives it in facsimile.

(4) The entrepreneur, who submitted a written report as provided for in Paragraph (1), shall submit the original written report to the Commission without delay.

Art. 2 [Notifying the Order of Submission and the Deadline for Submission]

The Commission shall, when it receives a written report as provided for in Paragraph (1) of the preceding Article, notify to the entrepreneur who submitted the written report the order of submission of the written report and the deadline by which reporting the facts regarding the violative act by using a written report of the

Form No.2 and submission of materials should be completed (hereinafter referred to as 'the deadline for submission')

Art. 3 [Reporting and Submission of Materials Prior to the Investigation Starting Date]

(1) An entrepreneur, who is about to make a report and submission of materials pursuant to the provisions of Article 7–2 (7) (i), 7–2 (8) (i), or 7–2 (8) (ii) of the Act, shall submit a written report of the Form No.2 and materials to the Commission by the deadline for submission.

(2) In the case of the preceding Paragraph, where the Commission deems the exceptional circumstances to be necessary for it with regard to substituting an oral report for the entries on the matters written in 'Note' of the Form No.2 in the matters to entry of that Form or substituting an oral statement for the Submission of the materials which is substitutable by an oral statement in the materials stipulated in that Paragraph, the entrepreneur may substitute the oral report or oral statement for the entries on the matters or submission of the materials. However it is limited to the case where the entrepreneur, who is about to make the oral report or oral statement, appears before the Senior Officer for Immunity from or Reduction of Surcharges (hereinafter referred to as 'the Senior Officer for Leniency Program') at the Management and Planning Division of the Investigation Bureau of the General Secretariat of the Commission and makes the oral report or oral statement by the deadline for submission.

(3) In the case of the preceding Paragraph, the Senior Officer for Leniency Program shall record the details of the oral report or oral statement.

Art. 4 [Reporting and Submission of Materials on or after the Starting Date of the Investigation]

(1) An entrepreneur, who is about to make a report and submission of materials pursuant to the provisions of Article 7–2 (9) (i) of the Act (including cases applicable *mutatis mutandis* under Article 8–3 of the Act; hereinafter the same), shall submit a written report of the Form No.3 and materials to the Commission by the deadline stipulated in the following Article.

(2) The written report as provided for in the preceding Paragraph shall be submitted by transmitting it in facsimile.

(3) The provisions of Paragraph (2) and (3) of the preceding Article shall apply to a case of Paragraph (1), and the provisions of Article 1 (2) through (4) shall apply to a case where a written report is submitted by the method stipulated in the preceding Paragraph. In this case, the term 'by the deadline for submission' in Paragraph (2) of the preceding Article shall be read as 'by the deadline as provided for in the following Article'.

Art. 5 [Deadline for Reporting and Submission of Materials on or after the Investigation Starting Date]

The deadline stipulated in the Fair Trade Commission Rules as provided for in Article 7–2 (9) (i) of the Act shall be the day that is passed by twenty days (the number of days listed in the item of Article 1 (1) of the Law Concerning Holidays of Administrative Organizations (Act No.91 of 1988) shall not be included in the calculation) reckoning from the day when either the measures indicated in Article 47 (1) (iv) of the Act or the measures as provided for in Article 102 (1) of the Act are first implemented regarding the case related to the violative act.

Art. 6 [Methods of Submission of a Written Report and Materials]

(1) A written report and materials as provided for in Article 3 (1) and materials as provided for in Article 4 (1) shall be submitted by using one or plural of the methods in the following items;

(i) Direct delivery to the Senior Officer for Leniency Program;
(ii) Sending to the Senior Officer for Leniency Program by registered mail, correspondence which includes undertaking and record of delivery as services of correspondence delivery as provided for in Article 2 (2) of the Law Concerning Correspondence Delivery by Private-Sector Operators (Act No.99 of 2002) by a general correspondence delivery operator as provided for in Article 2 (6) of that law or by a special correspondence delivery operator as provided for in Article 2 (9) of that law, or other methods similar to them; or
(iii) Transmitting in facsimile.

(2) The written report and materials as provided for in the preceding Paragraph may, notwithstanding the provisions of that Paragraph, be submitted by using an electronic information processing system in accordance with the Enforcement Rules on the Law Concerning Use of Information and Telecommunication Technologies in Administrative Procedures Related to Legislation under the Jurisdiction of the Fair Trade Commission (Fair Trade Commission Rule No.1 of 2003).

(3) The provisions of Article 1 (2) and (3) shall apply to the case where the written report and materials are submitted by the methods stipulated in Paragraph (1) (iii).

Art. 7 [The Order of Submission of a Written Report and Materials, and Others]

(1) If two or more entrepreneurs submit written reports and materials as provided for in Article 3 by the deadline for submission, which the provisions of Article 7–2 (7) (i), 7–2 (8) (i), or 7–2 (8) (ii) of the Act the report and materials fall under shall

be determined according to the order of submission of the written reports as provided for in Article 1 (1).

(2) If two or more entrepreneurs submit written reports and materials as provided for in Article 4 by the deadline as provided for in Article 5, the order of application for the provisions of Article 7–2 (9) of the Act to the entrepreneurs shall be determined according to the order of submission of the written reports as provided for in Article 4 (1).

Art. 8 [Duty to Keep Secret to Third Parties]

An entrepreneur who submitted the written report as provided for in Article 1 (1), Article 3, or Article 4 (1) shall not disclose thereof to third parties without justifiable reason.

Art. 9 [Terms]

(1) The written report as provided for in Article 1 (1), 3, and 4 (1) shall be prepared in Japanese.

(2) If the materials submitted to the Commission in accordance with the provisions of Article 3 and 4 (1) are not prepared in Japanese, a Japanese-language translation shall be attached to the materials.

FORM No.1 (Paper Size: JIS A4)

WRITTEN REPORT
REGARDING IMMUNITY FROM OR REDUCTION OF SURCHARGES

Date: _____ (Year) _____ (Month) _____ (day)

Submitted to: Fair Trade Commission of Japan
(Fax number: +81–3–3581–5599)

Submitted by:
Name or Title of Entrepreneur:
Address or Location:
Position Title of Representative: (Seal)
Name of Division for Contact:
Position Title and Name of Person in Charge:
Telephone Number:

We hereby make a report pursuant to the provisions of Article 7–2 (7) (i), Article 7–2 (8) (i), or Article 7–2 (8) (ii) of the Act Concerning Prohibition of Private Monopolization and Maintenance of Fair Trade (including cases where these articles shall apply *mutatis mutandis* to Article 8–3 of the Act).

Without justifiable reason, we shall not disclose to third parties the fact that we have made the following report.

1. Summary of the Violative Act to be Reported

(1) Goods or Services Targeted by the Said Act	
(2) Description of the Said Act	a. b.
(3) Name or Title and Address or Location of Other Entrepreneur(s) Participating in the Said Act	
(4) The Time of the First Implementation (The time of Termination)	______ (Year) ______ (Month) ______ (Day) (until ______ [Year] ______ [Month] ______ [Day])

Instructions for Completing This Form

(The following items correspond to the items on the Form No.1.)

Summary of the Violative Act to be Reported

1. Goods or Services Targeted by the Said Act

Enter in details for clarifying the range of goods or services targeted by the said act. If you do not know how to specify the name of goods, and others, please be based on the following instructions: For goods or services falling under 'Division F – Manufacturing Industry' indicated in the Standard Industrial Classification for Japan (Ministry of Internal Affairs and Communications Notice No.139 of 2002), specify in conformity with the industrial classification for the Census of Manufactures (the Ministry of International Trade and Industry Ordinance No.81 of 1951). For goods or services falling under other industries, specify in conformity with the segmented classification (four-digit classification) of the Standard Industrial Classification for Japan.

2. Description of the Said Act

(1) Enter the description of the said act (price cartels, bid-riggings, market allocations, and others) in 2. (1).

(2) Enter in detail in 2. (2) for clarifying, for example,

(A) in the case of price-raising cartels, the names of parties participating in the cartel agreement, the geographical region targeted by the price-raising, the time of implementation of the price-raising, and the range of the price-raising.

(B) in the case of bid-riggings, the parties participating in the bid-rigging, the contract awarding public agencies of the related projects, and others. If trade associations are involved in the said act, enter in 2. (2) for clarifying the title and details of the associations' involvement.

3. The Time of the First Implementation (The Time of Termination)

a. Enter the date when the arrangement regarding the said act was decided. If it is not clear when the said act was implemented for the first time, enter the earliest date when it is certain that the said act was being implemented, and append a note of 'at the latest'.

b. If the reporting entrepreneur has already ceased the said act, enter the date of termination in the parentheses.

Note

1. If a written report is prepared by an agent, enter the name or title and address or location of reporting entrepreneur, the description that the report is prepared by the agent, and the name of the agent, and put the seal of the agent in place of the seal of the representative of the reporting entrepreneur. In this case, a letter of proxy shall be required to be attached to the written report.

2. Where there is no space to write fully reporting matters of 1.and 2. on the Form No.1, use and attach extra sheets.

3. When this written report is transmitted in facsimile, do not mistake the fax number.

FORM No.2 (Paper Size: JIS A4)

WRITTEN REPORT
REGARDING IMMUNIT FROM OR REDUCTION OF SURCHARGES

Date: _____ (Year) _____ (Month) _____ (day)

Submitted to:
Fair Trade Commission of Japan

Submitted by:
Name or Title of Entrepreneur:
Address or Location:
Name and Position Title of Representative: (Seal)
Name of Division for Contact:
Position Title and Name of Person in Charge:
Telephone Number:

We hereby make a report pursuant to the provisions of Article 7–2 (7) (i), Article 7–2 (8) (i), or Article 7–2 (8) (ii) of the Act Concerning Prohibition of Private Monopolization and Maintenance of Fair Trade (including cases where these articles shall apply *mutatis mutandis* to Article 8–3 of the Act).

Without justifiable reason, we shall not disclose to third parties the fact that we have made the following report.

1. Summary of the Violative Act to be Reported

(1) Goods or Services Targeted by the Said Act	
(2) Description of the Said Act	a.
	b.
(3) Name or Title and Address or Location of Other Entrepreneur(s) Participating in the Said Act	
(4) The Time of the First Implementation (The time of Termination)	______ (Year) ______ (Month) ______ (Day) (until ______ [Year] ______ [Month] ______ [Day])

2. Position Titles and Names of Executives or Employees Who Have Involved in the Said Act at the Reporting Entrepreneur

Current Position Title and Division's Name	Position Title and Division's Name at Time of Involvement (The Time of the Position)	Name

3. Names and Others of Executives or Employees Who Have Involved in the Said Act at Other Entrepreneur(s) Participating in the Said Act

Name of Entrepreneur	Current Position Title and Division's Name	Position Title and Division's Name at Time of Involvement (The Time of the Position)	Name

4. Other Matters for Consideration

5. Submission of Materials

We hereby submit the following materials.

No.	Title of Material	Description of Material's Content (Summary)	Notes

Instructions for Completing This Form
(The following items correspond to the items on the Form No.2.)

1. Summary of the violative act to be reported

(1) Goods or Services Targeted by the Said Act

a. Enter in detail in 1. (1) for clarifying the range of the goods or services targeted by the said act. For example, where there are two distribution channels for a product—one for sales through distributors and the other for direct sales to users, if the price cartel is targeting only products sold through the latter distribution channel, enter for clarifying such matters. In the case of bid rigging, enter in detail for clarifying the contract awarding public agencies and divisions, the kinds of bids (open bids with limited conditions, bids competed by designated firms desiring to join the bid, bids competed by designated firms, and others), the type of construction, and others regarding ordered projects targeted by the said act.

b. If goods or services, within the range targeted by the said act, are specifically outside the target of arrangements (for example, goods or services for export, for specified uses, bidding projects competed by the designated specific firms, and others), enter in 1. (1) for clarifying such matters.

(2) Description of the Said Act

a. Enter the description of the said act (price cartels, bid-riggings, market allocations, and others) in 1. (2) a.

b. Enter in detail in 1. (2) b. for clarifying, for example,

(A) in the case of price-raising cartel, details of agreement (the time of implementation of the price-raising, and the range of price-raising, and others),

(B) in the case of bid rigging, details of the procedure (details of rules) for selecting an expected bid winner. If trade associations are involved in the said act, enter in 1. (2) b. details of the associations' involvement

(3) Name of Title and Address or Location of Other Enterpreneur(s) Participating in the Said Act

If trade associations are involved in the said act, enter in detail in 1. (3) for clarifying the title, address or location, and others of the trade associations.

(4) The Time of the First Implementation (The Time of Termination)

a. Enter the date when the arrangement regarding the said act was decided in 1.(4). If it is not clear when the said act was implemented for the first time, enter the earliest date when it is certain that the said act was being implemented, and append a note of at the 'latest'.

b. If the reporting entrepreneur has already ceased the said act, enter the date of termination in the parentheses. For example, if there is a date the entrepreneur decided to cease the said act as the organization, enter the date.

2. Position Titles and Names of Executives or Employees Who Have Involved in the Said Act at the Reporting Entrepreneur

While possible, enter not only executives and employees who are involved currently, but also were involved in the past.

3. Names and Others of Executives or Employees Who Have Involved in the Said Act at Other Entrepreneur(s) Participating in the Said Act

a. While possible, enter not only executives and employees who are involved currently, but also who were involved in the past. If the name and position title of the executive or employee is not found out, append a note to that effect.

b. If an executive or employee of trade associations is involved, enter the name and position title of the person.

4. Other Matters for Consideration

a. Enter other matters for consideration, for example, the situation surrounding the implementation of the said act, contact with other entrepreneur(s) participating in the said act, the profile of the industry, and the summary of related trade associations.

b. If the fact is deemed concerned with the involvement in bid rigging stipulated in Article 2 (5) (i) through (iii) of the Act Concerning Elimination and Prevention of Involvement in Bid Rigging and Others (Act No.101 of 2002), enter the details of the fact.

5. Submission of Materials

a. List on the chart and submit the materials leading to prove the matters indicated in 1. through 4. *above* :

(A) Memorandums of meeting related to the act, business daily reports indicating matters related to the said act, correspondence with other entrepreneur(s) participating in the said act, and others, and (B) Written reports related to the said act with the signatures and seals of the executives or employees involved in the act to be reported, and others. Where the materials are not prepared in Japanese, Japanese-language translations or abridged translations of the concerned parts shall be attached to the said materials.

b. For clarifying which matters indicated in 1. through 4. *above* are proven by the respective materials, appropriately organize the materials: For example, write '2.-(7)' in the Notes column of the seventh material leading to prove the matter indicated in 2. *above*.

Note:

1. 'Thee matters written in 'Note" (the matters which are substitutable for entering the Form by oral statements) stipulated in Article 3 (2) of this Rule is the matters indicated in 1. (2) b., 2., 3., and 4. *above.*

2.

(1) In the case of oral report or oral statement stipulated in Article 3 (2) of this Rule, the person who is about to report or state shall appear and do before the Senior Officer for Leniency Program by the deadline for submission stipulated in Article 2 of this Rule.

(2) The written report indicated in 5. a. (B) *above* is in principle 'the materials which are substitutable by an oral statement' stipulated in Article 3 (2) of this Rule. In this case, the person who should prepare the said written report shall make an oral statement.

3. If a written report is prepared by an agent, enter the name or title and address or location of reporting entrepreneur, the description that the report is prepared by the agent, and the name of the agent and put the seal of the agent in place of the seal of the representative of the reporting entrepreneur. In this case, a letter proxy shall be required to be attached to the written report. In case of making an oral report as provided for of in Article 3 (2), the letter shall be submitted at the time of report.

4. Where there is no space to write fully reporting matters of 1. to 5. on the Form No.2, use and attach extra sheets.

5. When this written report is transmitted in facsimile, do not mistake the fax number.

FORM No.3 (Paper Size: JIS A4)

WRITTEN REPORT
REGARDING IMMUNITY FROM OR REDUCTION OF SURCHARGES

Date: _____ (Year) _____ (Month) _____ (day)

Submitted to:
Fair Trade Commission of Japan
(Fax Number: +81–3–3581–5599)

Submitted by:
Name or Title of Entrepreneur:
Address or Location:
Name and Position Title of Representative: (Seal)
Name of Division for Contact:
Position Title and Name of Person in Charge:
Telephone Number:

We hereby make a report pursuant to the provisions of Article 7–2 (7) (i), Article 7–2 (8) (i), or Article 7–2 (8) (ii) of the Act Concerning Prohibition of Private Monopolization and Maintenance of Fair Trade (including cases where these articles shall apply *mutatis mutandis* to Article 8–3 of the Act).

Without justifiable reason, we shall not disclose to third parties the fact that we have made the following report.

1. Summary of the Violative Act to be Reported

(1) Description of the Said Act	a.
	b.
(2) Name or Title and Address or Location of Other Entrepreneur(s) Participating in the Said Act	
(3) The Time of the First Implementation (The time of Termination)	______ (Year) ______ (Month) ______ (Day) (until ______ [Year] ______ [Month] ______ [Day])

2. Position Titles and Names of Executives or Employees Who Have Involved in the Said Act at the Reporting Entrepreneur

Current Position Title and Division's Name	Position Title and Division's Name at Time of Involvement (The Time of the Position)	Name

3. Names and Others of Executives or Employees Who Have Involved in the Said Act at Other Entrepreneur(s) Participating in the Said Act

Name of Entrepreneur	Current Position Title and Division's Name	Position Title and Division's Name at Time of Involvement (The Time of the Position)	Name

		(The Time of the Position)	

4. Goods or Services Targeted by the Said Act

5. Situation Regarding the Implementation of the Said Act and Contact with Other Entrepreneur(s) Participation in the Said Act

6. Other Matters for Consideration

7. Submission of Materials

We hereby submit the following materials.

No.	Title of Material	Description of Material's Content (Summary)	Notes

Instructions for Completing This Form

(The following items correspond to the items on the Form No.3.)

1. Summary of the violative act to be reported

(1) Description of the Said Act

a. Enter the description of the said act (price cartels, bid-riggings, market allocations, and others) in 1. (1) a.

b. Enter in detail in 1. (1) b. for clarifying, for example,

(A) in the case of price-raising cartels, details of agreement (the time of implementation of the price-raising, and the range of price-raising, and others),

(B) in the case of bid-riggings, details of the procedure (details of rules) for selecting an expected bid winner.If trade associations are involved in the said act, enter in 1. (1) b. details of the associations' involvement

(2) Name or Title and Address or location of Other Entrepreneur(s) Participating in the Said Act

If trade associations are involved in the said act, enter in details in 1. (2) for clarifying the title, address or location, and others of the trade associations.

(3) The Time of the First Implementation (The Time of Termination)

a. Enter the date when the arrangement regarding the said act was decided in 1. (3). If it is not clear when the said act was implemented for the first time, enter the earliest date when it is certain that the said act was being implemented, and append a note of 'at the latest'.

b. If the reporting entrepreneur has already ceased the said act, enter the date of termination in the parentheses in 1. (3). For example, if there is a date the entrepreneur decided to cease the said act as the organization, enter the date.

2. Position Titles and Names of Executives or Employees Who Have Involved in the Said Act at the Reporting Entrepreneur

Enter not only executives and employees who are involved currently, but also were involved in the past.

3. Names and Others of Executives or Employees Who Have Involved in the Said Act as the Other Entrepreneur(s) Participating in the Said Act

a. While possible, enter not only executives and employees who are involved currently, but also who were involved in the past. If the name and position title of the executive or employee is not found out, append a note to that effect.

b. If an executive or employee of trade associations is involved, enter the name and position titles of the person.

4. Goods or Services Targeted by the Said Act

a. Enter in details for clarifying the range of the goods or services targeted by the said act,. For example, where there are two distribution channels for a product—one for sales through distributors and the other for direct sales to consumers, if the price cartel is targeting only products sold through the latter distribution channel, enter for clarifying such matters. In the case of bid-riggings, enter in detail for clarifying the contract awarding public agencies and divisions, the kinds of bids (open bids with limited conditions, bids competed by designated firms desiring to join the bid, bids competed by designated firms, and others), the type of construction, and others regarding ordered projects targeted by the said act.

b. If goods or services, within the range targeted by the said act, are specifically outside the target of arrangements (for example, goods or services for export, for specified uses, bidding projects competed by the designated specific firms, and others), enter for clarifying such matters.

5. Situation Surrounding the Implementation of the Said Act and Contact with Other Entrepreneur(s) Participating in the Said Act

Enter in detail for clarifying the situation surrounding the implementation of the arrangement related to the said act. For example, in the case of price-raising cartels, enter for clarifying the situation of information exchanges (the date and time, venue, content, and others), if they exchanged information in relation to the negotiations to raise prices, and also enter the time when transacting parties were notified of price-raising, details of the negotiations to raise prices, and the degree to which the price-raising have spread, and others.

Moreover, in the case of bid-riggings, enter for clarifying the process for determining the expected bid winner, details of communication in bid prices with other entrepreneurs in the case that you were selected as the expected bid winner, details of communication in bid prices from other entrepreneurs selected as the expected bid winner, projects for which the expected bid winner was decided and the entrepreneur actually received the order, projects for which the expected bid winner was decided and the entrepreneur actually could not receive the order, the situation of projects for which the expected bid winner could not be decided, and others in relation to the bid-rigging.

6. Other Matters for Consideration

a. Enter other matters for consideration, for example, the raw materials, manufacturing methods, the distribution channels, the method and parties involved in price negotiations, the official standards, the legal regulations, a profile of the industry, and the summary of related trade associations of the goods or services targeted by the said act.

b. If the fact is deemed concerned with the involvement in bid-rigging stipulated in Article 2 (5) (i) through (iii) of the Act Concerning Elimination and Prevention of Involvement in Bid Rigging and Others (Act No.101 of 2002), enter the details of the fact.

7. Submission of Materials

a. List on the chart and submit the materials leading to prove the mattersindicated in 1. through 6. *above*: (A) Memorandums of meeting related to the act, business daily reports indicating matters related to the said act, correspondence with other entrepreneur(s) participating in the said act, and others, and (B) Written reports related to the said act with the signatures and seals of the executives or employees involved in the act to be report, and others.
Where the materials are not prepared in Japanese, Japanese-language translations or abridged translations of concerned parts shall be attached to the said materials.

b. For clarifying which matters indicated in 1. through 6. above are proven by the respective materials, appropriately organize the materials: For example, write '2.–(7)' in the Notes column of the seventh materialleading to prove the matter indicated in 2. above.

Note

1. 'The matters written in 'Note" (the matters which are substitutable for entering the Form by oralstatement) stipulated in the Article 3 (2) of this Rule mutatis mutandis toArticle 4 (3) (hereinafter refer to as 'Article 3 (2) of this Rule') is the matters indicated in 1. (1) b., 2., 3., 5. and 6. above.

2. (1) In the case of oral report or oral statement stipulated in Article 3 (2) of this Rule, the person who is about to report or state shall appear and do before the Senior Officer for Leniency Program by the day that istwenty days (the number of days listed in the paragraphs of Article 1 (1) of the Law Concerning Holidays of Administrative Organizations (Act No. 91 of 1988) shall not be included in the calculation) reckoned from the starting day of investigation stipulated in Article 5 of this Rule.

(2) The written report indicated in 7 (a) of this Rule is in principle 'the materials which are substitutable by an oral statement' stipulated in Article 3 (2) of this Rule. In this case, the person who should prepare the said written report shall make an oral statement.

3. If a written report is prepared by an agent, enter the name or title and address or location of reporting entrepreneur, the description that the report is prepared by the agent, and the name of the agent and put the seal of the agent in place of the seal of the representative of the reporting entrepreneur. In this case, a letter of proxy shall be required to be attached to the written report. In case of making an oral report as provided for in Article 3 (2), the letter shall be submitted at the time of report.

4. Where there is no space to write fully reporting matters of 1. to 7. on the Form No.3, use and attach extra sheets.

5. When this written report is transmitted in facsimile, do not mistake the fax number.

[Translation]

Guidelines to Application of the Antimonopoly Act Concerning Review of Business Combination

31 May 2004
Japanese Fair Trade Commission

Table of Contents

Part V The Effect of Vertical and Conglomerate Business combination May be Substantially to Restrain Competition

1. Guiding Principle
2. The determining factors to decide the Substantial Restraint of Competition through the Vertical and Conglomerate Business Combinations

Part VI Measures to Remedy the Substantial Restraint of Competition

1. Guiding Principles
2. Type of the Remedies

   (Attachment 1) Prior Consultation

   (Attachment 2) Shortening of the Waiting Period

Introduction

Chapter 4 of the Antimonopoly Act (Act Concerning Prohibition of Private Monopolization and Maintenance of Fair Trade (Act No. 54, 1947), hereinafter referred to as 'the Act') prohibits such that acquisition or possession (hereinafter referred to as 'holding') of the stocks of a company (including shares of partnership) (Article 10 of the Act), interlocking directorates (Article 13 of the Act), stock-holding by a person other than a company (Article 14 of the Act) or a merger of companies (Article 15 of the Act), joint establishment type corporate split or absorption type corporate split (Article 15–2 of the Act) or acquisition of businesses (Article 16 of the Act) (hereinafter referred to as 'business combination') where the effect of such a business combination may be substantially to restrain competition in any particular field of trade, or where such a business combination is implemented through an unfair trade practice. Business combination to be prohibited is subject to elimination measures under the provision of Article 17–2 of the Act.

With regard to reviewing whether the effect of a business combination may be substantially to restrain competition in any particular field of trade (hereinafter referred to as the 'review of business combination' or the 'review'), the Fair Trade Commission has already clarified underlining principles through the Guidelines for Interpretation on the Stipulation that 'The Effect May Be Substantially to Restrain Competition in a Particular Field of Trade' Concerning M & As on 21 December 1998. However, in order to enhance transparency and predictability regarding the review of business combination, the Fair Trade Commission issues 'Guidelines to Application of the Antimonopoly Act concerning Review of Business Combination' (hereinafter referred to as 'Guidelines'), taking into account its experience of the review so far. These Guidelines, first of all, indicate the categories of business combinations which are to be reviewed under the Act (Part I). Second, they will indicate the criteria for defining a particular field of trade (Part II). Third, they shall clarify the meaning of 'the effect may be substantially to restrain competition' (Part III). And then, they will indicate the analytical framework and the criteria for assessing whether the effect of a business combination may be substantially to restrain competition in accordance with the categories of the business combination (Parts IV and V). Finally, they will illustrate remedial measures for resolving the problems involved in the business combination whose effect may be substantially to restrain competition (Part VI).

The Fair Trade Commission will review business combinations and determine whether or not the effect of a business combination may be substantially to restrain competition in any particular field of trade along with these guidelines, irrespective of whether it is subject to current reporting or notification requirement under the provisions of Chapter 4 of the Act. In addition, with the formulation of these guidelines, the Guidelines for Interpretation on the Stipulation that 'The Effect May Be Substantially to Restrain Competition in a Particular Field of Trade' Concerning M&A (including Supplement thereof dated 1 April 2001) is hereby abolished.

Part I
Subject of the Review of Business Combination

Chapter 4 of the Act prohibits a business combination if the effect may be substantially to restrain competition in a particular field of trade. The Chapter regulates business combinations because they can have an impact on competition in the market through the formation, maintain or strengthening of the relationship where more than one company conducts business activities in a united form, fully or partially by stockholding, mergers or other transactions (this relationship is hereinafter referred to as a 'joint relationship'). Accordingly, if two or more companies continue to engage in business activities as independent competitive units though there are stockholdings or interlocking directorates between them, and if these companies which have already had a joint relationship just alter merely the form of an organization, there is little impact on competition. Thus, these types of arrangements should be rarely prohibited. This part clarifies the categories of business combinations whose impact on competition should be reviewed.

1. STOCKHOLDING

(1) Stockholding by a Company

A. It is reviewed that a joint relationship is to be formed, maintained or strengthened between an acquiring company and an acquired one in the following cases.

(a) When the voting right holding ratio (the ratio of voting rights for stock held by an acquiring company to the overall shareholder's voting rights in a stock issuing company) exceeds 50 per cent. However, if the acquiring company establishes the acquired company and the former acquired all of the voting rights of the latter concurrently with the establishment, it usually falls outside the scope of the review of business combination (*see* (4) A *infra*).
(b) When the voting right holding ratio exceeds 25 per cent and the acquiring company is the sole leading holder of voting rights.

B. Other than the cases described *above*, when the ratio of voting right holding ratio exceeds 10 per cent and acquiring company is ranked among the top three voting right holders, the *following* items will be taken into consideration in order to determine whether a joint relationship is formed, maintained or strengthened.

(a) The extent of voting right holding ratio;
(b) The rank as a voting right holder, difference in the voting right holding ratios and distribution among the holders, and other relationships between holders;
(c) Cross-holding of voting rights (the acquired company concurrently holds voting rights of the acquiring company) and other mutual relationships between the companies involved (hereinafter referred to as 'parties');
(d) Whether officers or employees of one of the parties are holding the position of officers of the other parties;
(e) Trading relationship between the parties (including financial relationship);
(f) Relationships between the parties based on business alliance, technical assistance and other contracts or agreements; and
(g) Items (a) through (f), when including companies that already have joint relationships with the parties.

C. In the event of a joint investment company (a company which jointly established or acquired by two or more companies through a contract to pursue necessary operations in order to achieve mutual benefits; the same hereinafter), trading relationships between the parties and relationships based on business alliance, contracts, etc., will be considered in order to determine whether the business combination should be reviewed. (As far as a joint relationship between the investing companies is concerned, a joint relationship is indirectly formed, maintained or strengthened through the joint investment company. Accordingly, if the business activities of the stockholding companies are integrated through the establishment of the joint investment company, this fact itself indicates that there will be an impact on competition. (*See* 2 (1) C and 3 (1) D in Part IV later on))

(2) Stockholdings by a Person Other than a Company

'A person other than a company' means a person other than a joint stock company, mutual company, limited liability company, ordinary partnership, limited partnership or foreign company as prescribed by the Commercial Code and other laws and ordinances; it does not matter whether the person is an entrepreneur or not. Specifically, incorporated foundations, corporate juridical persons, special corporations, regional public bodies, cooperatives, associations, natural persons and all other persons that can hold stocks are included. The existence of stockholdings by a person other than a company will be examined in accordance with item (1) *above*.

(3) Scope of Joint Relationship

If a joint relationship is formed, maintained or strengthened between the parties concerned through the stockholdings, a joint relationship is also formed, maintained or strengthened among the parties and the companies which already have a joint relationship with the parties.

(4) Stockholdings which do not fall within the Scope of the Review of Business Combination

In the case of A *below*, a joint relationship is not formed nor strengthened so that, in general, it does not fall within the scope of the review of business combination. In addition, even in the cases of item B to item F as *below*, a business combination is not formed nor strengthened so that, in general, most of them are not considered to fall within the scope of the review of business combination. However, in the case of that a joint relationship is formed or strengthened between the Company V to Z and other shareholders, such joint relationship falls within the scope of the review of business combination.

A. The acquiring company establishes the acquired company and the former acquired all of the voting rights of the latter concurrently with the establishment (*see* (1) A (a) *above*).

B. A company acquires the voting rights of the subsidiary of its subsidiary (in these Guidelines, a 'subsidiary' means a company of which another company holds more than 50 per cent of its total stockholders' voting rights) (also *see* note 1).

C. A company acquires the voting rights of its sister company (in these Guidelines, a 'sister company' means companies of which the same company holds more than 50 per cent of their total stockholders' voting rights).

D. A company acquires the voting rights of a subsidiary of its sister company.

E. A company acquires the additional voting rights of another company more than 50 per cent of whose total stockholders' voting rights are held by the acquiring company and its sister company jointly.

F. A company acquires the voting rights of another company where two or more sister companies hold jointly more than 50 per cent of the total stockholders' voting rights of the acquiring and acquired company respectively.

Note 1 If:

(a) a parent company and its subsidiary hold jointly more than 50 per cent of total stockholders' voting rights of a company or;
(b) a subsidiary holds solely more than 50 per cent of total stockholders' voting rights of a company, the company is treated as a subsidiary of the parent company. This definition is adopted hereinafter except for the 'subsidiary' mentioned in 2 (4) B (a), 3 (3) A, 4 (4) A and 5 (4) A.

2. INTERLOCKING DIRECTORATES

(1) Scope of Officers

An 'officer' is defined in Article 2 (3) of the Act as 'a trustee, director, executive, partner with unlimited liabilities and executive power, an auditor or any person with a similar position, a manager or other employee in charge of business of the main or branch office'. Thus, officers are directors and auditors of joint stock companies, limited liability companies and mutual companies; managers defined by the Commercial Code (Article 37); and other employees in charge of business under the Commercial Code (such as the general manager of a head office, a branch manager, the head of a business division) and the like.

A 'person with a similar position' means a person, while not directors or auditors, with the title of adviser, counsellor, consultant or others who actually participates in the management of the company by attending board of directors' meetings or other measures. A person having only the title of division manager, department manager, section manager or supervisor is an employee, not an 'officer'. Further, the restriction on interlocking directors will not apply if an officer or an employee of a company completes retirement procedures and is then appointed as an officer of another company.

Note 2 Article 13 (1) of the Act defines in the parenthesis an 'employee' as 'a person other than officers in the regular employment of a company'. While temporary employments are not included, temporary transferees are included as employees.

(2) Joint Relationships through Interlocking Directorates

A. In the following cases, a joint relationship is formed, maintained or strengthened as an officer or an employee of a company serves concurrently as an officer of another company and that interlocking is within the scope of the review of business combination.

- (a) The officers or employees of one company comprise a majority of the total number of officers of another company.
- (b) Interlocking directorates hold the rights of representation of both companies.

B. Excluding item A *above*, the following items will be taken into consideration to determine whether a joint relationship is formed, maintained or strengthened.

- (a) Whether there is interlocking directorate formed by the full-time or representative directors;
- (b) The ratio of officers or employees of one of the interlocking companies to the total number of officers of one of the other interlocking companies;

(c) Mutual holding of voting rights conditions between the interlocking companies; and
(d) The trading relationships (including financial relationships), business alliance and other relationships between the interlocking companies.

(3) Scope of Joint Relationships

When a joint relationship is formed, maintained or strengthened between interlocking companies through interlocking directorates, joint relationships are formed, maintained and strengthened between companies including companies that already have joint relationship with the interlocking companies.

(4) Interlocking Directorates which are not within the Scope of the Review of Business Combination

A. In such cases as the following, a joint relationship is not formed, maintained or strengthened so that in general it is not within the scope of the review of business combination.

(a) No one but persons who do not have the right of representation serve concurrently as officers, and in either of the interlocking companies the ratio of officers or employees of the other company to the total number of its officers is 10 per cent or less.
(b) No one but persons other than full-time officers serve concurrently in companies with 10 per cent voting rights holding ratios or less, and in either of the interlocking companies the ratio of officers or employees of the other company to the total number of its officers is 25 per cent or less.

B. In the cases of item (a) and (b) *below*, a joint relationship is not formed or strengthened so that in general it is not within the scope of the review of business combination. In addition, even in the cases of item (c) to (f) *below*, a joint relationship is not formed or strengthened so that in general most of them are not considered within the scope of the review of business combination. However, in the case of that a joint relationship is formed or strengthened with other shareholders, such joint relationship is subject to the review of business combination.

(a) Interlocking directorates between a company and its subsidiary.
(b) Interlocking directorates between sister companies.
(c) Interlocking directorates between a company and a subsidiary of the company's subsidiary.
(d) Interlocking directorates between a company and a subsidiary of the company's sister company.
(e) Interlocking directorates between a company and a subsidiary whose total stockholders' voting rights are held, by more than 50 per cent, by the company and its sister company.

(f) Interlocking directorates between companies where two or more sister companies of an identical company hold jointly more than 50 per cent of the total stockholders' voting rights of the both interlocked company respectively.

3. MERGERS

(1) Mergers

In a merger, two or more companies combine to form a single company. Therefore, a merger is the strongest joint relationship that can be formed between companies. Consequently, even if a certain joint relationship formed through stockholdings or interlocking directorates may be deemed not to have a strong impact on competition nor cause a problem, such a joint relationship could be strengthened through a merger under the same set of circumstances, and the merger could present a problem.

(2) Scope of Joint Relationships

When a merger is conducted, a joint relationship is formed, maintained or strengthened between the parties and the companies which have already formed a joint relationship with the parties.

(3) Mergers which are not within the Scope of the Review of Business Combination

In the cases of item A to C *below*, a joint relationship is not formed or strengthened so that in general it is not within the scope of the review of business combination. In addition, even in the cases of item D to G *below*, a business combination is not formed or strengthened so that in general most of them are not considered within the scope of the review of business combination. However, if a joint relationship is formed or strengthened among other shareholders, such a joint relationship is within the scope of the review of business combination.

A. Mergers between a company and its subsidiary

B. Mergers between sister companies

C. Mergers implemented solely for the purpose of conversion of an ordinary partnership, limited partnership, limited liability company or mutual company to a joint stock company, conversion of a joint stock company to a limited liability company of mutual company, conversion of ordinary partnership to limited partnership, or conversion limited partnership to an ordinary partnership.

D. Mergers between a company and a subsidiary of the company's subsidiary.

E. Mergers between a company and a subsidiary of the company's sister company.

F. Mergers between a company and a subsidiary whose total stockholders' voting rights are held, by more than 50 per cent, by the company and its sister company.

G. Mergers between companies where two or more sister companies of an identical company hold jointly more than 50 per cent of the total stockholders' voting rights of the both merged company respectively.

4. CORPORATE SPLIT

(1) Joint establishment type corporate split/Absorption type corporate split

A joint establishment-type corporate split or an absorption-type corporate split (hereinafter referred to as the 'corporate splits') has an impact on competition similar to a merger in the sense that business (entire business or substantial part of it) which will be split off from the splitting company are integrated with the succeeding company. It is determined in the light of the criteria of Section 1 ('Stockholding') whether or not a joint relationship is formed, maintained or strengthened between the succeeding company and the company which is to be allotted the shares of the said succeeding company.

(2) Scope of Joint Relationships

If a joint relationship is formed, maintained or strengthened through corporate splits between the succeeding company and the company which is to be allotted the shares of the said succeeding company, a joint relationship is formed, maintained and strengthened between the succeeding and the allotted company and the companies which have already had a joint relationship with them.

(3) Substantial part of Business

The 'substantial part' mentioned *above* does not mean substantial part for the succeeding company but for the splitting company. Moreover, it is limited to the case in which the split portion of the business must function as a single business unit, and the portion is objectively deemed to have a value to the business of the splitting company.

Consequently, whether a split business constitutes 'substantial part' or not is examined on a case-by-case basis according to the actual state of the split business in the market. However, if the annual sales (or turnovers correspond to it). The same hereinafter of the split business does not exceed 5 per cent of the total sales of the splitting company nor one hundred million yen, this split business is not considered to be 'substantial part' in general.

(4) *Corporate Splits which are not within the Scope of the Review of Business Combination*

In the cases of item A and B *below*, a joint relationship is not formed or strengthened so that in general it is not within the scope of the review of business combination. In addition, even in the cases of item C to F *below*, a join relationship is not formed or strengthened so that in general most of them are not considered within the scope of the review of business combination.

However, in the case of that a joint relationship is formed or strengthened with other shareholders, such joint relationship is subject to the review of business combination.

A. Corporate Splits between a company and its subsidiary.

B. Corporate Splits between sister companies.

C. Corporate Splits between a company and a subsidiary of the said company's subsidiary.

D. Corporate Splits between a company and a subsidiary of the said company's sister company.

E. Corporate Splits between a company and a subsidiary whose total stockholders' voting rights are held, by more than 50 per cent, by the company and its sister company.

F. Corporate Splits between companies where two or more sister companies of an identical company hold jointly more than 50 per cent of the total stockholders' voting rights of the both corporate split company respectively.

5. ACQUISITIONS OF BUSINESS, ETC.

(1) *An acquisition of an entire business has an impact on competition similar to a merger in the sense that business activities of the transferring company are integrated with the acquiring company. Since the transferring company and the acquiring company are not related after the transfer, it is sufficient to examine conditions when the acquired business is newly added to the acquiring company. Acquisitions of substantial part of business or fixed assets of business are examined in a similar manner.*

(2) Scope of Joint Relationships

A joint relationship is formed, maintained or strengthened between companies including companies that already have a joint relationship with the acquiring company.

(3) Substantial part of Business

Concerning an acquisition of substantial part of a business or a fixed asset of a business, the idea of the 'substantial part' is the same as mentioned in item 4(3) *above*.

(4) Acquisitions of Business which are not within the Scope of the Review of Business Combination

In the cases of item A to C *below*, a joint relationship is not formed or strengthened so that in general it is not within the scope of the review of business combination. In addition, even in the cases of item D to G *below*, a joint relationship is not formed or strengthened so that in general most of them are not considered within the scope of the review of business combination. However, in the case of that a joint relationship is formed or strengthened with other shareholders, such a joint relationship is within the scope of the review of business combination.

A. Transfer of a business or fixed asset of business (hereinafter referred to as 'acquisitions of business') between a company and its subsidiary.

B. Acquisitions of business between sister companies.

C. Acquisitions of business which is a split-off of a corporate division effected through 100 per cent capital investment.

D. Acquisitions of business between a company and a subsidiary of the company's subsidiary.

E. Acquisitions of business between a company and a subsidiary of the company's sister company.

F. Acquisitions of business between a company and a subsidiary whose total stockholders' voting rights are held, by more than 50 per cent, by the acquiring company and its sister company.

G. Acquisitions of business between companies where two or more sister companies of an identical company hold jointly more than 50 per cent of the total stockholders' voting rights of the acquiring and acquired company respectively.

(5) Leasing of Business

Leasing of business (conduct of a lessee to manage a leased business under its name and calculations, and pay leasing fees to the lessor in fulfilment of a leasing contract), delegation of management of a business (conduct of a company to delegate management of a business to another company in fulfilment of a contract), and contracts to share the total profits and losses of a business (contracts between two or more companies agreeing to share the total profits and losses of a business for a specific period) will be treated as acquisitions of business similarly. Unlike what is described in item (1) *above*, a joint relationship can be formed, maintained or strengthened between companies and those which already have a joint relationship with them, depending on the content of the contracts.

Part II
A Particular Field of Trade

'A Particular Field of Trade' might be called a market. Every market will be defined as places where the business activities of all companies whose joint relationships are formed, maintained or strengthened by business combinations stipulated in Part I (hereinafter referred to as 'the company group') take place, and the impact on competition in each market by business combinations will be examined in accordance with Part III to V of the Guidelines. The criteria for defining the scope of a particular field of trade are clarified *below*.

1. BASIC POINT OF VIEW FOR THE SCOPE OF A PARTICULAR FIELD OF TRADE

The scope of a particular field of trade is defined in terms of goods traded ('goods' include services), trading areas (geographic range), stages of trade, a trading partner and other factors. Therefore, the goods traded are first enumerated for all of the businesses engaged in by the company group, and the product range is defined among the goods traded, then geographic range is defined for each of the product range. Here, the range of the trading partners of the company group and the range of competitors which compete for the said trading partners are the criteria for definition of the goods range and the geographic range and other factors. It can happen that a particular field of trade is constituted by a product range (or geographic range) in accordance with the type of trading, while at the same time another one is constituted by a wider (or narrower) product range (or geographic range) overlappingly.

2. PRODUCT RANGE

The product range of a particular field of trade is determined by goods which have similar functions and efficacy to the users. To determine whether the functions and efficacy of goods traded are similar to those of the other goods, it is considered whether, when the price of the goods traded increase or similar change of trading conditions occurs, the other goods can be the factor that prevent the price, quantity, or etc., of goods traded from varying freely because the users can purchase the other goods as a substitute. For instance, when the price of the product X increase, the presence of the product Y may prevent the price increase of the product X because the users purchase the product Y as a substitute for the product X, the sales of the product X decreases. Thus, the products X and Y are considered to have the same functions and efficacy. Here, the users mean those to whom business activities of a company group are directed. If a company group manufactures producers' goods, the users mean companies that process the goods into the next level of products. If a company group manufactures consumers' goods, the users mean general consumers. If a company group is a distributor, the users mean companies in the succeeding distribution level. For example, when a product X and a product group Y have similar functions and efficacy in a certain application and a product Z which belongs to the product group Y has strong similarity in its functions and efficacy to the product X for a specific application, then there is a case that the product range of a particular field of trade is comprised of the product X and the product group Y and simultaneously of the product X and the product Z. For the purpose of determining the product range of a particular field of trade, it is judged in light of the following viewpoint whether the functions and efficacy of a product are similar to those of the other goods from the view point of the users.

(1) Application

It is considered whether a product is, or is possible to be, employed for the same application to the product traded. To determine whether both products are employed for the same application, the following factors are considered: external features such as size and form, specific material character such as strength, plasticity, heat-resistance and insulation, quality such as purity, technical features such as standards and systems. (However, there is a case in which both products are considered to be for the same application even though the *above* factors are different to a certain extent. (*See* (3) later)) When the product traded is employed for several applications, it is considered for each application whether any other products are actually or possibly employed for the same application. For instance, the products X and Y may have similar functions and efficacy in a certain application and products X and Z may have those for another application.

(2) Changes of the Price, Quantity and so on

There is a case in which the difference of price levels, the changes of the price, quantity, etc., are considered. For example, the products X and Y can be used for the same application, but since the price levels of the products are different, the product Y is rarely used as a substitute for the product X. In such a case, it can not be considered that the products X and Y have similar functions and efficacy. In the meantime, the products X and Y can be used for the same application and the price levels are not different, but the product Y is rarely used as a substitute for the product X in practice because, to substitute product Y for X, some costs are required to change the facilities or educate the employees. In such a case, it can not be considered that the product X and Y have similar functions and efficacy. On the other hand, when the products X and Y have similar functions and efficacy, if the price of product X is increased, then users become to purchase the product Y and the price of product Y is likely to increase. Therefore, if the sales or the price of product Y increases in response to an increase in the price of product X, it can be considered that products X and Y have similar functions and efficacy.

(3) *Recognition and Actions of the Users*

There is a case in which the recognition, etc., of the users is considered. For instance, even though the specific material characters of the product X and Y are different, there could be a case in which users can use either of them as raw materials to produce the product Z of the same quality. In such a case, it is considered that the product X and Y have the similar functions and efficacy. It is also considered that whether a user substituted product Y for X when the price of product X was increased in the past.

3. GEOGRAPHIC RANGE

The geographic range of a particular field of trade is determined by whether, when in a certain region the price increase or similar change of trading conditions occurs on goods which is defined in accordance with Section 2 *above*, the producers in another region can be the factor which prevents the price, quantity or, etc., in the former region from varying freely because the users can purchase the goods from the producers in the other region as a substitute. For instance, when the price in the region X is being increased, if the producers in the region Y may prevent the price in the region X from increasing because it is expected that the users in the region X purchase from the producers in the region Y, then it is determined that the region X and Y belongs to the same geographic range.

Accordingly, similar to the case of the determination of the product range, there is a case in which the geographic range of a particular field of trade is determined as both the region X and the region Y, which is a part of the former, if the users in the region Y especially tend to purchase from the suppliers in the region Y.

In the meantime, even if the business area of the parties extends to foreign countries, the competition to be maintained by the Act is the domestic competition in Japan. Therefore, main focus of the review will be on the scope of the business activities of domestic customers. As a result, if the company group is on the supply side of the goods, the particular field of trade is not generally determined to include exports. To determine the geographic range of a particular field of trade, the following factors are considered.

(1) *Business Area of Suppliers, the Area for Users to Purchase, etc.*

The scope of the region where users can usually purchase the product is determined by the business area such as distribution network of suppliers, their supplying capacity and the area around which users purchase the product (purchase behaviour of consumers), etc. It is also considered from which region's suppliers the users purchased the product when the price of the products in a certain region was increased in the past.

(2) Features of Goods

The features of goods such as perishability, heaviness and fragility affect the range of transportation or the degree of difficulty to transport. Concerning this effect, it is considered in which regions the users can purchase the goods in general.

(3) Type or Cost of Transportation

According to the types of transportation, the proportion of the transportation cost to the price of goods, and/or the comparison between the transportation cost and the price difference between the regions of the original and the destination of the transportation, it is considered to what extent of regions the users can purchase the goods in general.

4. OTHERS

Depending on the reality of trade between the company group and its trading partners, distribution levels, character of each trading partner and so on are considered to delineate a particular field of trade on the same criteria of Section 2 and 3 *above*. For example, there could be a case in which the users who trade the product X with the company group are divided into large-scale customers and the small-scale ones, and peculiar trade conditions apply for respective customer group. In such a case, if the price of the product X for the small-scale customers is increased, they can not purchase the product X for the large scale customers because of constraints on transportation, etc., and the product X for the latter can not prevent the price increase of the product X for the former. Then, a particular field of trade for large-scale customers and small-scale ones are determined respectively. The difference of the facilities for supply or switching costs of them is also considered. If the time and the costs necessary to switch the facilities for supply or distribution network is small enough for the large number of the suppliers of the product X and Y, both products can be judged to be in the same particular field of trade.

Part III
The Effect May be Substantially to Restrain Competition

1. INTERPRETATION OF 'THE EFFECT MAY BE SUBSTANTIALLY TO RESTRAIN COMPETITION'

(1) Interpretation of 'Substantially to Restrain Competition'

In a precedent (decision of the Tokyo High Court on 7 December 1953 concerning Toho Company, Limited, et al), the following interpretation concerning 'substantially to restrain competition' was held.

A. Shin-Toho Company Limited (hereinafter referred to as 'Shin-Toho') was capable of distributing the films it produced through its own network. However, an arrangement with Toho Company, Limited (hereinafter referred to as 'Toho') consigned all film distribution to Toho and limited Shin-Toho solely to production of films. Shin-Toho continued to adhere to the terms of the arrangement even after the agreement had expired. However, in November 1949 Shin-Toho stated that it would independently distribute the films it produced because of the expiration of the arrangement, which caused a dispute with Toho. As a result of this dispute, hearing procedures were initiated by the Fair Trade Commission on the ground that the arrangement violated the Act. In conclusion, the Fair Trade Commission ruled in its decision of 5 June 1951 that the arrangement between Toho and Shin-Toho violated Article 3 (unreasonable restraint of trade) and Article 4–1–3 (*See* Note 3) of the Act.

Note 3 Article 4–1 of the Act (this provision does not exist in the current Act) 'Entrepreneurs shall not jointly engage in the following particular concerted practice' Article 4–1–3 'concerned actions to restrain technologies, products, distribution channels, or customers'

B. In response to the plaintiff's (Toho's) motion to quash the Fair Trade Commission decision, the Tokyo High Court ruled concerning substantial restraint of competition that 'substantially to restrain competition means to bring about a state in which competition itself has significantly decreased and a situation has been created in which a specific firm or a group of firms can control the market by determining price, quality, volume, and various other terms with some latitude at its or their own volition'.

(2) Interpretation of 'The Effect May Be'

The provisions of Chapter 4 of the Act differ from the provisions of Article 3 and 8 of the Act, and prohibit business combinations where 'the effect may be' substantially to restrain competition in any particular field of trade. This 'the effect may be' does not mean that substantial restraint of competition will inevitably result from the business combinations. Rather, it means that it is probable that conditions which could easily lead to substantial restraint of competition are furthered by the business combination. Consequently, if the market structure is altered in a non-competitive manner by the business combination, and conditions that would allow the company a certain latitude to manipulate price, quality, volume, and other conditions by unilaterally or acting cooperatively together with other companies are easily led to presence, then the effect of the business combination may be substantially to restrain competition in a particular field of trade, and it is prohibited by Chapter 4 of the Act.

2. TYPE OF BUSINESS COMBINATION AND SUBSTANTIAL RESTRAIN OF COMPETITION

There are various types of business combinations. Those are divided into the following categories.

(1) Horizontal Business Combinations. The business combinations between the companies in the same particular field of trade. The same hereinafter.

(2) Vertical Business Combinations. The business combinations between the companies which are in the different level of trade such as producers and its distributors. The same hereinafter.

(3) Conglomerate Business Combinations. The business combinations which are neither horizontal nor vertical ones. For instance, mergers between the companies which belong to the different categories of business, or stock holdings between the companies whose product range are in the same particular field of trade but whose geographic range are different. The same hereinafter.

Horizontal business combinations reduce the number of competing units in a particular field of trade. Thus they have the most direct effect on the competition and higher possibility to have the effect that may be substantially to restrain competition than vertical and conglomerate business combinations. On the other hand, vertical and conglomerate business combinations do not reduce the number of the units. Then they have less impact on the competition than horizontal ones and, except for some particular cases, the effect of them may not be substantially to restrain competition in general. Depending on the types of business combinations, the Fair Trade Commission uses different frameworks or determining factors to consider whether the effect of business combinations may be substantially to restrain competition. In the following Parts, the frameworks or the determining factors are explained for each type of business combinations, horizontal, vertical and conglomerate. In addition, if a business combination is composed of, for example, the horizontal and vertical aspects, the effects of each aspect are examined based on the frameworks or the determining factors for the horizontal and vertical combinations respectively.

Part IV
The Effect of Horizontal Business combination May be Substantially to Restrain Competition

1. GUIDING PRINCIPLES

As mentioned *above*, horizontal business combinations reduce the number of competing units in a particular field of trade. Therefore, they have the most direct effect on the competition and it is more likely that the effect of the combinations may be substantially to restrain competition.

There are two possibilities that the effect of the horizontal business combinations may be substantially to restrain competition: Through unilateral conducts by the company group and through coordinated conducts between the company group and its one or more competitors (hereinafter referred as 'competitors'). Individual cases should be reviewed in respect of these two conducts. Therefore, there will be a case, for example, in which the effect of a business combination may be substantially to restrain competition from a view point of a coordinated conducts even though it will not have such an effect from a view point of a unilateral conduct.

(1) Substantial Restraint of Competition by Unilateral Conduct

The typical cases in which the effect of horizontal business combinations may be substantially to restrain competition in a particular field of trade by means of unilateral conducts is as follows, depending on whether goods are homogenous or differentiated in the field.

A. Homogenous Goods

When goods are homogenous, if the company group raises the price of the goods and the other companies do not, the users of the goods will switch the suppliers to the other companies and, in general, the sales of the company group will decrease and the sales of the others will increase. Therefore, in many cases, it is difficult for the company group to control the price, etc., freely to a certain extent. However, due to reasons that, for example, the production or sales capacity of the company group is large whereas that of the other companies are small, if the company group raises the price of the goods, there are cases in which the other companies can not increase their sales without raising their prices or the users can not switch their suppliers to these other companies.

In such cases, a situation easily emerges where the company group can control the price, etc., freely to a certain extent. As a result, the effect of the horizontal business combinations may be substantially to restrain competition.

B. Differentiated Goods

When goods are differentiated by brands, etc., and the price of one brand of goods is increased, the users of the brand goods do not intend to buy the other brand goods indiscriminately instead of the brand goods. The users may buy another brand of goods which is next preferable to the first brand, in other words, which has the higher substitutability to the first one. In such a case, even though the company group increases the price of the first brand goods, if the group sells the second brand goods which have the high substitutability to the former, the increase of the sale of the latter compensate the loss of the sale of the former. Then, it is possible for the company group to increase the price without the decrease of the total sales of the company group. Therefore, when goods are differentiated by brands etc, if the business combinations will be made between the companies which sell the substitutable goods for each other, and other companies do not sell such goods, a situation easily emerges where the company group can control the price, etc., freely to a certain extent. As a result, the effect of the horizontal business combinations may be substantially to restrain competition.

(2) Substantial Restrain of Competition by Coordinated Conduct

The typical case where the effect of the horizontal business combinations may be substantially to restrain competition through the coordinated conduct is as follows. For instance, when company X raises its price, other companies Y and Z will try to increase their sales without raising their prices. In response to it, company X, in general, will cut its price to the same level as the previous one or the lower, and try to retrieve the sales from companies Y and Z. However, in addition to the reduction of the number of competitors, because of the market structure such as the concentration of the particular field of trade, the character of goods or the trade practices etc, there could be cases where the companies will be able to estimate behaviours one another with high predictability and the coordinated conduct bring the profits to them. In such cases, when the price rise by company X is followed by the other companies' raising their prices, even though company Y keeps the price to the previous level in order to gain the additional sales, the other companies will be able to detect the behaviour of company Y easily and likely to reduce their price to the same level as previous one or to the lower in order to retrieve the sales which was gained by company Y. As a result, the expected profit which would otherwise be gained by the company Y temporally when it keeps its price is much less than the expected profits which would be gained if company Y raises its price following the price rise by company X. Under such circumstances, it is much more profitable for each company to increase the price than to gain the additional sales by keeping the price to the previous level. Thus, a situation easily emerges where the company group can control the price, etc., freely to a certain extent by means of the coordinated conduct between the competitors and the effect of the horizontal business combinations may be substantially to restrain competition in a particular field of trade.

(3) The Effect may not be Substantially to Restrain Competition

It is decided in light of the factors described in Section 2 and 3 *below* whether the effect of each horizontal business combination may be substantially to restrain competition in a particular field of trade. However, when the market share of the company group after the combination (the total of each companies' shares in the company group) (*See* Note 4). If it falls within the condition either A or B *below*, the effect of a horizontal business combination may not be substantially to restrain competition in a particular field of trade.

A. The market share of the company group after the combinations is not more than 10 per cent

B. The market structure is not oligopolistic and the market share of the company group after the combinations is not more than 25 per cent (Note 5)

Note 4 The market share of each company is the percentage of its sales quantity (in case of the manufacturers) to the total sales quantity in a particular field of trade. However, when it is not suitable to calculate the share based on the quantity because there are considerable price differences among goods and sales achievements are usually calculated on monetary bases, the share is calculated by the amount of sales. When there are imports for domestic users, their market shares are calculated as domestic supplies. Concerning production capacity, percentage of exports or in-house consumption, there are cases in which these excess capacity, exports or in-house consumption will be directed to the sales for domestic market and in turn expanding the market share in response to the domestic demand. Then these excess capacity, etc., are taken into consideration if necessary.

Note 5 'The case that the market structure is not oligopolistic' means that the Herfindahl-Herschmann Index (hereinafter referred to as 'HHI') after a business combination is less than 1000. HHI is the sum of the squared market share of each company in a particular field of trade. When it is difficult to identify the market share of all companies and to calculate the accurate figure of HHI, estimated figure is used to decide whether the HHI is less than 1000 or not. This estimating figure is calculated by the following formula which is drawn up from the Production Concentration Study:

$$\text{HHI} = 69.5 \times \text{cumulative market shares of top three companies} \quad 2344.4$$

However, this does not apply to the case where the HHI with the identified market shares is obviously above 1000.

2. THE DETERMINING FACTORS TO DECIDE THE SUBSTANTIAL RESTRAINT OF COMPETITION THROUGH THE UNILATERAL CONDUCT TO DECIDE WHETHER THE EFFECT OF A HORIZONTAL BUSINESS COMBINATION MAY BE SUBSTANTIALLY TO RESTRAIN COMPETITION IN A PARTICULAR FIELD OF TRADE THROUGH THE UNILATERAL CONDUCT, THE FOLLOWING DETERMINING FACTORS ARE CONSIDERED COMPREHENSIVELY.

(1) The position of the company group and the state of competitors

A. The market share and the ranking

When the market share of the company group after the combination is relatively larger, it is more difficult for other companies in place of the company group, while keeping the same price level, to supply sufficiently in response to the company group's attempt to raise the price. Thus it could be said that the constraining power of the other companies for the price rise of the company group would be weaker. As a result, the larger market share of the company group or the increment of it after the business combination is, the greater the impact of the business combination on the competition is (Note 6).

Note 6 To calculate the change of a market share by a business combination, if it is expected that the market share will change drastically after the combination with respect to the recent sales quantity, the trend of sales or the change of the users' preferences, such expectation should be taken into consideration to review the impact on competition. Similarly, when the business combination puts the rank of the company group's market share at a high position or raises the rank to a great degree, the combination will have much more impact on the competition. For example, the business combination, when the companies concerned are at the high positions on the market shares, has much more impact on the competition than when they are at the low positions.

B. Competition among the Parties, etc., in the Past

There are cases where vigorous competition among the parties, or parties' actions which enhance market competition lead to the reduction of market prices or the improvement of the quality or variety of goods. In such cases, even though the combined market share of the parties or its rank is not high, the business combinations bring the large impact on the competition when this combination eliminates the possibility of the price reduction or the quality improvement as *before* mentioned. For example, there could be a vigorous competition between the parties such that the expansion of the market share of one party causes the reduction of the market share of the other party. In such a case, after the combination, the loss of the sales of the other party would be compensated by the increase of the sale of the former party. As a result, the parties will be able to raise the price of goods without losing the sales of the group as a whole, then this business combination has a large impact on the competition.

When goods are differentiated by brands and there is high substitutability between the goods sold by the parties, after the combination, the sales loss of one of goods would be compensated by the sales increase of the other goods. As a result, the parties will be able to raise the price of goods without loosing the sales of the group as a whole, then this business combination has a large impact on the competition.

C. Treatment of Joint Investment Company

If certain business department of the investing companies completely spun off by consolidation in the joint investment company, the connection between the business of the investing companies and that of the joint investment company would be considered to be weak. Therefore, when all of the business such as the production, sale, research and development, etc., for certain goods are spun off by the consolidation in the joint investment company, the market share, rank, etc., of the joint investment company itself would be considered in the review.

On the other hand, if a part of certain business departments of the each investing companies is transferred to the joint investment company, there is a possibility that the coordinated relationship between the investing companies would arise through the operation of the joint investment company. To determine whether the coordinated relationship between the investing companies would emerge or not, the specific contents of the investing contract, the actual conditions of the combination and the transactions between the companies are considered.

Suppose that, the production sections of goods are transferred to the joint investment company while each of the investing companies continue to sell goods. When the coordinated relationship between these investing companies would occur through the operation of the joint investment company, the impact on the competition is considered by taking such means as summing up market shares of the investing companies. On the other hand, even though the investing companies continue to sell goods after founding the joint investment company, when some measures are taken to prevent coordinated relationship between these investing companies from arising through the operation of the joint investment company, there will be much less impact on the competition (*See* 3 (1) later).

D. Market Share Differences from the Competitors

When the combined market share of the company group has relatively larger difference from those of competitors, it is more difficult for the competitors in place of the company group, without the price increase, to supply goods sufficiently in response to the company group's attempt to raise the price. Thus the competitors' constraining powers for the price rise of the company group would be weaken. Therefore, the larger the market share differences between the company group and the competitors are, the bigger the impact of the business combination on the competition is. On the other hand, after the business combination, when there are the competitors with the market shares equal to or higher than those of the company group, these competitors could be the factors which prevent the company group from controlling the price, etc., freely to a certain extent. Concurrently, in considering the market share differences from the competitors, the excess capacity of the competitors and the degree of substitutability between goods sold by the company group and the competitors are considered (*See* E *below*).

E. Excess capacity and the Substitutability of the Competitors

When the company group raise the price of goods, if the excess capacity of the competitors is not sufficient, it is not easy for the competitors, without increasing the price, to expand the sales of goods. Thus the competitors' constraining powers for the price rise by the company group could be weaken. In this manner, even though the market share differences between the company group and the competitors are not large, it could be considered that the business combination's impact on the competition would not be small when the excess capacity of the competitors are not sufficient. In the mean time, when goods are differentiated by brands and there is high substitutability between goods sold by the parties, the degree of substitutability between goods sold by the competitors and the company group is considered. When the substitutability is small, even though the market share differences between the company group and the competitors are not large, it could be considered that the business combination's impact on the competition would not be small.

F. The Case that the Effect of Business combination May not be Substantially to Restrain Competition

To decide whether the effect of a business combination may be substantially to restrain competition or not, the factors including those mentioned *above* and later in Section (2) and so on are taken into consideration in each specific case. However, in the following cases, the possibility that the effect of horizontal business combinations may be substantially to restrain competition in a particular field of trade through the unilateral conduct is usually thought to be small. (Nonetheless, this only applies to the cases where the business combination will not have any problem in respect of the previous condition of competition among the parties or excess capacity and the substitutability of the competitors. Concurrently, when goods are differentiated, the substitutability between goods sold by the competitors with 10 per cent and more market share and goods sold by the company group is considered.)

(a) The market structure is not highly oligopolistic, the market share of the company group after the combination is not more than 25 per cent, and there are one or more competitors whose market shares are more than 10 per cent (*See* note 7 and 8)

Note 7 'The market structure is not highly oligopolistic' means that the HHI after business combination is less than 1800. When it is difficult to identify the market share of all companies and to calculate the accurate figure of HHI, estimated figure is used to decide whether the HHI is less than 1800 or not. This estimating figure is calculated by the following formula which is drawn up from the Production Concentration Study:

HHI $= 69.5 \times$ cumulative market shares of top three companies $- 2344.4$

However, this does not apply to the case where the HHI with the identified market shares is obviously above 1800.

Note 8 To calculate the market share, the market share of import is treated as the market share of the competitors except for the import by the manufactures from its oversees subsidiaries.

(b) The market structure is not highly oligopolistic, the market share of the company group after the combination is not more than 35 per cent, and there are two or more competitors whose market shares are more than 10 per cent (*See* note 7 and 8)

(c) The increment of market share is in significant and there is one or more competitors whose market shares are more than 10 per cent (*See* note 8 and 9)

Note 9 'The increment of market share is insignificant' means that the increment of HHI figure by the business combinations is less than 100.

(2) Import

When there is sufficient pressure from imports, the possibility that the effect of business combinations may be substantially to restrain competition in a particular field of trade is usually thought to be small. When the amount of imported goods which are homogeneous with domestic ones is easy to increase, and the imported goods at lower price is likely to increase if the company group raises the domestic price of goods, the company group will not raise the domestic price taking into consideration that their sales will be taken by the imports. The following factors all together are considered in deciding whether the pressure from imports is sufficient or not.

(a) Trend of import, the relationship of the amount of imports to the price differential between the domestic goods and the imports

(b) Competitiveness of the imports with respect to price, quality, etc.
(c) Existence of the problems in distribution, storage facilities of import or so-called users' familiarity with domestic goods
(d) Major users' experience to use the imports
(e) Likelihood of import by leading foreign competitors, the number of such competitors and their excess capacity, etc.
(f) Demand and supply balance in the exporting countries
(g) Factors influencing the pricing of the imports, exports or domestic goods and the price difference between them
(h) Import tax system such as customs or other legislative regulations

To consider whether import can be the factors which prevent the company group from controlling the price, etc., freely to a certain extent, excess capacity of the imports is considered if domestic goods and the imports are homogenous. If those are differentiated, the degree of the substitutability between goods sold by the company group and the imports is considered.

Even though the current market share of the imports is small, if the users can increase the use of the imports easily when the price of domestic goods is raised, it is considered that there is pressures from import.

(3) Entry

When the entries into the markets are easy, they can be the factors which prevent the company group from controlling the price, etc., freely to a certain extent. When the entries are easy, and it is likely that some companies try to entry the market by selling goods at the lower price if the company group raises the price, the group will refrain from increasing the price taking into consideration that their sales will be taken by the entrants. To consider whether entries can be the factors which prevent the company group from controlling the price, etc., freely to a certain extent, excess capacity of the entrants is considered if goods are homogenous. If those are differentiated, the degree of the substitutability between goods sold by the company group and the entrants is considered. The following factors all together are considered to determine the possibility of entry.

(a) Existence of legislative entry regulations
(b) Degree of entry barriers in practice (e.g. the minimum scale of the capital for entry, the geographical and social conditions of location, technical conditions, conditions for the purchase of raw materials, sales conditions, state of the differentiation of goods, state of competitors such as entry and exit, change of the number of competitors, the trend of the change of the cumulative market shares of top three companies, etc.)
(c) Existence of companies that can supply goods without significant change in the production facilities
(d) Existence of entry plans by other companies
(e) Likelihood of the entry to the domestic market by foreign companies

(4) *Competitive Pressure from Related Markets*

Competitive conditions in markets related to the particular field of trade determined in Section 2 are also considered. Such markets are, for example, those geographically neighbouring to the defined particular field of trade, markets of the products processed from the goods defined as the particular field of trade, markets at the next level of transaction and markets of the products which have comparable functions and efficacy to the goods defined (such goods hereinafter referred to as 'competing goods'). For instance, when there is vigorous competition in the neighbouring markets, it will be evaluated as a factor which stimulates competition in the particular field of trade.

A. Comparable goods

When competing goods have comparable functions and efficacy to goods but have the separated market for it, these competing goods can be a factor which prevents the company group from controlling the price, etc., freely to a certain extent depending on the comparability of functions and efficacy from the view points of users, prices, distribution networks, etc.

B. Geographically neighbouring market

When a particular field of trade is limited geographically and there is another geographically neighbouring market where the same goods are supplied, the competition in the neighbouring markets can be a factor which prevents the company group from controlling the price, etc., freely to a certain extent depending on the closeness of location, distribution style, transportation, scale of the competitors.

C. State of the transaction at the next level

The competition in the markets situated as the next level to the particular field of trade can be a factor which prevents the company group in the markets from controlling the price, etc., freely to a certain extent through the transactions between these markets. As for the business combinations between raw materials producers, for instance, when the competition in the finished goods' markets is vigorous, the finished goods' producers who are the users of the raw materials try to purchase them as cheaply as possible in order to reduce the price of the finished goods. In this case, if the company group raises the price, they are likely to lose their sales significantly. Therefore, the competition in the next stage can be a factor which prevents the company group from controlling the price, etc., freely to a certain extent. Similarly, in view of the demand and supply balance of raw materials as well as major users' means of procurement, degree of diversity of their suppliers and their ease of switching trade partners, if the bargaining power in price of the producers of the finished goods is strong, it can be a factor which prevents the company group from controlling the price, etc., freely to a certain extent.

(5) Overall Business Capabilities

In addition to the market share of the company group after the business combination, changes in the overall business capabilities of the company group such as raw material procurement ability, technological capability, marketing capability, credit worthiness, brand popularity, and advertising capability will be examined. For example, if the raw material procurement ability, technological capabilities, marketing capability, access to credit, brand power, advertising capability and other business capabilities of the company group is enhanced after the business combination and the competitiveness of the companies increases greatly due to the combination, its competitors may have difficulty to take competitive actions as a result.

(6) Efficiency

Economy of scale, integration of production facilities, specialization of factories, reduction in transportation costs, efficiency in research and development and other improvements of efficiency caused by the business combinations are examined in terms of their impact on competition. When improvement of efficiency is deemed likely to stimulate competition (for example, a low-ranking company increases its cost competitiveness, financing capability, raw material procurement ability and other fundamentals through a merger, which leads to lower product prices and higher product quality, and in turn promotes competition with high-ranking companies), these positive impacts are considered.

(7) Financial Conditions of the Company Group

A. Poor Business Performance, etc.

To evaluate the business ability of the company group, the financial conditions such as poor business performance of a part of the company group or a business section concerned to the combination are also considered. Meanwhile, the possibility that the effect of the business combination may be substantially to restrain competition in a particular field of trade is usually thought to be small in such conditions as follows: a party to the combination is in excess of debt or unable to obtain loans for working capital and it is likely to go bankrupt and exit from the market in the near future; In addition, it is difficult to find any company that can relieve the party by a combination which gives less impact on competition than the other party to the combination.

B. Cases that The Effect may not be Substantially to Restrain Competition

Whether or not the effect of a business combination may be substantially to restrain competition is determined by the comprehensive considerations of all the relevant determining factors in each of the specific cases. However, in the following cases, it normally is not considered that the effect of a horizontal business combination may be substantially to restrain competition in a particular field of trade by unilateral conducts.

(a) Market share of the company group after the combination is not more than 50 per cent. In addition, a party to the combination is in excess of debt or unable to obtain loans for working capita and it is likely to go bankrupt and exit from the market in the near future. Furthermore, it is difficult to find any company that can relieve the party by a combination which gives less impact on competition than the other party to the combination.
(b) Market share of the business department in question of the company group after the combination is not more than 50 per cent. In addition, the business department of a party to the combination is in depression and likely to exit from the market in the near future. Furthermore, it is difficult to find any company that can relieve the business department by the combination which gives less impact on competition than the other party to the combination.

3. *The determining factors to decide the Substantial Restraint of Competition through the Coordinated Conduct*

To decide whether the effect of horizontal business combinations may be substantially to restrain competition in a particular field of trade through the coordinated conduct, the following factors are considered comprehensively.

(1) The position of the company group and the state of competitors

A. Number of the competitors

When there are few competitors in the particular field of trade or the market share is concentrated into a few leading companies, the behaviour of the competitors can be predicted with high reliability. Furthermore, when the companies sell homogeneous goods and have similar cost conditions, they tend to take coordinated conduct as they share common interests. In addition, it is easier to predict with high reliability whether competitors take coordinated conduct or not. Therefore, if the business combination brings such situations mentioned *above*, there will be large impact on the competition.

B. Competition among the Parties in the Past, etc.

In such cases where the parties have been scrambling for each other's market share or one of these parties has been aggressive in cutting prices, the fact that the parties have competed vigorously or their conduct in the market have invigorated competition may be deemed to contribute to the reduction of prices throughout the market, the improvement of qualities or the variety of goods. If the combination eliminates such conditions as *before* mentioned, it brings large impact on the competition even if the combined market share or the rank of the parties is not high.

C. Excess capacity of the Competitors

If a company does not have sufficient excess capacity, the opportunities to expand market shares by cutting prices or deprive competitors of their market shares are limited. As a result, the company can not earn large profit by such conducts, and it is likely to commit to a coordinated conduct with the competitors. On the other hand, if excess capacity of a company is large while that of competitors is small, when it reduces prices to gain sales, the sales to be deprived of by competitors through a price reduction in the near future is limited. Therefore, the incentive to commit to a coordinated conduct with the competitors will be smaller since profits from expanded sales are expected through reducing prices.

D. Treatment of Joint Investment Company

If certain business departments of the investing companies are completely spun off by consolidation in the joint investment company, the connection between the business of the investing companies and that of the joint investment company would be considered to be weak. Therefore, when all of the business such as the production, sale, research and development,, etc., for certain goods are spun off by the consolidation in the joint investment company, whether the joint investment company itself will be committed to a coordinated conduct with its competitors is examined. On the other hand, if a part of certain business departments of the each investing companies is transferred to the joint investment company, whether the investing companies are committed to coordinated conducts with their competitors is examined as well. To determine whether the coordinated conduct of investing companies with their competitors would emerge or not, the contents of the investing contract between the investing companies in terms of the joint investment, the actual conditions of the combination, and the transactions between the investing companies, if any, are considered. For example, when only the production sections of the goods are integrated into the joint investment company while each of the investing companies continue to sell the said goods, even though measures are taken to prevent coordinated relationship between the investing companies through the operation of a joint investment company, the production cost will become common. As a result, there will be less room for price competition and they will have incentive to commit to coordinated conduct with their competitors including the other investing company.

(2) Actual Situation of Trade, etc.

A. Conditions of Trade, etc.

When, for example, a trade association collects and provides such information of the member companies such as prices or production quantities, and each company can easily know the competitors' terms of trade, it is possible for each company to predict the behaviour of the competitors in high reliability, and also easy to know whether the competitors are taking coordinated conducts or not. Furthermore, under these circumstances, if a company cuts its price in order to increase the sales, its competitors are easily aware of it and they are likely to try to recover the sales taken by price cut of the company. As a result, the company has little incentive to take such an action. On the other hand, when trade contracts are not in regular bases and the volume of orders are in a large unit, large profit are expected by cutting price and getting such contracts while such opportunities for the contracts are limited. Therefore, the party has little incentive to take coordinated conducts with the competitors and it is difficult to predict the competitors' behaviour. On the contrary, if the trade contracts are carried out regularly and the volume of orders is small, the coordinated conducts with the competitors are likely to occur.

B. Trend of Demand, Technological innovation, etc.

When the demands are changing significantly or the technological innovation is frequent and the life cycle of goods is short, it is possible to get large profits by cutting price and increasing sales or depriving the sales of competitors. As a result, there will be less incentive to take coordinated conducts with competitors as well as it will be difficult to predict competitors' behaviour, so that coordinated conducts with competitors are not likely to occur.

C. Past Competition Conditions

To determine whether the coordinated conducts will be taken or not, the changes of the market shares or prices in the past are considered as well. For example, when these changes are large, the coordinated conducts with the competitors are not likely to occur because it is difficult to predict the competitors' behaviour. On the other hand, if these changes are small, it will be easier to predict the competitors' behaviour and the possibility is higher that the coordinated conducts will occur. And, for example, when there were coordinated conducts regarding the revision of prices of goods, possibility is higher that the market conditions for trade are prone to coordinated conducts.

(3) Competitive Pressure from Import, Entry or Related Market

When there is a significant import pressure, if the companies raise the domestic price, they will lose their sales because of the increase of the imports. Therefore there will be less possibility of the coordinated conducts. Due to the same process as mentioned *above*, it is difficult for the company group and the competitors to control the price, etc., freely to a certain extent. However, when the importers have established themselves as domestic players, such importers may take coordinated conducts with the competitors including the parties. The conditions regarding import described in Section of 2 (2) (a) to (h) *above* are considered comprehensively to evaluate whether there are import pressures or not. Entry pressures will have a similar influence on the possibility of coordinated conducts. Regarding the possibility of entries, the conditions described in Section 2 (3) (a) to (e) *above* are considered comprehensively. The competitive pressures from the related market may also be a factor which prevents the coordinated conducts from emerging or the company group and its competitors from controlling the price, etc., freely to a certain extent by the coordinated conduct. For example, in case where the bargaining power in price of the users is stronger with reflecting the demand and supply conditions, major users' means of procurement, degree of diversity of their suppliers and their ease of switching trading partners, it will often be difficult for the company group and its competitors to commit to coordinated conducts.

(4) Efficiency and the Financial Conditions of the Company Group

Efficiency and the financial conditions of the company group are evaluated based on Section 2 (6) and (7) *above*.

Part V
The Effect of Vertical and Conglomerate Business combination May be Substantially to Restrain Competition

1. GUIDING PRINCIPLES

As mentioned *above*, vertical and conglomerate business combinations do not reduce the number of the competitive units. Therefore, they have less impact on competition than horizontal ones, and the effect of them usually may not be substantially to restrain competition except for cases where substantial restraint of competition is caused by closures of or exclusion from markets by coordinated conducts, etc., Similar to horizontal business combinations, vertical and conglomerate ones are also reviewed from both view points of unilateral conducts and coordinated conducts.

(1) Substantial Restraint of Competition by Unilateral Conduct

The typical cases in which the effect of vertical and conglomerate business combinations may be substantially to restrain competition in a particular field of trade by means of unilateral conducts are as follows. When a vertical combination is completed, it is profitable for the parties to trade within the company group. As a result, there could be cases where other companies would in fact lose the opportunities to trade actually and the transactions among the company group may raise the problems of closure or exclusivity. Supposing, a manufacturer of finished goods has a large market share and purchases raw materials from many suppliers. When such a manufacturer merges with one of its suppliers and only uses the raw materials from it, the other suppliers are likely to lose their business opportunities with the manufacturer that is their large customer. On the contrary, a supplier of a raw material has a large market share and supply with many manufacturers of finished goods. When the supplier merges with one of the manufacturers and only supply the raw materials to it, the other manufacturers are likely to lose the business opportunities with their major supplier of raw materials. Similarly, when a strong manufacturer merges with a strong distributor, if it becomes difficult for the other manufacturers to enter unless they establish the distribution network by themselves, the merger will have a large impact on competition. In addition, even when the company group continues the business with its competitors after the vertical combination, if the competitors in more disadvantage position in their business with the group than before, the impact on competition will be significant since effective competition between them can no longer be expected. When the market share of the company group is large, a situation may easily emerge where the company group will be able to control the price, etc., freely to a certain extent resulting from closure or exclusivity on the trade within the company group by the vertical business combination. In such cases, the effect of vertical business combination may be substantially to restrain competition. A conglomerate business combination may raise the problem of closure or exclusivity when it increases the overall business capabilities of the company group. For example, if the combination increases the company group's business ability such as raw material procurement ability, technological capability, marketing capability, access to credit, brand power, and advertising capability etc, and its competitiveness is greatly enhanced, its competitors may have difficulty to take competitive actions.

(2) Substantial Restraint of Competition by Coordinated Conduct

The typical cases where the effect of vertical and conglomerate business combinations may be substantially to restrain competition in a particular field of trade by means of coordinated conducts are as follows.

For example, when a manufacturer and a distributor become combined vertically, manufacturer can obtain the competitors' information of prices and so on through the distributor. As a result, manufacturers which include the company group might be able to estimate the each other's behaviour with high reliability. In such cases, a situation is likely to emerge where the company group and its competitors will be able to control the price, etc., freely to a certain extent; thus the effect of vertical business combination may be substantially to restrain competition. The same may be true for conglomerate business combinations.

(3) The Effect may not be Substantially to Restraint Competition

It is decided in light of the factors described on Section 2 later whether the effect of each vertical or conglomerate business combination may be substantially to restrain competition in a particular field of trade or not. However, when the market share of the company group after the combination falls within the conditions A and B *below*, the effect of the vertical or conglomerate business combination may not be substantially to restrain competition in a particular field of trade.

A. The market share of the company group after the combination is not more than 10 per cent in all of the particular field of trade where the company group is involved.

B. The market structure is not oligopolistic and the market share of the company group after the combination is not more than 25 per cent in the entire particular field of trade where the company group is involved (*See* Note 5).

2. THE DETERMINING FACTORS TO DECIDE THE SUBSTANTIAL RESTRAINT OF COMPETITION THROUGH THE VERTICAL AND CONGLOMERATE BUSINESS COMBINATIONS

(1) The determining factors to decide the Substantial Restraint of Competition through the Unilateral Conduct

To decide whether the effect of vertical and conglomerate business combinations may be substantially to restrain competition in a particular field of trade through the unilateral conduct, the following factors are considered comprehensively.

A. The position of the company group and the state of competitors

After the combination, if the size of the market share of the company group is small and the rank of it is also in a low position, there is less possibility that the problems of closure or exclusivity arise. Also when the difference of the market shares between the company group and the competitors is small or excess capacities of the competitors are large, it is relatively easy for buyers from or sellers to the company group to find the alternative trade partners. Therefore, the possibility is smaller that the problems of closure or exclusivity arise. To decide whether the effect of each vertical or conglomerate business combination may be substantially to restrain competition or not, the determining factors including those mentioned later in Section B and so on are taken into consideration. However, in the following cases, the possibility that the effect of vertical and conglomerate business combinations may be substantially to restrain competition in a particular field of trade through the unilateral conduct is usually thought to be small.

(a) All of the particular field of trade where the company group is involved are not highly oligopolistic, the market share of the company group after the combination is not more than 25 per cent, and there are one or more competitors whose market shares are more than 10 per cent. (*See* note 7 and 8)
(b) All of the particular field of trade where the company group is involved are not highly oligopolistic, the market share of the company group after the combination is not more than 35 per cent, and there are two or more competitors whose market shares are more than 10 per cent. (*See* note 7 and 8)

B. Import, Entry, Overall Business Capabilities, Efficiency, etc.

These factors are evaluated in light of the same standard in Section 2 (2) to (6) in Part IV *above*.

C. Financial Conditions of the Company Group

This is evaluated in light of the same standard in Section 2 (7) A in Part IV *above*.

D. Other factors

It is also considered that the business combination will eliminate the possibility of new entries if a part of the parties are the potential competitors to the other part of the parties.

(2) The factors to decide the Substantial Restraint of Competition through the Coordinated Conducts

This is evaluated in light of the same standard in Section 3 (1) to (3), 2 (6) and (7) A in Part IV *above*.

Part VI
Measures to Remedy the Substantial Restraint of Competition

1. GUIDING PRINCIPLES

Even though the effect of business combination may be substantially to restrain competition in a particular field of trade, such restraint may be remedied by certain appropriate measures taken by the company group (such measures referred to as 'remedy(ies)' hereinafter).

It is considered on a case-by-case basis what kind of measures are appropriate as the remedies. However, the remedies basically should be ones which recover the lost competition after the combination in order to prevent the company group from controlling the price, etc., freely to a certain extent. In addition, the remedies should be completed before the implementation of the combination in principle. Even if the remedies are to be taken unavoidably after the implementation of the combination, the dead line for the remedies should be imposed appropriately and definitely. Moreover, to divest the whole or a part of the businesses as remedies for example, it is desirable to decide the partners who succeed the business in advance of the implementation of the combination. Otherwise, the parties are required to obtain the permissions from the Fair Trade Commission in regard with the divesting partners.

2. TYPES OF THE REMEDIES

Typical remedies are illustrated as follows. To make the remedies appropriate, those measures are taken independently or in combinations.

(1) Divestiture of Business, etc.

The most effective measures to solve the problems of the substantial restraint of competition by the business combinations are to establish new independent competitors, or to strengthen the existing competitors to be able to have the effective competitive constraint. Such measures include a divestiture of a part of or whole of the business of the company group or a dissolution of the business combination such as the cancellation of the voting rights holding, reduction of the holding ratio of voting rights or cancellation of interlocking directorates and so on in another company. When, as an exceptional example, it is difficult, because of the decrease of demand, to find a partner who takeover a part of or whole of the company group's business (e.g. section of production, sale or development), and research and development or services such as improvement of goods in response to users' requests are not important because goods are on a mature stage, it may be considered as effective remedies to give the competitors a right of trading at the price equivalent to the production cost of it (in other words, to make contracts of long term supply).

(2) Others

A. Measures to Promote Import and Entry

When the divestitures of business could not be taken as remedies because demand is decreasing and it is expected that a company which takes over a part of or whole of the company group's business do not appear easily, promotions of import or entry are exceptionally considered as remedial measures to solve the problem of the substantial restraint of competition in a particular of field.

For example, when the company group holds the storage facilities needed to import, the problems of the substantial restraint of competition in the particular of field would be solved by the promotion of import by means of making such facilities available to the importers. Alternatively, the problems could be solved by granting the licenses of company group's patents to the competitors or new entrants on their requests.

B. Measures concerning Actions of the Company Group

In addition to the cases in Item (1) and (2) *above*, the measures concerning the actions of the company group could be considered as the measures to solve the problem of the substantial restraint of competition in the particular of field. For example, when in a business combination goods are produced by the joint investment company but the sales of them are done by the respective investing companies, the problems of the substantial restraint of competition in a particular of field are solved by the measures which make it possible to block the exchange of information on each other's sales of the goods between the investing companies and between the investing companies and the joint investment company. (However *see* 3 (1) D in Part IV.) The problems of closure or exclusivity in markets could be solved by prohibiting discriminatory treatment of non-affiliated companies with regard to uses of essential facilities for the business.

(ATTACHMENT 1) PRIOR CONSULTATION

When the Fair Trade Commission receives inquiries from companies into whether the effect of an actual plan of business combination may be substantially to restrain competition in a particular field of trade, it will review the plan based on these Guidelines and respond whether the effect of the business combination will substantially to restrain competition in light of Chapter IV of the Act. Concerning the prior consultations, the Fair Trade Commission will handle them based on the guiding principle, ‘Policies dealing with prior consultation regarding enterprise combination plans’ (11 December 2002).

(ATTACHMENT 2) SHORTENING OF THE WAITING PERIOD

Article 15 (4) of the Act (including such cases where the said provisions are applied mutatis mutandis by Article 15–2 (6) and 16 (5)) prohibits any company from effecting a merger until the expiration of a thirty-day waiting period from the date of the acceptance of the notification of the intended merger (including joint establishment type corporate split, absorption type corporate split or acquisition of business, etc.). However, the same Paragraph authorize the Fair Trade Commission, when it finds it necessary to do so, to shorten the waiting period. The shortening of the waiting period will be granted, in principle, when the requirements of both A and B *below* are satisfied.

(a) It is evident that the effect may not be substantially to restrain competition in any particular field of trade. This requirement will be satisfied in those cases where the responses of the Fair Trade Commission to prior consultation indicates that the intended merger involves no problems under the Act and the notification is consistent with the consultation. Also, those cases which fall under the category of cases described in 1(3), 2(1)F and (7)B in the Part IV, 1(3) and the later part of 2(1)A of the Part V of these guidelines are very much likely to satisfy the requirement.

(b) There is a rational reason or reasons for the shortening of the waiting period. This requirement will be satisfied in those case where there is a probability that unless the merger is effected within a certain time limit, the business of one or more of the merging companies would be imposed (for instance, bankruptcy, desertion of employees, loss of customers, etc.).

SELECTED BIBLIOGRAPHY

Inoue, A, 'Liniency No Jitsumu' [Practice of Leniency – How to Protect Your Business from Antitrust Enforcement] (2006) *Lexis Nexis Japan.*

Inoue, A, 'B2B Compliance Bible' (2006) *Lexis Nexis Japan.*

Inoue, A, 'The Recent Amendment of the Japanese Antimonopoly Law', (2006) *Japan Business Law Review* Vol. 1, No.1.

Inoue, A., *The Great Step Forward: The Reform to the Japanese Antimonopoly Act,* (2006) Law Gazette (An Official Publication of the Law Society of Singapore), August 2006.

Inoue, A., *Japan tightens the rules of play*, (2006) Asian-Counsel vol. 4 Issue 5, July/August 2006.

Goetz, C.J., *Law and Economics Cases and Materials*, (1984) West Publishing Co.

Friedman, D.D., *Price Theory* (1990) 2 edn.

Ijuh, K., *Dokusenkinshihou No Tebiki* [The Guidance of the Japanese Antimonopoly Act] (1982) Tokyokeizaishinpousha.

Murakami, M., *Dokusenkinshihou* [The Japanese Antimonopoly Act], 1996, Hirobundou 2000.

Friedman, M., Price Theory, 1976, Aldine Publishing Co., Chicago.

Shiraishi, T., *Dokusenkinshihou Kougi* [Lectures on the Japanese Antimonopoly Act], 3 edn. 2005.

Shiraishi, T., *Dokusenkinshihou* [The Japanese Antimonopoly Act], 2006, Yuhikaku.

Kania, T., Yumio *Sensui and Noburu Kawanobe*, *Dokusenkinshihou,* [The Japanese Antimonopoly Act], 2006, 2d ed.

The Japanese Fair Trade Commission, *Dokusenkinshihoujouno Kigyoketugosinsa Nikansuru Unyohshisin* [*The Guideline Concerning the Examination on Merger and Acquisition under the Japanese Antimonopoly Act*], (2004), *available at* <http://www2.jftc.go.jp/pressrelease/04.may/04053101.pdf> (last visited 28 January 2007).

The Japanese Fair Trade Commission, *Dokusenkinshihou Kenkyukai Hokokusho* [*The Report by the Study Group Concerning the Japanese Antimonopoly Act],* (2003), *available at* <http://www2.jftc.go.jp/pressrelease/03.october/sochi2.pdf> (last visited 25 January 2007).

Kanazawa, Y, *Keizaihou* [Law of Economy], 1980, Yuhikaku.

Ryokaku, Y., *Kyosoh to Dokusenno Hanashi* [The Talk About Competition and Monopoly], 1978, Soukeisha 1978.

Index

References are to page number.

INTERNATIONAL COMPETITION LAW SERIES

1. Ignacio De León, *Latin American Competition Law and Policy: A Policy in Search of Identity* (2001) (ISBN 90-411-1542-0)
2. Wim Dejonghe and Wouter Van de Voorde (Eds.), *M & A in Belgium* (2001) (ISBN 90-411-1594-3)
3. Yang-Ching Chao, Gee San, Changfa Lo, Jiming Ho (Eds.), *International and Comparative Competition Law and Policies* (2001) (ISBN 90-411-1643-5)
4. Martin Mendelsohn and Stephen Rose, *Guide to the EC Block Exemption for Vertical Agreements* (2002) (ISBN 90-411-9813-X)
5. Clifford A. Jones and Mitsuo Matsushita (Eds.), *Competition Policy in the Global Trading System* (2002) (ISBN 90-411-1758-X)
6. Christian Koenig, Andreas Bartosch, Jens-Daniel Braun (Eds.), *EC Competition and Telecommunications Law* (2002) (ISBN 90-411-1814-4)
7. Jürgen Basedow (Ed.), *Limits and Control of Competition with a View to International Harmonization* (2002) (ISBN 90-411-1967-1)
8. Maureen Brunt, *Economic Essays on Australian and New Zealand Competition Law* (2003) (ISBN 90-411-1991-4)
9. Ky P. Ewing, Jr., *Competition Rules for the 21st Century: Principles from America's Experience* (2003) (ISBN 90-411-2006-8)
10. Joseph Wilson, *Globalization and the Limits of National Merger Control Laws* (2003) (ISBN 90-411-1996-5)
11. Peter Verloop and Valérie Landes (Eds.), *Merger Control in Europe: EU, Member States and Accession States,* 4th edition (2003) (ISBN 90-411-2056-4)
12. Themistoklis K. Giannakopoulos, *Safeguarding Companies' Rights in Competition and Anti-dumping/Anti-subsidies Proceedings* (2004) (ISBN 90-411-2254-0)
13. Marjorie Holmes and Lesley Davey (Eds.), *A Practical Guide to National Competition Rules across Europe* (2004) (ISBN 90-411-2295-8)
14. Sigrid Stroux, *US and EU Oligopoly Control* (2004) (ISBN 90-411-2296-6)

15. Tzong-Leh Hwang and Chiyuan Chen (Eds.), *The Future Development of Competition Framework* (2004)
(ISBN 90-411-2305-9)
16. Phedon Nicolaides, Mihalis Kekelekis and Philip Buyskes, *State Aid Policy in the European Community, A Guide for Practitioners.* Second Edition (2005)
(ISBN 90-411-2394-6)
17. Doris Hildebrand, *Economic Analyses of Vertical Agreements – A Self-Assessment* (2005)
(ISBN 90-411-2328-8)
18. Frauke Henning-Bodewig, *Unfair Competition Law – European Union and Member States* (2005)
(ISBN 90-411-2329-6)
19. Duarte Brito and Margarida Catalão-Lopes, *Mergers and Acquisitions: The Industrial Organization Perspective* (2006)
(ISBN 90-411-2451-9)
20. Nikos Th. Nikolinakos, *EU Competition Law and Regulation in the Converging Telecommunication, Media and IT Sectors* (2006)
(ISBN 90-411-2469-1)
21. Mihalis Kekelekis, *The EC Merger Control Regulation: Rights of Defence. A Critical Analysis of DG COMP Practice and Community Courts' Jurisprudence* (2006)
(ISBN 90-411-2553-1)
22. Mark R. Joelson, *An International Antitrust Primer: A Guide to the Operation of United States, European Union and Other Key Competition Laws in the Global Economy,* 3rd edition (2006)
(ISBN 90-411-2468-3)
23. Themistoklis K. Giannakopoulos, *A Concise Guide to the EU Anti-dumping/ Anti-subsidies Procedures* (2006)
(ISBN 90-411-2464-0)
24. George Cumming, Brad Spitz and Ruth Janal, Civil Procedure Used for Enforcement of EC Competition Law by the English, French and German Civil Courts (2007)
(ISBN 978-90-411-2471-5)
25. Jurgen Basdow (Ed.), Private Enforcement of EC Competition Law (2007)
(ISBN 978-90-411-2613-9)
26. Jung Wook Cho, Innovation and Competition in the Digital Network Economy: A Legal and Economic Assessment on Multy-tying Practices and Network Effects (2007)
(ISBN 978-90-411-2574-3)
27. Akira Inoue, Japanese Antitrust Law Manual (2007)
(ISBN 978-90-411-2627-6)